To Dad,

Merry Christmas!
I would just like to say thank you
for all the presents & things that you
have done for me over the holidays
& the year. Everything from college
applications to my Christmas presents
you have done w/ extra special care that
only you would do. This book is just
a reminder of how much I appreciate
all the things that you do for me.
Also maybe the tips will help you
so when I'm out of college we can
put some money on this golf game!

Love you, merry christmas

# Nicklaus

Other Books By Mark Shaw

*Down for the Count*
*Bury Me in a Pot Bunker*
*Forever Flying*
*The Perfect Yankee*

# Nicklaus

❖ ❖ ❖

Mark Shaw

TAYLOR PUBLISHING
Dallas, Texas

Copyright © 1997 by Six Dogs and Film Company

Published by Taylor Publishing Company
1550 West Mockingbird Lane
Dallas, Texas

**Library of Congress Cataloging-in-Publication Data**

Shaw, Mark, 1945–
Nicklaus / Mark Shaw.
p.    cm.
Includes bibliographical references and index.
ISBN 0-87833-961-2 (cloth)
1. Nicklaus, Jack.    2. Golfers—United States—Biography.
I Title.
GV964.N4S53    1997
796.352'092—dc21
[B]      97-501
CIP

Printed in the United States of America

10   9   8   7   6   5   4   3   2   1

This book has been printed on acid-free recycled paper.

*This book is dedicated to*
*Ed Tutwiler,*
*Bill Hyndman,*
*and*
*Jack Leer*
*Three of the greatest gentlemen to*
*ever play the game of golf.*

# Contents

# BOOK VII
## Nicklaus's Legacy

# Acknowledgments

From the germ of an idea for a book to the pages that follow, a literary work such as this is a joint effort of many.

A special thank you goes to Taylor Publishing and editor Michael Emmerich, who conceived the idea to have the first biography of Jack Nicklaus written, had faith in me to complete the book in five months, and nursed the book through numerous rewrites. Literary agents Frank Weimann and Scott Waxman of The Literary Group, who linked the author to the equation, also deserve thanks.

Other members of the Taylor Publishing team, including India Chumney, Jason Rath, and Carol Trammel, have been instrumental in the publication of this book and I thank them for their efforts. Special thanks go to Joe Grey, a talented editor who scrutinized the manuscript and made many helpful suggestions.

Throughout the research process, many have been helpful. Thanks go to Gray Autry, Ruth Martin, and Denise Taylor of the PGA Tour, Jo Ann Tocco of Britton Publishing, Craig Smith and Mia Romano-Brown of the United States Golf Association, Kip Erickson of The Memorial tournament, Peter Balestrieri of ASAP, Jorge Jaramillo of AP, photojournalists Rick Young and Kenny May, Jamie Roggero and Julius Mason of the PGA of America, Lee Gardner of The Brickyard Crossing Senior tournament, Buddy Antonopolous of The Medalist Golf Club, Joe Wilson of Crooked Stick Golf Club, Gary Boone, Marilee Leer, Havi Joslin, Micah Floyd, and Tricia Kinney, among others.

Thanks also go to Jim Ferriell, the highly respected head professional at Crooked Stick Golf Club; Alice Dye, the golf champion with a ready smile; golf historian Tom Meeks of the United States Golf Association; Kent Frandsen, a superb amateur player; and Tom Peterson, longtime friend and business associate of Jack Nicklaus; all of whom were kind enough to read early drafts of the book and provide expert comments and suggestions regarding the accuracy of the material.

The author would also like to thank Bill Hyndman, Alice Dye, Errie Ball, Jim Ferriell, Carol Mann, Mike Souchak, Chi Chi Rodriguez, Bob Charles, and Steve Hershey for their comments regarding selection of the greatest players in the history of the game.

Along the way, many people expressed their personal thoughts through interviews, providing an insight into the world of Jack Nicklaus. The author wishes to thank Gary Player, Chi Chi Rodriguez, Dave Stockton, Bruce Crampton, Gene Littler, Tom Weiskopf, Mike Souchak, Bob Charles, Phil Mickelson, Deane Beman, Brian Barnes, Gary Cowan, Tom Wargo, Phil Rodgers, Bob Dickson, Don Bies, Tony Perla, Carol Mann, Fuzzy Zoeller, Tom Watson, Tom Kite, Steve Jones, Raymond Floyd, Bob Murphy, Tommy Aaron, Errie Ball, David Frost, Ian Woosnam, Chip Beck, Tom Lehman, Ralph Terry, Kenny Perry, Colin Montgomerie, Donna Caponi, Don January, Angelo Argea, Jim Dent, Tony Jacklin, Miller Barber, Gene Littler, Downing Gray, John Konsek, Don Albert, Jack Hesler, Bill Hyndman, Carol Peterson, Tom Peterson, Alice Dye, Pete Dye, Jim Ferriell, Gary Koch, Mike Hill, Lou Graham, Bobby Weed, Vinny Giles, Dale and Martha Morey, Kent Frandsen, Nick Faldo, Steve Elkington, Dick and Lynne Taylor, Jimmy Roberts, Jack Leer, Phil Richards, George Peper, Richard Hinds, W.J. Ferguson, Steve Hershey, Jerry Potter, Ron Whitton, Robin Miller, Wayne Fusion, Rollie Schroeder, Jeff Schroeder, and Wayne Timberman, among others.

Certain longtime supporters of the author who also deserve thanks include Mickey and Janie Maurer, Bill Fox, Judy Deputy, Ray and Terry Browning, Jack and Sue Shaw, Anne Ott, Tom and Debbie Landis, Tracy and Connie Kemp, Ted and Lisa Roark, Charles and Patty Roark, Steve and Elaine Fess, David Brofsky, Charley Steiner, Scott and Sheri McKain, Jeff and Sarah Madsten, Mike Stipher, Bing and Suzi Pratt, David and Nancy Foley, David and Nancy Neal, Joe and Marsha Luigs, Jack Lupton, and Tom Meeks.

Certainly this book would not have been possible without the skills of Donna Stouder, a superb editor, trusted friend, and future author; Becky Howard, a dear friend and gifted editor; and Chris

Roark Shaw, a loving wife, mother extraordinaire, and talented editor whose encouragement through the writing process was essential.

The author wishes also to thank his four children, Kimberly, Kyle, Kevin, and Kent for their love and support. And his canine pals, Bach, White Sox, Snickers, Peanut Butter, Shadow, and Reggie Miller for their companionship at five A.M.

Above all the author wishes to thank the Good Lord, who continues to bless him in life like few others on the face of the earth.

MARK SHAW

*Talent develops in quiet places,*
*character in the full current of human life.*

JOHANN WOLFGANG VON GOETHE
German poet, playwright, novelist


*I want to be the best golfer*
*the world has ever seen.*

JACK NICKLAUS
1969

# Introduction

## *Jack Nicklaus Shocks Sports World—Wins United States Open at Age Sixty*

This will be the newspaper headline the day after the 2000 United States Open is held at Pebble Beach. Nicklaus will nip Phil Mickelson, Tiger Woods, Ernie Els, and John Daly by one shot when he drains a curling downhill 15-footer in dense fog by Carmel Bay. Once the putt drops, Jack will raise his putter toward the heavens, acknowledging yet another bionic triumph.

That dramatic win will provide yet another image of Jack Nicklaus for me, but several others have come to mind since I accepted the assignment to write the only biography to date of the Golden Bear.

These images are not of a golf journalist who has covered the game for half a century. Certainly such gifted men as Herbert Warren Wind, Dick Taylor, Dan Jenkins, Jim Murray, Ken Bowden, Rick Reilly, Jerry Potter, George Peper, Kaye Kessler, Steve Hershey, Larry Dorman, the late Charles Price, and Peter Dobriener, to name a few, were much more qualified to portray the life and times of Jack Nicklaus.

My observations will not be from the perspective of a championship golfer, for I am a shaky six handicap whose only claims to fame are par on the famous Road Hole at St. Andrews and birdie from the infamous bunker bordering the eighteenth hole at Seminole. Without a doubt, fine players-turned-journalists such as Ken Venturi, Gary Koch, Andy North, Gary McCord, Frank Beard, Peter Allis, and Johnny Miller could write more distinguished material from a competitive point of view.

In fact, I nearly turned down the opportunity believing that many of the talented men mentioned above should be the biographer. But, for whatever reason, they chose not to assume the project. In the end, I decided that it would be an honor to attempt to chronicle Nicklaus's life as I have previously done with former heavyweight boxing champion Mike Tyson, controversial golf course designer Pete Dye, legendary aviator R. A. "Bob" Hoover, and former New York Yankee right-hander Don Larsen, of perfect game fame.

My first recollection of Jack Nicklaus came when I was fifteen years old and aspired to gain a golf scholarship to Purdue University. I watched Jack battle the fine Purdue All-American John Konsek in 1960, the same year twenty-year-old Nicklaus made headlines in the United States Open by finishing runner-up to Arnold Palmer at Cherry Hills in Denver.

Thinking back, I recall the robust twenty-year-old Nicklaus booming tee shots one hundred yards past Konsek, who had a more accurate but less powerful swing. I also recall that Nicklaus's unbridled strength cost him the match: He often hit the ball too far, to places nobody thought possible, while Konsek split the fairways and posted lower scores. Despite seeing Nicklaus lose, I realized I had seen a player of immense talent and incredible promise. I remember telling my dad, "You wouldn't have believed it. Nicklaus hit the ball like King Kong."

During the past four decades, I have marveled at the way Nicklaus, dubbed the Golden Bear because of his burlish body and straw-colored hair, has overwhelmed golf's finest players. He quickly snatched the title of "golf's finest" from Arnold Palmer and then fended off such talented challengers as Gary Player, Lee Trevino, Johnny Miller, Tom Watson, and Severiano Ballesteros, among others.

My most striking recollection of Jack Nicklaus was not the fairy-tale-like 1986 Masters victory, in which Jack broke a six-year drought without winning a major, but his demeanor after the devastating loss to Lee Trevino in the 1972 British Open. His gentlemanly manner and tribute to one who had snuffed out the best chance he had at Bobby Jones's vaunted Grand Slam was exemplary. I came away with new respect for Nicklaus. This book will chronicle that courageous year when Nicklaus was at the pinnacle of his play.

Many years later, I saw a different image of Jack Nicklaus, the businessman and golf course architect. While researching the book *Bury Me in a Pot Bunker* with golf course designers Pete and Alice Dye, Pete took me to a never-to-be-forgotten lunch with Jack and his long-time friend golf instructor Jim Flick. Munching a turkey on wheat, I was mesmerized by the cumulative wisdom of Dye and Nicklaus as they talked about the game they both love dearly. Pete brought out Jack's best trait, his laughter, as they traded barbs of old when the two were associated with course design in the late 1960s.

Since I began writing this book, I have discovered fresh images of Nicklaus. When I first informed him of my commitment to write his biography, a month passed, then I received a terse letter from him urging me to abandon the project. He cited his work on his autobiography and the fear that I would not be accurate. He assured me that neither he nor Golden Bear, his organization, would cooperate. In the coming months, it became clear he had persuaded certain individuals that I contacted for interviews not to talk to me.

When I later learned that Nicklaus had been misinformed of my intentions, I asked mutual friends to talk with him and wrote Jack two additional letters requesting an interview. Neither produced alteration in his attitude toward potential cooperation.

Several of my journalist colleagues assured me that Jack meant nothing personal. "He simply has a distrust for things he cannot control," one told me. Another added, "Jack doesn't like surprises." Whether he would have been pleased if someone else had been the author, I do not know, but I regret that Jack would not speak personally with me so I could get a firsthand understanding of his thoughts about important events and their impact on his life.

To present the "voice" of Jack, I have instead included references from two books he has co-authored, two books that provided editorial comment by Jack, numerous magazine and newspaper reports, and material from over one hundred interviews with primary sources who shared their impressions of him.

To ensure accuracy, I have, wherever possible, corroborated the material by talking to current and former associates of Jack's or persons who witnessed the incidents chronicled. In addition, Tom Meeks, a respected official with the United States Golf Association, and Tom Peterson, Nicklaus's chief financial officer at Golden Bear, Inc. for over twenty years (longer than any other Nicklaus business associate), Alice Dye, two-time United States Senior Amateur champion, Kent Frandsen, a noted amateur golfer, and Jim Ferriell, former touring professional, reviewed drafts of the book and provided their insights about Jack and checked the facts.

The most recent recollections I have of Nicklaus involve his play and demeanor at the 1996 Memorial, United States Senior Open, British Open, and PGA Championship.

At The Memorial, his own coveted tournament at Muirfield Village, I watched Jack the frustrated golfer with a grumpy attitude to match. Perhaps his blemished play was the result of the announcement that several million dollars he hoped to receive through private funding for his Golden Bear conglomerate had fallen through.

On the Tuesday prior to the first round, I walked the fairways as Nicklaus competed in a nine-hole Skins Game with Ernie Els, Tom Watson, and Corey Pavin. Nicklaus did not play competitively against his rivals, though he did perform his trademark magic by holing a lengthy putt on the final hole, this time to win a skin.

Watching Nicklaus and Watson together in person was a dream come true for me, but the image of Jack was not what I expected. Unlike his television persona, Jack was drawn and appeared weary, nothing akin to the vital champion of yesteryear. Time has robbed him of his most potent weapon, strength, and often times he drove the ball well behind even the diminutive Pavin.

After the round, the spectators cheered the Golden Bear, but there was a sense that they were relieved the round was over and that Nicklaus would escape further embarrassment. Nicklaus made his way to the press tent where he noticed only a few journalists in attendance. Their questions set him off. He was short with answers and downright rude to one startled reporter.

Soon thereafter I saw Nicklaus at the United States Senior Open at Canterbury outside Cleveland. Whatever was bothering Nicklaus at The Memorial had vanished. He was humble and patient, playing practice rounds with little-known club professionals. Though his play in the tournament was spotty (sixteenth), he was affable with reporters and candid with remarks he made regarding the sorry state of his golf game. Jack was jovial and fun to watch. He appeared to be in better health and was having a good time, in spite of not being competitive.

Two weeks later, the same ebullient Nicklaus was blazing through the opening rounds of the British Open on television. His opening rounds of 69 and 66 at Royal Lytham and St. Anne's made his whole body smile. He played as if he had turned the clock back twenty-five years. Steve Hershey, the fine writer for *USA Today*, said Nicklaus was absolutely "giddy" during the bewitching round. I joined the masses in a universal congratulatory round of applause for the great champion.

At the 1996 PGA Championship at Valhalla, a Nicklaus-designed course, I watched Nicklaus play a practice round once again with Tom Watson. The Louisville area fans worshipped the two great champions, and Nicklaus, though sweat soaked and flushed, played well. On the thirteenth hole, a tantalizing little par four, Nicklaus strode to the green. I heard a proud father tell his son, "Now get his autograph. Tell Mr. Nicklaus you were born on the day of his last win in a major." The boy's eyes lit up as Jack approached, but unfortunately Nicklaus never saw him. Nevertheless, the image of Nicklaus, now an elder statesman of golf but still the idol of yet another generation, froze the moment in my mind.

During the tournament, I witnessed firsthand the character of Jack Nicklaus the champion. After opening the PGA Championship with a disheartening 77, the five-time winner catapulted back to within striking distance of making the cut with several early birdies in the second round. By the end of sixteen holes, fifty-six-year-old Jack knew one more birdie would permit him to play the weekend, meaning Nicklaus would have played in all four rounds in each of the major championships in 1996.

Although he was only attempting to make the cut rather than move into contention for a sixth PGA Championship crown, Nicklaus fought in the 100 degree heat with a ferocity and spirit that was undeniable. Grinding out one superb shot after another, the golf gladiator nearly met the challenge, only to be defied by a balky putting stroke that left him one birdie short. Although he displayed a beet-red face and hunched shoulders as he left the eighteenth green, the roar of appreciation from the crowd for his effort brought a smile and wave.

Because Nicklaus has been a fine amateur player, a champion as a professional golfer, a successful businessman, a respected golf course architect, and a man dedicated to his wife and family, there are many facets of the legendary golfer for me to portray. To present his story, I will weave the tapestry of his life around the magical season of 1972, a year that best encapsulates the personality and uncommon talent of Jack Nicklaus.

During that season, he expected the best, achieved it, reached beyond the definitions of success, experienced the depths of loss and despair, and then battled to regain prominence. Through it all, he challenged himself as never before and learned as much about his mettle as in any other time in his life.

So come take to the fairways with Jack Nicklaus, and enjoy five decades of the finest golf ever played in the history of the game. Along the way you'll meet Jack's family, his friends, and his competitors and gain a sense of why he is indisputably one of the great sportsmen of all time and a true inspiration for the aspiring athlete of today.

# BOOK I

# Destiny's Child

❖ ❖ ❖

# CHAPTER 1

# Crosby—1972

On January 16, 1972, Jack Nicklaus stood on the tee of the finest finishing hole in golf, the oceanside eighteenth at Pebble Beach, California, in the final round of the prestigious Bing Crosby National Pro-Am. During nine seasons on the PGA tour, the thirty-two-year-old golfer had notched more tour victories than many golf greats had in their careers: nine major championships (including two United States Amateur championships, three Masters, two United States Opens, two PGAs, and two British Opens), as well as triumphs in thirty-four PGA Tour events, four World Series of Golf titles, two Australian Opens, and the Picadilly World Match Play Championship, among others.

On that day in 1972, Nicklaus was attempting to start the new year with a bang. Based on his superlative performance in 1971 (he'd won four of his last five tournaments), Jack Nicklaus was consumed by a singular thought: Could he win all four majors in one year and achieve the miracle Grand Slam performance made famous by his boyhood idol, the legendary Bobby Jones in 1930?

The potential for a Grand Slam dominated conversation in golf circles. Experts analyzed his chances, figured the odds, and pronounced him ready for the assault. His performance at Pebble Beach would say a lot about his chances; he was determined to show the world he was ripe for the challenge.

Most experts knew what Nicklaus knew: The four majors in 1972 were scheduled to be played on courses favored by the Golden Bear. Augusta National, the site of the Masters, played well to

Nicklaus's strengths: power, ability to draw the ball on cue, and an adept putting touch. This combination resulted in Nicklaus Masters victories in '63, '65, and '66. Five months after the Crosby, the second major, the United States Open, returned to Pebble Beach. Nicklaus dearly loved the seaside links. "If I only had one round left to play," he said, "it would be at Pebble Beach." He had won the 1961 United States Amateur and the 1967 Crosby Clambake there.

The third major, the British Open, would be staged at legendary Muirfield in Scotland. Nicklaus not only knew the course but had also admired it since he first played there during the 1959 Walker Cup. He won the British Open there in 1966. Later, he would pattern his own Memorial course after Muirfield, giving it the same name. Finally, Nicklaus would test "The Monster," Oakland Hills, in the PGA Championship. It was a lengthy course where his powerful long game gave him a distinct advantage. He had competed there in 1961 as an amateur in the United States Open and tied for fourth.

Despite Nicklaus's past successes and promising future, some sportswriters were understandably skeptical that he could capture the Grand Slam, a phrase coined by a close friend of Bobby Jones's biographer O.B. Keeler. After all, only one golfer had ever done it. Before the season began, *Golf Digest* polled a panel of nine experts, including noted writers Dick Aultman, John May, and Ken Bowden, who would later collaborate with Nicklaus on many fine golf publications. Aultman chose Nicklaus to win both the Masters and British Open, placing Jack second in the United States Open and PGA. John May picked Nicklaus to win the United States Open and the PGA, noting Lee Trevino was better suited for the Masters and British Open. Ken Bowden picked Jack to win the British Open, place second in the United States Open, and finish off the pace in the PGA and Masters, where he picked Lee Trevino to break through.

The consensus among the nine writers was that Nicklaus would win the Masters ("Nicklaus is due after five winless years," they wrote), the United States Open ("Nicklaus is best in the big tournaments"), and the PGA ("The course is built for a big man and Nicklaus's fast green putting ability gives him an advantage"). The writers agreed that Trevino was the favorite to win the British Open, noting, "He's inspired by British fans."

When asked about his chances at the Grand Slam, Nicklaus told *Golf Digest*, "The Slam is a goal of mine. I suppose the odds are a million-to-one against anyone achieving it . . . but I don't believe you should set easy goals for yourself." He added, "I really believe I'll have my best chance at the Slam this year. I couldn't pick four courses I like better or that challenge and inspire me more."

Lee Trevino, interviewed in the same article, said, "I don't think it's [Grand Slam] possible for me, but it may be for Jack."

The Grand Slam seemed a formidable task, even for someone as superbly talented as Nicklaus. Of Bobby Jones's feat, noted journalist Charles Price had written, "Jones had broken the game's sound barrier, flown into its ionosphere, touched its fourth dimension. He had gone so far into golf-space that only afterward did the public feel that what he had done needed a vernacular handle."

In the final segment of the interview with *Golf Digest*, Nicklaus told of his plans for 1972 and the challenge he faced. "You have to bring your concentration to an enormous pitch [for the majors]. Ultimately, we'll all be measured largely by our performance in major championships. . . . The essence of Bobby Jones's greatness was his ability to play his best in truly important events. He has always been my hero."

In all, Nicklaus planned to compete in nineteen tournaments on the 1972 PGA Tour, with the majors his prime targets. The season would prove to be a trial by fire year that he would never forget. He would play golf as well as he had ever in his life, but the challenges he faced would test his physical and mental capabilities nearly to the breaking point.

To prepare himself, Nicklaus had trained with the dedication of an athlete attempting to win a gold medal at the Olympics. Nothing but victory would satisfy him.

By examining his play at the Crosby, Doral, the Masters, the United States Open, the British Open, the PGA Championship, Westchester, the United States Pro Match Play, and the Disney Open and weaving his professional and personal life around these tournaments, a full portrait of Jack Nicklaus emerges.

Jack Nicklaus was impatient for the start of the 1972 season and the battles ahead, those with rivals Arnold Palmer, Gary Player, Lee Trevino, Tom Weiskopf, Chi Chi Rodriguez, Miller Barber, Frank Beard, Johnny Miller, and Tony Jacklin.

He had skipped the season-opening Glen Campbell-Los Angeles Open, won by George Archer. The Crosby Pro-Am would be his coming out party for 1972. The 1972 edition of the tournament was noteworthy because money winnings would be counted for the first time on the official PGA money list. It also was the first Pro-Am in which amateurs were required to play with regulated handicaps. The Pro-Am featured such notable players as balladeer Glen Campbell; astronaut Alan Shepard, sporting the six-iron he used for his moon shot; and Minnesota Democratic Governor Wendell Anderson, who said that Pebble Beach "was so hard it must have been designed by a Republican." Arnold Palmer must have agreed. He passed up the 1972 tournament, the first Crosby he had ever missed as a professional.

Lee Trevino, who with partner Don Schwab ran away with the Pro-Am Championship in 1972 with thirty-two under, admitted he couldn't keep his eyes off the colorful galleries. "I ain't seen so many pretty girls since I left El Paso," he said.

The weather at the 1972 Crosby, called by *Golf World*'s Art Spander "an exercise in one-liners and three-putts," was straight out of wonderland. Instead of the usual cold and damp conditions typical for southern California in mid-January, the temperatures were so balmy the greens had to be watered for the first time in the tournament's history.

Nicklaus recognized the pressure he faced from the first tee shot of the tournament. "Everybody in the world of sport, except me, seemed to be talking about the Grand Slam from the first minute of January onward," he recalled later. "Even before the Masters in April, I seemed to have become the focus of constant attention, the guy in the middle of the merry-go-around."

Nicklaus opened the tournament, which was played at Pebble Beach, Cypress Point, and Spyglass Hill, with a startling 66, to lead Lee Trevino by three and Jacklin by four. A second-round 74 resulted in a tie with Tony Jacklin at 140. Johnny Miller shot 68 to tie Trevino (74) for second, three shots back.

Miller fired a super 67 to take the third-round lead at 210. Tony Jacklin matched Nicklaus's third-round 71, and they stood at 211. Trevino was at 213. Bruce Crampton and Dan Sikes lurked four shots behind.

When Nicklaus entered the final round, he could draw for help on a reservoir of memories of the famed oceanside course. Eleven years earlier he had competed there in the 1961 United States Amateur. His final-round opponent was Dudley Wysong. Nicklaus drove him into the ground with an eight and six victory.

That triumph came two years after Nicklaus's first victory in a major. In a squeaker at Broadmoor Golf Club in Colorado Springs, he had defeated Charlie Coe, the defending champion from Oklahoma, one-up.

The two United States Amateur crowns put the cap on an amateur career topped only by Bobby Jones. Ironically, Jack Nicklaus's early fascination with the game of golf was a direct result of his father's obsession with Jones, the greatest amateur ever to play the game.

# CHAPTER 2

# The Nicklaus Clan

The clubhouse attendant took one look at the stout man approaching, sporting knickers and slicked-down hair parted in the center, and said, "Go right on in," in a reverent tone. The man tipped his hat to the attendant and entered as if he belonged.

He didn't, but for the next few hours Jack Nicklaus's dad, Lewis Charles (Charlie) Nicklaus Jr., hobnobbed with several of the greatest golfers who ever lived. In both his attire and his physical appearance, Charlie Nicklaus was a dead ringer for the legendary Bobby Jones. The clubhouse attendant was not the first one to make the error in identification.

The golfers were gathered to play in the 1926 United States Open at Scioto Country Club in Columbus, Ohio. The tournament featured Walter Hagen, Gene Sarazen, Tommy Armour, and defending champion Willie McFarlane, who had beaten Jones in a double playoff for the Open Crown the previous year.

But the star was amateur Bobby Jones, a player without peers who was still four years away from his Grand Slam year. Just as Jack Nicklaus was forty-five years later, Jones was the favorite each time out and was expected to win the 1926 Open.

Scioto, a Donald Ross masterpiece built in 1915, was playing as if it hated the competitors. Heavy rains had soaked the course and the rough was so high that Jock Hutchison said, "I lost my ball, dropped another, and then while looking for it, lost my caddie!"

Spirited Brit James Braid, one member of the Great Triumvirate with Harry Vardon and J.H. Taylor, echoed his thoughts, "They should mow that blooming, bloody hay."

Along with the cries of anguish, the tournament became a dogfight between Jones and Joe Turnesa, one of seven golfing brothers. Turnesa birdied the final hole for 294. Jones needed a birdie to win.

His drive on the eighteenth hole measured 310 yards. A "mashie-iron" delivered the ball to within twenty feet of the hole from where his putter, "Calamity Jane," produced the winner. Famed writer Grantland Rice called the ending, "the most dramatic of all golf championships."

Witness to Jones's extraordinary play that day was Charlie Nicklaus, a sixteen-year-old drugstore clerk. Jones had made an indelible impression on Charlie. "All I heard about when I was growing up was what Bobby Jones did [in the 1926 Open]," Jack later said, "where he hit it, how he had trouble with the ninth hole and the tree overhanging the right side."

John William Nicklaus, or Jack, as he was called from an early age, was born on January 21, 1940. Franklin Delano Roosevelt beat Wendell Wilkie for a third term as president and Joe DiMaggio hit safely in fifty-six consecutive games that year.

The year was also an eventful one on the PGA Tour. Flamboyant Jimmy Demaret won the Masters, Lawson Little defeated Gene Sarazen in a playoff at Canterbury in Cleveland for the United States Open Crown, and Byron Nelson nipped Samuel Jackson Snead one-up for the PGA Championship. The British Open was shelved due to World War II.

The Nicklaus family could trace their history to Peter Nicklaus who lived in the Alsace-Lorraine area of eastern France in the early nineteenth century. Peter's grandchildren came to America and settled in Ohio and Kansas.

The name Nicklaus was first pronounced Nick-*loss*. It eventually became pronounced Nickl-us, with the accent on the first syllable.

Jack Nicklaus's great grandfather was a steel-hard boilermaker who founded the Nicklaus Boiler Works in Columbus, Ohio. His son Louis was a boilermaker like his dad. Louis married Arkie and they had five children, the second oldest being Jack's father, Charlie.

Love of sport and strength of character were indigenous to the Nicklaus clan. Jack's grandfather and his father were baseball catchers. Charlie won eleven letters in high school. He was a fullback on the football team, a guard in basketball, and a tennis player who won the 1935 Columbus Public Courts Championship.

Charlie Nicklaus's introduction to golf came through an employer, Fred Mebs, called "Doc" because of his avocation as a pharmacist. Mebs gave eleven-year-old Charlie a job as a clerk when he convinced him he could handle work intended for a much older boy. After finishing his paper route delivering the *Ohio State Journal*, Charlie worked at Mebs's pharmacy.

Doc Mebs not only influenced Charlie Nicklaus but also indirectly influenced his son, Jack. It was Mebs who asked Charlie to caddie for him and a few buddies when they played golf at the local army depot. And it was Mebs who gave Charlie tickets for the 1926 United States Open at Scioto, where the young man fell in love with the golf game played by nineteen-year-old Bobby Jones. It was Charlie's love for golf and stories about Bobby Jones that would in turn inspire Jack.

It was also Mebs who sold Charlie his first set of woods and irons, once used by Bobby Jones, for fifteen dollars. They were a perfect fit for Charlie's long-looping swing, patterned after his idol. That swing worked, and Charlie often shot in the mid-70s as the top man on the South High School golf team.

After graduating from high school, Charlie Nicklaus followed in Mebs's footsteps by entering the school of pharmacy at Ohio State. His stout, solid frame—which Jack would inherit—enabled him to play end on the football team. His career was over before it began when he refused an operation on his appendix that was required before he could join the team. Charlie knew the long recovery time would take away from his studies, a priority at the time, so he got up and left the hospital, much to the chagrin of the physicians. Charlie did play briefly for the Portsmouth Spartans of the National Football League.

Charlie Nicklaus's main goal was a degree in pharmacy, which he attained in 1935. Two years after graduation, he met and fell in love with Helen Schoener, a lovely woman who understood the importance of family and home. Later, Helen encouraged Charlie to accompany Jack to golf tournaments, while she stayed at home with their daughter, Marilyn. Neighbor Woody Hayes, the irascible Ohio State football coach, famous for his torrid temper and a stickler for family virtue, said of Helen, "I realized the [Nicklaus] story was more than Jack and his dad. There was a very important third part of this, the strong mother in the house."

While Helen kept the home fires burning, Charlie spent several years working in sales for Johnson & Johnson before purchasing a Walgreen Pharmacy in Columbus in 1942. During the following two decades, his business acumen resulted in the ownership of four pharmacies in the Columbus area. Doc Mebs even worked for Charlie at one of the stores when he became semi-retired at the age of sixty-four. The Nicklaus family never forgets their friends.

Although some were quick to accuse him, Jack Nicklaus disputed those who said he was "born with a silver spoon in his mouth." "My father wasn't poor," he once told *Golf Digest*, "but he certainly wasn't wealthy. He worked hard and was successful, but he had a middle-class income. When I started playing golf, he was probably a $16-18,000 a year man. By the time I turned pro in 1961, he might have been making twice that. . . . He had to make a heck of a lot of sacrifices to allow me to do what I did."

Whenever Jack Nicklaus is asked about his dad, his face lights up. There is no question that Charlie was a warm, compassionate, loving father, and a devoted friend and confidante. He had a close relationship with both of his children, but the ties that bound father and son became even stronger when, in 1950, the same year Ben Hogan won the United States Open Championship, Charlie Nicklaus introduced golf to his ten-year-old son.

# CHAPTER 3

# Learning the Game

J ack Nicklaus shot 51 on the first nine holes he ever played. From there, the scores ballooned into the high 60s and 70s before young Jack got down to business. By the end of that summer, the ten year old showed promise by breaking 100 for eighteen holes.

Nicklaus played at Scioto Country Club in Columbus, where Charlie had become a member in 1948. Charlie referred to his play at that time "tolerable." A beat-up ankle had hindered his progress through the years.

If not for an orthopedic surgeon named Dr. Jud Wilson, Jack Nicklaus might have made his mark elsewhere. After an operation on Charlie's ankle in 1949, Dr. Wilson suggested that he "give the foot as much movement as he could, the type one gets when walking on soft ground."

So Charlie took to the fairways at Scioto, dragging with him son Jack, to whom he had given a cut-down set of Hillerich and Bradley golf clubs. "[Dad] couldn't get a golf game," Jack said later. "I carried the bag and he'd play one hole and sit down, and while my dad was resting, I'd chip around the green and putt and hit a few shots and fool around like any ten year old would."

The sport of golf was new to Jack. His passion was football, which he played with zest, even around the house. The Nicklaus family maid, Annie, had been a victim of one of Jack's ground-level tackles. Battered and bruised, she promptly hailed a taxi cab and left, to return only when Jack's mother promised her son would save his tackling for the football field.

Even though Jack had a talent for football (the coach told Charlie his son would be the starting quarterback as well as a place kicker and punter), one expert discouraged him. Woody Hayes told Charlie

Nicklaus, "Your son has a great talent in golf. Keep him as far away from football as you can."

Though Charlie Nicklaus respected Hayes, he never discouraged Jack from playing any sport. As fate would have it, the arrival of a new golf professional at Scioto County Club influenced young Jack's life in ways no one could have predicted.

Although Dr. Jud Wilson is credited for resurrecting Charlie Nicklaus's interest in golf and for his introduction of the game to Jack, it was Scioto golf professional Jack Grout who recognized and nurtured the innate talent of Jack Nicklaus.

Grout was a native Oklahoman who spent several years as an assistant professional to his brother Dick at Glen Garden Golf Club in Fort Worth, Texas. He was a fine player who had a knack for spotting young talent, such as two teenage players who frequented Glen Garden, Byron Nelson and Ben Hogan.

The job of assistant professional at that course had consumed most of Grout's time in the early thirties. He then moved on to become assistant to Henry Picard, the 1938 Masters Champion, at the Hershey Country Club in Pennsylvania.

In 1950, Grout, whose willowy frame was more typical to a dashing South American hero in a romance novel than to a golfer, moved to Columbus at the recommendation of a member who knew of an opening. He was appointed head professional at Scioto the year Jack Nicklaus and golf discovered one another.

Jack Grout was profoundly influenced by Henry Picard, a disciple of Alex Morrison, a controversial West Coast professional with a peculiar way of teaching the interlocking-grip where the left thumb was positioned off the shaft. Like Picard, Grout believed in teaching the fundamentals; it was those teachings that molded young Jack Nicklaus into a champion by age fourteen.

Grout's methods were sound. "He was as good as you'd want . . . just solid," said Bill Thomas, the golf coach at Upper Arlington High School in Columbus when Grout was pro at Scioto. "He gave Jack the good things he needed to know."

The first meeting between Grout and Jack came when Charlie Nicklaus enrolled his son in Grout's weekly two-hour junior golf class. Jack's enrollment came after the gangly professional wandered into the Nicklaus drugstore in search of medication for a family member. "Charlie Nicklaus introduced himself to me," Grout recalled later. "He'd heard I was starting a junior golf class. . . . He told me he had a ten-year-old boy who wanted to play."

"When we started" Grout added, "the first little boy on the tee was Jackie. He was just out there slamming away, like little boys do." It didn't take long for the golf professional to see that he had a prize pupil. Soon, Grout was using Jack to demonstrate certain points of the golf swing for his classmates.

Nicklaus said later that experience provided him with great self-esteem and confidence. But giving his ego a boost wasn't the sole reason Jack played. "The reason I took up golf in the first place was because you could play it by yourself."

Although Jack Grout was capable of competing successfully on the PGA Tour, he preferred teaching. When Charlie signed his son up for private lessons, the professional gave Jack individual attention involving every aspect of the game.

Jack Grout and Jack Nicklaus spent endless hours working on fundamentals. Jack's natural abilities were in part hereditary, but it was Grout who mined the gold, making a promising player into a formidable one within three years.

A quick thinker with an analytical mind, Grout preached the importance of keeping the head still, stabilizing foot action, and developing a full arc swing by using a wide shoulder turn.

Keeping the head still meant disregarding the old adage to "keep your eye on the ball," which was possible even if the head wasn't stable. Grout believed since the head was "the balance center" for the swing, it had to be rigid from address to follow-through.

Jack Nicklaus learned that lesson the hard way.

A year into his private lessons, Jack, age eleven, was still a "head-bobber." One summer afternoon Grout, by all accounts a mild-mannered man, grew frustrated and called for Larry Glasser, an assistant professional. When Jack addressed the ball, Glasser was instructed to grab a lock of the prized student's blonde hair and hold on while Nicklaus made swing after swing.

Nicklaus's mother Helen was not pleased with the stern method the pros used, especially after learning the lengthy and painful teaching sessions had left Jack in tears. The tactic worked, however, and Jack learned to keep his "noggin" still, even cocking his head in a fashion that became his trademark.

Jack Grout's philosophy about footwork was simple. Conventional wisdom dictated that during the backswing a player should move up onto his left toe as his weight shifted toward the right foot, with the opposite occurring on the downswing.

Nicklaus was taught that the key to shifting weight was with the ankles, rolling them properly throughout the swing. During the backswing, the right foot acted as a brace while the left ankle rolled in later-ally. Coming down, the right ankle rolled laterally and the left became the brace. Grout taught all his pupils to keep their heels to the ground throughout the swing.

In interviews later in his career, Nicklaus said that whenever he experienced swing problems, he'd go back to Grout's fundamental of keeping his heels on the ground. He pointed out that Ben Hogan used the same technique. If it was good enough for Ben, it was good enough for Jack.

The Nicklaus full arc swing that would influence thousands of golfers evolved at an early age; in fact, it might be his greatest contribu-tion to the game.

What Jack Grout taught was simple: A full shoulder turn, as full as possible, was best.

Grout's philosophy on the matter was explicit. A young golfer who swings hard with a full shoulder turn exercises and expands his muscles. Grout was an advocate of hitting the ball as far as possible with accuracy coming later.

Grout's belief in distance over accuracy was perfect for Jack. By the time he reached his teens, he had developed a strong, compact body with powerful legs. He was 5' 10" and weighed 165 pounds at thirteen. In high school, Jack ran the 100-yard dash in eleven seconds, an out-standing time for a boy his age. Using his strength, Jack could tee the ball high and let it fly.

Nicklaus learned quickly that the golfer who hit the ball farthest had a distinct advantage. "You could see he had a chance to be spe-cial," Jack Grout said. "I never saw a kid hit it that far and that hard."

Some have wondered what would have happened if young Jack Nicklaus had learned from a professional who taught the finesse game. But Jack was built for power and his mentor knew it. Grout had him swing hard and with such a full arc that soon he was hitting the ball so long that one Scioto member called him "Superboy."

Besides worrying about head movement, foot action, and devel-opment of a wide swing arc, young Jack learned to curb his temper. When the occasion presented itself, Charlie Nicklaus made a point that his son never forgot. On the fifteenth hole at Scioto, Jack hit an eight-iron shot into a green-side bunker. Furious, he promptly threw his club. Charlie Nicklaus marched over to his son and said, "Young man, that will be the last club I'll ever see you throw or hear of you throwing, or you're not going to be playing this game."

Nicklaus later recalled his dad's words. "[They] said more than just criticizing my actions or temper at the time. Golf is a game of integrity, sportsmanship, humility, and respect. Dad helped me realize that early on."

In addition to respect for the game of golf, Jack learned much more from his dad. "[He] rarely offered me advice without invitation, but when I did ask for his thoughts, I listened to them carefully because he was extremely knowledgeable in all facets of the game. . . . My father's great gifts to me were his selflessness and the solidity of his character."

With his dad and Jack Grout guiding him, Jack Nicklaus enjoyed a solid foundation. Together, the three of them never wavered off course, but no one could have imagined the incredible adventures ahead.

# CHAPTER 4

# Molding a Champion

J ack Nicklaus shot his first 69 when he was only thirteen years old. He eagled the par-five eighteenth hole at Scioto by draining a thirty-five-foot putt so late in the day that he could barely see the tops of his shoes.

Two years earlier, he had shot an 81 in the Columbus District Junior Championship using his first set of standard golf clubs, a set of Bobby Jones woods and irons.

The legendary status of Bobby Jones had been everyday conversation to the young Nicklaus from the first day he showed an interest in the game. When Nicklaus entered the locker room in the Scioto clubhouse in 1950, there was a large framed photograph of the champion. Several Scioto members were Jones worshippers, and they often spun yarns about his golfing exploits.

The most exuberant spinner of Bobby Jones tales was a Scioto member named Stanley Crooks. His stories about Jones's strategic play made a lasting impression on Nicklaus. He told the young boy where Jones placed his drives on every hole, how he manipulated the ball onto the greens, and the methods he used to decipher Scioto's fast, undulating putting surfaces. Nicklaus spent hours grappling with the techniques his hero used to hit shots from different positions, recounting incidents such as when Jones rifled the pinpoint iron shot to within twenty feet of the eighteenth hole during the 1926 United States Open.

Jack Grout was also a Jones disciple. He never tired of demonstrating Jones's swing technique, believing it to be the finest of the day.

In later years, Nicklaus paid tribute to Scioto by calling it "a great training ground." The course, designed by Donald Ross, required superb play with each club in the bag.

If that wasn't enough, Nicklaus was able to gain a firsthand look at the finest golf professional the game had to offer. When Scioto hosted the 1950 PGA Championship, Ben Hogan, among other greats, competed. As testament to his great athletic spirit, earlier in the year Hogan had won the United States Open just sixteen months after an automobile crash. At Scioto, however, Chandler Harper emerged the champion. Regardless, ten-year-old Jack Nicklaus couldn't have made out any better; Skip Alexander, a touring professional, took Jack into the clubhouse, allowing him to collect autographs from nearly every player. Despite Hogan's presence, Nicklaus said "riverboat gambler" Lloyd Mangrum and a "scowling and silent" Sam Snead impressed him the most.

At age twelve, after eight consecutive rounds of 80, Jack Nicklaus finally broke into the seventies by carding a 74. The first 69 came a year later, the same year he received the scare of his life.

At thirteen, Jack was diagnosed with polio. Severe headaches, loss of weight, and an aching back puzzled his parents and doctors. When his sister, Marilyn, was stricken with polio, they feared Jack was infected as well.

Fortunately, Jack's case was mild, and although he lost twenty pounds (going from 165 to 145), effective treatment prevented long-term effects. Watching Marilyn suffer was difficult for the entire family, especially when she lost the use of one leg. Fortunately, that loss was temporary and Jack felt blessed that the epidemic hadn't crippled him or his sister permanently.

Nicklaus's zeal for practice and his willingness to listen to Jack Grout resulted in progressive improvement in his play. His parents built a driving range in the basement of their home, coinciding with Scioto's erection of a half Quonset hut that allowed golfers to practice in the winter. His father footed all the bills, including private lessons and fifteen buckets of balls at the practice range on Friday after the swing class. Later, Grout got so involved with improving young Jack's game that he finally quit charging Charlie for the lessons and the practice balls.

Young Nicklaus's work ethic added to the equation. He squeezed every bit of daylight out of each day, practicing or playing until it was too dark to see the ball. "I was one of those kids who didn't come home at night until my mom grabbed my ear and pulled me in," he said.

Nicklaus later admitted he was fortunate that his swing was "pretty much locked in a groove" at an early age, which was the result of Grout's vigilance to his game. "I'd tee off before eight o'clock and get in eighteen holes. Then I'd spend all afternoon on the practice range and the practice green until I could go back out and play another eighteen holes." Nicklaus added, "[Then] I'd walk in from playing and Grout would say, 'How'd you do, Jackie boy?' and I'd say 'I hit 'em, really hit 'em good, Mr. Grout, but I hit a couple of bad shots,' and he'd say, 'Let's go out to the practice tee.'"

Nicklaus practiced vigorously at Scioto. His game progressed so much that he'd begun some refinements: hitting a series of tee shots that went right-to-left (draw) and then left-to-right (fade). His favorite hole was the tree-lined twelfth, a 554-yard par five that featured a creek bed to the left and a wall to the right. "I loved to start [the ball] at those trees and cut it, practice those cut tee shots," Jack later said.

That several of the holes at Scioto were set left-to-right with small greens demanding high, lofted approach shots was a blessing for Nicklaus. The left-right shots forced Jack to learn ball control. He also learned to hit the ball high and let it descend on a vertical plane so as to produce a shot that stopped within a few feet after landing. On the 377-yard, par-four third hole, he practiced hitting left-to-right with short irons from out of the rough onto the green that sloped from back-to-front. On the 425-yard, par-four sixteenth, Jack would cut his second shots over the edge of the bunker and let them float down on the green.

Scioto members remember Jack vividly. Bob Hoag, a fine amateur player and Jack's partner later at the Bing Crosby Clambake, recalls the first time he heard his name. "I was playing the sixteenth hole one day and if you drove the ball to the top of the hill, you were a pretty long hitter." Hoag had walked up the hill, hit his second shot, and then walked toward the green. "All of a sudden," he said, "a golf ball rolled between my legs. I said 'Who the hell is that?' and the guy playing with me said, 'That's the thirteen-year-old kid. Jackie Nicklaus is his name.'"

Later, Bob Hoag prophesied to anyone who would listen that a new challenger to the professionals was on the horizon. "I used to play with Dow Finsterwald all the time and with Arnold Palmer quite a bit. When I came back to Scioto and played with Jack, I knew he could hit the ball better than they could. I kept telling people that."

Although Bob Hoag was talking about Jack's shotmaking ability, what impressed Robin Obetz, another fine player at Scioto and later Nicklaus's best man at his wedding, was the young golfer's mental capability. "Starting early," Obetz said, "[Jack] has always been mentally and emotionally mature. He could always control his emotions. . . . He had the ability to reason very well and to block out extraneous matters."

Just as Nicklaus always remembered his days at Scioto, the membership never forgot his early years there either. Jack Hesler, a championship caliber amateur, gathered a collection of memorabilia of Nicklaus's career, and it is now encased in glass along a wall of the Nicklaus Library. The collection includes Nicklaus's driver from his two United States Amateur wins, the wedge he used to win the 1986 Masters, replicas of trophies from all the majors, trophies of Nicklaus's triumphs from his early days as a junior golfer, and a wonderful picture of Jack and his parents.

By the time Jack Nicklaus was thirteen, he was beating the socks off other golfers, first the older members at Scioto and then youngsters his own age in Columbus area tournaments.

His first victory came in the Ohio State Juniors Tournament in Toledo, where he shot 161 for thirty-six holes. He then won the Columbus Junior Match Play Championship before testing his skills as the youngest qualifier in the USGA Juniors at storied Southern Hills in Oklahoma. He won three matches before being defeated. His visit to Southern Hills was the first of many for the young Nicklaus. Charlie wanted to give him valuable experience on championship layouts.

"That's where I first saw him," future amateur and professional champion Deane Beman recalled. "And I was quite impressed."

Nicklaus's handicap at age thirteen was a three. A startled teacher at school brought this to his attention, "Jack, I looked in the paper this morning. They printed all the handicaps in the area and you're the lowest."

Jack didn't always live up to his low handicap. While playing with the immortal LPGA golfer Patty Berg, the United States Women's Open Champion in 1946, Jack shot an ugly 53 on nine holes. He caught a case of the "shanks" and was embarrassed by his performance for several weeks.

At age fourteen, Nicklaus recorded his first hole in one while winning the Columbus Juniors but lost in the second round of the USGA Juniors in Los Angeles to Hugh Royer, a future Tour player. At that tournament, he attended a clinic given by Byron Nelson. "The caddie never moved sideways," Nicklaus said, impressed with Nelson's ball striking ability and the fact the caddie shagging balls remained nearly stationary.

Nicklaus's fifteenth year, 1955, was marked by additional victories and an astounding five 63s on the nearby Ohio State Gray course.

More important was his chance meeting with Bobby Jones at the Country Club of Virginia, where Nicklaus had qualified for his first United States Amateur Championship.

Bobby Jones spoke at the player's banquet honoring the twenty-fifth anniversary of his final appearance in the tournament. That had been 1930, the year of his Grand Slam.

During the Amateur, Jones saw Jack reach the green of the monstrous 460-yard, par-four finishing hole in two. He was the only contestant to do so. Upon learning from reporters that Nicklaus was just fifteen, the legendary golfer invited Jack and his father for a chat.

One can only imagine what it felt like for Charlie and Jack to stand beside Jones's golf cart and talk with him. Jack later called it a tremendous thrill. Here was their god of golf, a man both idolized like no other.

Toward the end of the conversation, Jones threw young Nicklaus for a loop. "I'm coming out to watch you play a few holes," he said to the gaping boy.

Few times in his career has Jack failed to live up to his billing. This was one of them. One up after ten holes against Bob Gardner, a future Walker Cup player, Nicklaus lost three straight holes. He managed to square the match after Jones bid adieu but eventually lost on the eighteenth hole.

When Jack Nicklaus notes his list of disappointments, the dismal display he put on in front of Jones ranks at the top. Charlie Nicklaus must have been disturbed, too. Showing off his son at the top of his game to Bobby Jones would have made him immensely proud. Little did he know that Jones *was* impressed, as was another talented amateur player named William "Bill" Hyndman.

"I first saw Jack play in the '55 Amateur," Hyndman said. "He had tremendous ability. So big and strong. And he was very long. He just stepped up and hit the ball as hard as possible."

Nicklaus continued to improve through 1956 and 1957. His biggest win came in the Ohio State Open in 1956. Nicklaus shot 76 and 70 in the first two rounds and then flew to Urbana, Ohio, where he played an exhibition match with Sam Snead at the Urbana Country Club, a course designed by Paul Francis Dye, father of famed course designer Pete Dye.

Snead beat Jack 68 to 72, constantly vexing the young prodigy during the round by calling him "Junior." Sam's smooth game, however, must have stuck with Nicklaus. The next afternoon he shot 64 and 70 to whip the best amateurs and professionals the state had to offer in the Open.

"I saw Jack play in the Ohio State Open in 1956," Deane Beman said. "It was evident he was going to be a very good player."

Jack Nicklaus met up with Bobby Jones again in 1957. They were photographed together at the International Jaycees Junior Championship played at Ohio State. That same year, Nicklaus played with future United States and British Amateur Champion Vinny Giles, who recalled, "Jack was overpowering the ball. He was 75 yards ahead of me all the time. It was very discouraging."

Jack's length proved to be of little help at the United States Open in 1957, his first year to qualify. In 1956, at age sixteen, his score made him second alternate, but he was denied a chance to play when no one withdrew.

In 1957, Nicklaus started play in the Open as if he could teach the professionals a thing or two.

By all accounts, Jack had been wide-eyed prior to the competition. If so, he certainly didn't show it in his early play. Nicklaus's playing companions were Tour players Tommy Jacobs and Fred Wampler. Jack hit a three-wood off the tee on the first hole, a seven-iron onto the green, and then holed a birdie putt from thirty-five feet. When he parred the second and the third, Jack Nicklaus's name appeared on the leader board in a major championship for the very first time.

Unfortunately, Nicklaus drove into the left rough on the fourth hole, flubbed his second and third shots, and made double bogey. Quick as a wink, the letters of Nicklaus's name disappeared from the scoreboard.

The same year Jack played in the Open, Bobby Jones visited Scioto and asked Jack Grout for a look at his prize pupil. "Mr. Jones gave Nicklaus a great deal of attention that day," Grout said, "and then advised me not to make any changes in the young man's style. He said Jack had such good balance and such a good sense of fundamentals, including an excellent head position, and was certain the necessary transitional adjustments would come naturally later."

Grout took to heart Jones's words. "Although other professionals later urged me to alter Nicklaus's style," he said, "I followed Jones's advice, and I'm glad I did."

Besides Jack's physical skills, there was evidence that he possessed a strong mental makeup.

In junior high school, Jack was not only a good runner for the track team but, as expected, he was also the starting quarterback, punter, and place-kicker on the football team. Playing those three positions required mental toughness and an ability to perform under pressure. Successful at each position, Jack proved he was a leader with an even temperament.

Jack also played baseball in his teens, having taken up the sport while competing in a Boy Scout league. His position was catcher, forcing him to be a field general who controlled play for his team.

In high school, Nicklaus started three years on the varsity basketball team. As a senior, he averaged eighteen points a game and was named "all-league" and honorable mention "all-state." More importantly, Nicklaus showed the ability to concentrate well under pressure, once hitting twenty-six consecutive free throws.

In the classroom and in the social arena, Jack also excelled. Longtime friend Robin Obetz said, "Jack was no average kid. He was never average. He was a much better than average student (3.25 average), much better than average personality, his athletic abilities were exceptional; he was popular socially, and had a good balance between golf and social."

Despite abilities in other sports, Jack knew golf was more than a game for him, and he spent every possible moment he could with Jack Grout.

During Nicklaus's high school years, they worked on two additional facets of the game: hitting the ball high and developing better expertise in hitting the left-to-right, or fade, shot. Jack's ability to master both would assist him in becoming a dominant player.

Bobby Jones's words regarding hitting the high shot were gospel to Grout and Nicklaus. Hitting the ball high, Grout told his protégé, would enable him to land the ball softly, almost vertically, on hard greens with difficult hole locations. This would be particularly helpful in major tournaments when officials positioned the pins in places only the most accurate players could reach.

By positioning the ball forward and adjusting his angle, Nicklaus virtually "swept" the ball off the ground.

The need to hit a high fade was the result of Grout's disgust for the "hook," which he called the worst shot in golf. He knew when a player came over the ball and snapped it, the result would be a speeding, overspinning, out-of-control bullet headed for disaster.

When a mistake was made by the left-to-right player, a bad slice resulted, the slice being the lesser of two evils. As Grout explained, "You can hit a duck-hook, but not a duck-slice. The ball may find trouble, but normally it's at least playable." Later on, Nicklaus recalled Grout's wisdom, pointing out that Ben Hogan never became a great player until he learned to hit the ball left-to-right.

The lessons Jack learned from Grout were specifically crafted to prepare him for major tournaments. As Jack approached his college years, his mentor had provided him with the fundamentals for greatness.

Bobby Jones knew Jack was a winner. In fact, his admiration of Nicklaus became apparent in 1959 when Jack was about to face off with Robert T. Jones III, Bobby's son, in the United States Amateur in Colorado. Young Bobby told Jack his dad was thinking about coming out to watch him play, but when he learned of the pairing against Nicklaus, he changed his mind. "He told me it wasn't worth it to just come watch me play one round," young Jones said.

And he was right. Jack dusted young Bobby off seven and six. It was the year Nicklaus made a serious bid to win his first major championship.

BOOK II

# Jack's Amateur Days

❖ ❖ ❖

# CHAPTER 5

# Glory in the Mountains

J ack Nicklaus stood eight feet away from a major tournament victory. "Not much break," caddie Bob Valdes told him, sizing up the
putt. "Left edge, if anything." The nineteen year old took one more
long look at the line to the hole from behind his ball, and then
crouched low over it, a position that was to become familiar to golf
fans for the next forty years.

Watching nervously at the side of the green was the defending
United States Amateur Open champion, Charlie Coe. The thin, soft-
spoken Oklahoma oil broker had won the Amateur Championship at
the Olympic Club in San Francisco in 1958 where he had defeated
future Masters champ Tommy Aaron five and four. Now, one year
later, a teenage collegian from Ohio State was one putt away from
stealing his crown.

The upstart and thirty-five-year-old veteran had battled each
other at Broadmoor Country Club in Colorado Springs for thirty-five
holes. *Golf Journal* later described the match as a "classic drama."

Charlie Coe knew from the first tee that he would have his hands
full. He had begun with a strong statement of his skill, making birdie
on the first three holes, but Nicklaus countered with two of his own.
Jack refused to fold and was just two down after the first eighteen holes
of the thirty-six-hole match.

Despite the lead, Coe was far from confident. As captain of the
American Walker Cup team earlier in the season, Coe had seen firsthand how good the teenager was when Jack helped the Americans
defeat the British at Muirfield in Scotland. Now Coe faced Nicklaus
and the old-fashioned hickory-shafted putter that the young golfer had
purchased during the United States-British matches.

That putter had been magic during Nicklaus's early rounds. He had putted brilliantly all week, especially in the semifinals against Californian Gene Andrews. On the thirty-fifth hole of their match, Nicklaus attempted to take advantage of a following wind, the thin mountain air, and the hard surface and *drive* the 613-yard, dogleg par five. The result was a bad hook followed by two more errant shots. His fourth shot landed the ball on the green, but twenty-five feet above the hole. Andrews was on in three and looked to square the match with par. Nicklaus then hit what was one of the first crucial shots that could make or break his chances in a major championship.

Surveying the putt carefully, he noticed that the grass on the seventeenth green was heavier than that on other holes. He hit a firm putt over a severe hump and squarely into the hole to tie. "There was no way that ball could get into the cup," a stunned Gene Andrews later told reporters after being eliminated by Nicklaus on the eighteenth hole. "Just no way it could be done."

In the afternoon round of the final match against Charlie Coe, Nicklaus drove long and straight while Coe found the rough on several occasions. By the twenty-first-hole, the two golfers were even. The next fourteen holes produced a tie heading into the deciding, thirty-sixth hole.

On the 430-yard, par-four eighteenth, Nicklaus drove six yards ahead of Coe, who used a three-wood off the tee. The Oklahoman then hit an eight-iron that bounded over the green, leaving himself a challenging chip shot.

Nicklaus first chose an eight-iron, but after watching Coe's shot, he switched to a nine. Playing the ball back in his stance, he hit a low punch shot that landed on the front portion of the green and rolled to within eight feet of the hole.

Coe's deft short game produced a sensational chip that stopped a half-turn from the cup. Nicklaus circled his ball, sizing up the distance and break of the green. He crouched beside the ball, took three practice swings, set the putter behind the ball and drew back. The stroke was straight and true, dropping the ball in the right side of the hole. With it, Jack Nicklaus had won the 1959 United States Amateur Open, his first major tournament, becoming the youngest champion since Willie Fownes Jr. who won the tournament in 1910 at age nineteen. Charlie Coe, despite being a fierce competitor, was a graceful loser, impressing Nicklaus with his gentlemanly manner, a trait Nicklaus sought to emulate throughout his career.

Jack Nicklaus's win in the Amateur brought an end to a hectic two years since Nicklaus entered Ohio State. Jack hadn't competed on the Ohio State golf team until his junior year, being ineligible as a freshman (they weren't allowed to compete) and unable to play as a sophomore because of a tour in Scotland with the Walker Cup team during the spring quarter when collegiate play occurred.

Academics and golf were not the only things in Jack's life at Ohio State. Shortly after the 1959 United States Amateur Championship, he met his bride-to-be, Barbara Bash, an intelligent, attractive graduate of North High School in Columbus. Barbara, an elementary education major, met Jack when he was elected Snow Ball King during an interschool winter carnival, beating out the competition from her school. Barbara teased him about influencing the judges, but Jack won her over and the two became a steady couple.

The relationship blossomed when Barbara's father, a high school mathematics teacher, tutored Jack for an algebra and trigonometry exam. A score of one hundred resulted and Jack aced the course.

Nicklaus's major was pre-pharmacy, but he could not sustain his zeal to push pills and finally ended up pursuing a degree in insurance. To this day, Nicklaus regrets that he didn't complete his degree from OSU, but he was intensely focused on playing golf and attaining a proficiency level that would make him competitive with the best players.

Nicklaus's reputation began to spread throughout the nation in 1958. That was the year, at age eighteen, he won the Trans-Mississippi Championship. That tournament, the Western, and the North and South Amateur—were not as prestigous as the United States Amateur, but they were still important tournaments that attracted the country's best amateurs.

The Trans-Mississippi Tournament was played at Prairie Dunes, a popular course designed by Perry Maxwell near Hutchison, Kansas. In the semifinals, Nicklaus faced a thirty-two-year-old aspiring golf architect named Pete Dye.

Dye, who would design, along with his wife Alice, such magnificent layouts as Harbour Town, Oak Tree, Crooked Stick, the Stadium Course at TPC, Oak Tree, and Teeth of the Dog in the Dominican Republic, fought a good fight but to no avail. "Midway through the front nine, my confidence wavered when I found myself being outdriven by thirty yards on every hole by this young kid half my age," Dye said in his autobiography, *Bury Me in a Pot Bunker*. "After he dusted me off, Jack went on to become the youngest champion in the history of the Trans-Mississippi."

After the loss, Pete Dye remembers asking Nicklaus a favor before he left Kansas. "I flew back to Ohio," Dye recalled, "but I asked Jack to bring my clubs back in the trunk of his dad's car. He might have won the tournament, and his incredible memory lets him recall every shot he ever hit, but he forgot my clubs. Left them out in the middle of Kansas."

The Trans-Mississippi victory (Nicklaus defeated Dick Norville nine and eight in the finals) was combined with solid performances by Nicklaus in the Rubber City Open in Akron, Ohio, his first PGA event, and the United States Open held at Southern Hills in Tulsa.

At Akron, the teenage Nicklaus fired rounds of 67 and 66 to take the lead from future PGA Tour players Charlie Sifford and Jerry McGee. Paired with "Terrible" Tommy Bolt and leader Art Wall in the third round, he was distracted by Bolt's shenanigans and shot 41 and 35. Smooth-swinging Julius Boros was his playing companion in the final round. The eighteen-year-old Nicklaus rebounded with 68, finishing twelfth.

Growing confidence from the final round spilled over into the United States Open. Jack had qualified for a second time in 1957 but missed the cut. In 1958, rounds of 79 and 75 permitted him to play on the weekend. He shot 73 and 77 for a total of 304. He finished seventy-two holes tied for forty-first, twenty-one shots behind Mr. Bolt.

The trip to Olympic's Lake Course for the 1958 United States Amateur did not bring victory but instead folklore. Among the membership was Bob Rosburg, who at age twelve beat the irascible baseball great Ty Cobb seven and six in the club championship; Ken Venturi; and Johnny Miller. There also was a player named Johnny Swanson, who "dressed like Archie Bunker and played like Minnesota Fats," according to *Golf Magazine* editor George Peper.

Swanson and Nicklaus hooked up on the first tee of a practice round. Nicklaus asked his opponent, "How many strokes do you want?" To which Swanson replied, "Strokes? Listen, fat boy. I don't need anything from you. It's you and me, belly to belly, for all of your trophies."

The match was a heated one. By the end of sixteen holes, Swanson was one up, but the eighteen-year-old Nicklaus finished the last two holes with an eagle and birdie to prevail.

Despite his triumphant practice round, Nicklaus couldn't beat two-time champion Harvie Ward in the second round of the United States Amateur. Ward had thirteen one-putt greens and rattled Jack with scrambling shots that included "getting up and down from a hot dog stand." Jack said later that he learned that day to stay focused on himself and not to pay attention to the other guy's game.

In spite of that defeat, Nicklaus had a stellar year by anyone's standards. The next year would prove to be even better.

# CHAPTER 6

# Jack in Scotland

In 1959, Jack Nicklaus won the United States Amateur, won the North and South, won the Trans-Mississippi (again), played in the Masters for the first time, qualified for the United States Open, won the Royal St. George's Challenge Vase in England, and went to the quarterfinals in the only British Amateur he ever entered. Not bad for a nineteen year old!

Nicklaus's first trip to the Masters was an eventful one. Experiencing the aura of Augusta was something Jack called "the thrill of a lifetime." Unfortunately, his play left something to be desired. He missed the cut and headed home.

Despite his poor play, one future opponent of Nicklaus's was quite impressed. "I watched Jack at the '59 Masters," Jim Dent said. "I remember he was a little chubby, but he sure could play. And he was long, *really* long. Amateurs weren't supposed to knock it as far as the pros, but Nicklaus was outhitting them all. Jack was strong as a bull. He knocked it right over the bunker at number one. Nobody else was doing that." Dent also added, "And Jack was doing it with bad golf balls and mediocre equipment compared with what we have today."

The highlight of the year for Nicklaus was the Walker Cup matches against Great Britain. The event had a long and distinguished history, dating to 1922 when the United States defeated the British eight and four at the National Golf Links of America in Southampton, New York.

Based on his performance in 1958, Nicklaus thought he had a shot at making the team. The team members were announced in January of 1959. They included Harvie Ward, future PGA Tour Commissioner Deane Beman, Charlie Coe, Billy Joe Patton, Bud Taylor, Tommy Aaron, Ward Wetlauffer, Bill Hyndman—and Jack Nicklaus.

The selection was heady stuff for a nineteen year old, and it proved to be an invaluable experience with lasting memories.

For starters, Jack was swept off his feet for the second time in less than a year, but he knew Barbara would understand. It happened the moment he saw the Honorable Company of Edinburgh Golfers at Muirfield, Scotland, the seaside links course off the Firth of Forth, crafted by the legendary Old Tom Morris.

Nicklaus's interest in the history of the game and golf course design in his early years is pure conjecture, but Muirfield's beauty no doubt opened his eyes to the traditions of golf. Besides gaining respect for the history of the sport, he was impressed with the many facets of the Muirfield design. The course's bunkers, in particular, caught his attention. "There are something like 190 bunkers at Muirfield," Jack said. "The most fastidiously built bunkers I had ever seen, the front walls faced with bricks of turf fitted together so precisely that you would have thought a master mason had been called in."

Nicklaus also liked the way that "trouble" was ever-present. His fascination with the deep-set bunkers and the honesty of the course is evident when one considers his own later design at Muirfield Village in Dublin, Ohio, named and styled after the famed Scottish course.

The teenage Nicklaus suffered a rude awakening, however, when he attempted to land his high, floating iron shots on Muirfield's cement-like greens. Rain had not blessed Scottish soil in May, and the surface of the greens repelled the small British ball like hail on a tin roof.

Jack's practice partner for the matches was twenty-three-year-old Ward Wetlauffer, an affable man with a ready smile. He was a quarter finalist in the 1958 United States Amateur and, like Nicklaus, Beman, and Tommy Aaron, was playing in his first Walker Cup.

The British press dubbed the younger players the "Whiz Kids." Together with the veterans, they were expected to challenge what was being billed as one of the strongest British squads in several years. Irishman Joe Carr, a two-time British Amateur Champion, led the squad along with Guy Wolstenholme and young Michael Bonnallock, who went on to win the British Amateur title five times.

"The British were primed and ready," said Bill Hyndman, who finished second to Harvie Ward in the United States Amateur Championship in 1955. "The great Henry Cotton tutored their squad to get them ready."

But the Americans were ready too, at least the younger ones. "When we arrived the old guys went to bed," Deane Beman recalled. "The Whiz Kids hit the course."

The Brits got their first look at Nicklaus in a practice round when several members of the British team approached the 349-yard, par-four second green just as Nicklaus was teeing off. "They watched in wonder as the ball arched against leaden sky, cracked against the brick-hard fairway and bounded onto the green." one report said. "Like a flock of birds reacting to a mysterious signal, they turned as one and marched smartly and silently back to the clubhouse and straight into the bar."

"That may be true," Deane Beman recalls, "but I think it was the third hole, a relatively short par four. Ward hit a huge tee shot on the front part of the green. Then Jack launched it onto the green twenty feet from the hole. The British players headed for the clubhouse, as if to say, it's over."

There were those who doubted young Nicklaus's potency in the unpredictable wind. Among them was Pat Ward-Thomas, a noted writer for the *Manchester Guardian*. "I myself wrote," he later told *Golf Digest*, "that Ward Wetlauffer might have a great deal of recovering to do when the winds caught Jack's high shots." His view was not shared by the famed journalist Bernard Darwin who was quoted by Ward-Thomas as saying, "Nicklaus struck me as a tremendous player of the future who hits, in the old phrase, like a kicking horse."

Hitting the bump and run shot and gauging distances in the blustery seaside winds presented new challenges for Nicklaus. The 6,806-yard Muirfield course played short but was not well suited to the youngster who liked to hit high shots with full impact.

Despite the fact that he and Wetlauffer were four down at one point in their first thirty-six-hole match against law student Alec Shepperson and his partner, Michael Lunt, they rebounded to win two and one. By day's end, British hopes for victory had been dashed as the Americans won every match to take a four to nothing lead.

The next day's singles match for Nicklaus against balding Scot Dickson Smith, twenty-two years his senior, was a cakewalk. Jack built up a five-hole lead with a 70 in the morning round, and then won the first three holes in the afternoon to go eight up. He fended off four birdies by Smith and coasted to a five and four stampede of the outclassed Scot.

Nicklaus's resounding victory, added to those of his teammates, provided the Americans with a nine to three win. The British team was stunned, their fans in shock.

"I remember that Walker Cup well," Bill Hyndman said. "In the alternate shot, Tommy Aaron asked me to drive off the first tee because he was too nervous. Later, I made three at eighteen to win our match over Joe Carr and Guy Wolstenholme. But even more memorable was watching Nicklaus play. He was strongly mature for his age. Had great common sense. Could really manage his game. He wasn't cocky, just supremely confident. So confident he felt he was unbeatable, even when he played bridge or gin, which he did well."

When asked by a sportswriter about Nicklaus's chances if he turned professional, Hyndman said, "He can't miss."

Nicklaus's impression of international play was evident with comments he made years later. "International team events are the most enjoyable in golf. If the game has one drawback, it is its individuality, its self-concernedness, its selfishness, to be blunt about the matter."

The team celebration was long and loud. Nicklaus had now been introduced to the challenge of links golf and the competitiveness of international tournaments.

But another lesson had also been learned. Nicklaus proved to himself that he could compete successfully on foreign courses and against foreign competition—and under conditions different from the United States. For the Scots, it was their first glimpse of Jack Nicklaus. Some saw promise in his game, but none predicted the international championships that Nicklaus now knew were possible.

Before he left the continent, Jack Nicklaus recorded a stroke-play victory and a match-play defeat. He won the Royal St. George's Challenge Vase in Sandwich, England. At the awards ceremony writer Ward-Thomas said it "was the only time I have seen Jack seem a little shy." He then lost four and three to Bill Hyndman, the crusty veteran, in the quarterfinals of Nicklaus's only British Amateur. Afterwards, Hyndman said Jack's dad Charlie told him, "This will be good for Jack."

Deane Beman, a diminutive player who resembled a pepper pot, beat Hyndman in the final three and two, sweet revenge for being bypassed in the team matches at the Walker Cup.

When Jack Nicklaus, described by Hyndman as "having a lot of stomach" at an early age, returned to Columbus, members at Scioto noticed a change in his demeanor. He seemed more sophisticated and cognizant of the honor of representing one's country. His dad traveled with him, making the experience even more meaningful. Jack was maturing, and the sight of him competing so ably in Scotland filled his father with great pride.

"It is chiefly a matter of having gained experiences and experience is an elusive quality to define," Nicklaus later commented on the Walker Cup matches. "After Muirfield, though, I know I had a deeper confidence in my ability to produce a good golf shot when I had to. . . . I had more confidence, too, about my capacity to function under pressure."

Nicklaus was now confident in his ability to play well anytime, anywhere; however, he quickly learned that pride goeth before a fall.

The 1959 United States Open was played at Winged Foot in Mamaroneck, New York, the A.W. Tillinghast course built in 1923. Tillinghast once said, "A controlled shot to a closely guarded green is the surest test of any man's golf." And Winged Foot surely tested Nicklaus's golf that year.

When Jack Nicklaus arrived at Winged Foot, he was a hot golfer, full of callow self-assuredness. Two 77s quickly threw cold water on his spirits. Later, when Nicklaus was asked by reporters to rate the fabled course using a scale of one to ten, he replied, "Eleven, maybe twelve." When asked about the difficulty of the finishing holes, he added, "The last eighteen are pretty tough."

Just as the Walker Cup had bolstered his confidence, Winged Foot shook his composure. He was paired with Doug Ford and Gene Littler for the first thirty-six holes. Both were fighting their games; Ford shot 141 and Littler 143.

Because Nicklaus would soon test his mettle against the Tour Professionals on a regular basis, he realized that serious work was ahead.

"I decided right then and there I had better start learning how to get my figures [good scores] on those days when I wasn't playing well," Nicklaus recounted. "While I was about it, I had also better start learning how to adapt quickly to new conditions, as the touring pros do who play a different layout each week."

Despite his poor play, Nicklaus had impressed Gene Littler, the precise player with the picture perfect swing who would become the United States Open champion in 1961. "Jack was powerful," Gene recalled. "He had a big shoulder turn, his hands were really high. He also had an air of confidence about him. Like he was going somewhere."

Following the Open at Winged Foot, a new phrase was added to Nicklaus's vocabulary: golf course management. He could hit it far and hit it straight and his short game was adequate, but he began to work hard on the more subtle aspects that had to be a part of any golf champion's arsenal. He knew he needed to hone his skills at lag putting, pinpoint placement off the tee, and positioning iron shots so an errant one was left in good position to gain par. He now understood the importance of figuring percentages of when to play safe or when to charge, and the necessity of finessing bunker shots into short range of the cup on the "right" side of the hole. In short, Jack Nicklaus was learning about how to play more intelligently so that when he was playing poor golf mechanically, he still gave himself a chance to win.

During three other PGA tournaments that summer, the Gleneagles-Chicago Open, the Buick Open, and the Motor City Open, Jack continued to learn more about these facets of the game. Three top professionals, Ken Venturi, Art Wall Jr., and Mike Souchak, won those tournaments respectively. Nicklaus's best finish was in the top fifteen at the Buick Open, but he observed the professionals and how they manipulated the ball into a favorable position on the course. Jack turned each experience into a learning one.

"Because of his great amateur record, I watched him closely," recalls Motor City Open champ Mike Souchak. "At the Motor City Open, Jack was everywhere. I could tell he was really trying to see how the pros played certain holes. Obviously, it didn't take him long to learn how we did it."

At the Buick Open, Bruce Crampton, who would later battle Jack in several major championships, watched Nicklaus for the first time. "Jack was chubby at the time, but I knew he had tremendous talent," Crampton said. "I realized it was only a matter of time until we saw him on Tour."

# CHAPTER 7

# Magic at the Open

Because Jack Nicklaus was already competing nationally and internationally against the best golfers of the day, some considered Jack's turn to collegiate golf as a sideshow. In 1960, his junior year at Ohio State, Nicklaus became a member of Ohio State's team. He and coach Bob Kepler had one thing in common. Both possessed the full turn, high arc golf swing. They also found common ground in another sport when Kepler introduced the twenty-year-old college student to the merits of fly-fishing.

The Buckeyes' main college rival was Purdue University, led by John Konsek, Jack's constant nemesis. Known for his precision, Konsek won three consecutive Big Ten Championships. Duels between the two became legendary, but like few others before or since, Konsek held his own.

"During that era, we played home and away matches against most of the Big Ten schools," Konsek remembered. "But I'd seen Jack play earlier when we were juniors. He was incredibly intimidating then, head and shoulders above the rest of us. Besides his length, which was overwhelming, he had maturity and composure beyond his years."

Konsek thought Jack was a more intimidating player as a junior than as a collegian. "He had so much knowledge of the game," Konsek said, "it gave the rest of us an inferiority complex. In those days, we had no chance, but then, in college, he found that the great length he had got him in all kinds of trouble. He actually would knock himself out of play. He didn't know how to harness his strength, and since players like me had matured and knew better how to manage our games, we could beat him, especially on shorter courses where it took placement and not strength to score well."

Another witness to Nicklaus's collegiate career was Tom

44

Weiskopf, a freshman at Ohio State when Jack was finishing up his collegiate play. "I had watched the pros at Firestone and in the Open, but I'd never seen anyone with more brute power, controlled power, than Nicklaus," Weiskopf recalled. "But there was more that made him special. He had the ability to evaluate a golf hole, plan his strategy, and implement it with precision. He knew what club to hit from the tee and so forth, and then he'd execute his plan flawlessly. And he always picked the right club. I've only played with three players who always did that: Hogan, Lee Trevino, and Jack. But he was doing it before he hit twenty."

Although Weiskopf's freshman status forced him to watch from the gallery, John Konsek fared well in college matches with Nicklaus. "He beat me at the long Ohio State Scarlett course," Konsek said, "and then I returned the favor at the Purdue South Course, where all the short doglegs favored a straight hitter like me. At the Big Ten Championship at Michigan State, where we played thirty-six holes two days in a row, I led by one shot going to the final hole. He boomed two shots hole-high on the par five, but I hit a wedge a foot from the hole to win the crown."

Konsek said that playing with twenty-year-old Nicklaus was an event. "It was a real circus. He had a 'name' then and there was a lot of 'oohing and aahing' at his strength. It was hard to believe how long he was. He's hitting an eight-iron; I'm hitting a five. He was flashy, a real crowd pleaser. I don't know if he knew how good he was, but I did."

Konsek, who later became a respected physician in Wisconsin, graduated in 1961, the year Nicklaus trampled the Big Ten field by twenty-two strokes. Ohio State University was the team champion by five. Nicklaus lost in 1960 in the second round of the NCAA but then captured the crown in 1961 at Purdue, giving him a United States Amateur Championship, a Big Ten title, and the NCAA Championship before he was twenty-one years old.

Even though he was a collegian, Nicklaus began 1960 with a respectable performance in the Masters at Augusta, won for the second time by Arnold Palmer, who birdied the last two holes to defeat Ken Venturi. Nicklaus tied Walker Cup teammate Billy Joe Patton for low amateur at thirteenth place. The finish was the first time Jack proved he could play competitively with the professionals in a major event.

But the growing pains were not over. More came in the 1960 United States Open when Ben Hogan, Arnold Palmer, and Nicklaus faced-off for golf's most prestigious championship in what many experts believe is the greatest tournament ever played.

The 1960 Open was held at Cherry Hills, a course just outside of Denver designed by William S. Flynn in 1923. Flynn loved spectator sports so much that he became a part owner of football's Philadelphia Eagles. He was also a futuristic thinker, designing "forward tees" instead of "ladies tees" and suggesting strongly that a limit be placed on the distance a golf ball could travel, a belief Jack Nicklaus advocated many years later.

At first glance, Cherry Hills did not seem to be a course that would favor Nicklaus. It wasn't long so accuracy was required more than power.

Prior to the Open, Nicklaus went through a ritual at Scioto. Former club manager E. Hugh Davis, a.k.a. "Sockeye," told Jack that if he could tee off where Nicklaus hit his booming drives, he would be a great player, too. Jack said he'd still beat him even if he played from the spot where Sockeye drove his tee shots.

Sockeye proved the loser, scoring in the mid-40s while Jack broke 40 even though he saw parts of the golf course he never knew existed.

Based on his practice rounds and the state of his game, Nicklaus felt good about his chances in the Open. Prior to the opening round, Charlie Nicklaus told Jack the odds makers put him at 35–1 to win. "Would you like to make a bet?" Charlie asked his son. "You're damn right I would," young Nicklaus said. Charlie then laid $20 on his son to win, meaning Jack would collect $700 if he won the tournament.

By this time, Nicklaus's length off the tee was approaching Paul Bunyon standards. Like Purdue's John Konsek, the members of Scioto were in shock. Jack regularly drove the seventh green, a 342-yard par four. One day Bob Hoag saw him hit a drive and eight-iron to the 527-yard, par-five sixth hole.

Nicklaus's prodigious length was about to be tested against the best players in the world, including Ben Hogan and Arnold Palmer. Nicklaus was certainly well aware of both. Bobby Jones was his idol, but Nicklaus called Hogan the "best shotmaker I'd ever seen. No other modern player . . . has approached his control of the swing, and I wonder if any player in any era has approached his control of the golf ball. Ben has probably hit more good shots and fewer poor shots than any man in history." Jack Nicklaus had first laid eyes on Arnold Palmer in 1954, at the Ohio Amateur in Sylvania, Ohio. Jack was fourteen. Palmer was twenty-four.

"It was pouring down rain, and when I came off [the course], there was one guy out on the practice tee, hitting balls, drilling them about waist high," Nicklaus told the *Orlando Sentinel Tribune*. "I just sat back and watched him for about an hour."

Nicklaus added, "I didn't know who he was, but someone said, 'That's Arnold Palmer, the defending champion,' and I said, 'Man, oh man, he is strong.'"

Palmer remembered seeing Nicklaus at an exhibition celebrating "Dow Finsterwald Day" in Athens, Ohio. "We had a driving contest, and I beat him by a bit. After that I kept an eye on him and was aware of what he was doing in golf. You never know how someone's game will develop, but with Jack I figured it was just a matter of time."

The first round of the 1960 United States Open was full of thrills and spills. After Arnold Palmer's tee shot splashed into a creek on the first hole, he had a double bogey en route to a 76. Ben Hogan opened with a dull 75 duplicated by "Slammin'" Sammy Snead. Mike Souchak had only twenty-four putts to shoot 31 and 37, seventeen shots better than Tommy Bolt. Tommy's temper boiled over when he hit a tee shot out-of-bounds at eleven and a dunked shot into the water on the par-three twelfth. Two more wayward balls fell into the lake at eighteen for a back-burning 85. The club that he propelled into the air on the final hole was his straightest effort of the day. In another tournament, after Bolt missed a short putt, playing companion Ed "Porky" Oliver, a character himself, grabbed Bolt's putter and threw it over the gallery into the water. "Just wanted to help him out," Oliver told the press.

Colorful Doug Sanders also got into the act. Needing a four on the eighteenth hole to tie Souchak, he instead made six when an enthusiastic fish had the audacity to create a huge splash right in the middle of his backswing on a mid-iron approach shot. "I thought somebody was unloading a truckload of empty beer cans," he told reporters.

Nicklaus opened with 71 and duplicated it in the second round. Hogan fired a 67 to tie Jack at 142, seven shots behind the leader, the broad-shouldered Souchak. Thirty-six grueling holes faced the competitors on the final day.

At the 1960 Open, Ben Hogan was eleven years removed from that car crash that nearly killed him on Groundhog Day 1949. But the Wee Ice Mon made a remarkable recovery and by 1950 was back in competition, starting with the Los Angeles Open.

He returned strong, winning the '51 and '53 Masters, the '51 and '53 United States Open, and the '53 British Open. His game almost produced another Open Championship in 1955 at fabled Olympic in San Francisco. So sure of victory was Hogan that he had already given the golf ball he used in the final round to Joe Dey for the USGA Golf Museum; however, the crown was stolen away from him by Jack Fleck, an obscure municipal course player from Davenport, Iowa, who teed off at 1,000 to 1 odds.

A win at the '59 Colonial boosted Hogan's confidence. He felt he could win another major. He was forty-seven years old when the '60 Open began at Cherry Hills. His game was sharp, and best of all, a putting stroke that often drove him crazy seemed to be behaving.

When Jack Nicklaus learned of his pairing with Ben Hogan for the final thirty-six holes, he was pleased but cautious. Stories of Hogan being a difficult playing companion were widespread. As the hour approached for their tee time, Nicklaus became more and more nervous. "What should I say? What should I do?" he wondered. He didn't even know how he should properly address Hogan. If he called him Mr. Hogan, it might seem too stiff and formal. But could a twenty year old call him Ben? After all, Hogan had won nine majors and had a film produced about his life starring Glen Ford in the lead role. All these questions, as well as others, concerned Nicklaus, especially because he knew Hogan sometimes played entire rounds without uttering a single word.

The thin Colorado air gave a chilly edge to the sun-lit Saturday when Hogan and Nicklaus teed off. They both shot 69. To his great relief, Nicklaus found the Texan to be a delightful playing companion. "He didn't talk a great deal," Nicklaus said, "but whenever I produced a better than average stroke, he'd say, 'Good shot,' and in a way you knew he meant it. In a word, he treated me like a fellow competitor, and I liked that."

The two 69s brought both men within three shots of Souchak, who carded an erratic 73. Now the game was on. Hogan was in the hunt for a record-breaking fifth Open win while the amateur Nicklaus pursued his first.

On the back nine of the final eighteen holes, ten men were in a position to win. Souchak kept coming back into the field, and Arnold Palmer, Julius Boros, Jack Fleck, Dow Finsterwald, Don Cherry, Dutch Harrison, Ted Kroll, Ben Hogan, and Jack Nicklaus were all within one or two shots of the lead.

Nicklaus's thoughts of that memorable nine holes were indicative of his mind-set at the time. He was twenty years old and twenty-seven years the junior of his playing partner, but to hear him tell it, he was loose as a goose, out for a Saturday game with the guys. "The prospect of possibly winning the Open didn't faze me at all," he said. "All I had to do, I said to myself, was to continue hitting my shots well and let the rest take care of itself." He added, "I was *glad* to be paired with Hogan. It gives you a firm sense of reality when you look across the fairway and see his familiar figure walking to his ball as you walk to yours."

Although Nicklaus may recount his day with Hogan as a walk in the park, the more realistic view is that young Jack was scared to death of playing with the legendary champion. One account says Nicklaus slept little and ate nothing on the Friday night before the Saturday round. On the first tee, Jack paced nervously, staying as far away from Hogan as possible. Later, an incident at thirteen lent credence to Jack's less-than-calm manner around the dour Texan.

Nicklaus had played well during the opening eighteen holes on Saturday and for the first twelve holes of the final round, but that changed as he reached the thirteenth hole, a nondescript 385-yard par four. Nicklaus actually led the pack of professionals at that point by a precarious one-stroke margin. He rifled a three-wood straight down the fairway, and a solid nine-iron shot landed the ball to within twelve feet of the cup. If he birdied the hole—and it was definitely possible—Nicklaus would have a two-shot lead.

At that point, providence must have decided that Nicklaus was good but not yet ready for prime time. After a missed putt for birdie, he found himself staring at a two-footer from behind the hole for par.

Nicklaus inspected the near-"gimme" and was shocked to see a small indentation in his line. "Spike mark or ball mark?" he wondered, with logic pointing toward asking Hogan his opinion. He was about to do so but for whatever reason decided otherwise. Instead, he chose to just ram it over the mark and into the hole.

Whether he pulled it, as some say, or whether the ball nicked the indentation, no one but Nicklaus really knows, but he went from a potential six under to four under in a matter of ninety seconds. He was now tied for the lead with Julius Boros, Arnold Palmer, and Jack Fleck with five holes remaining.

Three putts for bogey at fourteen quickly changed that, dropping Jack to three under. When Hogan drilled a twenty-footer at fifteen, having hit an incredible thirty-two consecutive greens in regulation, the Texan was tied for the lead with Palmer and Jack Fleck.

Both men missed birdies at sixteen, Nicklaus misreading a delicate five-footer. The young lion then parred the par-five seventeenth, resisting the temptation to flirt with a hole location only five paces beyond the edge of a water hazard in front of the green.

The bell tolled for Hogan, however, when a risky wedge shot from twenty-five feet spanked the bank. The ball tumbled back into the water, and despite a valiant water recovery shot, Hogan carded a fat six that broke his spirit.

Ever the sportsman, Nicklaus later agreed with Hogan's decision to go for it with the gambling wedge. He believed Hogan felt he needed to win outright and not face the rigors of a playoff, especially after just playing thirty-six grueling holes.

Perhaps Nicklaus was just being diplomatic, but the bottom line: The twenty-year-old kid played the right shot, and the living legend hit the ball in the water at the most critical time in the world's most important tournament. Nicklaus kept his composure; Hogan didn't.

Shaken, Hogan then took seven on the final hole. Nicklaus finished with a five after a botched approach shot. Jack's 282 was two shots higher than Arnold Palmer's, yet the lowest score ever recorded by an amateur in the long history of the event.

The second-place finish spurred talk of Nicklaus's unlimited potential. For Palmer, the victory was a crown jewel. For Hogan, it was a devastating defeat. Three men. Three very different stages in three great golf careers.

Nicklaus, whose memory borders on photographic, later recalled each detail of that day outside Denver. Time and time again he would describe every shot, every emotion, and every nuance that occurred from the first shot through completion of the final hole. It was as if he and Hogan were playing in a vacuum, frozen in time, unaware of the significance of the moments they shared.

Nicklaus said later what everyone knew: his play in that tournament was exemplary. "That week I fell into a way of playing which I've never been able to recapture," he said, "though goodness knows I've tried a hundred times. The main thing was the feeling I had at address. I felt that my right knee was directly under me, setting up my pivot nicely. . . . I was hitting my shots a little like Hogan. . . . I was strong through the ball, and my irons were flying on a high trajectory with a touch of cut on them."

Lost in the moment until years later was the realization of what Nicklaus had actually accomplished. His performance against the big boys of golf, the best the world had to offer in 1960, is difficult to comprehend. It is one of the greatest performances by a twenty-year-old amateur athlete in the history of the sport. Only the performance of

John J. McDermott, who won the 1911 Open at age nineteen, can compare with Nicklaus's achievement at such a young age.

Sportswriters who covered the event lauded Nicklaus with the "next great player" tag. Competitors hoped Jack would decide to follow in Bobby Jones's footsteps by remaining an amateur.

If Nicklaus didn't realize the significance of the moment, Ben Hogan did. "I didn't win today," he told reporters, "but I played with a kid who should have won this championship by ten shots."

# CHAPTER 8

# The Miracle at Merion

Journalist Herb Graffis said it best when he wrote, "Jack Nicklaus has done a number of smart things in his life, but the smartest thing he ever did was marry Barbara." The two were married on July 23, 1960, during Jack's busy tournament schedule, and after thirty-six years and counting, they are still, as golf champion Alice Dye puts it, "one of golf's great love stories."

Nicklaus played sporadically following the '60 U.S. Open. He was defeated in the second round of the NCAA tournament, played without luster in the America's Cup victory, and then lost his United States Amateur crown when defeated by Charley Lewis five and three at St. Louis Country Club. That defeat came after he pummeled future Tour Professional Phil Rodgers in the third round by throwing seven birdies at him in the first thirteen holes. "Jack shot 29," Rodgers recalled. "I played pretty well and got beat six and four. Then he played Charley Lewis and shot a hundred [not actually]. Jack learned to not put all his eggs in one basket."

The marriage to Barbara Bash (they became engaged on Christmas Eve) took place on the same weekend Jay Hebert won the PGA Championship at Firestone Country Club in nearby Akron. Despite his great love for Barbara, Jack still loved his golf, so he, Ward Wetlauffer, Bob Hoag, and Don Albert, a gifted amateur and former Big Ten Champion at Purdue, sauntered out to Scioto for eighteen holes before the wedding.

Nicklaus's score is unknown, but according to Don Albert, the groom-to-be announced boldly on the eighteenth tee, "Fellows, this is my last tee shot as a single man; I'm really going to smack it." That said, he proceeded to dribble the ball into the creek fifteen yards in front of the tee, much to the delight of his companions.

After saying their wedding vows, the newlyweds headed for New

York City. The honeymoon trip proved that Jack had married an understanding woman. Along the way to the Big Apple, she didn't object
when Jack stopped at the Hershey Country Club in Pennsylvania, where
Jack Grout first apprenticed under professional Henry Picard. With
Barbara following every shot, as she continued to do whenever possible
for the next three and a half decades, Jack posted a 71.

At twenty years of age, Jack Nicklaus was married, a college student, a touring amateur golfer, and a part-time insurance salesman
earning less than $8,000 a year. New York City prices were an eye
opener for both Jack and Barbara. Taxi fare and the price of a cup of
coffee bought dinner for four in Columbus.

During the trip, Nicklaus realized he could count on a rather
hefty expense over the years, one he hadn't expected. He had been surprised when Barbara packed what he called "enough shoes on the trip
to last a lifetime." He was even more surprised when she asked to buy
more pairs in New York. "Compared to Barbara," Jack later said,
"Doug Sanders [a golf shoe aficionado] is a barefoot boy."

The trip to New York was high stakes for the new Mrs. Nicklaus,
whose hopes for the future were summed up later when she told *Golf
Journal,* "We just hoped to live the modest middle-class life our parents
had lived."

Whether it was pre-planned or not—Nicklaus never said—as they
packed their bags for the trip home, Jack suddenly ached to see the
Mecca of golf courses, Pine Valley, just down the New Jersey turnpike.

Built in 1912 by George Crump on 184 acres of sand hills near
Clementon, New Jersey, Pine Valley has consistently been rated the
finest course in the world. Its penal nature makes it extremely difficult
to play, but it should be every avid golfer's dream to play Pine Valley
once before leaving for the hereafter.

To test his game at Pine Valley, Nicklaus called upon a friend who
was a member of the course. Because women were only permitted on
Pine Valley's course one day a week, and the day they chose to play was
not one of them, Barbara was forced to watch Jack battle par from a
car on a private road that surrounded the course. Nicklaus lost that day
to Pine Valley when the best he could do was 74. Sometime later he
would return and shoot a 66.

The planned two-week honeymoon was cut to one for budgetary
reasons, and Jack managed to turn it into a golf trip. But Barbara was a
great sport, proving to be truly the perfect partner for her husband.

Two months after the honeymoon, Barbara became pregnant.
During her pregnancy, Jack made another important stride in edging
his golf game toward the caliber necessary to challenge golf's elite com-

petitors. Just as Nicklaus's finish in the 1960 United States Open was a foreshadowing, his play in the World Amateur Team Championship in September of 1960 at Merion marked the signal moment when the golf world knew he was destined for greatness.

Merion, outside of Philadelphia, was designed and built by Hugh Irwine Wilson, a Princeton graduate who was captain of his golf team. Ben Hogan had been victorious in the 1950 United States Open played there, but considering Hogan's seven-over-par score, some say the course actually won.

Like Cherry Hills, Merion didn't seem suited to Jack Nicklaus's power game. Called by *Golf Magazine* Editor George Peper "a dowager, a damsel, a siren, a sorceress, and the Princess Grace of fairways and greens," Merion is a narrow course (built on less than one hundred acres, half the normal land allotted) that requires precise shots. Its less than 6,700 yards are filled with shifty doglegs and more than a one hundred strategically placed bunkers. The premium was on placement and conservative, patient play.

Those traits were especially necessary when it came to hitting the greens. The approaches were narrow, requiring excellent judgment in shot selection. The ball had to be precisely placed on a particular ridge or it wouldn't stay on the putting green.

The greens at Merion are akin to moonscape terrain. Once the ball rested on the green, the game had just begun. Every putt, long and short, was a test of will. In championship play, the greens played as slick as bowling lanes, and many top players shook their heads in disbelief as they watched their balls scamper past the hole.

Nicklaus had always admired Merion. "Acre for acre," he later said, "it may be the best test of golf in the world."

The United States team of Nicklaus, new United States Amateur Champion Deane Beman, Bill Hyndman, and Bob Gardner challenged selected squads from all over the world. Australia, England, Canada, and South Africa were the most formidable competitions in the chase for the Eisenhower Trophy.

Prior to the tournament, Jack Nicklaus and Bill Hyndman flew to Merion from St. Louis, where Deane Beman had just defeated Bob Gardner to win the United States Amateur championship. "Jack wanted to know about Merion," Hyndman recalled. "'If you don't keep your shooter in the ring, you can have a million,' I told him, meaning you have to hit the ball straight."

After some reflection, Nicklaus continued the conversation. "Jack asked me what par was," Hyndman said, "I told him it was 70. He thought a minute and then said, 'I'll definitely break 270.'"

Hyndman normally would have dismissed the comment because that was at least ten under par on one of the world's toughest golf courses. "But the way Jack said it made me believe it was gonna be a hell of a week," Hyndman said.

If anyone bet the competition would be close, he went bankrupt. Superb play by all four of the Americans resulted in a 42-stroke victory. In the third round, Beman shot 69, but his score did not count because Hyndman shot 67 and Gardner and Nicklaus shot 68s under a format where the best three scores were aggregated.

Just as he had predicted, Jack Nicklaus stole the show and made headlines around the world. He shot 66, a new course record for amateurs, in the first round, followed by 67, 68, and 68. He won the individual championship by 13 shots over Beman and his total of 269 was 18 strokes better than Hogan's total ten years earlier in the 1950 United States Open. Several pundits said the course was not as difficult for Nicklaus because the fairways were a bit wider, the roughs were not as tall as they were at the Open, and the pin placements were not as severe. Yet, the improved conditions only made the course play a few shots easier, at best. Nicklaus bested Hogan by nearly twenty strokes.

"After Jack's performance, I thought to myself, I've still got a lot to learn about this game," Bill Hyndman, a veteran of scores of amateur and professional tournaments, observed. Deane Beman said, "After Merion the perception of Jack changed. I was in absolute awe of what he had done."

"I had never dreamed I could get it going like that over seventy-two holes at Merion" Nicklaus later observed. "Everything just came together for me. Every time I stepped up to the ball, I knew I was going to hit a good golf shot. . . . I was so comfortable before the ball I never gave a thought to the mechanics of my swing; all my attention was riveted on producing the shot I decided to play. To top it off, my concentration was astonishing."

Later Nicklaus added, "I wonder if I have ever hit the ball as squarely or sustained my shotmaking at as high a level as I reached at twenty [years old] at Merion." Ironically, though he tried on several occasions, Jack never won a major championship there.

Respected golf journalist and television commentator Jack Whitaker remembered Jack at Merion in 1960: "It was the first time I ever saw him play. I watched him on the fifteenth hole of the third round. It was a misty day, but I could see Jack's power was awesome.

Other parts of his game got lost in those days. He was so strong and hit the ball so far and so straight."

Nicklaus's play at Merion marked a definite turning point in his career. His power game coupled with his deft putting stroke had made a mockery of Wilson's masterpiece course. At age twenty, Jack Nicklaus had exhibited dominance. His astounding performance sent an unsettling message to the Tour professionals, who sensed that there was something extraordinary about this kid who would be joining them presently.

# CHAPTER 9

# Major Win Number Two

During the winter months of 1960, speculation was rampant about when Nicklaus would decide to shed his amateur stripes and head to the professional Tour. His attention was on amateur golf and married life, but his heart was with the PGA Tour. He had conquered every obstacle the amateur golf world could place before him. What was left to prove?

Nicklaus thought seriously about turning professional in the early months of 1961, the same year Gary Player won the Masters and Gene Littler the United States Open, but elected not to. Instead, he continued his assault on the amateur golf record book, tantalizing the professionals as he went. His philosophy was simple. "I just hit the ball as far as possible off the tee, found it, hit onto the green, then hit it into the hole," he said. "Rough wasn't any great problem. . . . I was usually close enough to the green and/or strong enough to just bulldoze the ball out of anything I found myself in, short of a young forest."

There is no doubt that at age twenty-one, Jack Nicklaus was enjoying every golfer's dream. He was the little guy (though not in stature), an underdog, the amateur, and a constant threat to the kings of the game. He could hit the ball farther than most who had ever played, so hard that he broke the face inserts on *nine* drivers.

Many saw Jack Nicklaus as the second coming of Bobby Jones. To most amateur golfers, low and high handicap alike, he was paladin. With April and the Masters coming, there was a buzz in the air. Could Nicklaus win at Augusta and become the first amateur to do so? The answer was no. A second-round 75 that year sunk any chances he had. His tournament total was 287, low amateur but seven strokes behind winner Gary Player.

Even though Nicklaus was playing well, he admitted he was out of shape. His love for food had started to produce excess baggage, and his frame began to resemble the Pillsbury Dough-Boy, double-chin and all. In an effort to lose the extra pounds, Nicklaus played thirty-six holes a day prior to the United States Open at Oakland Hills.

As much as Jack had been impressed with Ben Hogan at Cherry Hills, Hogan had been impressed with him. To Nicklaus's delight, Hogan had set-up two practice rounds with him. Nicklaus told friends later that they never played a stroke or match play game of chance but made an occasional bet based on who hit the fairways and greens. "Guess who won?" he said, not letting on how many dollars he'd lost to Hogan.

Nicklaus was a contender in the 1961 Open, playing the type of golf that once again showcased his potential. He opened with a 75 but then shot a 69 and 70 to place him three shots behind Sanders. For the second year in a row, Nicklaus would be in the finals group in the last round of the Open.

By the time he hit the twelfth tee in the final round, Nicklaus was just one shot out of the lead. Hitting his tee shot on the twelfth, a long 560-yard par five, in that final round, Nicklaus flirted with the notion of winning. His prodigious power produced a mammoth drive in the fairway. When he pulled a three-wood from his bag, the gallery leaned forward in anticipation.

Unfortunately, Nicklaus caught an unfavorable wind just as his ball took flight, and the result was a sinister shot that hit a limb on a tree down the right side of the fairway. The ball dropped straight down. Nicklaus managed a short-iron to within thirty feet, and then the debacle that had occurred on the thirteenth hole at Cherry Hills repeated itself. Instead of a birdie, he three-putted for a bogey.

That, for all practical purposes, ended Nicklaus's challenge. His fate was sealed further by a bogey at seventeen and the inability to make a birdie on the final hole. He finished fourth, only three shots away from Gene Littler's winning score of 281. Little did Nicklaus realize he had blown his last chance to win a major professional event as an amateur golfer.

Prior to the Masters, Nicklaus had won the prestigious Western Amateur. That year he would also win the NCAA, the Walker Cup matches in both foursome and singles matches, tie for thirty-eighth in the Colonial National Event won by Doug Sanders, tie for twenty-third in the Buick Open won by Jack Burke Jr., tie for fifty-fifth in the American Golf Classic won by Jay Hebert, and best of all, win his second major, another United States Amateur Championship.

The 1961 U.S. Amateur took place at Pebble Beach, a renowned course designed by John Francis Neville, a five-time California State

Amateur Champion, and Douglas Grant, a fellow state champion. When it opened in 1918, the layout was called Del Monte Golf and Country Club, but years later it became known as Pebble Beach, one of the most beautiful courses in the world.

The year 1961 marked Nicklaus's first visit to the legendary links along Carmel Bay. He had seen some of the great courses of the world: Pine Valley, Merion, Augusta, and Muirfield. Jack Nicklaus took one look at Pebble Beach and was smitten.

"I tried to bear down every moment, to think out and execute each shot just as deliberately when I had a comfortable lead as when I didn't," Jack said. "That week, for instance, my concentration was practically invulnerable, and I believe that my golf was every bit as good as it was at Merion—that is, slightly over my head."

With the physical part of his game also in peak form, Nicklaus was a virtual juggernaut. Two close matches in the middle rounds were a threat to Nicklaus's thunderous march toward the title, but in the end he prevailed. The semifinals and finals, both thirty-six holes, were mismatches. Nicklaus defeated Marion Methvin nine and eight, then a helpless Dudley Wysong eight and six.

Later, writer Pat Ward-Thomas said, "[Nicklaus's] victory in that championship was so commanding, so ruthless and so assured, it seemed pre-ordained."

Sweet memories of Pebble Beach remained with Nicklaus throughout his playing days. For the 112 holes played that pivotal week in 1961, Nicklaus was an astounding 20 under par.

Though he didn't know it at the time, Jack's appearance at Pebble Beach would mark his last United States Amateur Championship. Overall, he was 24-5 in USGA amateur play with a winning percentage of .828, which ranked behind only Lawson Little and Bobby Jones.

Jack's early memories of Pebble Beach, where he captured his last win as an amateur, were renewed as he competed in the last round of the 1972 Crosby Clambake, his first tournament of the year. Heading into the final round, Johnny Miller led by one. Tony Jacklin and Nicklaus were each one back.

Most of the contenders fell by the wayside since Pebble Beach played tough on Sunday. "Everyone was chopping so bad out there, it was amazing," Johnny Miller said. "That's what this course does to you. It jumps up and grabs you."

Tony Jacklin, wearing what writer Art Spander called "knickers and pastel pants," ballooned to 77, and Lee Trevino and Bruce Crampton shot erratic 73s. That left Miller, the homegrown California favorite, and Jack Nicklaus.

The two were dead even after fifteen-holes. Miller made all the hackers in the gallery and on television feel right at home when he shanked his approach shot at sixteen and bogeyed. That shot came after he said to Nicklaus, "It's taken me sixty-nine holes to figure my problem out. But I've got it corrected now."

The shank put Nicklaus one ahead, but Jack uncharacteristically three-putted the par-three seventeenth from thirty-five feet, squaring the competition once again.

When they parred the final hole to tie at 284, two ahead of Lee Trevino, it meant a sudden-death playoff. They returned to the 397-yard, par four fifteenth. Although a victory for Miller would be significant, Nicklaus knew he had to win the tournament to serve notice that 1972 was going to be his year and his year alone.

True to his character, he canned an eighteen-footer square in the hole to beat Miller, who jokingly told Nicklaus, "You're off to a bad start again, Jack. One tournament, one victory." The win was worth $28,000 to the new champion from a total purse of $140,000. It might not seem like much money in present day terms, but back then it was a small fortune.

The two contenders talked about their golf games after the tournament. Miller recalled his unfortunate shot at sixteen, and Jack recalled his problems with putting. "It was a perfect shank. If you've never seen one, that was it," Miller observed, while Nicklaus said, "I didn't play so badly. I [just] missed a ton of short putts."

"It was a day of who wants to win it," Nicklaus later told *Golf World*. "It really wasn't that tough out there, but Pebble Beach has a history of doing that to people."

Although the Tour headed to the Dean Martin Tucson Open, played in the third week of January of 1972, Nicklaus began thinking of his next two tournaments, the Jackie Gleason Inverrary and the Doral-Eastern Open. Winning at Pebble Beach placed him right on schedule. Now it was time for sunny Florida and a prayer that the sun would continue to shine through April when he played his first major at Augusta.

# BOOK III

# Jack Nicklaus, Golf Professional

❖ ❖ ❖

# CHAPTER 10

# The Rookie

"If I was playing well, I thought I might as well get paid for it. . . . I wasn't born a rich kid. Money like they were offering on the professional Tour seemed like all the money in the world." Those were the sentiments of twenty-one-year-old Jack Nicklaus in 1961, eleven years prior to his play in the final round of the Doral-Eastern Open in March of 1972.

Heading into the tournament, Nicklaus had a goal. Ten-years-plus on the Tour had produced official winnings of $1,447,286. That left him $23,940 short of the total won by Arnold Palmer. First prize in the Doral-Eastern Open was $30,000. If Nicklaus could win, he would top Palmer by $6,060 and become the Tour's all-time money leader.

In nine previous attempts at the 7,065-yard Blue Monster in Miami, Florida, Jack had never won.

And this time he'd be facing a blue-ribbon crowd: veteran Tour players Bob Rosburg, Lee Trevino, Julius Boros, Johnny Miller, and Sam Snead. Jack opened with two uneventful 71s to trail Trevino by four strokes.

In the third round, torrential rains replaced the Florida sunshine. Early rounds of 68 by Bob Murphy, Tom Weiskopf (coming off a win at the Jackie Gleason Inverrary), and Tony Jacklin were literally washed away. To accommodate television, officials cut the field from eighty competitors to fifty-two, causing several professionals to complain that TV had too much influence over schedules. Nonetheless, a thirty-six-hole final was scheduled, barring more interference from Mother Nature.

Nicklaus led the field with 64 in the third round, and he and Lee Trevino, who had shot 69, 69, and 68, took the fifty-four-hole lead with a ten-under 206. Snead, the tireless wonder, and Paul Harney were each one shot back.

Heavy afternoon rains postponed the final eighteen holes until the

following day. Nicklaus would have a night to think about breaking
Palmer's money record. More importantly, he knew a win could continue the momentum he needed for the Masters in April, the first major
tournament of the year.

As Nicklaus attempted to win his second tournament of 1972, in
as many tries, he could point with pride to a ten-year record on the
PGA Tour that was unmatched by anyone.

The question in 1961 of turning professional had been at the fore-
front of Nicklaus's mind for months. Nicklaus's thoughts reflected a
man in turmoil. "It was becoming clear that some big decisions had to
be made," he said. "I still greatly enjoyed the world and atmosphere of
amateur golf, but actually competing was becoming less fun the more I
was expected to win, which by then was every time I teed up."

He also wanted desperately to complete his education at Ohio
State. Jack Nicklaus was a man who finished things he started. Quitting
wasn't part of his make-up. Lodged against that wish was the realization that he faced financial responsibilities with the birth of Jack
William II in September of 1961.

"I was comparatively well off for those days, earning about
$24,000 a year from insurance sales and promotional work for a slacks
company," he recalled later. "But it was hardly secure income, especially in light of our recent parenthood. . . . There was the nagging question of how to continue to develop and maximize my talents as a golfer
and still be able to meet all my other responsibilities and work toward
my other goals."

With these thoughts in mind, Jack made a phone call. He sought
advice from Mark McCormack, the shrewd business manager who had
catapulted Arnold Palmer to million-dollar earnings *off* the golf course.
McCormack was a lawyer-turned-promotional wizard, and his
Cleveland-based organization, IMG (International Management
Group), was just beginning to gain notoriety for its ability to promote
professional athletes.

Nicklaus's consideration of a professional career in 1961 coincid-
ed with McCormack's leading effort to establish the sport's agent profession. More than anyone else, he had seen the opportunity to bond
sports figures with business opportunities.

Not content as a business attorney, McCormack edged into sports
management by booking exhibitions for professional golfers. He was
interested in golf more than basketball, football, or baseball because of

its superior potential as a participation sport, which would mean high demand for the dozens of products available to the thousands taking up the sport recreationally.

McCormack also knew that although consumers couldn't play basketball, baseball, or football with the greats of the game, they *could* play golf with PGA professionals. He envisioned potential for interaction with corporate entities and sponsors who wanted high-profile associations with professional athletes.

While setting up exhibitions with the professionals, McCormack formed close ties with Arnold Palmer. When Palmer asked him to handle his business interests away from the course, as well as to manage his private affairs, McCormack welcomed the opportunity. He sold his interest in his exhibition business to his partner, and the lawyer-turned-agent set out to promote his only client.

"That deal," *Los Angeles Times* writer Bill Shirley observed, "sealed by a handshake, made both men millionaires and changed the face of sports agentry and merchandising."

Later, Shirley's colleague Jim Murray put Mark McCormack's influence in perspective. "You look at the billion dollar business sports has become in this country, you look at the multi-million dollar salaries," Murray said, ". . . and if you had one man to thank (or curse), that man would be Mark McCormack."

Not content to have just Palmer as a client, McCormack signed Gary Player in 1961. When Jack Nicklaus phoned to say he "wanted advice" about turning professional, McCormack was only too happy to talk to the young Buckeye.

In response to Nicklaus's invitation, the endorsement whiz flew to Columbus in the early fall of 1961 and mapped out gold paved streets for young Jack and his family. He promised revenues in excess of $100,000, substantial money in 1961, in addition to anything Nicklaus won on the Tour.

In the sixties, aspiring professionals had to show the PGA that they were financially stable. That meant having $13,000 in the bank or proof that their sponsor was capitalized for that amount. Since Nicklaus had little savings and no sponsor, McCormack told him he could finalize a deal with Revere Knitting Mills to endorse sports shirts and sweaters. He also promised to close a lucrative deal for a book by Nicklaus.

McCormack's words were welcome ones. Jack knew financial stability could be his before he ever teed it up on the Professional Tour.

By all accounts, the moment McCormack left, the decision was made. As the years went by Nicklaus recalled it differently.

"I was still very much an amateur at heart," he said. "I had virtually made up my mind to remain one . . . but then I started looking ahead and planning all the things I wanted to do with my golf game, and quickly the sheer impracticability of my goals became sharply evident. I called a family council and also sought the advice of a number of good friends in amateur golf, and suddenly I made up my mind."

Although these words may reflect Jack's state of mind later, the decision was actually an easy one. His parents and wife voiced opinions, but in the end the chance to challenge the professionals and make money outlasted the desire by Jack's mom that he finish college.

The announcement that Jack Nicklaus would turn professional came on November 8, 1961. Not even a cable from Bobby Jones urging him to reconsider could change his mind. He would leave college and his insurance job to compete as a professional in 1962.

The news was not surprising. Several professionals were excited at the prospect of dueling the upstart youngster, but there was one who knew Nicklaus would be a direct threat to his lofty status. Thus began the greatest rivalry sports has ever known: Jack Nicklaus versus Arnold Palmer.

# CHAPTER 11

# Testing the Tour

Arnold Palmer captivated golf fans around the world when he joined the Tour in 1949 at the age of twenty. By the start of the '62 season, he had won twenty-six times, including two Masters, one United States Open, and the British Open in 1961.

With such momentum, many wondered whether Palmer might take dead aim at Bobby Jones's Grand Slam record in 1962. By sheer coincidence, Jack Nicklaus would join the Tour the very year Palmer was expected to play the best golf of his career.

Palmer's hard-driving, charismatic, tug-of-the-pants style endeared him to nearly everyone in the gallery, many of whom became members of "Arnie's Army," so labeled by Augusta, Georgia sportswriter Johnny Hendrix. Alice Dye said, "Palmer made direct eye contact with all the fans. He played golf like tennis: fast and furious. He made the gallery really believe he knew every one of them."

Alice Dye's description of Palmer's pace of play echoed that of Tour veteran Doug Ford, who observed, "Palmer has two 'speeds' for playing, a normal pace and high gear for when he's trailing [in a tournament]."

Palmer's aggressive play produced eight victories on the Tour in 1960 and five more in 1961. He led the Tour in winnings in 1960 with $75,263 and was second in 1961 with over $61,000. Those totals must have made Bob McCall shudder. He was the Navy chum of Palmer's who turned Arnold down when he suggested "Let's you and I go on the Tour and split all the money we make between us."

Besides Palmer, the field Nicklaus would face when he first joined the Tour included such established names as Art Wall Jr., Fred Hawkins, Walter Burkemo, Stan Leonard, Jay and Lionel Hebert, Doug Ford, Gary Player, Gene Littler, Johnny Pott, Jack Fleck, Dow Finsterwald, and Mike Souchak (who with Arnold Palmer, Gene Littler,

Billy Maxwell, Don January, and Dow Finsterwald had been the first collective group to come straight from collegiate competition to the Professional Tour).

There were also the veterans such as Ben Hogan, Ted Kroll, and Tommy Bolt, as well as newcomers Phil Rodgers, Tony Lema, Bobby Nichols, and Dan Sikes.

Despite the collection of talent looming on the Tour, amateur Bill Hyndman boldly predicted, when asked by a sportswriter about Nicklaus's chances on the professional Tour, that "He'll win a major championship his first year." Hyndman later recalled, "The guy looked at me like I was crazy."

The PGA Tour in the early sixties hosted tournaments with purses ranging from $20,000 to $35,000, but a few, such as Doral, the Western, and the Indianapolis 500 Open offered total prize money of $50,000 or more. The new Thunderbird Classic was the Tour's first tournament with a $100,000 purse.

Phil Rodgers's description of the Tour in the early sixties provides a sharp contrast to today's professional circuit. "The players weren't playing for much," Rodgers said. "Everybody was scratching out a living. We drove from tournament to tournament. The Tour was more feisty then, too. You had to fight and scrape to make it. Most players gambled and made money other ways to make ends meet."

By all accounts, Arnold Palmer welcomed Nicklaus to the Tour, but he was determined to beat his pants off. He would show the kid that professional golf was a different game. It had taken him four years as a professional to win his first tournament. Jack would have to crawl before he walked, too; Palmer was positive of that.

And crawl Nicklaus did. He made his first Tour appearance in 1962 at the Los Angeles Open. Later he said he never played well in Los Angeles, and his performance that year was a portent of the troubles to follow in the City of Angels.

The tournament was not held on a plush country club course like Nicklaus was accustomed to playing. Instead, the professionals competed at Rancho Park Municipal Golf Course, a high handicapper's haven that was designed in 1947 by William P. Bell, a former caddiemaster and greenskeeper. Mike Souchak had made his Tour debut there a few years earlier, telling reporters later, "I was so nervous I didn't have the strength to push the tee in the ground. I hit a hook that went so far out of bounds, I almost killed a horse in some stables a cab ride from the first fairway."

At Rancho Park, Jack's official first round total as a card-carrying member of the PGA Tour was 74. Course conditions were rough at best. Playing MacGregor clubs under an endorsement contract he'd signed in January of 1962, Nicklaus tied for last place. He pocketed a humbling $33.33 for the four days of work, far behind winner Phil Rodgers, whose final-round 62 produced a nine-shot victory worth $7,500.

"I never let Jack forget that I won and he finished dead last," Rodgers jokingly remembered. "It was the last time I was ever ahead of him."

Nicklaus quickly warmed to life as a PGA professional. "I found a very high level of what you might call 'competitorship' on the Tour," he said later. "Each man regarded the men he was paired with as equals. We were all out to make a living, and if you happened to be playing better that week than the next guy was—well, good luck to you. There was a minimum of pettiness and, I thought, a strong basic sense of fairness and sportsmanship."

Nicklaus may have been the only one who viewed the Tour so romantically.

It was the professionals' meal-ticket. Few of the players had endorsement contracts, and, with the exception of Palmer and Gary Player, none had Mark McCormack out scouting for deals. As Phil Rodgers pointed out, they ground it out each week, many hoping to cash a big enough paycheck to pay the electric bill at home.

Nicklaus's presence meant one more serious competitor the professionals didn't need. All courtesy to his face aside, many of them hoped Jack Nicklaus would fall on his duff, fail, and head back to Ohio.

Nicklaus was surprised to learn of this attitude in the media, which had always been cordial to him. When a California writer penned, "The pros resent the intrusion of this highly publicized newcomer," it made Nicklaus stop and think. His adverse reaction to the comments precipitated, unexpectedly, a somewhat testy relationship with the media.

Although Nicklaus would later put a positive spin on his last-place finish in his first professional tournament, he was embarrassed by his play. Despite the fancy clothes, new golf clubs, and endorsements Mark McCormack provided, Nicklaus knew he had a great deal to learn about competing successfully with the big boys.

The professionals' reaction to Jack's play was predictable. Mike Souchak knew of Nicklaus's great amateur record but said, "Playing on Tour was a different ball game. Jack was a rookie. He would have to prove himself like any other player."

Jack followed his Rancho Park performance with finishes that won him $550 at San Diego, $450 at the Crosby Clambake, and $62.86 at the Lucky International where he was dead last again. To correct his problems, Nicklaus took a practice session at the Olympic Club in San Francisco. He tried to straighten out his driving by changing the shaft of his driver, and he took a putting tip from Jackie Burke that altered his grip. Nothing worked as he won only $164.45 at the Bob Hope in Palm Springs.

In his first five tournaments, Jack Nicklaus won $1,260.64. He was making $252.12 a week, certainly not enough to support a wife and child. Worse, Jack Nicklaus was used to winning golf tournaments, not being an "also ran." His psyche suffered considerably, and he began to think about returning to Columbus.

Jack was frustrated most by his inconsistency with the putter. A chance meeting with George Low changed that. Most of the professionals believed Low was a genius on the short grass. Tour player Doug Ford simply put it, "He's the best putter I've ever seen."

George Low is a folkloric figure in golf. A fixture on the Tour for years, he fashioned a great career not in competition but in clipping opponents on practice greens around the world. Doug Ford claims to have seen Low take $35,000 from an unsuspecting Cuban on a putting green in Havana. Besides his uncanny accuracy with the putter, Low was just as gifted with other means of putting. "He could putt with his foot and beat anyone," Ford told *Golf Digest*. "He'd also turn over a wedge and putt with the back of it and win. Any wedge."

George Low told Nicklaus his Ben Sayers model putter was too light for the varying speeds of the greens on Tour. Low recommended his own George Low Bristol model, and Jack saw immediate improvement. Bolstered by new confidence on the greens, Nicklaus tied for second at Phoenix with Billy Casper, Bob McCallister, and Don Fairfield. Arnold Palmer lapped these four by twelve shots, but Jack received $2,300 for the second-place finish, his biggest paycheck to date.

The first significant finish of his professional career saw Nicklaus celebrate as if he'd won the Masters. More importantly, Jack's confidence was restored. Another bad finish might easily have increased his self-doubt. But after Phoenix, his confidence was on the rise, carrying Jack across the Mississippi to New Orleans.

Golf is the cruelest of all games. Just when the swing is in sync, the touch perfected, and the putting stroke tried and true, they all go south. No wonder Gary Player said, "Golf is the most difficult game in the world . . . the margin for error is minimal."

Jack Nicklaus was reminded of that in the city of clams and bouillabaisse.

The result was an opening round of 80 at New Orleans, the first of its kind for Nicklaus. Once again his confidence was battered, and his ensuing poor play in New Orleans and Baton Rouge showed the effects.

At the Pensacola Open, Jack shot three mediocre rounds that placed him back in the field but recovered by shooting his first low round on Sunday, a 64, to finish tied for eleventh.

After a quick lesson in Florida to correct what was being called a "flying elbow" (Jack Grout disagreed), Nicklaus finished in third place at the Doral Open, two shots behind Billy Casper. Momentum was building as Nicklaus readied himself for his first Masters as a professional golfer.

Even though his first weeks on the Tour had been inconsistent and for the most part uneventful, the pundits made Nicklaus a *co-favorite* at the Masters with Arnold Palmer. That didn't set well with Arnie's Army. After all, what had Jack done to deserve equal footing with their hero?

Nicklaus came up a bit short of pre-tournament expectations with a solid but inconspicuous 74, 75, 70, 72–291 finish. It earned him a tie for eleventh. Palmer cranked out a third Masters victory by defeating Dow Finsterwald and Gary Player in a playoff.

The victory triggered an incredible run by Palmer, whose popularity reached its zenith. The Latrobe, Pennsylvania, welter-weight won the Texas Open, the Tournament of Champions, and the Colonial, all with last-minute heroics.

While Arnie and his Army were busy conquering courses throughout the Tour, Nicklaus came close to bagging his first Tour victory at the Houston Classic, but lost in a playoff with Bobby Nichols and Dan Sikes. Off his best finish, Jack readied himself for his first trip abroad as a professional to play in the Picadilly Stroke Play Tournament in England. Rounds of 79, 71, 70, and 78 (298) denied him a trophy, but Nicklaus learned the importance of preparation for an overseas tournament. Those included an allowance to adjust to the time difference between Europe and the United States and learning to play the small British ball.

With the 1962 United States Open approaching, Nicklaus's mental state was fragile. The year had been more of a struggle than he had ever expected. He had no victories, something that shocked him, and the regimen of Tour life was draining. His days were consumed with playing golf, discussing business deals with Mark McCormack, running up huge phone bills calling Barbara in Columbus, and fending for himself like a first-year college student.

The worst part about being a Tour Professional was the long periods away from Barbara, his life support, and their son Jackie. His father Charlie was at his side for several tournaments, but Nicklaus found the Tour to be lonely. He wasn't prepared to fend for himself, unaccustomed to menial tasks. "My chief regret," he later said, "was that I had not signed up [to represent] a good Chinese laundry and a nationwide we-pick-it-up-anywhere dry cleaning service."

Despite his reservations about his golf game and the hassles of the Tour, Nicklaus looked forward to the Open. It would be played at Oakmont, near Pittsburgh, and Jack was determined to prove to the world that all the hoopla surrounding him was not hollow rhetoric.

# CHAPTER 12

# The 1962 United States Open

Jack Nicklaus served notice that his golf game was coming around at the Thunderbird Classic in New Jersey, a week before the 1962 United States Open. During that tournament, he practiced hard, especially with his driver, to make certain that his left-to-right fade could handle the tight fairways at Oakmont.

At the Thunderbird, Jack followed a 69 with a 73, and then a brilliant 65 to tie Dow Finsterwald for the third-round lead. Unfortunately Gene Littler fired birdies on seven of the first eleven holes in the final round, and Jack finished second. He won $10,000, his biggest paycheck to date.

Nicklaus now headed to Oakmont, site of three previous Opens in 1927, 1935, and 1953. Brimming with confidence, Jack told *Golf Magazine*, "I was ready going in. I felt I should have won it [the Open] the previous two years as an amateur, so I felt '62 was the year I should win."

Tommy Armour aptly called Oakmont "the final degree in the college of golf." The course, opened in 1904, was designed by three-time United States Amateur Champion Henry Fownes to simulate a British moorland layout. That meant there were few trees and no water, making it an unappealing site for the first-time observer.

What Fownes featured on his dream course were bunkers—two hundred and twenty to be exact. And he had them groomed with a tri-angular toothed rake that made them appear ready for spring planting.

If a golfer managed to escape the ferocious bunkers, they had to deal with Fownes's lightening-fast greens. "Putting on Oakmont's greens," *New York Times* writer Jimmy Powers said, "is like putting down a marble staircase and trying to hole out on the third step from the bottom."

Tour veteran Mike Souchak, while calling the greens as "true as any he ever played on," said striking the ball on them was like "putting on a billiard table."

At Oakmont, television commentators told their audience he was "checking his scorecard" during play. But Nicklaus was really checking yardage distances and other meticulous notes written on a notepad that had become his course bible. At the suggestion of Deane Beman prior to the '61 U.S. Amateur, Jack used the practice rounds the week before to pace off the course, helping him to gauge distance better in the tournament. That dictum would become a Nicklaus trademark in future major events.

"I played with Gene Andrews in the 1958 Amateur," Deane Beman recalled. "And I noticed he had a little book he kept in his back pocket. He didn't keep yardages, but only what club he hit from certain places on the golf courses. Sometimes if a tree had been cut down or a landmark moved, he'd have trouble."

Beman took Andrew's idea one step further. "I did what Gene did for awhile," he said. "Then I went to a football field and measured off how long my steps were. To the yard. I also paced off how far I hit each of my clubs. That was the key. You had to know how far you hit each of them."

When Nicklaus saw what Beman was doing, he was interested but wary. "Jack can be stubborn at times," Beman said. "He laughed at first, scoffed at the idea. Then he realized it was an extra tool. He paced everything off himself. Since he could hit his clubs a precise distance every time, it was a great advantage for him to use a yardage book."

Before that golfers had "eyeballed" distances, but now Nicklaus jotted down notes in a yardage book. Many members of the media reported that he was the first to do so in tournament golf, but Andrews and Beman beat him to the punch.

Nicklaus's playing companion for the first two rounds was Arnold Palmer, a favorite because Oakmont was only thirty miles from his hometown of Latrobe. Arnie's Army was big and loud for four days running.

Nicklaus had seen evidence of Palmer's popularity before in major tournaments, but now he witnessed it weekly. He told Barbara that Palmer was treated like a movie star. The fans loved him and hated anyone who threatened to beat their champion.

What people forgot, Nicklaus noted, was that Palmer was ten years his senior. They had divergent lives, backgrounds, and perspectives. The fans assumed Nicklaus wanted to steal Palmer's thunder, but what Jack really wanted was to play good golf and establish his own presence. His aim was never to be disrespectful. His dad and Jack Grout taught him otherwise. They drummed home the theme that a golfer played the course, not the man. Golf was an impersonal game. You didn't root against anyone. You merely posted a score and the lowest score won.

When he came on Tour, Jack knew Palmer was king. Arnold deserved to be among golf's royalty. He'd earned it. Jack wasn't seeking a rivalry. He just wanted to compete against the best. Now he was hooked up in a duel with a matinee idol and an army of fans who began to typecast him as an enemy.

In his first few months on Tour, Nicklaus experienced small doses of Palmer's fans' resentment of him. But at Oakmont, Arnie's Army turned vicious. "I thought I was at a wrestling match," said Tom Fitzgerald of *The Boston Globe*. A wrestling match might have been more civil than the galleries at Oakmont. Signs read, "Jack's a Pig" and "Miss it—fat gut." Some fans ignored the customary silence provided a golfer during his address and play of the ball. The crowd noise even continued during Jack's preparation to putt. And sometimes the crowd greeted him with a foot-stomping. It was classic hero-villain stuff and Jack was shocked to learn he was the proverbial black knight. A lesser man would have voiced his objection to an official. Nicklaus never squawked, even though his shabby treatment was unprecedented.

Many golfers were aghast at Nicklaus's treatment, including future United States Women's Open champion Carol Mann. "I thought it was awful," she said. "I felt sorry for Jack. That [the poor conduct of the fans] wasn't golf. But I never heard Jack say he was victimized. He just shook his head in disbelief and bore down more than ever."

His ability to handle situations like that, Mann said, "was due to Jack's upbringing. His dad, Jack Grout, and his hero Bobby Jones were all gentlemen role models. They all showed Jack that you do your talking with your clubs."

Palmer didn't encourage his fans, but he did rile Nicklaus with a pre-Open comment. "Everybody says there's only one favorite, and that's me," he told reporters, adding "but you better watch the fat boy." When Nicklaus learned of Palmer's words, he was furious. "I'll show him," Jack warned. "I'll show him what the fat boy can do."

Palmer's comment was significant. It marked a turning point in their professional relationship. Palmer had made fun of Jack on occasion behind the scenes, but this comment was for public consumption. Battle lines had been drawn, and from the very first day of the 1962 United States Open, Jack Nicklaus vowed to topple King Arnold from his throne.

The remark by Palmer also triggered a change in the men's personal relationship. Being cordial to one another in public was essential for both, but off the course, Nicklaus and Palmer chided one another.

Both men were represented by Mark McCormack, and Nicklaus knew Palmer was the agent's priority. Jack could handle that for the present, but he wondered whether McCormack condoned Palmer's taunts.

Despite suggestions he do so, Nicklaus never confronted his lawyer/manager. McCormack was, after all, the key to lucrative endorsements. But friends of Jack said it bothered him that McCormack never told Palmer to tone down his rhetoric.

Despite Nicklaus's desire to strike back, Palmer won their thirty-six-hole first and second round "matches" at the '62 Open, 139 to 142. Bob Rosburg shared the lead with Palmer. Billy Maxwell was at 141. Bobby Nichols and Gary Player were tied with Jack for third.

Displeased with his play around the greens, Nicklaus worked on his short game after the second round. Oakmont members recall Jack on the putting green well after eight at night, chipping practice shots and tapping ten-footers in the twilight.

Palmer and Rosburg played in the group behind Nicklaus and Maxwell for the final thirty-six holes. Arnold shot 73, giving him 212 and a tie with Bobby Nichols. Phil Rodgers, who often partnered with Nicklaus in bets with other professionals in practice rounds, was at 213. A third-round 72 placed Nicklaus at 214, trailing by two strokes.

For a time, it looked as if Palmer would charge ahead and dust the field. He led Jack by three after eight, but a six on the par-five ninth sliced Arnold's margin. When Nicklaus birdied eleven, the lead was one, and when Arnie bogied thirteen, they were dead even. Pars down the stretch brought them both to 283, necessitating a playoff.

To get that far, however, Nicklaus showed remarkable poise for a twenty-two year old. He had been forced to hole two short, tricky putts on the pavement-hard greens of the last three holes. The first occurred at the sixteenth when he left himself a three and a half-footer from below the cup. His solid stroke drove the ball dead center.

On the seventeenth, dubbed by journalist Herbert Warren Wind as "an ugly mongrel of a par four," Nicklaus attempted to find a sliver of an opening just left of the green with his drive. The par-four hole played fewer than 300-yards long, and Nicklaus's awesome strength permitted him to attempt to reach the green from the tee. He blocked the shot just slightly and the ball came to rest in one of Henry Fownes's famous bunker furrows. His play from there fell short of the green, leaving a delicate chip from the high rough infamous to the United States Open.

Nicklaus faced a critical moment because there was little green between his ball and the flag stick. A fluff shot would leave the ball in the rough, and a scalded one would catapult the ball over the green. Either way, double bogey loomed large.

Though not known for an adept short game, Nicklaus was prepared to hit the type of shot that faced him. Before the tournament, he'd sought out Art Wall, a master around the greens. The Tour veteran told Nicklaus the way to execute the shot, and Jack practiced it relentlessly in practice rounds.

Remembering Wall's tip, Nicklaus now gripped a sand wedge firmly with his left hand. He opened the club face and hit down and through the ball with a slow, steady pace. The ball broke cleanly, landed softly on the green and rolled to within four feet of the cup.

The means by which Nicklaus canned the ugly putt would later bring a letter of congratulations from Bobby Jones. He saw on television what Nicklaus did, that while there was a slight right-to-left break, the hole was perched on a slope that fell off to the right.

Throughout his career, Nicklaus became known as a player with a great touch on fast greens. Tour player Jim Ferree said that Nicklaus's ability on fast greens was mainly responsible for his great play in the majors. Ferree's comment has merit, but Nicklaus went on to win majors on many different putting surfaces, making the observation too narrow.

On this occasion, touch was not the issue. Nicklaus was faced with the task of hitting a pressure-packed four-footer firm and straight toward the center of the hole. If it veered off, the next putt would be from well past the hole.

After great deliberation, Nicklaus steadied himself and stroked the ball solidly into the hole. The shot was a courageous answer to the pressure of a major, a trademark that became emblematic of his play during crunch time in the years to come.

The dead heat between Arnold Palmer and Jack Nicklaus forced an eighteen-hole playoff on Monday, and Jack became the villain once again. Palmer's loyal followers whooped and hollered, but Nicklaus tried to ignore them. He also combated their curse with one of his own.

Based entirely on superstition, he wore for the fifth consecutive day a pair of $8.95 olive-green pants. Barbara later said the pants "were quite ripe by then."

An interesting incident occurred prior to the playoff. Both men confirmed later that Palmer approached Nicklaus in the locker room and offered to split the purse for first and second no matter who won, a practice permitted in those days but illegal on the Tour now. Although Palmer's gesture was gratuitous, it largely served to build Nicklaus's confidence. Here was the "King," offering a compromise to a youngster. Later at the inaugural World Series of Golf, the two men would split a purse, but in the Open Nicklaus declined, much to the displeasure of Palmer, who later told others, "Nicklaus acts like a spoiled brat."

As is often the case in sports when the action doesn't live up to the hype, the playoff for the 1962 United States Open Championship was nearly over by the end of six holes. Palmer played dreadfully and fell behind by four. He then rallied and cut Jack's margin to one after the twelfth, where Palmer sent the crowd into near hysterics by almost hitting the 598-yard par five in two.

Just when the momentum was shifting, Palmer three-putted the par-three thirteenth. Nicklaus was two strokes up with five to play. Arnie's Army was restless.

"A two-stroke lead is an entirely different thing than a one-shot lead with five holes to go," Nicklaus later commented on his strategy during the last holes of the playoff. "Except for the seventeenth, none of those [last] five holes was what could be called a birdie hole. I felt that if I could match par, hole by hole, I would not be tied."

Deciding to make five pars and doing it under the pressure-cooker atmosphere of a playoff for a United States Open Championship was a stout task, especially before thousands of Palmer's fans and an international television viewing audience. But when the cool and collected Nicklaus came to the 462-yard, par-four eighteenth, he had carved out four pars and still led by two.

Then, Jack did the unthinkable. He hit one of those ugly hooks that must have shortened Jack Grout's life. It was a ducker that ended up where it shouldn't have, in heavy rough making the next shot nearly impossible to hit to the green.

With Palmer in the fairway, the Army envisioned a birdie-bogey, two-shot swing for a possible finish. But Palmer dashed those hopes when he half-chunked a three-iron shot that fell like a wounded duck off to the right of the green in the rough. That critical miss convinced

Nicklaus he could win with bogey. Jack hit a pitching wedge out into the fairway just short of a large fairway bunker and 75 yards in front of the green. The approach shot positioned the ball twelve feet from the hole.

Palmer's last hope fizzled when his chip shot whistled by the flag stick. If he had holed it, Nicklaus would have been forced to drain the twelve-footer for the win, but the shot was just right. When the scores were posted, Jack had shot 71, Palmer 74. The king had been defeated. Jack Nicklaus was the 1962 United States Open Champion.

The victory put Jack Nicklaus on the cover of *Time*. A hometown parade in the more friendly confines of Columbus, among other things, preserved the moment. Jack now had a major win in his pocket to go along with his two National Amateur Championships. It had come in his eighteenth professional event.

Although Nicklaus would dub 1962 "my longest year," it was a successful one. He won two more Tour events, the Seattle World's Fair and the Portland Open.

At Portland, he beat George Bayer by one shot despite being penalized two strokes for slow play. Joe Black was the official who made the ruling after timing Nicklaus for several holes during his round. As Jack headed toward the scorer's tent, Joe passed by him. "Whatever you had, Jack, just add two strokes to it," Black said. Nicklaus started to object, but Joe kept on going. The next morning, Black approached Jack in the locker room and told him the reasons for the penalty. Nicklaus had cooled off by then and said that although he did not think the penalty proper, he would accept Black's decision.

Mike Souchak, who finished second by four, jokingly told tournament officials in the locker room, "You didn't penalize Jack enough. You should put four or five strokes on him."

Despite his woes at Portland, Nicklaus later won the Inaugural World Series of Golf in 1962, defeating Palmer, who had won the Masters and British Open, and PGA Champion Gary Player. The scorecard for that year showed three victories and three second-place finishes. Jack ended up third on the money list with more than $62,000 and was named "Rookie of the Year" on the PGA Tour.

But it was the win at Oakmont, like the earlier one at the United States Amateur, that marked the twenty-two year old for future greatness. He had beaten the best professionals in the world and in doing so became the first golfer in history to win a major as his first tournament victory.

Arnold Palmer knew what was in store for the PGA. "I'll tell you something," he said, "now that the big guy is out of the cage, everybody better run for cover."

# CHAPTER 13

# Jack and Arnie

J ack Nicklaus entered the professional golf arena with the fury of a wild stallion. Just as he had done with his amateur career, he rose to the top of the mountain so quickly that many had to be reminded that he was just twenty-two years old.

By making the United States Open his first victory, Nicklaus stood alone until Lee Trevino and Donna Caponi (in the U.S. Women's Open) matched the feat. Jack's early successes prompted Bobby Jones to suggest that his record thirteen major championships was in danger of falling. If they hadn't before, every professional golfer in the world realized Jack Nicklaus would now be a contender in each tournament he entered. He had exhibited nothing but awesome strength, a deft touch, and grace under pressure.

The man most affected by Nicklaus's sublimity was Arnold Daniel Palmer. He had been a prominent figure since his first Tour victory in 1955, but eight wins, including his first Masters in 1960, made Palmer the most commanding figure in golf.

Palmer's charisma was endearing to all. Galleries adopted him as a loving son and heartily cheered the Pennsylvanian whenever he mounted one of his famous charges. His play-hard, go-for-broke style brought with it so much drama, it made him a darling of the media as well. Nicklaus might be the pretender to the throne, but Palmer was the sentimental favorite every time he picked up his clubs.

Biographer Thomas Hauser put it this way:

The reasons for Palmer's popularity were many. First, he was an immensely likable man with an enormous amount of natural warmth and friendliness. He didn't have to work at getting along with anyone; it was instinctive. People liked Arnold because they sensed he liked them. He genuinely enjoyed shaking hands, bantering with the gallery, and making people feel good. He was a common man in the best sense of the word; uncomplicated, stable, one of the guys.

Television and Arnold Palmer were made for one another. His magnetic personality and all-American looks aside, he provided what every viewer craved: high drama. No matter how far behind he fell in a given tournament, Palmer always provided the sense that he would pull a whirlwind finish to unravel the spirit of those players ahead of him. With his army pounding out high decibel explosions of cheers, Palmer hitched up his pants and took on the bad guys with the fervor of Alan Ladd in the classic film *Shane*.

Palmer's chief adversary before Nicklaus was South African Gary Player. Player exhibited signs of greatness by winning the '59 British Open at Muirfield (he came from eight shots back after thirty-six holes), the '61 Masters, and the '62 PGA Championship.

Nicklaus's arrival as a champion made the so-called Big Three he formed with Palmer and Player as exciting as the triumvirate of Harry Vardon, J.H. Taylor, and James Braid at the turn of the century.

Although matches between Player and his two adversaries were always entertaining, the competitions between Palmer and Nicklaus became classics, reminiscent of Walter Hagen and Bobby Jones, Walter Hagen and Gene Sarazen, Walter Hagen and Sam Snead, Sam Snead and Ben Hogan, and Carol Mann and Kathy Whitworth. In later years, well-publicized rivalries between Bill Russell and Wilt Chamberlain, Jerry West and Oscar Robertson, Jimmy Conners and Bjorn Borg, Magic Johnson and Larry Bird, and Pete Sampras and Andre Agassi would only pale in comparison to the Palmer-Nicklaus clashes. Although these were compelling rivalries, none produced as many dramatic moments or lasted as long as the one between Arnie and Jack.

Because of their respective positions, the rivalry between Nicklaus and Palmer is probably most similar to the relationship between baseball great Roger Maris and his more popular Yankee teammate, Mickey Mantle. When Maris joined the Yankees in 1960, Mantle, as Palmer, was a living legend who had already performed Herculean acts. Like Nicklaus, Maris attempted to unseat Mantle, especially during the chase to break Babe Ruth's magical home run mark in 1961. Amazingly, Maris's record sixty-one home runs that year made him a villian to the New York fans who worshipped Ruth and Mantle.

Although Maris and Nicklaus had amazing careers, neither ever achieved the heart-felt love fans bestowed upon Mantle or Palmer. In several ways, Roger and Jack were unwanted heroes, forever overshadowed by their adversaries.

Pundits have tried to put their own spin on the Nicklaus-Palmer relationship for decades. Certainly, much of the tension between the two was a result of their sharply contrasting personalities and playing styles.

On the one hand, Palmer was outgoing to a fault. He was built like a chiseled steelworker, a feisty character who always seemed ready to put-up-his-dukes and fight anyone bare-knuckled who dared challenge his golf score. His slapdash play was urgent and furious as if there was a time limit on completing his round. His clothes were often ill-fitting, the muscles bulging under the sleeves of a rumpled, sweat-stained shirt. Every shot seemed laborious, and "oohs" and "aahs" awaited the result after he'd ripped through the ball as if he had a personal grudge against it.

Palmer's sex appeal was unparalleled. "When he looked at a woman, she felt like she was naked," the wife of a prominent amateur said recently. "Those eyes of his. They were piercing. He was sexy as hell."

Then there was Nicklaus, who looked more like an opulent, overweight man-child. With short hair, bulging cheeks, and a waistline that tumbled over his belt, Jack was not sexy. He was meticulous and a "too good, too soon" prodigy who made the game of golf look too easy. "He was not homespun like Sam Snead, not funny like Trevino," *Sports Illustrated*'s Rick Reilly said of Nicklaus. "His pants didn't need hitching like Palmer's. . . ."

Years later, David Kindred of *The Washington Post* captured the Nicklaus-Palmer contrast most vividly. "In the early years of his Everestian career," he wrote, "Nicklaus was cast as the mechanical heavy—an overweight blob in a dumb hat—opposite Arnold Palmer's sexy, sweating, grimacing-on-every shot hero."

Although Nicklaus did not grow any taller than the 5' 10" height he reached at thirteen, he added forty-five pounds. His wife, Barbara, playfully called him "Fat Boy," and his fraternity brothers at Phi Gamma Delta at Ohio State referred to him as "Blob-O."

To some, the labels attached to Jack might have been terms of endearment. But Nicklaus wasn't attempting to become just another PGA professional; he was trying to beat the pants off the celestially popular Arnold Palmer and become the best player in the world doing it.

Instead of trekking out to see Jack Grout about his golf swing, Nicklaus needed a conference with a weight-reducing expert or time spent with a fashion consultant, for if he wasn't going to lose weight, his too-tight wardrobe required an overhaul.

But Nicklaus ignored the advice to slim down, even when it came from Barbara and Mark McCormack.

By not attempting to improve his public image, he set himself up for ridicule by not only fans of Palmer's but also members of the press who could find little else to criticize. Then he did the unforgivable, he beat Arnold Palmer in his home state near his home town in the U.S. Open, the world's most prestigious golf tournament. In doing so, Jack Nicklaus poured acid in the wound and turned the next few years into ones where he became so disconcerted with the behavior of fans that he considered giving up the game.

In addition to being overweight and beating Palmer, Jack Nicklaus's method of play caused resentment. Many fans felt it wasn't fair for Nicklaus to drive the ball to smithereens, hit pin-point iron shots that dropped as soft as blanket fuzz, and then stand over unsinkable putts for lengthy intervals before steering them directly into the center of the hole. Commenting on Nicklaus's meticulous nature, *Los Angles Times* columnist Jim Murray said, "Nicklaus picks up things on a course like a German housewife picking up lint off a suit." Years later, Nicklaus said he recognized these shortcomings. "I had come up too fast some people felt," he said. "I had things too easy. . . . I seemed cold and teutonic and too darn sure of myself. . . . The best thing about my golf is my golf."

Later, Nicklaus summed up his feelings for biographer Thomas Hauser:

> Being as honest as I am, I think of myself as fundamentally companionable: a shade more sensitive than I appear to be, a bit too direct on occasion, a bit too stubborn on others: but a good deal less cold and grim and cock-sure than some people read me as being. I'm aware that I'm not the matinee idol type. Rooms don't light up when I enter.

Nicklaus's threat to Palmer, along with a slightly discernible aloofness, impeded his ability to ingratiate himself to spectators and television viewers. The notion that he regained popularity among many of those early dissenters is a false one. Most who viewed him as a cold fish in the early sixties never changed their opinions. There is something about Nicklaus's attitude and detached persona for which they will never care. "Nicklaus just never got close to people," a golf insider said recently. A reporter put it another way. "Jack was stuffy. He made the gallery, especially young fans, feel like they were bothering him."

*Indianapolis Star* writer Robin Miller remembered seeing Jack at the Speedway 500 tournament in the sixties. "My dad and I ran into him," Miller said. "Dad asked for an autograph, but Nicklaus never looked at us and kept going." Top amateur golfer Chip Gagnier said, "I just never liked to watch Jack play. I still don't."

United States Women's Open champion Carol Mann said, "In his first years as a professional, I didn't like to watch him because he was so deliberate. Besides, I was such a huge fan of Arnie's. He was 'the guy.'"

Three-time Indiana State Amateur Champion Kent Frandsen said he liked to watch Nicklaus play in his peak years but believed Jack "unintentionally encouraged slow play on the part of others." He added, "At the PGA at Crooked Stick, I watched Mark Brooks stand over a chip shot for what seemed an hour. I think Jack's deliberate play made many golfers try to emulate him."

Gifted writer William Price Fox wrote in *Golf Digest*, "A lot of us never personally liked him. He was the bully on the block who owned the bat and the ball, he had the first car, got the first girl. . . . He was too much . . . too aggressive, trained too hard, and said dumb things to the press, but worst of all he was fat."

That point was emphasized in the mid-60s by Bruce Ogilvie, a professor of psychology at San Jose State University. At the Tournament of Champions, he conducted several interviews with golf fans only to discover that one player on Tour "inspired unflattering remarks, snickers, cackles or similarly expressed bad feelings. He was repeatedly subjected to what I considered real fan abuse. . . . The much-maligned golfer was none other than Jack Nicklaus."

In a report to *Golf Digest*, Dr. Ogilvie sought to answer the question. "Why should a fine golfer such as Nicklaus stimulate such ill will among golf enthusiasts?" The answers he found were divided into four basic categories.

The most common complaint was that Nicklaus was considered to be a mechanical man, one "who played like a robot." One spectator said, "I like my heroes to be human."

His body type was listed as a second reason. "He doesn't look like an athlete," one fan observed. "He is built more like a football player." Another said, "I like my heroes to look more like Cassius Clay."

Many golf fans complained that Nicklaus didn't care about the galleries who watched him. "[Nicklaus] is too cool," said one spectator. "He's personally cold, unwilling to give anything of himself. . . . He's unconcerned about the fans." Regarding this complaint, Ogilvie commented that Nicklaus was similar to other athletes who never garnered fan support. "The hero is expected to communicate affection to the fan, so that the fan can feel needed, indeed important, to the athlete."

The fourth reason for the anti-Nicklaus sentiment, Dr. Ogilvie concluded, was based on his relationship with Arnold Palmer. "Many fans mentioned Arnold Palmer as their particular idol and viewed Nicklaus as a direct threat to the man with whom they so strongly identified," Ogilvie wrote. "They took any threat to Arnie as a very personal threat to themselves."

In summary, Dr. Ogilvie concluded, "Nicklaus's noxious combination of 'machine like' characteristics and his 'cool' or neutral personality made him an ideal target for fan abuse. His high physical proficiency opens a door in the mind of a certain kind of fan and flashes a bright light on that fan's personal inabilities. At the same time, Nicklaus's bland personality invites this disgruntled fan to hang any characteristics on the athlete that will belittle him or reduce him to the fan's small stature."

Dr. Ogilvie pointed out that the fans' perception of Nicklaus seemed at great odds with how he was perceived by his fellow golf professionals. "The men who know him best—his fellow pros, for instance, describe him as warm, friendly, helpful, good-humored— hardly the anti-hero he has become in the eyes of many golf fans."

Tour veteran Phil Rodgers's terse observation about the early Jack Nicklaus probably says it best, "Jack was never a people person in his early years."

# CHAPTER 14

# Sparring Partners

One man who observed the Nicklaus-Palmer rivalry up close was Chi Chi Rodriguez, who began to make his mark on the Tour in the early sixties. "I think the rivalry was good for the game," he said. "Golf needed the kind of rivalries like Snead and Hogan, Nelson and Hogan, and so forth."

Mike Souchak echoed those sentiments. "Golf welcomed a rivalry like Jack and Arnold's at that time," he said. "It was great for all of us." United States Open Champion Carol Mann added, "They were good for each other. Each brought their game to a new level. It was the bold slasher versus the conservative, methodical technician."

Rodriguez also believed that Nicklaus and Palmer handled themselves well when they were going head to head. "It was a healthy relationship," he said. "They weren't like two fighters. They were gentlemen."

Gary Player recalled being shocked at how Nicklaus was treated. "I don't think Arnold liked it either. At Baltusrol one year, they were cheering when Jack made bogey. That wasn't right. But Jack never moaned and groaned. When it happened at Augusta in the sixties, Jack and I were walking up the third fairway. He looked at me and said, 'The more they [gallery] do that, the better I'll play.'"

Tour veteran Jim Dent said Nicklaus told him he never read newspapers so he wouldn't notice nasty comments about him. "He didn't want to get involved in the Arnie against Jack business," Dent explained. "He just wanted to play golf, but I don't know how he did it. One year at the Hope I heard the gallery boo when Jack hit a good shot. That had to bother him but he didn't show it."

To that end, Nicklaus said, "I always had Arnold's gallery to fight, but I never had to fight Arnold." Mann said that Nicklaus's reaction to the hostile galleries made her realize "that perhaps we had a better sportsman than we'd ever seen."

Nicklaus was not the only one who battled Palmer's fans. "When Palmer hit an errant shot," Phil Rodgers said, "the gallery closed together like a steel wall. The ball never got through. When a competitor hit one toward them, they parted like the Red Sea. That was especially true when Jack was paired with Arnold."

Rodgers witnessed firsthand Palmer's interaction with the galleries. "It was no wonder the galleries helped Arnold," he said. "While Jack looked straight ahead or up and down, Arnold's head was moving side to side. He had a look of flare and aggressiveness on his face, and he established contact with all of those fans who adored him. Everybody was touched by Palmer. He brought the person off the street to watch golf."

Rodriguez and Nicklaus's generous comments to the contrary, the rivalry was not all tea and crumpets. When Nicklaus arrived, Arnold was an immensely popular champion. To many he *was* golf, and he possessed an ego to match his popularity.

Palmer recognized immediately that Nicklaus was a threat to his dominance of the game. Nicklaus might be overweight, unattractive, and methodical, but Palmer spotted a raw talent in Nicklaus that unnerved him. He struck back with private jokes and unflattering remarks about Nicklaus, many of which were not indicative of Palmer's true feelings. In truth, Palmer relished the challenge Nicklaus presented, because it made him work harder at his game.

Many journalists attempted to root out the rub between the two rivals, relying on gossip and rumors. Better evidence of the truth exists in the words of Angelo Argea, Nicklaus's long time caddie who was closest to the Palmer and Nicklaus rivalry.

Argea's reflections mainly refer to Jack's reactions during the Byron Nelson Classic in 1970, but they are indicative of the sparring that occurred between the two men for over two decades. At the tournament, Palmer and Nicklaus were playing together and exchanged the lead during the final round. Argea said Jack tried to tune out the blustering applause every time Arnold made a birdie or merely winked at the crowd.

Argea also remembered Nicklaus's mindset at the time. "Jack didn't mind [the] show of favoritism, mainly because by that time he was used to it—that is, he didn't mind it until he got to the eighteenth green. Needing only a par to win the tournament, he bogeyed the hole, forcing a play-off between him and Palmer and sending the gallery into thunderous cheers for Arnie. Now, *that* made Jack mad."

As the two made their way to the first extra hole, Argea watched Nicklaus carefully. "[Jack] didn't say anything, but I could just tell that his pilot light had suddenly turned into a Bunsen burner."

Nicklaus took care of matters on the first playoff hole. He busted his drive fifty yards past Palmer and ended up winning the hole. "And that's how Jack got a little sweet revenge," Argea said, putting to rest Nicklaus's claim that the unruly crowds and Palmer's inability to control them never bothered him, something Jack later confirmed to journalist Herbert Warren Wind.

Although the relationship between Palmer and Nicklaus was testy, or "uncomfortable" as Argea put it, Nicklaus always put the proper spin on it. "I'm often asked," Jack said later, "how friendly Arnold and I have really been over the years. The short answer is we've been as good a friends as two guys could be who've tried as hard and as often as we have to beat each other and who are as different as we are in non-golfing tastes and interests."

Later, Nicklaus mellowed even more when he commented on how Palmer dealt with their rivalry in the early years. "Looking back now, I have even greater respect for [Palmer's] qualities," he said, "because I am not sure that in a similar situation I could be quite as gracious as he was at the time."

Obviously, Nicklaus's words reflected that he had forgotten that Palmer had called him "fat boy" and tacitly supported a boisterous Army who hoped Jack would self-destruct.

"I think our relationship is good," Palmer said of Jack. "We're friends. But we are competitive and we will always be that. Whatever we do, wherever we are, we will be competing against each other."

Nicklaus's personal feelings toward Palmer were mixed ones, but he respected Palmer's abilities as a golfer.

Jack believed Arnold's finest year as a golfer came in 1964. When Palmer won wire-to-wire in the Masters with superlative rounds of 69, 68, 69, and 70, Nicklaus was highly impressed. He rated it on a level with Arnold's win at Troon in the 1962 British Open. "Never, before or after, has Arnold's swing, to my mind, possessed such perfect tempo as it did in 1964 at Augusta," Jack said.

Regarding Palmer's talent on the greens, Jack said, "Arnold

doesn't think he's as good a putter as he used to be. Maybe so, but he's still excellent on the greens. . . . I never did see Bobby Locke, but Arnold's the best putter under pressure I've ever seen."

Nicklaus also respected Palmer's play under adverse conditions. "He's the best bad-weather golfer I know. Every time it's raining or chilly or blowing hard, he has a definite advantage over the field," Nicklaus said. "Part of this comes from his determination not to let things distract him, part of it comes from his confidence in his ability to function in any weather, and the rest comes from an extraordinary physical strength and stamina."

Palmer's feelings about Nicklaus the golfer are a bit fuzzy. When asked about Jack in the early sixties, however, he said, "I think he should play faster," and later, "He stands over a putt for one or two eternities." He even filed a complaint about Jack's slow play with the USGA during one United States Open.

Later, Palmer was so incensed with an isolated incident where he felt Nicklaus's behavior toward fellow professionals was in bad taste, he called Nicklaus "the one guy in history who has put himself above the game." When asked about the comment, he professed to having been misquoted.

Palmer was also not pleased with Nicklaus one year prior to the World Series of Golf. Despite not having a victory to qualify, Palmer was invited. "If this is a contest for champions only," Nicklaus boldly protested, "then Arnold doesn't belong here. Arnie's strictly an also-ran in major events. The World Series should have winners, not also-rans. Isn't that right, Arnie?" Nicklaus later said he was kidding. Palmer didn't laugh.

Despite Palmer's complaints about Nicklaus's slow play, meticulous nature, and presumed arrogance, he did recognize Jack's talent, telling his brother Jerry that he "very much respected Jack's ability." And as mentioned, Palmer knew instantly that this ability of Nicklaus's would pose a threat to his reign. So intense was the rivalry that it extended beyond the golf course to their business interests, particularly their respective PGA golf tournaments. Palmer always felt the Bay Hill Classic, played at the Bay Hill Country Club in Orlando, which Palmer owned, would surge to a prominence just behind the majors. When Jack's upstart tournament, The Memorial, began play at Muirfield years later, he felt the same.

The Bay Hill Classic never rose to a lofty status for several reasons, but The Memorial consistently elevated its respectability. That didn't set well with Palmer.

In 1976, Nicklaus attacked Palmer's beloved Bay Hill Club. "It's a good golf course," he told reporters, "but not that good. I don't think the golf course is geared for tournament play."

Palmer was quick to respond publicly. "I'm a little befuddled as to why he would say those things about Bay Hill. . . . He hasn't played here for eleven years." In private, however, he lambasted Nicklaus as "too big for his britches."

In the early eighties, the two enjoyed a fist fight through the media. Nicklaus incensed Palmer when he said that he was skipping the Bay Hill Classic because his sons were playing in a basketball tournament. Palmer informed a PGA official, "You can tell Jack I won't be at The Memorial this year because Riley [Palmer's golden retriever] is in a show that week."

Of the many memorable Palmer and Nicklaus confrontations through the years, a special one occurred at the 1980 Masters. Both were out of contention after three rounds, but Nicklaus's 218 and Palmer's 219 paired them together for the 11:32 starting time.

Palmer had an extra incentive that day at age fifty. Nicklaus, just forty, had snubbed Palmer's Bay Hill tournament again that year, choosing to play at the nearby Doral and at Jackie Gleason's Inverrary.

For Arnold, it was revenge time and birdies at two and three brought him to life. The gallery was more respectful by this time, but the two rivals bore down on their games as if their reputations were at stake. Hole after hole they challenged one another, reminding observers of the great days of old. It was like a classic movie to be savored for the ages.

By day's end, Palmer had a 69, 73, sweet victory over the befuddled Nicklaus. Jack was gracious as always in defeat, but his shoulders slumped noticeably when he left the golf course.

That evening Palmer celebrated like he'd won another major. Beating Jack made it seem like New Year's Eve.

Despite the fierce competitiveness on the course, many thought Palmer brought out the best in Nicklaus on a personal level. When Arnold loosened him up, the fans and media saw a side of the Golden Bear they weren't familiar with.

The incident that brought the most laughs between the two legends occurred during dinner and drinks at an entertainment club after one round of the Bob Hope Classic.

Both men were enjoying the night, and the mood was light. What happened next illustrates the tense dynamics between the two, how each postured for control. According to Arnold, he was the instigator. He entered the bar and restaurant, saw Nicklaus at a table with mutual friends, then bumped a woman as he made his way across the dance floor. "I knocked her wig off her head," Palmer said. "Her hair was in curlers. She was terribly embarrassed. . . . I picked up the wig and put it on my head."

Palmer said that Nicklaus saw him, laughed, and blew him a kiss. "I asked [Jack] to dance," Palmer said. "He got up and came to the dance floor. . . . And that's when I took the wig off and put it on his head."

Jack Nicklaus's version had him as the instigator. According to Jack, he left the table where he and Palmer were enjoying a drink to use the bathroom. On the way back, he knocked the wig off a woman's head. "I picked up the wig," Jack said, "put it on Arnold's head, and led him out to dance. Then he put it on my head, and we danced some more. We laughed, and it was kind of fun, although the lady whose wig it was didn't think it was all that funny."

Regardless of who did what to whom, the sight of the two rivals tripping the light fantastic was astounding. Though Jack could let himself go on occasion, to do so in a public place was uncharacteristic. No one who had seen Jack as the proverbial choir boy could believe he could conduct himself in such a manner.

Another incident, this time involving Palmer and the other "Big Three" member, Gary Player, confirms that Jack had a lot of "kid" in him.

In the early sixties, the three men were staying in a three-bedroom suite while filming a television series at Royal Montreal Golf Club in Canada. When food and drinks arrived later that evening, Palmer, Nicklaus, and Player began to behave like out-of-control dormitory kids.

"We had those tall bottles of Canadian beer," Gary Player recalled. "Arnie was on the phone to Winnie, and I picked one up, opened it, and shook it up while holding my thumb on the opening. Then I let Jack have it, and Arnie too. Arnie told Winnie he'd have to call her back, and by that time Jack had the other bottle and was squirting both of us. There was a big pitcher of iced tea and it spilled and got all over the curtains. We laughed all night. The three of us were gigglers. We had a great time. Then we told the manager what we'd done next morning."

Later, Player added, "It shows how famously we all got along in those days, even Jack and Arnold. Too bad it didn't last between those two," obviously aware that the two bickered in the coming years.

True to a Player comment that "time is the great eraser," the passing of years healed any deep wounds between Nicklaus and Palmer. The turning point, according to longtime Nicklaus business associate and friend Tom Peterson, came when Nicklaus honored Palmer at his Memorial Tournament in 1993. On that occasion, Nicklaus told the *Cleveland Plain Dealer*, "[Palmer] came along when golf needed a shot in the arm. [He] did it with a hitch in his pants, a fast walk, and a quick swing. It seemed like he hit it where [the fans] hit it. But Arnold always got it onto the green with a chance to score."

"That really meant a great deal to Arnold," Peterson said of Jack's tribute. "And he and Jack have been closer ever since that happened."

Today the men are rivals in business, if not in competition. At tournaments, Nicklaus still wins; Palmer can't. Nicklaus grieves at scores above par; Palmer enjoys playing even when he shoots 76 or 77.

From time to time, the two cross paths, and they enjoy one another's company. The continual friendship of Barbara Nicklaus and Winnie Palmer helps to maintain an air of lightness about the relationship, but just as they used to do with golf scores, Jack and Arnold keep an eye on what the other is up to.

In looking back it's clear that Nicklaus had great admiration and even awe for Palmer when he first came into prominence. For awhile, Jack was extremely jealous, unable to understand why he became unpopular with fans while Palmer stole their hearts. Palmer's sharp comments about Jack unsettled him, and he responded with petty comments. In the years after 1962, Nicklaus worked hard to change an image most saw as dour at best. The truth of the matter was, despite all the victories and all the money, what he wanted most was to be loved like Arnold. Only time would elevate him toward the stratospheric heights of admiration fans had for Palmer, but Jack the realist knew becoming an equal in a popularity contest with his chief rival was an unachievable goal. After all, try as he might, there never was a Nicklaus's "Army."

## CHAPTER 15

# Making His Mark

In all, Jack Nicklaus won thirty official PGA tournaments in the 1960s, Arnold Palmer twenty-nine. Nicklaus left a distinct impression on everyone who saw him play.

Nicklaus's record in the sixties was a dynamic one. In 1963, his second year on Tour, future United States Women's Open Champion Donna Caponi remembers seeing him for the first time.

"I was eighteen and my dad took me out to Rancho Park," Caponi said. "Jack was paired with Arnold Palmer, who won the tournament. But I remember seeing this very large, round man with blonde hair. I was impressed with how far he hit the ball, but he also had a good touch. When I heard him speak, I was surprised he had such a high-pitched voice, but he sure could play."

The squeaky voice was something Jack was self-conscious about to the point of deliberately attempting to learn to alter it. A former associate of Nicklaus's provided an example of the lengths he went toward correcting the flaw. The incident also showed how gullible Jack could be at times.

In an interview with ABC commentator Chris Schenkel, who had a voice quality Jack envied, Nicklaus asked the reporter, "How'd you get that deep voice?" "By smoking two packs of Marlboros a day," Schenkel replied.

Those words were gospel to Nicklaus. The next day Schenkel noticed that Jack was toting a pack of Marlboros.

The irritation with his voice, however, didn't keep Nicklaus from playing well in 1963, the year a seemingly unfortunate incident resulted in an improvement in his play. It took place just prior to the Lucky International tournament in San Francisco when bursitis attacked Jack's left hip.

In an effort to lessen the pain Jack said he "had to slow down his hip action through the ball." The swing adjustment made his hands and arms close the club face sooner than normal, causing him to say later, "For the first time in my life I was [intentionally] obliged to play a right-to-left draw."

The bursitis subsided, and Nicklaus was ecstatic about what had occurred. "I learned that I could do something that I had never tried to do before: play successful golf from right to left. . . . If it had never happened, I doubt I would have ever changed my method. And if I hadn't I wouldn't be as good a player as I am today."

And he was good. With his incredible length, he overpowered the opposition in 1963. Learning to "draw" the ball made him even more formidable.

In the fifth tournament that year, Nicklaus won the ninety-hole Palm Springs Classic in a playoff with Gary Player. It was the first tournament where Jack employed the services of A.G. Argeropoulos, better known as Angelo Argea, the former Las Vegas cab driver and gambler who attained celebrity status as Jack's caddie. Angelo remembered "having a sharp picture of Jack continually outdriving Player by forty and fifty yards and hitting eight-irons where the South African was using fives."

In addition to the Palm Springs victory, Nicklaus won his first Masters in a playoff over Player, 65 to 73 (see page 273). He captured the Tournament of Champions and then scalded the field to win his first PGA Championship at Dallas Athletic Club (see page 212). Jack had won three major professional titles in two years on Tour. He also won at the World Series of Golf (for the second year in a row) and the Sahara Invitational.

During the Sahara and the Tournament of Champions, caddie Argea was at Nicklaus's side. The Greek, or "Angero" as Nicklaus called him, brought Jack good luck because he won five of the first six tournaments with his wire-haired companion in tow.

After his success on the American Tour, Nicklaus capped off the year by winning the Canada Cup individual crown played outside of Paris. Jack sank a long putt that excited the Duke of Windsor so much he fell off his walking stick.

In his second year on the Tour, Nicklaus earned $100,040. Arnold Palmer won seven events for the second year in a row and $128,230 in prize money. Jack ranked second with five wins.

In addition to his impressive play on Tour, Jack Nicklaus was now the father of two. On April 11, 1963, Barbara gave birth to their second son, Steven Charles Nicklaus.

Nicklaus played in twenty-one events that year, and in '64 and '65 he competed in a combined forty-eight more. Nicklaus did not capture a victory in a major during '64 (he finished second three times), but he did win five times, including the Tournament of Champions, the first of six Australian Opens, and the White Marsh Open. There he holed out two eight-iron field shots in the final round to beat "Big Three" rivals Palmer and Player.

The Palmer-Nicklaus battle for supremacy reached its peak in 1964, the same year a boxer named Cassius Clay won the heavyweight crown. Within two months, Jack and Arnie faced each other in six tournaments, with neither man finishing lower than fifth.

The dramatics they provided in head-to-head competition caused a virtual tie for the money earnings title as the year came to an end. Palmer knew he needed to finish ahead of Nicklaus to ensure his status as the number one player. Nicklaus understood the significance of the money title, too. Beat Arnold, he knew, and a true changing of the guard would take place.

Their year-long joust would be settled at the Cajun Classic, held in Lafayette, Louisiana. On the final green, Gay Brewer needed a twenty-foot putt for birdie. If he made it, Nicklaus would finish third in the tournament, five shots behind winner Miller Barber. That meant Palmer would take the money crown.

Gay Brewer said he walked over to Jack and asked, "How much is it worth to you to miss my putt?" Instead of responding, Jack handed Gay his wallet in jest. Brewer took his time and once again surveyed the putt. "I tried, but the putt slid by," Brewer said. This miss made Jack Nicklaus the 1964 money earnings champion.

Nicklaus had beaten Palmer in earnings by exactly $81.13. Few, however, missed the significance of the moment, especially Palmer, who seethed all winter about missed opportunities.

Although he was pleased to win the money title, his second-place finishes in three majors (Masters, British Open, PGA) and three other tournaments caused Nicklaus concern. "[1964] was a bitter-sweet season for me," he observed, " . . . I had shown a lack of strong finishing punch on several occasions."

Jack's play in the majors that year centered on memories of a shanked eight-iron at the twelfth in the third round of the Masters, which Palmer won for his last major victory, and what he called "atrocious" putting during the Saturday round of the United States Open.

More optimistically, Jack recalled a brilliant course-equaling 66 in the final round of the British Open that left him a shot behind Tony Lema. He also recorded a three-stroke, second-place finish with Arnold

Palmer to Bobby Nichols in the PGA held at the Columbus Country Club in Jack's hometown.

Less than a month after Ken Venturi's grueling victory in the 1964 United States Open, Nicklaus decided to make life easier for himself. He purchased a twin-engine Aero Commander 680 F1, a plane that became popular when aerobatics genius R.A. "Bob" Hoover lit up the sky with one for North American Rockwell. It seated seven in addition to the pilot and copilot.

Nicklaus found that having his own plane permitted him, like Arnold Palmer, to take control of his travel schedule. Avoiding commercial planes meant he could also shorten the time it took to travel from Ohio to golf tournaments and back. With more time to be a homebody, Jack could see Barbara and the two boys for longer periods of time.

At times, Nicklaus piloted the new plane, but only as a student apprentice, since he wasn't licensed at that time. Later, he traded the plane in for a model 24 Lear twin-engine jet that cruised at 550 m.p.h. In the 1990s, Jack bought a Gulf Stream IV to carry him from place to place.

In 1965 Nicklaus took his second Masters crown (see page 241), earned four additional Tour victories, and welcomed the third Nicklaus child, Nancy (Nan) on the 5th of May.

The Masters win for Nicklaus was especially disturbing to Arnold Palmer. His goal was to become the first Masters champion to repeat, but second place was the best he could do.

Despite his success, Nicklaus uncharacteristically threw away a potential tournament win that year at the Buick Open. Just when a late back-nine charge brought him to within one shot of Tony Lema, Nicklaus duck hooked a tee shot on the eighteenth hole that hit a tree and vanished. "I was stunned," Lema, the winner, said. Nicklaus's reaction was rather nonplussed. "I took a chance and got caught," he told reporters.

Nicklaus's bane was the occassional fatal hook. In the summer of 1965, he'd received advice from Tour rookie Tom Weiskopf. "When Jack is hitting the ball flush," Tom told *Golf Digest*, "the back of his left hand and his left forearm form a straight line at the top of his backswing. . . . I played a practice round with him and noticed he was cupping his left wrist up there. . . . When he cupped his wrist, he usually hooked."

Nicklaus agreed with Weiskopf's assessment but couldn't remedy the problem quickly. Sometime later he did, but by then he had to deal with other problems as well. "Now my putting and chipping has fallen off," he told *Golf Digest*.

That year, in the short-lived National Challenge Match, Nicklaus, Palmer, and Gary Player were pitted against amateurs Bill Campbell, Deane Beman, and Dale Morey. No one seems to remember who won, but Beman acknowledges he "went home with the trophy."

During this time, Nicklaus was defeated by another amateur golfer, his business manager Mark McCormack, at Pine Valley. A sterling 34 on the back nine by the IMG boss permitted him to savor a four and two victory over his client, who was not amused.

Nicklaus's play on Tour saw rough going at the '65 American Golf Classic where rounds of 82, 69, 79, and 75 (305) left him far behind the pack. After the third round, he irrationally threw away a pair of golf shoes he'd worn in that round and the first, blaming them for the poor performances. Despite brief lapses into bad play, Nicklaus again won the money title with $140,752. He also finished in the top ten a phenomenal twenty times in twenty-four events.

Although Nicklaus was contending nearly every time out, Arnold Palmer's game was falling apart. To please his wife Winnie and others who cared for his health, Palmer quit smoking. Immediately, he gained fifteen pounds, but that was the least of his worries.

Palmer's main concern was with a putting stroke that was inconsistent at best and awful most of the time. He could still handle the long putts but admitted that his hands shook when he attempted the short ones.

The result was a year in which Palmer prevailed in but one tournament, the Tournament of Champions. His earnings dropped to little more than $55,000. With Nicklaus at the top of his game, some felt the Arnie and Jack rivalry was finally coming to a close.

In 1966, the year Billy Casper ventured to Vietnam to entertain the American troops and Bob Murphy won the United States Amateur, Nicklaus captured his third Masters (see page 245), his first British Open (see page 225), and the Sahara Invitational. He also won the National Team Championship with Arnold Palmer, who rebounded from his dismal season in 1965 by capturing three Tour victories and more than $110,000 in earnings, less than a $1,000 behind Jack. At thirty-six years old, Palmer wasn't ready to be buried quite yet.

One victory did slip away from Nicklaus that year. He finished second at the Philadelphia Classic to Don January but should have won given the breaks he received. He recorded two eagles, the results of holed-out shots from the fairway on par fours at the second and eighth in the final round.

Nicklaus enjoyed Lady Fortune's favor when an errant one-iron approach shot headed out of bounds, struck a spectator, and ricocheted to the fringe of the green at the fourth. A tee shot hooked at the eleventh struck another fan, and dropped down safely in front of a tree. Nicklaus shook his head at that point and told an official, "You either get an eagle or you get a spectator." But he wasn't through. At four-teen, an approach shot soared over the green, destined for a creek. It hit *another* fan and stopped short.

That year Nicklaus also tangled with the eighteenth hole at Pebble Beach in the Crosby and came out second best. In the fourth round, he hooked two tee balls toward the beach. Despite the efforts of two military servicemen who aided in the search, the balls were appar-ently missing in action. "Imagine losing two balls on one hole. I've never lost one since I turned pro," Nicklaus exclaimed, forgetful of a lost tee shot at the Buick Open in 1965.

Besides his errant shot there, Nicklaus had also struck a wayward one that hit the left breast of Mrs. Lenora Steinberg at the Memphis Open in 1965. That incident resulted in a lawsuit against Jack for $5,000. It wasn't personal, though. Mrs. Steinberg said that Jack was her favorite player. The suit was eventually settled.

Nicklaus probably felt like suing Gary Player, who soundly defeated him in the 1966 Picadilly World Match Play Championship. The four finalists that year were Nicklaus, Palmer, Player, and Casper, then considered to be the four finest players in the world.

In the semifinals, Nicklaus was six-up on Casper, before the wily veteran scored five threes in seven holes, providing some last-minute heroics. After the round, Nicklaus told reporters, "I wasn't scared, just totally panic stricken." He finally prevailed one-up but then lost to Player six and four. That finale showcased the only two active players at the time to have won the four Grand Slam tournaments.

The match with Player also produced an incident Nicklaus want-ed to forget. At the ninth, a 460-yard par four with the London Ascot electric railroad tracks bordering the whole left side, Nicklaus hooked a drive into a ditch just short of the tracks. One-down to Player at the time, Jack dropped out with penalty, then spied a billboard sporting an ad for Picadilly cigarettes in the rough fifty yards ahead in his direct line of flight.

Nicklaus asked for a drop, but former Walker Cup captain and referee Tony Duncan refused the request since the billboard was permanent, not a "temporary immovable obstruction." Nicklaus fumed and chopped the ball a few yards before picking it up. At the tenth, Duncan asked if Nicklaus wanted a change in officials. "I'd like one who knows the rules," Jack bellowed, embarrassing Duncan. The change was made as Duncan left the course. Many fans were critical of Nicklaus's impudence.

Jack later acknowledged the mistake in judgment, but it was years before he returned to the tournament.

"I'd never seen that side of Jack before," Gary Player recalled. "We all make mistakes we're sorry for, and Jack made one. The thing I remember is that the press the next day said the incident upset Jack. It must not have been too bad. He won the next hole."

# CHAPTER 16

# More Victories

Nicklaus's fifth year on Tour, 1967, was marked by the first real debate about whether he could win the Grand Slam. In an article for *Golf Digest*, noted writer Nick Seitz examined Jack's potential. He quoted Las Vegas oddsmaker Jimmy "The Greek" as laying down the odds against Nicklaus winning the Masters, United States and British Opens, and the PGA Championship.

"A good average odds for Jack in any one tournament is 7-1," Snyder explained. "Arnold Palmer used to be 7-1, but he's like 10-1 now. Billy Casper is 8-1, Doug Sanders 12-1. Nobody is in Nicklaus's category." To find the chances for the Grand Slam, he said, "I multiply seven time seven times seven times seven to get odds of winning all four tournaments, which comes to about 2400-1. I knock that down to 2000-1 because Jack is tough under pressure in the big ones."

Other prominent professionals gave Seitz their two cents' worth. Tony Lema told Seitz "Jack wouldn't surprise me by winning the four big ones in one year. . . . He has the skill and he has the desire. To do it, he will have to condition himself mentally more than anything else, and Jack is the best at bearing down when a great deal is at stake."

Byron Nelson speculated how capturing the Grand Slam would affect Nicklaus's future on the Tour. "Jack has to have a goal. Keeping his interest will be a problem."

Nicklaus, who was twenty-seven, had his own thoughts. "You would have to have everything going for you," he said, ". . . including a lot of luck. But it can be done."

Nicklaus's chief challengers in the mid-60s included Billy Casper, Tony Lema, Julius Boros, Doug Sanders, Gene Littler, Gay Brewer, Ken Venturi, Chi Chi Rodriguez, Bruce Devlin, Bruce Crampton, Bob Charles, and Tom Weiskopf. Ever pragmatic, Nicklaus continually sized up the competition. Understanding the strengths and weaknesses of those who battled him was a Nicklaus trademark. Although he told everyone he played against the golf course, Nicklaus was always aware of the potential of the opposition, especially when playing the final holes in major tournaments.

Nicklaus said of Billy Casper, whom he would later honor at The Memorial tournament, "Casper looks phlegmatic but has an intense drive and fire. He is a stupendous pressure golfer . . . a super competitor. He never plays a foolish shot." No wonder Casper earned fifty-one official Tour victories, winning three majors and five Vardon trophies, a mark Nicklaus never equalled because although he had the lowest scoring average four times, he never played enough rounds to qualify for the trophy.

Regarding Tony Lema, who beat him in the 1964 British Open, Nicklaus said, "[He] was just about the prettiest player of the 1960s." Jack described Julius Boros as "a perfect example of a professional athlete who found a method that worked for him and who stayed with it."

Of Doug Sanders, Nicklaus made a surprising comment. "Everybody talks about [him] having a bad golf swing. That isn't true at all. His club travels on the correct path more regularly than any other player's."

Nicklaus offered other comments about chief competitors, including Gay Brewer ("Can show you some great shots"), Ken Venturi ("Of all the post-Hogan era, Ken without a doubt possessed the best talent"), and Chi Chi Rodriguez ("The longest driver pound for pound there ever has been").

According to Nicklaus, Bert Yancey was "a better player than he thinks he is." Dave Stockton "has overwhelming confidence," and George Archer is the "top putter in golf today."

Nicklaus's thoughts regarding Tom Weiskopf were a bit more subjective. "When he gets his emotions more under control," Nicklaus said, "he'll become one of the best players of all time."

On the other hand, Jack's competition had their own ideas about his ability as a golfer. "When Jack prepared like only he could, nobody could beat him," Lee Trevino said. Bruce Crampton agreed, "Jack was the man to beat," he said. "Every time out." The wife of a prominent opponent added, "The Tour players knew Jack could win anytime he really wanted to."

Tom Weiskopf's thoughts about Nicklaus were guarded. "Jack's always in there," he told *Golf Digest*, ". . . but he really doesn't scare me. I don't have to defend my game against his. If I play well, I can beat him." Later, Weiskopf told the *Cleveland Plain-Dealer*, "I never wanted to be the 'next Nicklaus,' only half as good."

Even later reflection caused Tom to say, "Jack was an inspiration to me. I had the luxury of watching him up close for several years after we both left Ohio State. The key was his supreme confidence. He'd stand on that first tee and look at you with those icy blue eyes and you knew he knew that you knew he was going to beat the shit out of you."

Weiskopf was also impressed with Nicklaus's ability to motivate himself like none other on the Tour. "He loved to compete," Weiskopf said. "Every time out. That was a constant. New players came along, but he just kept beating them. First it was Arnold, and then Jack was the man. Until the next challenger came out, Jack tried to overcome himself, be better, stay on top, never let down. He had an insatiable desire to remain the best. That was as evident in the mid-sixties as it is today. Young players today have no idea how phenomenally good Jack was."

Despite Weiskopf's admiration for Nicklaus, he and the other players never gave up. Tom even learned karate, believing the discipline would be good for his game. He tried to impress his fellow professionals with his new concentration by breaking a brick. Instead he almost broke his hand.

Although Jack Nicklaus has commented on the playing ability of his fellow competitors over the years, he has rarely shared his personal thoughts about them. "Essentially," Jack said, "all of us are individualists who respect and defend a common right to do our best without interference from others who are doing the same. Everyone pulls for himself, but without actively pulling against anyone else."

Regarding specific relationships, Nicklaus added, "Much of it promotes camaraderie and casual companionship, however, the Tour isn't conducive to the formation of very deep friendships. . . . I make an effort to be as friendly as I naturally can with everyone on Tour, and to the best of my knowledge, I don't have any enemies out there."

And Nicklaus didn't. Though some were jealous of his play, the way Jack handled his success produced nothing but respect. He was humble and kept a proper distance between himself and the other players, most of whom were reluctant to approach him.

Although Nicklaus was named PGA Player of the Year in 1967, his quest to win the Grand Slam was doused at the Masters. Nicklaus was attempting to win three times in a row, but with opening rounds of 72 and 79, he failed to make the cut.

Nicklaus did win five times that year: at the Crosby, the Western,

Sahara, Westchester (the total prize money at Westchester of $250,000 was the largest in Tour history), and at the United States Open (see page 263). Winnings of nearly $200,000 brought him his third-consecutive money title. Arnold Palmer won four tournaments and just $14,000 less than Jack.

Nicklaus had opened the season winning the Crosby by five shots (despite going double-bogey, double-bogey, double-bogey, and par to finish the third round), with birdies on twelve, thirteen, fourteen, sixteen, and seventeen on the way in. That round of 68 came despite early morning back spasms that continued throughout the day.

The win at Sahara demonstrated Nicklaus's ability to block out distractions. A third-round 62 matched the lowest score he ever recorded in a PGA event. At eight o'clock in the morning on the final round, a very pregnant Barbara awoke Jack to tell him they needed to leave for the hospital. Shortly after arriving there, Barbara miscarried. Despite the emotional trauma, she insisted Jack complete the fourth round. When he was assured she was in no danger, Nicklaus played the final round, shooting 71 to win the $20,000 first prize.

Although 1967 was a banner year, Nicklaus found frustration with an incident that occurred at the Champion's Tournament in Houston, a tournament conceived by Jack Burke and Jimmy Demaret. After an opening-round 77 that included a "snowman" 8 at the fourteenth hole, Nicklaus shot 69—or so he thought.

That score was increased by two when PGA Tournament Director Jack Tuthill assessed Nicklaus, Al Geiberger, and Cary Middlecoff two shots each for slow play. Jack said later the penalty was appropriate but criticized the PGA for pairing three "slow" players together. "When you take a player who's as slow as Cary," he observed, "and stick him with a player who's as slow as me and add a player like Al Geiberger who's not exactly a speed merchant—well, you've got trouble my friends."

Later on in the year, Nicklaus nearly was penalized again. During final-round play in the 1967 PGA Championship, Don January, partnered with Jack and Bob Goalby, was approached by a PGA official. "You're gonna have to speed it up," January was told. Motioning toward Nicklaus, January replied, "Go talk to the reason we're behind." Later January said, "But the official didn't. He was scared to death of Jack."

There were consistently complaints about Jack's slow play, but Mike Souchak pointed out they usually came from competitors who weren't playing well. "If everything was going great, I didn't care how

deliberate Jack was," he said. "But if I was hacking around, it bothered me."

Prior to the PGA Championship, Nicklaus had captured the
United States Open crown. It gave Jack seven major wins in just six
years on the Tour. Coupled with the two United States Amateur titles,
Jack had nine majors, just four short of Bobby Jones's record. He had
also accumulated six second-place finishes in majors during those early
years on Tour.

Although Nicklaus had produced good numbers in 1967, he
wasn't altogether pleased with his performance, especially when it
came to driving the ball. He found himself hitting too many second
shots from the deep rough.

An occasional duck-hook still plagued him, but Nicklaus's inconsistent play now emanated from a new shot he developed that started
right and continued right. Swing changes did little good, and it wasn't
until Nicklaus changed to a new driver, similar to the one Byron Nelson
used, that he could keep from hitting the ball too far to the right.

With that change, Nicklaus found he could hit the ball straight,
but he wasn't pleased. "I am still convinced," he said, " . . . that the
percentages are on the side of the golfer, be he a fader or a drawer, who
can aim down the side of the fairway and so have almost the full width
of the fairway at his disposal."

Ever in search of perfection, Nicklaus continued to tinker with his
swing. Normally, he could find the answer quickly and return to form,
but as the '68 season approached, Jack was about to learn what the
term "slump" meant for the first time in his career.

# CHAPTER 17

# The Slump

In 1968, Jack Nicklaus followed his first book, *My 55 Ways to Lower Your Golf Score*, with *Take a Tip from Me*. The book sold for $4.95. In *Golf Digest*, an advertisement for the book boasted "The new Jack Nicklaus book helps you look good—even in the rough."

The advertisement was tinged with irony, for after six brilliant seasons as a professional golfer, Nicklaus was playing golf as if *he* was stuck in the rough.

With twenty-five tournament victories, including seven major titles behind him, no one would have thought a slump possible. At just twenty-eight years of age, the future looked brighter than ever.

Of course, for anyone else a 1968 season filled with two second-place finishes in majors, two Tour victories, an Australian Open Championship, and second place on the money list with more than a $150,000 would not have been considered a slump.

Nicklaus also recorded a second-place finish at the Canadian Open. "Jack, Billy Casper, and I were in the last threesome," Bob Charles remembered. "Jack was hitting it by us forty to fifty yards, but he and I were tied heading into the last hole. I had a seven iron for my second [shot] and he had a wedge. But I hit the ball a foot from the hole and Jack missed the green. I tapped in for the win."

Such erratic play was the reason that for the first time in his professional career Nicklaus did not win a major event. For Jack and a public that perceived him as the number one player, that meant disappointment.

"Nicklaus focused on the majors," Bob Charles recalled. "While the rest of us were out there trying to make a living playing thirty to thirty-five tournaments, Jack was playing maybe fifteen. I think he was the first player to do that. He was doing things 'his way' and it worked for him."

But not in 1968. Although caddie Angelo Argea was by his side full time for the first time, Jack played erratically. He blamed it on continued problems with the driver and an incorrect take away that crept up at just the wrong time.

Try as he might, Nicklaus couldn't correct his swing problems. Even playing with Arnold Palmer didn't help matters. Winners so many times before, they befuddled their golf legions with a lackluster finish in the PGA Team Championship at Quail Creek. Bobby Nichols and George Archer won with 23 under, and the Nicklaus-Palmer tandem finished eight shots back in eighteenth place. Nicklaus told reporters, "We were in places where we could have hunted real quail. . . . We covered enough acres to build a thirty-six hole course."

During the winter between the 1968 and 1969 years, Nicklaus dissected the state of his play. "Many shortcomings had been apparent in my game," he said " . . . I began to perceive more clearly not only why I had failed in the tournaments I had a crack at winning but also why there had been so many other tournaments in which I hadn't scored well enough to become even a secondary factor."

Nicklaus also scrutinized a side of his game that had always been a strength. "My [course] management had been poor on a large number of occasions, much less sound than it had been in my younger days." The man known for conservative, calculated play also added, "A high percentage of my gambles hadn't been sensible. No wonder I had run into so many big holes for the first time in my life—those sevens and eights crush your chances."

Nicklaus took a look in the mirror and didn't like what he saw. "I . . . began to realize at this time that, while many people still referred to me as 'Young Jack Nicklaus,' I wasn't so young any more, certainly not in terms of golf. I was twenty-eight, the same age Bobby Jones had been when he retired from tournament play in 1930 following the Grand Slam. . . . I was already in my seventh season as a professional. It was about time I grew up a bit."

Nicklaus also questioned whether he had been playing "smart" golf and if he was making the proper adjustments to correct his swing technique during rounds when his play was inconsistent.

The 1969 season, marked by the miracle win by the amazing New York Mets in the World Series, began with a blessing at home. Gary Thomas Nicklaus, Jack's third son, was born on January 15. There were now four young Nicklauses—Jackie, Steve, Nan, and Gary, named after Nicklaus's friendly foe Gary Player.

Determined to improve on his performance in '69, the year Joe Namath correctly "predicted" the Jets would beat the Colts in the Super Bowl, Jack Nicklaus won the Kaiser, Sahara, and at San Diego, had eleven top-ten finishes in twenty-three events, and compiled $140,167 in money earnings.

The measuring stick for Jack, however, was the majors, and for the second straight year, he was shut out.

The wins at Sahara and the Kaiser were the first ones for a new, svelte Nicklaus. He lost twenty pounds during the '69 season and explained to *Golf Magazine* how he did it. "The way I played golf during that period was to take five or six clubs and run the course as I hit balls." That must have been quite an image.

Despite Nicklaus's solid year by most players' standards, Tour veteran Frank Beard caused a stir when he criticized Nicklaus in a book he wrote. The essence of Beard's comments, which he later claimed were misinterpreted, was that Nicklaus was washed up. Although some players would have been deeply affected by a comment like that, Jack used Beard's criticism as inspiration.

There were others, though, besides Beard who noticed that more than Nicklaus's girth had changed. An issue of *Golf Digest* carried the headline, "What's Bugging Big Jack?" Written by journalist Kaye Kessler, the article enumerated the reasons Nicklaus's game had hit rock bottom.

The most blunt of the observers quoted was Jack Grout, Nicklaus's longtime mentor. "His swing isn't the same as it was when he was winning everything," the teacher said. "His backswing has slowly deteriorated." These were tough words. Nicklaus was surprised and a bit hurt by them. Was everyone abandoning ship?

Tour golfer and Nicklaus's Florida neighbor Gardner Dickinson saw a different problem. "Jack is unwilling to dedicate himself to practicing enough or playing enough to get tournament tough. . . . He sets up games, but then he decides to fish or run up to Vero Beach or Hilton Head to see one of his courses or take his two elder boys and watch them beat balls." Dickinson added, "I love to play golf—but I don't think Jack does. . . . If he'd just sublimate every effort to golf like Hogan did, it scares me to think how good he'd be."

Gary Player had a different perspective. "Jack's doing what he should do, taking time for his family. . . . He's too preoccupied . . . to be totally absorbed in golf, but I think that's wonderful." Jack's dad, Charlie Nicklaus, told Kessler, "With all Jack's other interests now, the swing is the thing he doesn't get a chance to work on."

Nicklaus seemed unaffected by all the hubbub about a "slump." "I'm not happy with the way I'm playing," he observed in the same article. "But I know you're going to have periods when you're up and periods when you're down. This period has been a little more prolonged than I'd like." Later he added, "But I don't enjoy playing bad golf. I get tired of golf. There are periods when I can't make myself work . . . shooting 73 and 74, this burns me up. Then I do go back to work. Only trouble is, I haven't been able to get my game back as fast as I once did when I was a teenager."

The Jack Nicklaus at age twenty-nine who spoke those words hinted to Donald Rearson of *Golf Digest* a year earlier why his game had gone south. "I practice a lot at Lost Tree [his Florida home]. If you play, you only hit thirty-odd full shots during a four-hour round. I can practice for an hour, hit all my clubs, and spend the other three hours fishing."

Later on, Nicklaus, the true sportsman, would tackle hunting and nearly every other sport known to man. But fishing was Jack's current passion, and the competitive attitude that once inspired him to conquer the golf course now inspired him to conquer fish. He was most proud of the three large tarpon he caught off the coast of Nicaragua with Curt Gowdy and Lee Wulff, a fisherman of some renown, during a segment of ABC's *American Sportsman*. He also won third place in the *Field and Stream* fishing contest by catching a 124-pound tarpon in 1967.

Kay Kessler's *Golf Digest* article provided great insight into how Nicklaus's pride and resolve enabled him to bounce back from poor play. The challenge was to rekindle the fire and reshape his golf game to be competitive once again.

To illustrate how Jack operated, Kessler pointed to a story Charlie Nicklaus told him about Nicklaus's early years:

> I remember when he was in eighth grade and wanted to go out for football. [Jack] said he wanted to play in the backfield. I told him he better go out for guard. Oh boy, this really got him. . . . I said to him, "Run for me, let me see how fast you are." And I laughed at him, I guess. Boy, this got him. He went to our high school track coach and asked him to let him work out with the team. Well, they had a track meet with the eighth grade against the ninth and tenth. Jack won the 100, 220, 440, was on the winning 880 relay, and took third in the broad jump. He got a bunch of blue ribbons, brought them to me and said, "Now am I fast enough for the backfield?"

Charlie Nicklaus then added, "It was my needling that got him and still does. Nothing makes him madder now than to have me say to him, 'Why don't you just give it up? You've lost your edge.' Damn, that really burns him. But the challenge isn't over for him despite all his accomplishments. He's just having a hard time realizing it."

In addition to trying to get his game back together, Nicklaus gained many supporters in 1969, some of whom had previously found him stiff and uncaring. This support came from an incident that occurred at the Ryder Cup matches at Royal Birkdale. After Jack had holed out a tricky putt to ensure a tie with Tony Jacklin, he conceded the British star's two and one-half-footer. The act of sportsmanship was highly publicized, though some members of Nicklaus's team were less than thrilled since the result was a final-score tie at sixteen.

The gesture was classic Nicklaus. Even in the throes of a slump, he was the gentleman golfer. He knew there was a standard of conduct, a code that every player needed to follow. Forcing Jacklin to make the short putt in the Ryder Cup was not in keeping with Jack's interpretation of the code. In fact, Nicklaus was befuddled when some questioned his right to do so.

Who was the best player of the sixties? It was clearly a three-man race, with Jack's choice a bit of a surprise: Gary Player. Nicklaus sported seven major wins, Arnold Palmer five (the last one in 1964), and Gary Player four. But Jack Nicklaus was an arrant Gary Player advocate. "With the exception of Ben Hogan," Jack said at the time, "who's in a class by himself, Gary Player is the most accomplished technician in the game today. I would certainly rate him as the most consistent striker of the ball; every shot looks like it's been struck with the same hitting action, and the flight of his shots is extremely uniform." More specifically, Nicklaus said, "Gary is solid in every department. He's as good as they come with fairway woods, he's a top-class putter, and as I see it, he's the best sand-player in golf."

Nicklaus seemed more at ease with Gary Player then with any of his competitors during this era. When Nicklaus began competing on the PGA Tour in 1962, Player was the top money winner. Before long, the two developed a close friendship. Jack admired Player's tenacity and what he called the "sheer breadth" of his accomplishments in winning "repeatedly in just about every country where golf is played professionally."

As Nicklaus headed toward his second decade on Tour, Gary Player was still a formidable opponent. Like the rest of the competitors, he was bent on keeping Jack Nicklaus out of the winner's circle in a major tournament.

# CHAPTER 18

# Thin Jack

From the first day of 1970, thirty-year-old Jack Nicklaus was determined to regain his position as the finest golfer in the world. Since his win in the 1967 United States Open, Jack had competed in ten major tournaments without a victory. Worst of all, his play in 1969 rarely put him in contention. He had finished the four majors twenty-fourth, twenty-fifth, sixth, and eleventh.

Over the winter months, the golf experts continued to question Nicklaus's ability to recover the magic. They said he was bored and that his competitive edge was gone. He had become complacent, they said, unable to generate the enthusiasm necessary to win. His practice sessions seemed lackadaisical and tournament play uninspired. In forty-one events in 1968 and 1969, he'd won only four times.

Sportswriters, in fact, for the first time in several years, dismissed him as a true contender for the majors in 1970. *Golf Digest* picked Gary Player to win the Masters, Player or Billy Casper in the United States Open, Casper in the British Open, and Lee Trevino in the PGA Championship.

In pre-Tour interviews, Nicklaus agreed with his critics, admitting that during 1968 and 1969 his golf game did not improve. He said it was the only time during his career that had happened.

The Jack Nicklaus that greeted golf fans in 1970 was the "thin" version. In the preceding year, he had started the "Nicklaus make-over" by letting his blonde hair grow long and flow freely. "I guess my hair first started to get longer when my kids started wearing theirs longer," Nicklaus told *Golf Digest*. "They didn't want to have it cut—they wanted to be in the swing with the other kids—so I guess I just started to let mine grow a bit longer with them." Both the pundits and the people in the galleries liked the change, and Jack was happy with that.

Just after the Ryder Cup matches in late 1969, Jack told Barbara he wanted to lose weight. At the time, he weighed more than two-hundred pounds, prompting continued use of the unflattering nick-names "Ohio Fats," "Fat Jack," and worse.

Nicklaus's love of food was common knowledge, and fellow golfers often witnessed Jack's appetite firsthand. Chi Chi Rodriguez had this pleasure at the '62 Masters. "Jack and I were having dinner," Chi Chi recalled later. "And I was cutting the fat off my steak. 'What are you doing?' Jack asked. 'That's the best part.' I gave him the por-tion I'd cut off, and he ate it."

By all accounts, Jack Nicklaus wasn't a discriminating eater. Friends and business associates say that although he ate "salads and good stuff" in public, he was prone to return to the office and gobble down an entire package of cookies. One time Jack became enthralled with milk shakes made with avocado. "He downed six or seven of them," a friend said, "and then complained of having diarrhea. When he told Barbara of his problem, she just laughed."

When he decided to shed the pounds, Nicklaus battled excess poundage as if it was an unruly par four. With the help of a strict Weight Watchers diet, Jack shed nearly thirty pounds, dropping from 210 to 180, and lost six inches around the hips and two from his waist. Fortunately, he could afford a new wardrobe since the old one had to be pitched.

Barbara told writer Dick Taylor the weight loss was due to a steady diet of swordfish. When Taylor reported in an article that Jack and Barbara both looked great, he received a seething phone call from Jack explaining sternly that "Barbara has always looked great" and that "it was only he who needed improvement." Taylor laughed at the incident but clarified his remarks in a later article.

The Nicklaus medical history (his dad weighed nearly 350 pounds at one point and his uncle reached 375—and none of the men in his immediate family lived past sixty) would account for Jack's later pas-sion for physical fitness as well as his constant drive and determination to do all and see all when he hit his mid-fifties. In 1996, Nicklaus com-mented, "I'm going to attend the birth of one of my grandchildren because I was never there to see my own kids born, or any of the other grandkids." Nicklaus wanted to make up for lost time and to experi-ence everything possible before hitting the sixty-year mark.

The weight loss Jack experienced between 1969 and 1970 did require some adjustments for Barbara. Nicklaus apparently became a bit narcissistic while shedding the pounds, prompting his wife to tell *Sports Illustrated*, "There is nothing worse than a reformed slob."

The new hair style and thinner frame brought about a third

change. He'd been admittedly nonchalant, even flagrantly aloof, with his fans, but Jack now started to be downright friendly. Spectators responded to his outgoing nature and relaxed attitude. Reporters noticed the change and wrote about the "new" Jack. A fresh personality was emerging, and Nicklaus the "stuffed shirt" was becoming attractively casual.

Former United States and British Amateur Champion Vinny Giles noticed Jack's transformation. "Nobody worked harder at changing their personality than Nicklaus did," he observed. "From the clothes, the hair, the whole nine yards. Jack was not a guy who didn't want to be liked, never a bad sport. He just wanted to better himself."

Nicklaus acknowledged the changes, especially in his relationship with fans. "Being . . . by nature a fairly private and not a particularly demonstrative type of person," he said, "it simply took me awhile to learn that you have to give the fans a little more of yourself than just a golf game. Greater experience and maturity have, I think, allowed me to do that without, I hope, needing to be dishonest or unnatural in my behavior."

*Golf World* writer Dick Taylor later summed up Nicklaus's new image when he said, ". . . a metamorphosis occurred. [Jack] took off that silly hat and his flaxen Nordic hair became bleached; his baby blues were observed, and then he dropped all that weight, and at Tulsa during the '70 PGA Championship, he suddenly had 'birds' in his gallery, pretty things who didn't know a feathered fade from a Sassoon razor cut."

Nicklaus's metamorphosis was also appreciated by one of the companies he endorsed, Hart, Schaffner, and Marx. "When I first went with [them]," Nicklaus told *Golf Digest*, "they'd give me drawings of how they planned pictures for the ads. They were always shooting me from the waist up—showing the jacket only—not the pants. My legs were so beefy, they just couldn't use them. Now they're using pictures of all of me."

The challengers Nicklaus faced in the seventies included many of the same ones from the sixties: Palmer, Player, Casper, Lema, Boros, Doug Sanders, and Gay Brewer. But he also faced a few new ones, including Tom Weiskopf, whom Nicklaus said was "the best swinger and the best striker in the [new] group." He also singled out Ray Floyd, whom Nicklaus said "can hit the ball a mile and . . . fade and draw it," as well as Terry Dill, Rod Funseth, Bob Lunn, and Marty Fleckman.

Ben Hogan wasn't as impressed by the group as Nicklaus was. "I've noticed some of them are off balance when they swing," Hogan told reporters, "Too much hair." Whether "The Hawk" included Nicklaus in the too-much-hair group is unclear. Jack's transformation rejuvenated him, and his spirit came back during the British Open at St. Andrews in 1970. He hadn't played well at the Masters (won by Billy Casper) or at the United States Open held at Hazeltine in Minnesota, a course professional Dave Hill referred to as a cow pasture.

In fact, through the first twenty-seven Tour tournaments of the year, Nicklaus had only one win, the Byron Nelson Classic. Skeptics continued to discount him, and he had been unable to prove them wrong.

The United States Open, played under conditions that historian Herbert Warren Wind called "more suitable to hunting caribou than playing golf," was won by Tony Jacklin, making him the first British golfer to do so in fifty years. Nicklaus was never a factor, shooting a four-round total of 304 that included a 43 and 38, his highest round ever in a United States Open. Afterwards, he brushed by reporters, saying, "Excuse me while I go and throw up."

A return to Scotland saw him triumph over a classy field. Doug Sanders's famous faux pas, a four-foot miss on the final hole, gave Nicklaus the victory in a subsequent playoff and major championship number ten (see page 229).

The triumph was a result of Nicklaus's hard work. He produced a new set up that permitted a smoother take away. Problems with the driver, which had caused him to play from the rough so much of the time, were corrected.

More than anything, whatever "slump" Nicklaus had experienced seemed to have disappeared with the lengthening of his hair and loss of weight. The hitch in his giddy up seemed a bit more spry.

In addition to the win in Scotland, as well as the Byron Nelson Classic, Jack won the National Team Championship with Arnold Palmer, the Picadilly World Match Play title, and the World Series of Golf.

His superb play inspired author Nevin Gibson to write, "No one hits the ball farther off the tee, or higher, and straighter with more consistency. No one has his game so finely tuned to the power lurking in the massive arms and shoulders. No one has been able to master courses as he has with his sheer strength."

The British Open victory unleashed the floodgates of media adulation once again, especially with regard to Jack's ability to overpower the opposition at age thirty.

Nicklaus's performance throughout the seventies bordered on the unbelievable. From '71 to '75, he won twenty-two times on the United States Tour, including four more majors, breaking Jones's record. He also recorded four more second-place finishes in major tournaments.

Although Arnold Palmer had a resurgence in 1971, winning four times with what would be his last great play on Tour, Nicklaus was most threatened by a new contender. His name was Lee Buck Trevino, a fast-talking hombre from El Paso who'd learn to play on hard-pan Texas courses that country club boys like Nicklaus and Palmer never knew existed.

The world first became aware of Trevino when he qualified for and then finished fifth in the 1967 United States Open. Before that, no one had heard much about a Mexican hat dancer who played golf with a pop bottle while beating the socks off of his challengers.

Trevino was an ex-Marine who scraped through the ball with an inside-out swing that made golf purists cringe. He was one of the best at chipping and putting. When he astounded the world with a four-shot United States Open victory over Nicklaus at Oak Hill, Jack found a competitor who stuck to him like Super Glue.

Trevino's own estimation of his game was coy. "My swing is *bad-looking*," he said to *Golf Digest*. "But the point is it works for me. . . . The vital point every time is how well a person can master a swing, not how pretty it looks to other people."

*Golf Digest* writer Roger Schiffman, who first saw Trevino in 1970, is one who would agree with that assessment. "I was shagging balls for the cigar-chomping Billy Maxwell, my bag for the week," Schiffman said, "when suddenly Trevino's caddie was standing twenty feet to my left. Back on the practice tee, his man started stamping out nine-iron facsimiles that never rose higher than your shoulder. The shots all seemed to be aimed directly at me, then faded toward the caddie, landing at his feet. The shagger would let the ball hop once, catch it in a towel, wipe the ball clean and drop it in the bag. He hardly had to move."

Trevino became Nicklaus's newest nemesis, a player who pushed him to the edge much as Nicklaus had pushed Palmer. Their match-ups became classics. Early on Jack told Lee, an effervescent man with a quick wit, "You don't know how good you are."

Nicklaus said of Trevino, "He's a great fellow: honest, straightforward, very hardworking, a great competitor. . . . Lee likes his fun, but don't let that clowning fool you. There's a very serious and intelligent man behind it, and a very good one."

Trevino, whose followers became known as "Lee's Fleas," said Nicklaus inspired him. "Jack brings out the best in me every time. I match him shot for shot, and nothing pleases me more. I could care less about anybody else in the field. I don't even care who is leading the tournament, as long as I beat him when we're paired together."

The Merry Mex, never one to hide his bravado, told *USA Today*'s Steve Hershey, "If you match me with Nicklaus, I'd beat him eight times out of ten. The reason is that I'd match him shot for shot; the better he hit it, the better I'd hit it." On a day when his senses returned he reversed his thoughts, saying, "[Jack's] a freak . . . he might even beat two people. Beat their best ball."

Through 1975, Trevino, who Dick Taylor said, "had a degree in street smarts," amassed twenty-two victories, including five majors. Whether he toppled Nicklaus from his perch as the best player in world at that time is debatable, but he was a proven contender every time out. As Tom Weiskopf said, "Jack could beat anyone, but Lee Trevino had his number."

# CHAPTER 19

# Johnny Miller

Nineteen seventy-one was a banner year for Nicklaus, even though he mourned the death of his idol Bobby Jones. He became a double Grand Slam winner (having won all of the professional majors twice) when he captured the PGA Championship, his eleventh major championship victory, at PGA National Golf Club in Florida.

Nicklaus was also victorious in the Tournament of Champions, the Disney World Open, the National Team Championship, and the Byron Nelson Classic. He won the PGA money title again with $244,490, a new record.

On the international scene, Nicklaus shot a course-record 65 in the third round of the Australian Open and won by eight shots. It was the third time he had won the event. He captured the Dunlap International by seven shots, shooting a third-round 62 that by *Golf World*'s account, had "the bustling, hustling galleries roaring like a football mob." Nicklaus then teamed with Lee Trevino to win the World Cup by twelve while defeating house guest Gary Player for individual honors by seven shots. He now had three World Cup victories. For those twelve rounds of play, he was 50 under par. He also won five matches out of six for the victorious Ryder Cup team. By all accounts, it was an incredible year.

The World Cup victory, played on the East Course of the PGA National Golf Club in Florida, was especially significant, because it foreshadowed great things to come in 1972. Nicklaus, now thirty-one, was at the top of his game. "It's probably three of the best weeks I've ever played in a stretch," he told *Golf Magazine*.

Using the 1.62" British "small" ball (the American ball is 1.68") permitted in World Cup play, Nicklaus shot 271, seventeen under par, to beat house guest Gary Player by seven shots. Trevino and Nicklaus won the team title by twelve.

When asked by *Golf World* his opinion of the "small" ball,

Nicklaus said, "The large ball requires better shotmaking, the small ball is more fun to play. But it shortens courses, will make them obsolete. And playing the [small] ball tends to make me sloppy."

As for the state of the relationship between Nicklaus and his chief rival Trevino at the time, *Golf World*'s Dick Taylor said, "It was a delight to see these two titans of world golf openly admire one another's talents . . . and Nicklaus enjoyed the quick-witted retorts of his partner. There has to be a genuine rivalry between them, but it hasn't gotten in the way of friendship."

Taylor was right. Trevino sometimes irritated Jack with chatter and schoolboy shenanigans. Lee also shared many of Palmer's characteristics. He was a swashbuckling, go-for-broke player and had Palmer-like charisma with galleries who loved his merry ways. Lee's Fleas emulated Arnie's Army though their numbers never approached that of Arnold's worshipers. Even so, there was none of the behind-the-back sniping that pockmarked the Palmer-Nicklaus rivalry.

The difference was that by the time Trevino came along, Nicklaus was a changed man. There were fans who still cared little for Jack, but his new hip look was attractive. Jack had also improved his demeanor on the golf course. He still got the Nicklaus "look" on his face when he was concentrating, but the bounce in his walk and his willingness to smile more made him somehow more acceptable to the fans.

Throughout the '71 season, Nicklaus's golf game was simply superb, and spectators seemed to appreciate it more. He no longer seemed to be "a mechanical man" but a player crowds actually cheered for when he made one of his famous runs at a championship.

And Trevino? He had come along at just the right time. Golf once again needed a rivalry and Lee became Jack's foil. His great play inspired Nicklaus and vice versa. When Jack needed fresh motivation, Lee provided it.

During the week of the World Cup, Trevino was named PGA Player of the Year. In defiance, Nicklaus blistered the course, causing Lee to comment, "Jack could have beaten everybody else hittin' a basketball. . . . He was crackin' that thing so loud I had to stuff cotton in my ears." Trevino added, "If he played that small ball on the Tour, he'd shoot in the fifties half the time."

When asked in 1971 to articulate whether he agreed with the theory that a golfer reaches his prime at age thirty-five, Jack told Phil Tresidder of *Golf World*, "I certainly hope so. I had a reasonable amount of success in my twenties and now I'm asking myself whether I'll improve in my thirties like Palmer, Player, Hogan, and Snead. I think I'm getting better. I'm a better player from tee to green, more consistent, and I make fewer mistakes. My swing feels the same but a lot more things are falling into place."

Golfers who wanted to witness that swing for themselves could purchase "Jack Nicklaus on Golf," a fifteen-minute instructional 8 millimeter color film on which Nicklaus collaborated with noted writer Herbert Warren Wind.

There was one playoff loss that provided insight into how important winning was to Jack. It took place when Nicklaus shot 70, 71, 67, and 72 (280) to tie Bobby Mitchell at tournament's end. Mitchell, a twenty-year-old Virginian, drew the green on the first extra hole while Nicklaus hooked a four-iron into the La Costa rough. Nicklaus chipped to within eight feet, but Mitchell was true with his twenty-foot birdie putt and Nicklaus was second fiddle for the week.

Afterwards, Mitchell, an obscure professional clawing for the limelight and calling himself "the invisible man," said he won because "maybe Jack didn't see me." Nicklaus's second-place purse of $19,000 gave him $153,000 for one-third of the year, but Jack wasn't smiling when he said, "I was counting on it being $167,000" (first prize was $33,000). Whether it was Arnold Palmer or Lee Trevino or a journeyman player like Bobby Mitchell who beat him, Jack Nicklaus was never pleased with second place.

In 1973, Nicklaus won seven more times, giving him an astonishing fourteen victories in the thirty-seven events he entered between 1972 and 1973. He was named PGA Player of the Year for the second consecutive year and the third time in his career. He won $308,365 and recorded an incredible 69.81 scoring average.

Nicklaus's scores at the majors in 1973 were consistently outstanding. He tied for third in the Masters, tied for fourth in the United States Open, finished fourth in the British Open, and won the PGA (see page 218).

Even though he won two majors in four different years ('63, '66, '72, and '75), these finishes marked his most consistent play in any one year other than in 1973.

Nicklaus's other triumphs in 1973 came in the Crosby, the New Orleans Open, the Tournament of Champions, the Atlanta Classic, the Ohio Kings Island Open, and the Disney World Open, which he won for the third straight year.

The Tournament of Champions victory was significant because Nicklaus was reluctant to play after his disappointment in losing the Masters. "That was the only tournament Barbara ever made me go to," Nicklaus told *Golf Magazine*. "She said, 'You are going, your plane reservations are here, and this is where you're going to stay.'"

In addition to the Tour wins in 1973, Nicklaus and Johnny Miller won the World Cup. Jack went four, one, and one in the Ryder Cup. He also found time to shoot 59 in an exhibition at the Breakers Hotel course in Palm Beach. The layout was short by Tour standards (par 70, 6,008 yards), but neither Sam Snead (69), Kathy Whitworth (69), nor Kathy Ahern (74) scored as far below par as Jack did.

Between Nicklaus's competition in the American Golf Classic and the Westchester tournament, another significant event occurred. On July 24, Michael Scott, the youngest of the Nicklaus troupe, was born.

Even though Nicklaus notched no major victories in 1974, he was victorious in the Tournament Players Championship and The Hawaiian Open. That year he was inducted into the PGA World Golf Hall of Fame, one of thirteen original inductees.

Nicklaus's win in Hawaii was his payback to business advisors who chastised him for buying a painting of elephants by wildlife artist David Shepard. The painting cost him $12,000, bringing cries of "You can't afford that" from his associates. Singed by their criticism, he entered the Hawaiian Open, shot 271, and won the first-place purse of $44,000, more than enough to cover the cost of the painting.

Nicklaus was a consistent factor throughout 1974, the same year in which twenty-seven-year-old John Laurence Miller assaulted the PGA Tour with eight wins. Miller, a Californian with surfer-boy looks, won at the Crosby, the Tournament of Champions, and the World Open, among others.

Miller was a San Francisco native with a penchant for shooting lights-out scores that left competitors and those in the gallery breathless. Dubbed the latest "new Nicklaus", he first played on the PGA Tour in 1969. By 1974, he'd only compiled three Tour victories, but one of them was the 1973 United States Open at Oakmont, where he shot a phenomenal 63 in the final round. He would add another major in 1976 at the British Open and end up compiling twenty-four career wins before returning to the sidelines.

Miller may have been the hottest player on the '74 tour, but by 1977 his game cooled considerably and he was never able to regain the magic touch that led him to so many dramatic victories.

To Nicklaus, Miller was an enigma. "I can understand a fellow with his talent getting a little bit off his game at times," he observed, "but frankly, getting as far off as he appears to have been in the past couple of years is beyond my comprehension. My guess at this problem is that he hasn't been able to work out a formula that allows him to balance the various compartments of his life—most notably his keen desire for privacy and a full family life—to his total emotional satisfaction."

Nicklaus offered insights into his own game with the publication in 1974 of *Golf My Way*, a classic to this day. Written with collaborator Ken Bowden, it chronicles Nicklaus's career (to that point), presents tips for those wishing to learn the game of golf and play it better, and most importantly, features Jack's insight into his own manner of play.

Nicklaus believed at the time that the curtain on his twelve-year professional golf career was actually drawing to a close. "Given my present health," he wrote, "I believe that I can continue to sharpen and improve my game in the physical sense for at least another five years." Since Nicklaus was thirty-four at the writing of the book, it appears he felt he could play competitively only until he was forty.

Toward the end of the book, Nicklaus provided a discerning analysis of his game. "My highest rate of failure occurs, of course, in execution. Maturity and experience have brought me to a point where, when I'm concentrating properly, objective shot analysis presents few major problems. How much I compromise depends on my confidence level, but when it's high I can be pretty resolute about attempting the proper shot."

Nicklaus did not shy away from self-criticism. "I feel the nearest I've ever gotten to the goals I set for myself is about 75 percent," he wrote in the book. "At my worst, I probably do not reach 33 percent. Over-all, day in and day out, at the present time I'm probably averaging about 60 percent."

Here was the man who had won fourteen major golf championships and forty-eight professional golf Tour titles by the end of 1974. Could he really only be operating at "about 60 percent"?

If Nicklaus truly believed that, he saw room for much improvement in his game. More likely, Nicklaus was simply attempting to motivate himself, as was his custom. He should have spoken to writer William Price Fox, who wrote in *Golf Digest*, "Nicklaus is wiser, smarter, better, and he will win unless something like a brick wall or a subpoena server gets in front of him. There will be no stopping him."

In 1974 Nicklaus was the complete player, a better one than at anytime in his career. Every part of his game was sharp.

With the driver, Nicklaus not only hit the ball as far as he ever had, but his power had also been harnessed and he was straight off the tee. He could both fade and draw the ball on cue and hit a low booming shot, but the ability to hit the high floating tee shot was still his greatest asset.

Jack recognized the advantage he had, especially with his power, telling Tour competitor Jim Dent, "Whatever you do, don't let them ever take your distance away." Dent knew what Nicklaus meant. "He was saying, 'Don't let them change your swing so you can't hit it as far as you do'," Dent recalled. "That was a great tip."

Carol Mann, the 1965 United States Women's Open champion, saw the advantage that Nicklaus had with his power (his club speed was estimated to be 120 miles per hour at impact) and his ability to hit the high shot. "In the mid-sixties," Mann said, "Jack and Doug Sanders were pitted against Kathy Whitworth and me in an exhibition in Baltimore, my home town. Kathy and I were one up going to eighteen, which was a lengthy dogleg up-hill par-four. Needing birdie, Jack hit a high driver up over the trees onto the back of the green. I couldn't believe how strong he was. And how high he could hit the ball."

There is an aside to that story, Mann reported. Even though Jack two-putted for birdie to give "the boys" a halve, the newspapers reported the next day that Nicklaus and Sanders had won. "I was furious," Carol said, "Kathy just shrugged her shoulders, but I couldn't believe either Jack or Doug told reporters they'd won. I guess they just couldn't stand losing to us gals."

In addition to witnessing Jack's proficiency with high shots and his power, Carol Mann saw what everyone else did, that Jack was a great three-wood player. "Jack was the first player I saw who regularly used the three-wood off the tee," she said. "He realized that the driver wasn't always required. He left his ego in the lockerroom."

When it came to long iron play, Nicklaus was simply the best in the game in the early- to mid-seventies. Once again his ability to strike the ball with crisp precision and hit it high proved an enormous advantage. "When a player hits the ball high like Jack did," Carol Mann said, "they can fly it over creeks, trees, all the hazards. It makes golf an easier game." Chi Chi Rodriguez agreed. "I was a shotmaker, hit lots of different types of shots," he said. "But Jack hit the ball the same way every time. He hit it so high it floated down. My shots bounced all over the place. Jack's just landed and stopped."

Deane Beman saw Nicklaus's ability to hit the ball high as one of four reasons Jack was a superior player. "He was the first really long hitter who could control his shot enough that it was an advantage. And Jack was as great a putter as ever lived. He also played every shot the same. Never played a careless shot. But the fact that he could hit the ball high, so far in the air, with both woods and long irons, was the key. Others hit it low and ran it. But Jack hit it over everything, all the bunkers, everything. He didn't intimidate short hitters like me. He intimidated the long hitters 'cause they couldn't keep up with him."

Observations about Nicklaus's play with middle and short irons varied, but there is no question that he was a fine mid-iron player. "My percentage of misses is small," Nicklaus said, "and I can play a wide variety of . . . shots." His observation was correct as competitors who watched him play the 150- to 180-yard par-threes would confirm. Nicklaus was deadly with a mid-iron in his hand.

Jack wasn't as proficient from within 150 yards, however, but Nicklaus had improved his eight- and nine-iron play when he dominated in the mid-seventies. Still Jack was not pleased. "I'm better in this area than I was three years ago," he said, "but I still lack the finesse—the total ball control—that I think I should have."

The words were emblematic of what a perfectionist Jack could be—ever ready to be self-critical. "One aspect of my personality that has at times helped my career and at times brought me a lot of heartache," he said, "is my desire for perfection in all things." Never was that more true when he assessed his own ability at golf.

Nicklaus's perception of his chipping game in the mid-seventies spoke volumes about his ego. "I don't miss a lot of greens," he said, "thus I don't get to chip the ball a lot under competitive conditions." On cue, Jack Nicklaus could rationalize a shortcoming, for he knew that the weakest part of his golf game was chipping.

The truth was that Jack wouldn't listen to others who offered advice, and he wouldn't practice the art of the chip shot. Doing so bored him. The power game was much more exciting.

As a bunker player, Nicklaus had at least one shortcoming. "Jack could play well out of firm sand," Chi Chi Rodriguez said, "but soft sand—not as good." Jack acknowledged the problem but felt his sand play had improved with age.

Tour veteran Mike Souchak said that "a good putter can handle any type of putting surface, but a mediocre one like me is always much better on fast greens." The comment was significant when applied to Jack Nicklaus. He believed himself to be a poor putter on slow greens and a good putter when the surfaces ran fast. "Realistically," he said, "I'd rate my putting somewhere between 70 and 80 percent, with lows of about 30 percent and occasional highs of about 90 percent." Leave it to Nicklaus to rate his putting so severely.

When all of Jack's comments about his game were added up, the grade was no higher than C+. But overall performance didn't mean a thing. Jack hit the shots he had to hit. More important, he made the putts he had to make. Carol Mann believed Nicklaus was chiefly responsible for a resurgence in interest among fans about putting. "Jack brought attention to that part of the game," she said. "Hogan and Nelson hated it, but Jack rounded out the game by turning putting into an art. He was a great role model that way."

Nevertheless, Jack called putting an "in and out game for me." He vowed improvement in that area, and in other areas as well, as he approached his thirteenth year as a professional golfer in 1975.

# CHAPTER 20

# Tom Watson

I n 1975, Jack Nicklaus won five times, including victories at the Masters and PGA Championship. Still, he wasn't satisfied.

"[It's] the year I lost the Grand Slam by three shots," he said later. "I won the Masters and PGA, lost the British Open by one, and lost the U.S. Open by two after double bogeying the 16th hole in the final round.

"Had I won [the Grand Slam], I probably would have gotten out of the game. . . . I had a better chance that year than I ever had. The U.S. Open [tied for 7th] I gave away, and the British Open [tied for 3rd] was almost given to me."

Nicklaus's opposition wished he *had* won, so they could be rid of him for good. Jack's fifth Masters title (see page 248) and his fourth PGA Championship (see page 219) were his fifteenth and sixteenth major championships. He also won at Doral, the Heritage Classic, the Walt Disney World Open and added a fourth Australian Open victory that year. With a total of $298,149 Jack led the money list for the seventh time, and his scoring average of 69.87 ranked number one. Nicklaus tied Ben Hogan's record when he was named PGA Player of the Year for a fourth time and was also honored with the prestigious USGA's Bobby Jones Award for Distinguished Sportsmanship in Golf.

Despite the year's successes, Nicklaus suffered humiliation in the Ryder Cup matches. He was 2-2-1 overall, but two defeats (4-2, 2-1) came in one day at the hands of the effervescent Scot Brian Barnes. The matches (won by the U.S. 19-13) were played at Laurel Valley Golf Club in Ligoner, Pennsylvania, near Arnold Palmer's hometown.

Barnes, who later became an American Senior Tour regular after battling a bout with alcoholism, remembered the day well. "The first time I won, he didn't seem to mind," said the man who once marked his golf ball in a major championship with a beer bottle, "but the second defeat pissed him off. Jack was gracious, though, I give him that."

Losing to the colorful Barnes, possibly the only man to wear a kilt while competing on the European Tour, was an embarrassment to Nicklaus. Jack might have been gracious to his opponent, but he was fuming at the losses.

Just when Lee Trevino's game began to sour a bit, Jack faced another formidable challenger, twenty-six-year-old Tom Watson, a Huck Finn look-alike from the Show-Me State of Missouri.

The Stanford grad had begun to play among the Tour leaders in 1974, and even led the United States Open in the final round before closing with 79. That year he won the Western Open, but the breakthrough tournament for Watson came at Carnoustie in the British Open in 1975. He rallied to gain a tie with Australian Jack Newton and then won in a playoff to record his first major win.

In the late seventies, Nicklaus said of Watson, "He isn't, in my estimation, quite as naturally talented physically as Weiskopf and Miller, but he sure makes up for it in a lot of other ways. Perhaps the most impressive of these are his self-confidence, his maturity, and his tremendous determination. Tom knows where he wants to go, and he's going there in the straightest possible line and the shortest possible time—almost to the point of having blinders on."

Watson, who amassed thirty-nine Tour victories from 1974 to 1996, including seven major championships, had his own opinions about Nicklaus during that time. "He may not be the best ball striker ever," he told reporters, "but he is the greatest at course management, the best with long irons, and the best in big tournaments." Golf commentator Jack Whitaker said Watson's comments surprised him. "I always thought of Jack in terms of ball-striking ability, but Watson was right. He wasn't as good as the others, but his total game just outlasted everyone."

For many years, Nicklaus and Tom Watson had an uneasy and jealous relationship, as they were frequently head-to-head in competitions. Writer Thomas Boswell says the rivalry became so intense after the 1977 Masters championship that Nicklaus and Watson had harsh words behind the eighteenth green.

The disagreement was a result of Watson's belief that Nicklaus, playing one group ahead on the final day, had waved at him on the thirteenth hole after draining a birdie putt as if to say, "Take that." Nicklaus denied it so strongly that Tom backed off.

From 1976 until 1985, Watson caught and eventually passed Jack Nicklaus as the dominant player on Tour. Trevino still made occasional visits to the winner's circle, but the fiercest battles were between Jack and Tom, two players who joined the elite group of athletes known instantly by the mention of their first names.

Even though he didn't win a major championship, 1976, a year that saw Tour rookie Jerry Pate win the United States Open, was a good year for Nicklaus. He won his second Tournament Players Championship at Pete Dye's TPC Sawgrass course in Ponte Vedra, Florida, against a field as good as any that had ever lined up for a major. He also won the World Series of Golf for the fifth time and with $266,439 led the Tour in earnings, the last year that he would do so. Through the end of 1976, Jack had made the cut in 105 consecutive starts over six years on Tour.

Nicklaus also captured a record fifth Australian Open title. Second-place finishes in the Canadian Open and at Doral rounded out the year, and he was named PGA Player of the Year for a record fifth time, including four of the past five years.

In 1977, Jack won his own tournament, the Memorial, as well as the Jackie Gleason Inverrary and the Tournament of Champions. His sixty-three victories on Tour surpassed Ben Hogan's count, placing Jack second in all-time victories, behind Sam Snead.

At the British Open he and Tom put on a historic competitive display not soon to be forgotten (see page 231), but Nicklaus eventually finished second to Watson in both the British Open and the Masters. Watson's win in the British Open and the Masters and his position at the top of the money list (Jack was second) seemed to signal a changing of the guard. Was Tom Watson supplanting Jack Nicklaus, fans wondered, as Nicklaus had Palmer?

Nicklaus was aware that Watson had the capacity to overtake him not only as the best touring golfer but eventually in the record books.

"I would like to extend those records as far as possible, not only for my own satisfaction," Nicklaus said, "but also to provide an exciting target for other golfers, present and future."

Nicklaus added, "I'm one heck of a better shotmaker with every club in the bag than I've ever been. The key factor then is the matter of desire. I am convinced that this is simply a question of pacing, of orchestrating my life in such a way as to keep myself 'hungry' on the golf course."

Jack's dedication to excellence contributed to his win in the

British Open in 1978 (see page 233), his seventeenth major. The victory boldly told competitors, especially Watson, "Hold on a minute, don't close the door on me yet."

By winning, Jack became the first player to be victorious in the four majors three times over. He also won three times on the regular PGA Tour and recorded his record sixth and final Australian Open title. When Nicklaus was named "Sportsman of the Year" by *Sports Illustrated*, journalist Frank DeFord claimed Jack had attained "mystic oneness . . . with the game of golf itself during that long span and with courses on which it is played."

However, the victory at the Australian Open was not without a struggle. A few days before the tournament, Nicklaus battled a 15' 6" black marlin for six and a half hours. Jack prevailed, entering the fishing record books with the catch, but the marlin's fighting spirit wrenched his knees.

Then, after a first-round 73 at the Open, Jack played tennis and injured his shoulder. "I was taking Butazolidin, which they only give to horses anymore." He later told *Golf Digest*, "I didn't know if I was going to be able to play the next day." He did and, amazingly, shot 66. Battered and bruised, Jack eventually cruised by the field with a six-shot win.

The Tour win at Inverrary was most significant. During the final round, Jack birdied the last five holes to douse dispirited Grier Jones's chance for victory. After Inverrary, playing companion Lee Trevino said, "Those five consecutive birdies . . . is like Reggie Jackson hitting three consecutive home runs in the World Series, Leon Spinks beating Ali. It was the most remarkable thing I've ever witnessed in my life." Later, Nicklaus told *Golf Magazine*, "The next year, in the first round, I birdied [the last] five holes again."

While Tom Watson was playing his heart out to win the money earnings title in 1977 and 1978, in addition to winning the two majors, another compelling face arrived on the professional tour. Severiano Ballesteros captured his first major, the British Open at Royal Lytham and St. Annes. As many other young winners, the colorful Spaniard was labeled the "next Nicklaus." The constant comparisons to Nicklaus prompted author Brad Herzog to write, "There was Nicklaus and Palmer, Nicklaus and Player, Nicklaus and Trevino, Nicklaus and Miller, Nicklaus and Watson, Nicklaus and Ballesteros. But always there was Jack Nicklaus."

Although Ballesteros had success winning a major in 1979, Nicklaus endured a year he would rather forget. At thirty-nine years of age, he had only a fourth-place finish in the Masters as a highlight. He was completely shut out of the victory circle (his best finish was a tie for third in the Philadelphia Classic), and for first time in his seventeen years as a professional Jack appeared to have fallen off his throne. Weary of answering questions about his bad play, he became testy with the media. "You answer questions a lot different when you're thirty-nine than when you were twenty-five," he said. "At twenty-five, I was brutally honest; at thirty-nine, I'm carefully honest."

Things got so bad that Nicklaus became less than excited about playing at all. After barely making the cut at the United States Open at Inverness, he admitted to *The New York Times* that he'd made the remark, "I guess I've got to go out and play tomorrow."

By year's end, his despondence had subsided, and Nicklaus was ready to do what he did best—motivate himself.

"I was out here [Nicklaus's lighted putting greens in his Florida backyard] putting with some friends on New Year's Eve," Nicklaus told the *Times*, "and at 11:59, we went inside for a toast. Then we came out again. I had a thirty-foot putt, and I told myself, 'First putt of the year; this will be indicative of the year.' I knocked it in. The next morning I came out to hit some chip shots. . . . On the first shot, I knocked it in the cup. Another omen."

# CHAPTER 21

# Jack at Forty

When Jack Nicklaus turned forty in 1980, he was determined to rebuff those skeptics who said, "Jack is dead." To do so, he realized that without power as his dominant weapon, he needed to sharpen his skills at pitching, chipping, and bunker play, areas he had sorely neglected. Rationalizing his play as he sometimes had in the past wouldn't help. He needed advice. With the same sensible and systematic approach he used to improve other facets of his game, he sought advice from those he respected.

The decision to do so had been long overdue. "By Tour standards, [Nicklaus] is not a great chipper," PGA Champion Dave Marr said. "He never would take advice." Jack knew Marr was right.

In the mid-seventies, Nicklaus had recognized his problems with the short game. He opined that he was the only golfer on Tour who was better with long irons than short irons. "I'm a Little Leaguer . . . compared to a major leaguer like Deane Beman," he said.

When the realization finally set in that improvement was necessary, Nicklaus contacted a master of chipping and wedge play: Phil Rodgers.

Sessions with Rodgers, who correctly said, "Golf is not a game of great shots . . . It's a game of great misses," were a result of conversations Nicklaus had with Touring professional John Schroeder. "I wasn't looking forward to 1980," Nicklaus told *The New York Times*. "I hadn't played well in '79, and I didn't see any prospect of improving. I wanted to play, but I didn't know how to. I didn't like my swing. I didn't like my short game. I never had a good short game anyway."

The exact time Nicklaus finally decided to seek help is subject to conjecture. Apparently he realized that unless he did, being competitive, always the Nicklaus bellwether, was a thing of the past.

Fortunately, Schroeder told him he should talk to the master of chipping and wedge play, Phil Rodgers. The two finally met up at the Los Angeles Open at Riveria, a difficult course where, ironically, Nicklaus never posted a win. "That Friday afternoon," Jack told the *Times,* "we went over to another course and he [Rodgers] started showing me the basics."

It's difficult for some to believe that Jack Nicklaus, winner of seventeen major championships and sixty-six Tour victories, needed to get back to basics with a facet of golf as important as the short game. But the knowledge Rodgers imparted made an immediate difference.

Rodgers's instruction involved several aspects of the short game, but the most beneficial concerned Jack's wedge play. One of the shots Rodgers taught involved positioning the weight of the body on the left side and crouching the upper body, while keeping the head position to the right. Utilizing a relaxed grip and sufficient wrist action, the open-faced sand wedge lifted the ball vertically and permitted the ball to stop as if it had brakes.

Rodgers also worked with Nicklaus on wedge shots from short distances in the fairway to the green. Results of his tutelage began to show right away. "The next morning," Nicklaus told the *Times,* "back at Riveria, I had a little thirty-yard chip for my third shot on the par-five first hole. I told myself, 'Here goes. If I'm going to learn it, I've got to do it.' I hit it up there about six feet away. But it took me until May to find out how hard to hit it, to really know what I was doing."

Nicklaus's new passion to learn the wedge shot came at a time when there was no such thing as the high-degree loft wedge. That wedge didn't appear until the nineties. Players carried a pitching wedge and a sand wedge, not three wedges as is normal today. Two-time United States Women's Open champion Donna Caponi commented recently, "I've always been proud of the fact that like Nicklaus, my first Tour tournament win was an Open. But Jack and I also shared something else. Neither of us had very good short games. I'm sure both of us would have won many more tournaments if we had had the 60 degree wedge."

"I tried to stimulate Jack's imagination with the short game," Phil Rodgers explained of his work with Jack, "by showing him how to hit different shots, low ones and ones with different spins. Basically, Jack was a methodical one-way player. To be a good short game golfer, you have to know options. When I met him, Jack's short game was like his long game that featured power and touch."

Rodgers, who learned his short game from legendary Tour player Paul Runyon, later commented, "I knew Jack had a good touch.

What I wanted to do was give him confidence, give him a variety of ways to hit the ball from short distances in."

Rodgers's perception of Nicklaus's attitude toward the short game was insightful. "Jack never liked to chip shots. He hated to practice them. It's the only part of his game that ever came close to defeating him. I asked Jack once after we had worked together how things were going. 'I'm alright around the green,' he said. 'I can visualize the shot and execute it. But just short of the green, in the fairway, I have too many options.'"

Overall, Phil Rodgers's efforts were successful, and Jack acknowledged his contribution. "Jack was always willing to give credit to others who helped him," Rodgers said. But had Nicklaus been willing to help other players through the years? According to Rodgers, his relationships were always cordial, if not friendly. "Jack let everybody be themselves. He was not pretentious."

Many of Jack's competitors never approached him for words of advice or help with their swing, but if they did, he always gave them his two cents' worth. Tom Meeks, longtime official with the United States Golf Association, remembers one such occasion. "Gary Player and Jack were in the scorer's tent at the U.S. Open one year," Meeks recalled. "I was standing right there, and I heard Gary say something like, 'I'm not playing well. I just can't figure out what's wrong.' Jack said, 'Well, I see something,' and off they went talking about it."

Over the years, Jack was even known to assist players who were being touted as the "next Nicklaus." Two of the best known were Hal Sutton and Greg Norman. Nicklaus briefly became a bit of a father figure to those players, but eventually a cordial, arm's-length relationship prevailed.

The split between Norman and Nicklaus remains unexplained. For a time, Greg rode to the Masters with Jack in his jet and sought his advice with business matters. The two have remained cordial, but the relationship certainly isn't the one that caused writer Thomas Boswell to observe, "Norman has praised Jack with such reverence that it borders on worship."

At times Nicklaus was disappointed that new "stars" on the Tour didn't seek his advice. One such disappointment was John Daly. When he was experiencing rocky times in his private life after his PGA Championship win in 1991, he and Jack were paired in a shoot-out prior to the Doral Open. After both were eliminated on the early holes, Nicklaus suggested that they play the back nine.

With a contingent of exuberant fans following them, Jack and John played along. By round's end, Jack was flabbergasted that Daly had not taken advantage of his experience and knowledge. "He didn't ask me one damn question. No advice. Nothing."

Nicklaus was helpful to fellow competitors, but he expected loyalty from them. When Tony Jacklin came out of hiding to play the Senior Tour, Jack and Barbara went to great lengths to assist him. Jacklin and his wife stayed at the Nicklaus guest house while looking for a home of their own. Jack's management company secured endorsement contracts for the British player, and bartered a deal that enabled Jacklin to play at will for free on a nearby course.

Despite the enormous friendship Nicklaus showed, eventually Jacklin joined Mark McCormack's stable of players at IMG. Nicklaus was hurt by Jacklin's about-face but, as usual, made no public comments about the incident.

If his play was any indication, Jack Nicklaus had gone back to school with Phil Rodgers and earned outstanding marks. As his short game improved, he gained more confidence. He was also inspired in 1980 by another factor, one that was to motivate him throughout his career.

"I've always needed somebody pushing me," Nicklaus told *The New York Times*. "At first it was Arnold Palmer, and then Gary Player, then Lee Trevino, Tom Weiskopf and Johnny Miller, and now Tom Watson. It was always, 'Here's the guy who's going to take over Nicklaus's spot.' I always enjoyed that. I always reacted to that."

And react he did in 1980, first by winning the U.S. Open at Baltusrol (see page 274) and then by winning the PGA at Oak Hill (see page 211), becoming the first golfer since Ben Hogan (in 1948) to win both in one season. *Golf World* named Jack "Player of the Year." He now had eighteen major championships and twelve second-place finishes to his credit. Had the crowning of Tom Watson as Nicklaus's heir taken place too soon?

As Dave Kindred of *The Washington Post* saw it, Nicklaus's ability to win was another sign of perseverance, especially after the disappointments in 1979. "The lovely thing is, he didn't quit," Kindred wrote. "The powers of concentration yet burned brightly. He put his swing back together, he learned new tricks with the wedge. And in times when people asked him if he was dead, Nicklaus made every putt he needed to, as sure a sign of life as there is."

Unfortunately, the tendency toward better play didn't continue. Lean years were to follow between 1981 and 1985, especially in comparison to the wealth of victories Jack had enjoyed the previous season.

In 1981, Jack mounted a charge at only one major, the Masters, where he finished tied for second behind Tom Watson. He had runner-up finishes at Doral and Inverrary but played superbly in the Ryder Cup (his last appearance as a player), winning all four matches in which he competed. His Tour scoring average was 70.70, the best in four years. Winnings of $178,213 brought his total to $3,759,426, an average of slightly less than $200,000 a year for twenty years as a Tour professional.

During 1982 Jack captured PGA Tour victory number sixty-nine. It came at the Colonial Invitational, earning Nicklaus $63,000 for first prize. A second-place finish at Arnold Palmer's Bay Hill Classic head-lined his other play, which resulted in seven top-ten finishes in fifteen appearances. Tom Watson spoiled Nicklaus's bid for a twentieth major championship with his magic chip at Pebble Beach's seventeenth hole (see page 269).

At the PGA Championship in 1983, it was Hal Sutton who kept Nicklaus from the elusive twentieth major. Jack's sparkling final round of 66 at Riveria fell short by one shot to Sutton's, another player labeled the "next Jack Nicklaus." Nine top-ten finishes in sixteen tries produced more than a quarter of a million dollars in earnings but only one victory—at the Chrysler Team Championship with partner Johnny Miller. That year also marked Jack Nicklaus's first appearance as a cap-tain of the Ryder Cup team. In 1969, Nicklaus's first year on the team, play resulted in the first tie in history. Sam Snead was the captain, and Nicklaus produced a lackluster one, two, and one record, which includ-ed a four and three loss and the famed half with Tony Jacklin at Royal Burkdale when Jack said "that's good" to the two-and-a-half-footer.

In 1971, Nicklaus amassed five points of the American's eighteen and a half as they beat the British at Old Warson Country Club in St. Louis. Muirfield was the site of Nicklaus's third Ryder Cup in 1973, which resulted in a nineteen and thirteen U.S. win. An unlikely foe named Maurice Bembridge fought Nicklaus virtually to a standstill, los-ing one-up and halving with the American champion.

At Laural Valley Golf Club in Pennsylvania in 1975, Nicklaus lost two matches to Brian Barnes (see page 125), but the Americans were victorious behind captain Arnold Palmer, twenty-one and eleven. Royal Lytham and St. Anne's was the site of the 1977 matches won by United States twelve and a half and seven and a half. Nicklaus scored one point when he and Tom Watson won five and four over Tony Horton and Mark James.

Not chosen for the '79 team, Nicklaus competed in 1981 for the Americans at Walton Heath Golf Club in Surrey, England. In a classic match, he and Tom Watson beat Nick Faldo and Peter Oosterhuis four and three. Nicklaus won his other two team matches and a singles encounter with Eamonn Darcy in true championship fashion, to go four and zero. The Americans won eighteen and a half and nine and a half, the last time they were to dominate the Europeans.

Well into his mid-forties, Nicklaus won only once in 1984 and 1985. A second victory at his own Memorial Tournament was a highlight, but except for sixth-place tie in the '85 Masters, Nicklaus's performance in the majors was undistinguished.

Nicklaus was runner-up in four tournaments during those two years and received the largest check of his career, $240,000, in the Skins Game.

The early months of 1986, Jack's twenty-fifth year as a professional golfer, gave no indication that he was about to do something special. But then came the Masters, and the Golden Bear awoke from his lengthy hibernation—and captured the hearts of the golf world—stunning the field at Augusta and winning his fifth green jacket (see page 281).

# CHAPTER 22

# Moments of Splendor

A month after winning the Masters in 1986, Nicklaus made another chase for victory that brought back memories of his former championship play. The Nicklaus renaissance occured at his own Memorial Tournament.

In the final round, Hal Sutton, the eventual winner, enjoyed a substantial lead. Jack played in a threesome with Peter Jacobsen and Andy Bean. The front nine produced little play of note. However, Jack began the back nine with three consecutive birdies, and Jacobsen saw him enter, as he later called it, "the Twilight Zone."

"Nicklaus always analyzes the totals after fifty-four holes and picks a number he'll need to shoot in the final round to win," Jacobsen wrote in his book, *Buried Lies*. "After that birdie on the twelfth, I could sense that he was thinking of a number like 65."

Jack came close to realizing 65 when he hit a drive and a mid-iron to within eight feet at thirteen, then made the birdie putt. "Now," Jacobsen said, "[Jack] really had that 'look'—intense but slightly glazed—that great players get when they're in a zone of perfect concentration."

At the fourteenth hole, Jacobsen saw the confidence that was the core of Nicklaus's success. Seeking his fifth straight birdie, Jack hit his second shot to within fifteen feet from the hole. Jacobsen was in the left bunker and Bean about twelve feet from the hole.

Despite his predicament, Jacobsen hit his bunker shot to within four feet. Then something unusual happened. Nicklaus was away, but Andy Bean putted first. He made it and the crowd politely applauded.

Jacobsen knew that Bean had hit out of turn. Just as he was trying to figure out what to make of it, Jack turned to him and said, "Peter, do you want to go ahead and putt out?" Jacobsen looked at

Jack, and said, "Why would I putt out, Jack? You're away." Without any hesitation Nicklaus replied, "Because when I make this putt, the people here are going to go crazy."

Jacobsen was dazed. He took a moment to gather himself. Finally, he said, "You go ahead, because I have to learn to deal with these types of situations." Peter then stood back and watched Nicklaus assume the hunched position above the golf ball that had become so familiar.

The putt was a fifteen-footer with a huge break from left to right. Nevertheless, Jacobsen knew what was coming. "It was a darn tough putt," he said, "but I could tell from his eyes that he had absolutely no doubt that he was going to make it."

And, of course, Nicklaus did make it—his fifth straight birdie. Jacobsen somehow holed his par putt in the confusion that ensued, and the three headed for the par-five fifteenth, where Nicklaus knocked his second shot onto the green, just twenty feet from the hole. "At that point," Jacobsen recalled, "I thought, 'This guy's gonna shoot 27 on this nine.' As he stood over the eagle putt, Jack knew he was going to make it, and Andy knew he was going to make it, and I knew he was going to make it, and 10,000 misty-eyed Nicklausites knew he was going to make it."

But the eagle wasn't to be. The ball rolled up just short of the hole and stopped.

Even though Nicklaus recorded his sixth straight birdie, his momentum had ebbed. Try as he might, he couldn't regain his inner drive, and he bogeyed the final three holes.

In spite of the let-down, Jacobsen would never forget that round with Jack. "It was . . . the most interesting nine holes of golf I've ever seen," he said later. "At least for a few short hours, I was seeing the best that ever was playing as good as he could."

By year's end, Jack had reached another monumental point in his life. While his Masters victory was the last time Nicklaus headed into the victory circle on the regular PGA Tour, the PGA Championship marked Nicklaus's one hundredth appearance in a professional major tournament—he had won eighteen of them, nearly 20 percent.

In 1988, Nicklaus was named "Golfer of the Century" by golf experts and journalists and became the first player to break the $5,000,000 mark with official winnings on the PGA Tour. A further honor was the creation of the Jack Nicklaus Award by the Golf Coaches Association of America for yearly presentation to the out-standing player in collegiate golf.

In 1989 Nicklaus won slightly more than $96,000 on the regular PGA Tour, but he was even more successful in promotional events, earning more than $500,000 overall. More than a quarter of a million dollars came from the Australian Skins Game.

That year Nicklaus experienced back problems that caused him severe pain. The problem was a reoccurrence of the same injury that had prevented Jack from playing in the 1983 Masters.

Two herniated discs in the lower lumbar areas were the culprits. They produced stiffness and numbness in his left leg and cortisone treatments proved unsuccessful. As Jack approached fifty, he was unable to swing a golf club properly, play tennis, or ski, all favorite passions of his.

The pain was so severe that Nicklaus shot 49 for nine holes on his forty-ninth birthday. Fortunately, a consultation with Peter Eqoscue, a noted kinesiologist, brought Jack relief. "Nicklaus was not only the best at what he did," Tour contemporary Bruce Crampton said, "but he knew how to find the best experts, and that was what Peter was."

In 1990, Jack Nicklaus began playing on the Senior Tour, though many questioned the logic of doing so.

Asked by *Sports Illustrated*'s Tim Rosaforte if there was a point to facing the same players he competed against on the regular Tour, Nicklaus replied, "The challenge is the challenge of me. I've always felt that challenge, whether it be the seniors, regular golf, amateur golf. My challenge has always been preparing Jack Nicklaus to play, not whether I beat the field."

However, Nicklaus did not endear himself to many of his fellow players when he was quoted by writer Jamie Diaz as saying, "The problem for me is that the guys who are competing in the Senior Tour are the same guys I have beaten for thirty years."

The criticism was fast and furious. Dave Hill, called "straight-forward" by some and "a jerk" by others, responded, "I used to have a lot of respect for Jack. But he forgot what humility was like." Don Bies saw the comment a different way. "I don't think Jack thought he said anything wrong," Bies said. "He's having a hard time turning fifty. I think that's part of his problem." Lee Trevino added, "There was a lot of tough talk in the locker room. . . . 'I'm going to say this to him, I'm going to say that,' but there's too much respect for this man for any of that. . . . Everyone welcomed him aboard."

The unfortunate quote by Nicklaus was a reflection of his indecision about playing the regular Tour, the Senior Tour, or both. In 1989, he had said, "The Senior Tour has become a significant part of the game, both from the fans' standpoint and the players', and I think some support is almost an obligation on my part. I will cut down when I am no longer competitive. I think I can be competitive on both Tours."

As to being competitive on both Tours, Jack was only successful in part. He experienced great results on the Senior Tour and mixed ones on the regular Tour.

In 1990, on cue, Nicklaus won the first tournament he entered on the Senior Tour, a major championship, The Tradition, which echoed his effort twenty-eight years earlier when he won the United States Open his first year as a professional.

Besides The Tradition, Nicklaus also won the Senior Players Championship, finished second in the Senior Open, and tied for third at the PGA Senior Championship. Since that auspicious beginning, Nicklaus has won eight Senior major championship titles, two more than either Gary Player or Sam Snead, and rival Arnold Palmer has five. Through 1995, Jack had won nearly $2 million.

However, play on the regular Tour was a disappointment for Jack, who had set a goal to become the first golfer to win on both the Senior Tour and regular Tour in the same year. His play was especially disappointing to those such as Greg Norman, who had said, "No question, [Jack] can still win [on the regular Tour]. Jack is still an extremely good putter. That's the key. What happens to most of the Seniors, the putter sort of fails first under pressure and then works into the rest of the game. Jack still is a great putter."

Norman's thoughts aside, Nicklaus could not muster a win on the regular PGA Tour during the first six years of the nineties. Through 1995, his best finish in a major championship was sixth at the 1990 Masters.

In 1996, Nicklaus pushed hard to be a contender, and his efforts produced significant results but mixed reactions as to the state of his golf game.

Aspiring Senior Tour player Tony Perla, swept into a dream pairing with Jack in a practice round prior to the 1996 Senior Open, observed that Nicklaus was "all business, congenial, but businesslike. He's like a mechanic out there, taking the ball down the left side of the fairway or the right setting up shots." Perla, who caught Nicklaus on a bad day and put eight dollars of "Jack's money" in his pocket, added that the Golden Bear still reminded him of a "scoring machine."

Former Tour player Gary Koch, now a golf commentator for NBC, said, "[Jack's] unfortunately really starting to show his age. He doesn't have his power anymore. He's pretty frustrated, can't be as consistent as he wants to be. The constant up and down is beginning to take its toll. I get the impression that when he doesn't have a legitimate chance to win, he'll quit."

Fellow competitor Tom Weiskopf preferred to put aside Nicklaus's physical condition and deal with the mental aspect. "I think that win [in the '86 Masters] was a big deal from the standpoint that it was the pinnacle of Jack's career," Weiskopf said. "I didn't see the same intensity or ferocity or determination after he won that."

Dick Taylor professed amazement at what Nicklaus had to go through physically to compete in his mid-fifties. "Up until now," he said, "Nicklaus was convinced he could still play with the kids, but it's been painful the last two to three years . . . and he works his ass off, exercises, strenuous exercises. . . . I think he's going to have a heart attack . . . but somehow he does them." When asked in 1996 whether Nicklaus should give up competitive golf, at least on the regular Tour, Taylor said, "He'll play the British Open. Then he should play in the PGA, then that's it. Just play the Senior Tour. Take care of his dignity. Keep his dignity. Be a winner in front of the public."

In addition to the opinions of Taylor and the majority of the sportswriters who cover the regular and Senior Tours, Nicklaus had also listened to Barbara's voice of concern. "She's telling him it's time to step aside," related the wife of a close friend of the Nicklauses. "Time to move on."

With forty United States Opens, thirty-seven Masters, thirty-five British Opens, thirty-five PGAs, and more than 525 PGA Tour events behind him, Nicklaus's ability to compete at any level at age fifty-seven has been severely reduced. Although he did win the 1996 Tradition, his eighth Senior Tour major event (a record), to garner his 100th career win, results for the year were mixed. At his beloved tournament, The Memorial, crowds urged him on, but the shot quality wasn't there. Of course he had a perfect right to play, but a young player with a chance to win deserved to take his place, a fact Nicklaus acknowledged after a tournament when he missed the cut for the third straight time, shooting 77 and 75.

In the majors, Nicklaus tied for forty-first with nine over par at the Masters, then played well at the United States Open with a tie for twenty-seventh at Oakland Hills recording rounds of 72, 74, 69, and 72 (287). Just as pundits were ready to write him off for the year, he shocked the sporting world with opening rounds of 69 and 66 at the British Open at Royal Lytham and St. Anne's, where previous finishes of third, sixth, third, and second brought more heartaches than pleasant memories. It was as if Jack was saying once more, "Don't count me out, you've done that before and look what happened."

The rounds that seemed to "turn back the clock" came after Nicklaus thought he might have to withdraw due to his painful back injury. A call to his therapist in the United States provided him with new exercises to try, and Jack was able to step up to the first tee for the first round of his thirty-fifth British Open. At the end of thirty-six holes, he trailed by one stroke, combining accurate driving and a masterful putting stroke to annihilate the hardpan course where good weather was a pleasant surprise.

As was the case with previous majors where Nicklaus had provided heroics, he gave others credit. This time it was Jack's son Gary, an aspiring Tour professional, who helped him conquer an alignment problem with his putting stance.

The superb play caused *Golf Digest* to report, "For one more time in his astonishing career, Nicklaus was Gable, Hemingway, Bogart, Sinatra—The Man." Unfortunately, the third round saw "The Man" duplicate what had become his "Saturday at the majors pattern." Since his last win at the 1986 Masters, he had averaged 73 in the third round of the majors. This time the score was worse, 77, which left him at one under par, fifteen shots behind runaway leader Tom Lehman. The score was also the eleventh time he had shot 76 or higher in the third round, something Jack Nicklaus never did in his prime.

In the fourth round, Nicklaus shot a marginal 73. His four-round total at one under pushed him far down the standings. The winner was journeyman Lehman, whom ABC's Brent Musberger called "the working man's champ." The new British Open winner's golf game did have a Nicklaus "connection"—Lehman's loyal teacher was Jim Flick, Jack's partner in the golf center business and the man to whom Nicklaus gave credit for resurrecting his game.

The PGA Championship was played in August at Valhalla, a Nicklaus-designed course in Louisville, Kentucky. Jack opened with 77, then fired a second-round 69 that left him one stroke short of making the cut. He had missed his chance to say he'd played all four rounds of the majors at age fifty-six.

Although Nicklaus's goal for the year to play all four rounds signaled that his competitiveness was still there, it was tempered with an admission that he no longer possessed the game to challenge for a major championship. That was in evidence on the Senior Tour as well, where his record revealed the win at The Tradition but no challenges at the PGA Senior's Championship, United States Senior Open, or the Senior Players Championship.

By year's end, Nicklaus said he'd take stock over the winter months and decide what tournaments he would play in 1997. His brain will probably tell him it's time to end his string of playing in thirty-eight consecutive Masters, yet it is difficult to imagine Nicklaus not teeing it up at Augusta when spring welcomes the best that golf has to offer.

The effort to produce the thirty-seventh of Nicklaus's victories at the Doral-Eastern Open in 1972, twenty-four years removed from his play in 1996, was not an easy one.

In the chase for the $30,000 first prize the next day, Nicklaus, Rosburg, Trevino, and Snead battled until the final hole. Rosburg fired a superlative 68, and Trevino and Snead, 72. Nicklaus mustered an up-and-down 70, but he played the last five holes two-under to pull out a two-stroke victory.

With the victory, Nicklaus moved past Arnold Palmer on the career money list. Afterwards he commented about his new position at the top to *Golf World*: "The money is great but it was the last thing on my mind, and still is. . . . I expect Arnold and I will trade this thing back and forth. . . . I'd like to continue playing golf for a long time and set a record in this area, but no matter how much I win, someone will come along and make more."

# BOOK IV

# The Nicklaus Method

❖ ❖ ❖

# CHAPTER 23

# The Masters—1972

Attempting to win the 1972 Masters, and thereby add the first leg to his quest for the Grand Slam, Jack Nicklaus did the unthinkable. He three-putted three greens on the back nine in the final round, including one that meant double bogey at the fifteenth hole. It put him in a surly mood. He knew major tournaments were not won by three-putting, especially when being challenged by Tom Weiskopf, Bruce Crampton, Gary Player, and Bruce Devlin.

That year Nicklaus was trying to win his fourth Masters. *Golf Digest* had him as a 5-1 favorite, describing Jack as "strong, intelligent, determined" and citing his "overpowering presence." The magazine set odds of 6-1 for George Archer, Johnny Miller, and Lee Trevino. At 7-1 were Miller Barber, Gary Player, and Bob Murphy. Forty-two-year-old Arnold Palmer, who would shoot 81 in the final round, his worst score at Augusta, was listed at 10-1.

In the first round of that Masters, Jack Nicklaus's play was uncharacteristic. He nearly dug himself into a hole even he couldn't escape from.

Thirty-seven on the front nine and a bogey at ten left him at two-over and in a downward spiral. Augusta National was beating the Bear. But then, as if the drama had been scripted especially for the fans, Jack's game came alive.

The first scene of his heroic turnaround came at the 455-yard, par-four eleventh. Upset with his play, Nicklaus decided that a jump-start was needed. The opportunity presented was a hole location on the extreme left side of the green. With water fronting the green, pinpoint accuracy was required.

With a five-iron, Nicklaus lofted the ball away from safety toward the dangerous portion of the green and the flag stick. The ball crossed safely over the water and nearly rolled into the hole, but stopped ten feet away. The putt was true, and the birdie put a smile on Jack's face.

Pumped up by his turn at eleven, Nicklaus manufactured two more birdies at twelve and thirteen, parred fourteen, and then ripped his second shot, a 235-yard one-iron, over the lake on the par-five fifteenth to within thirty feet. When Jack holed that putt for eagle, drained another one for birdie from the fringe at sixteen, and parred seventeen and eighteen, he turned a two-over-par round into a four-under-par 68 to lead a frustrated field in which no one bettered 72.

That uncanny ability to gather himself was symbolic of Nicklaus's play on Tour. Time and time again, Jack steadied a shaky ship to keep himself in contention.

Nicklaus's ability to post good scores after bad starts or to transform a mediocre round into an excellent one was based on two important factors. He was not only a superb golfer in terms of swing mechanics, but he was also a superior player in the mental aspects of the game.

Nicklaus's swing, one observer said, "may need a minor tune-up from time to time but never needs a major overhaul," and Jack admitted that his swing was "grooved" at an early age. Guru Jack Grout helped Nicklaus hone that swing, and Nicklaus acknowledged his contribution. But it was Jack who practiced to "groove" the swing, which was based on three fundamentals: keeping the head still, using proper foot position, and developing a full arc. Nicklaus repeated that fundamentally sound swing so many times that it never varied.

Unlike Hogan or others of that ilk, Nicklaus never hit golf balls until his hands were bloody. He practiced *each and every shot* as if it was a real one on a real course under real tournament conditions. His practice sessions were relatively short, astounding those competitors who pounded balls for hours on end.

On the Saturday before the third round of the 1972 Masters, Nicklaus took twenty minutes to correct what he said was a flaw in his swing. "Even before a round, when you'd think I'm just loosening up, I'm really learning as I practice," he said. "The range may be one hundred yards wide and I might be scattering balls from one side to the other. It might look like I'm hitting some absolutely horrible golf shots, but I'm really not. I'm experimenting to find out exactly what I can do that particular day. Then I won't be apt to try something on the course that I can't pull off."

When Jack's play was off kilter, he remembered what Bobby Jones had told him in 1962, his first year on Tour.

Jones's comments were the fruit of his experiences playing in a number of major tournaments. "I matured to the point where I understood my game well enough to make my own corrections during the course of a tournament," Jones had said, "and that's when I say I became a good golfer."

Jones explained that prior to that revelation, he always had to run back to his teacher, Stewart Maiden, when problems occurred. While many of the great professionals in history, such as Arnold Palmer, Ben Hogan, Byron Nelson, and Sam Snead, had no professional teacher in their early years, Nicklaus relied on Grout in times of trouble. But Grout would not always be there. Jones had given Nicklaus invaluable information: Know your game so well you can fix it yourself right in the middle of a tournament.

Nicklaus took Bobby Jones's words to heart. Jack realized an experienced player needed to "instruct himself" in the midst of major tournaments when things went sour. After many rounds, Nicklaus would traipse to the practice tee, where he'd hit a few choice shots to correct a flaw he'd noted. "That was intimidating to many of us," one fellow professional said. "Here we're out there shakin' our heads for hours trying to figure out what's wrong, and Jack takes five minutes and cures all."

Nicklaus's general feelings about his golf swing, which he discussed in his books *Golf My Way* and *Golf, the Greatest Game*, were rather elementary. He believed the best way to play involved a club face that started square with the ball, opened a bit on the backswing, and then closed as the downswing propelled the club face through the ball. "This opening and closing is neither excessive nor contrived," he said, "but simply the natural response to a one-piece take-away, a generous turn of the body, a free swing of the arms and a reflective hinging or cocking of the wrists on the backswing, and a reciprocal set of actions on the forward swing."

Jack wrote poetically of the swing, "There is often about it an element of abandon, or freedom, in the way the club releases through the ball: almost as though it were whistling along of its own volition. Over all, to me, this open-to-closed type of golfer makes the game look graceful, physically easy—sometimes, you might say, almost symphonic."

Although both of Nicklaus's books are insightful, the bible on Nicklaus's swing technique was *Let Me Teach You Golf the Way I Taught Jack Nicklaus*, by Jack Grout, published in 1975.

When Grout wrote the book, the teacher was sixty-five and had been Nicklaus's mentor for twenty-five years. To understand the passion for golf that he passed on to young Jack, Grout described a day when, as an eight year old, he followed his three brothers to see where they went every morning. "Finally, they came to a fence, jumped over it, and disappeared," Grout recalled. "I . . . took a peek over it. On the other side was the most beautiful site I'd ever seen. It looked like a huge pasture of lovely green grass with trees and lakes. People were strolling around, hitting little white balls with sticks. Fascinated, I stayed there drinking in the scene for many minutes."

Grout's love for golf led to a career as a teaching professional at age sixteen. When Jack Nicklaus took up golf in 1950, Grout was destined to cross his path.

Jack Grout's opening words in his 1975 book were a powerful statement about his instructional philosophy: "The person who relies solely on natural athletic talents and normal instincts will sooner or later surely reach a point where improvement *stops*. To build a golf swing only on natural instinct is to build a golf swing full of golfing flaws. You can practice hard and long and play frequently, but if your swing is not based on golfing fundamentals, you will merely ingrain your mistakes."

Jack Nicklaus certainly got an earful of that philosophy as a young player. "There's a million things Jack [Grout] told me to do," Nicklaus said, "but he always told me why to do them." One included never altering his propensity to use the interlocking grip instead of the conventional and misconstrued overlapping Vardon grip. Young Jack used the interlocking grip, and still does today, because he felt his hands were too small to use the overlap. Grout never made a change with that part of Jack's game.

Later, Nicklaus said he felt there was great curiosity about his hands. He told reporters he had stubby hands with short fingers. "I wear a men's small golf glove," he said. "Actually, my wife Barbara has stronger hands than me from doing the dishes. . . . You won't be surprised to learn that I regard as bunk that hoary old maxim about big, strong hands being essential for good golf."

The swing that Jack Grout taught Nicklaus has been described by many experts, but none more succinctly than Ken Venturi, the 1964 United States Open champion and current color commentator for CBS television.

"Jack makes very intelligent use of his body configuration," Venturi said. "He has short, thick fingers, and so he uses an interlocking grip. His one-piece take-away, the club going straight back from the ball with no break of the wrists, remains 'of a piece' longer than most because he is on such a solid foundation he doesn't have to worry about swaying off the ball."

Many observers thought the "flying elbow" syndrome tarnished Jack's upright swing. Ken Venturi, however, said the argument was hogwash, that Jack's technique merely permitted him to hit the ball with a high trajectory. "To further extend his backswing," Venturi explained, "Jack lets his right elbow go away from his right side. . . . [His] elbow doesn't actually fly—the gap between his arms at address remains almost constant throughout the swing. . . . Nicklaus simply drops his hands downward as he starts back to the ball and his elbow falls naturally in close to his right side."

Tour player Don Bies said the flying elbow was simply a necessary element of Jack's swing. "With his hands so high, the elbow had to fly. He had a big shoulder turn, and that gave him his power. Most golfers adhered to the technique that, first, the right elbow had to stay close to the right side during take-away to make sure it was there at impact and, second, that the swing path must be from inside to out at impact. Jack was an exception to the rule. The way he played, how could anyone fault his swing?"

Ken Venturi pointed out that those who chose the method Bies described generally hit low trajectory shots that curved right to left. Drawing or hooking the ball was acceptable for the non-irrigated courses where distance off the tee was essential. But just as Nicklaus was coming on Tour, softer fairways necessitated the need to propel the ball farther on the fly off the tee, and better maintained greens required that the ball be hit high to stop on those surfaces.

Jack's stout nature and 5'10" height made him a natural to play that type of shot, but Venturi saw another factor in the equation. "It has always been said of Jack Nicklaus," Venturi observed, "that his power comes from the strength of his legs. This is true, but I think another factor about Jack's legs that is just as important as their sheer strength is that they are not long for a man his size. This is why Jack can take a relatively narrow stance, which allows him to make a very full turn of his waist, and get his hands high, both of which have a lot to do with his power and the high trajectory of his shots."

From his downswing through contact with the ball, Venturi said, Nicklaus exhibited power everywhere: "The hands dropping and the legs driving create the log-pump/piston movement that is also a major factor in his power. . . . Jack can keep his body low to the ground and retain the flex of his knees throughout impact—two more contributions to both his power and his high-flying shots."

Jim Ferriell, former touring professional and longtime head professional at Crooked Stick Golf Club, site of the 1991 PGA Championship, said Nicklaus's flying elbow actually enhanced his power. "Nicklaus had great leg action for a big guy," Ferriell said. "The flying elbow wasn't a flaw. WHen Jack started down, his huge hip turn pulled the right elbow into the right position. Then he had tremendous release with his hands. I call Nicklaus one of the great 'leg players' of all time. What power he had."

Several of Jack's fellow professionals were asked to assess Jack's swing in the early seventies, when his game was at peak performance. Dan Sikes took the easiest, if not the most precise, route: "Jack Nicklaus gets the best results," he told *Golf Digest*, "so Jack Nicklaus has to have the best golf swing."

CHAPTER 24

# Self-Analysis

While most competitors were hoping for some semblance of decency with their golf games, Jack Nicklaus set higher goals for himself. "At the back of your mind you continue to see perfection," he observed, "and now and then, the law of averages will be on your side, and you will produce an almost uninterrupted sequence of practically perfect swings and practically perfect shots."

No wonder Phil Rodgers said, "Jack Nicklaus was the only golfer I was ever afraid of. I knew I could beat the rest, but not Jack."

Nicklaus possessed the ability to fully know his swing like few before or since. When Jack Grout wrote his instructional book in the mid-seventies, Nicklaus, as a contributing editor, offered slivers of knowledge that were critical to understanding his method.

Nicklaus's greatest insight concerned the set up. Jack called it "the most important maneuver in golf." He correctly believed that even if a golfer made a great swing, poor set up would alter the shot so drastically that it would produce a poor result.

One only had to watch Nicklaus go through his characteristic pre-swing ritual to understand that he practiced what he preached.

Nicklaus's preparation was precise and repetitive. His approach to hitting the ball never varied, his pre-swing routine as predictable as the rising sun. From behind the ball, the Golden Bear would survey the shot, sizing up the ball location, the distance to the intended location, existence of trouble spots, and wind conditions. Then Jack would amble up to a location beside the ball, plant his feet in the intended position, glance down in front of him and up from ground level through the line he had chosen for the shot, and waggle the club once, twice, and a third time before placing the club just slightly above the ground before the ball. Elevating the club was a habit he picked up from playing on the long grass in his early days at Scioto.

With head cocked back and a mini-forward press, Nicklaus would then pull back the club and repeat the swing that had produced so many brilliant shots. Everything was done in virtual slow-motion, for Jack Nicklaus knew that hurrying any part of the set-up or swing meant disaster.

Regarding the take away, Nicklaus said, "I believe you cannot start the golf club back too slowly. . . . The harder I want to swing, the slower I try to start back."

At this, Nicklaus was superb. Nothing was rushed. When his head was cocked at just the right angle, the backswing began. He knew that timing was everything, each part of the swing crucial to the whole. As directed by Grout's teaching, Nicklaus played from the "insides" of his feet.

"I put in many, many hours of exercises—like rocking sideways on my ankles—designed to teach me to stay on the inside of my right foot going back and the inside of my left coming down," Nicklaus said.

At the top of the swing, Nicklaus was determined for his hands to be high. "I like to have the feeling, as I near the top of the backswing, of trying to thrust them through the clouds," he said, aware that doing so meant a swing with a wide arc.

Of all the swing components, the downswing caused Nicklaus the most concern. Although his brain tried to signal his hands to take their time, his tendency was to bring the club down toward the ball before the rest of the body was ready. "My method of keeping these limelight-botters [hands] backstage," he said, "is to try to feel that they are not moving any faster on the first half of the forward swing than they did during the final phase of the backswing." When the hands behaved, Nicklaus hit the golf ball farther than nearly any golfer of the late sixties and early seventies.

Jack's penchant for long, high drives was not lost on players like Carol Mann. "Jack introduced 'high ball power' to the game," she said. "Nobody had ever seen anything like it." Nicklaus's Tour contemporary, Phil Rodgers, added, "Jack did what Tiger Woods is doing in the mid-nineties. He hit the ball twenty to thirty yards farther than anyone else. . . . It gave him a dramatic advantage. During an average round of golf, it meant he was playing twenty to thirty yards less per hole than the rest of the field was. That adds up."

Phil Rodgers recalled two instances where Nicklaus's power was mind-boggling. "At Lakewood Country Club in New Orleans in the mid-1960s, Jack had a 215-yard shot to a par five," Rodgers recalled. "Between his ball and the green were seventy-five-foot to one hundred-foot tall huge swamp cypress trees. I figured he'd lay up, but he hit a

three-iron so high and so far over those trees I couldn't believe it. It settled in the middle of the store [the green] and he two-putted for birdie.
It was one of the single greatest shots I ever saw."

At Augusta, during a practice round Rodgers and Jack were
playing with Dow Finsterwald and Arnold Palmer, Phil Rodgers challenged Nicklaus. "Dow, Arnold, and I hit our drives on the par-five
thirteenth. I turned to Jack and said, 'Hit a shot for me. Take a three-
wood and see if you can knock it over those pines down the left side.'
He did, and the ball was hit so high it cleared those towering trees
with ease. From his ball location, he had an eight-iron left to the
green. Couldn't have been more than 140 yards from the green. What
a power source he had."

Based on his own observation, Rodgers knew why Nicklaus could
hit the ball so high. "Jack played the ball way forward," he said. "His
weight was on his back foot. I called him a sweeper. The angle of his
swing mashed the ball in the club face, and he hit it with upward climb.
Not only did the swing produce such a high shot, but Jack put great
spin on the ball. He clipped it so the ball just soared and then floated
softly down."

Jim Ferriell was impressed with Nicklaus's power for another reason. "At the Canadian Open in 1973," Ferriell recalled, "Chuck
Courtney and I played with Jack. He was hitting the ball fifty-five to
sixty yards past us, but he seemed to be able to turn the power off and
on. That day he was hitting what looked like a heel fade. When I hit
the ball 250, it was all I had. When Jack hit it that far, he was taking
some off. He had all kinds of speeds."

Don Bies, a Tour veteran and contemporary of Nicklaus's, first
saw Jack play at the 1961 Walker Cup matches in Seattle.

"Jack was better than anyone I'd ever seen," he said. "He had
what I'd call controlled power. He could hit the ball harder than anyone. Jack got his left shoulder behind the ball—almost in line with the
right foot—and then let go."

Bies saw firsthand how Nicklaus's power worked to his advantage. "I was in contention at the American Golf Classic at Firestone in
1968," he said. "At the last hole, a monstrous par four, I hit a drive as
good as I could hit. I remember hitting a four-iron to the green that
plugged the ball in a bunker. Jack was so far past me he hit *seven*. I
missed the playoff. Jack won by one shot."

The veteran Bies saw Nicklaus's power favored him in yet

another way. "I always felt Jack had an advantage in the majors. They'd let the rough grow, but Jack had the power game going, so he was always hitting much less club than we were. That really helped in the deep rough."

David Leadbetter, successful golf guru to great players like Nick Faldo, saw the Nicklaus power swing as being significant in the annals of golf. "You could say that Jack Nicklaus had the first really modern swing," Leadbetter said. "He developed a technique that used the big muscles to a great extent—a wide one-piece take-away, a tremendous pivot in which he'd wind his shoulders around 100 degrees, coil up like a spring, then use his lower body to impart amazing speed to the ball. It was amazing how far he hit the ball."

Examples of Jack's power abound during his career. Former United States Amateur champion and Senior Tour player Gary Cowan remembered a practice round in the Masters with Jack in the early seventies. "The thirteenth is a sharp dogleg. Most of us just hit the ball out into the fairway to set up a second shot. Jack stepped up and said, 'This is the way I used to play the hole.' Then he proceeded to hit the tee shot so high and so far over the trees on the left I couldn't believe it. I was pretty long then, but I'd never even thought about that shot."

Senior Tour player and 1966 United States and British Amateur champion Bob Dickson recalled a round he played with Nicklaus and Dave Hill at the Atlanta Golf Classic in 1968. "There were four par fives, and at the end of two rounds, Jack had two-putted for birdies on *seven* of them. Dave and I were just looking at ourselves. Jack was so long it was unbelievable."

To understand just how far Nicklaus's "maximum velocity at impact" propelled the ball, Frank Hannigan, a former executive director of the USGA, checked the record books. "What I found was that Nicklaus's driving average in 1968 was 275 yards," he told *Golf Journal.* "Only ten players were longer on the 1995 Tour. And Nicklaus was using his wooden McGregor driver in those days."

Though power was paramount to his game, Nicklaus remembered well the best piece of advice Jack Grout ever gave him. "I regard keeping the head very steady, if not absolutely stock still, throughout the swing as THE bedrock fundamental of golf," he said. "If you can't or won't learn to keep your head steady . . . there is nothing that I or anyone else can do for your golf game." Obviously Nicklaus never forgot the days the assistant professional at Scioto grabbed his hair and held on to it so Jack would keep his head still.

When golf competitors, experts, and fans in future years marvel at Nicklaus's record, they will ask themselves several questions.

Why didn't the experts ever say Jack Nicklaus had the greatest golf swing ever seen? Or that he was the best driver of the golf ball, or for that matter, the best short- or long-iron player or the best putter or chipper or bunker player who ever lived?

When great golf swings are discussed, Ben Hogan, Sam Snead, Mickey Wright, or Byron Nelson will get the nod. Discussions of the finest players off the tee will include Harry Vardon, Nelson, Lee Trevino, and Arnold Palmer.

Iron-play aficionados will mention Hale Irwin, Tom Watson, Bobby Jones, and Ben Hogan when they're challenged to pick the best. Discussions of top chippers include Paul Runyon, Jerry Barber, Dave Stockton, and Phil Rodgers, while commentary on the best putters will always bring forth names like Walter Travis, Jerry Travers, Horton Smith, Walter Hagen, Bobby Jones, Billy Casper, Ben Crenshaw, and Bobby Locke, a former Bomber pilot who once told professional Ernie Ball he was taking so much time to line up a curling ten-footer because "I missed one of these once."

Jack Nicklaus will in all likelihood receive no votes for the best swing. He may get some mention with the driver, a bit regarding iron play, none with bunker play or chipping, and surprisingly little when debates about the best putters are contested. History will probably record that Nicklaus is the proverbial Jack-of-all-trades but is not a master of any individual component that makes up the ideal golfer.

Although this will be true, Nicklaus's success is a result of one area of mastery: tempo. His ability to properly pace his swing is the best way to explain why he was able to use every club in his bag with precision when the pressure was boiling hot.

To hear Nicklaus tell it, tempo differs from rhythm. "Tempo is the rate of speed throughout the golf swing," he observed. "Rhythm is the flow, the cadence, that knits the various elements of the swing." To that end, Nicklaus and Jack Grout built a perfectly tempoed swing that withstood the test of time, one that permitted him to hit more meaningful shots than any golfer in history.

In many ways, that smooth swing echoed Nicklaus's manner of living. He was a quick thinker but slow to act without sufficient facts. When he made snap decisions, they often backfired. "Jack Nicklaus was slow and deliberate like me," Don Bies said. "Both with his golf swing and his private life."

Phil Rodgers observed, "What makes great players is how close they play to 100 percent of their personality. Jack was a calculating, methodical person. Very organized. Well-planned. He never played a shot before he was ready. He played like he lived."

Nicklaus's comments support the Rodgers theory. "I've learned increasingly to go along with my basic instinct, which is to reason things out and reflect a little bit before I act. And I think this has rubbed off on my golf swing because . . . my swing tempo . . . is slower than it's ever been."

The tempo Nicklaus enjoyed provided unparalleled accuracy. Even during 1968, when Nicklaus's game was sub-standard, he still produced great results. Frank Hannigan of the USGA recently observed, "I discovered Nicklaus led the PGA Tour [that year] in the critical category of greens in regulations in 1968, hitting 75.6% of his greens in regulation. The Tour has not recorded one player in the intervening three decades as hitting as many greens in regulation as he did in 1968. . . ."

In 1972, when Nicklaus was at peak performance, *Golf Digest* presented several thirty-three-millimeter movie frames of the swings of Nicklaus and his main rivals, Gary Player and Arnold Palmer. On close inspection, the elapsed time between take-away and impact for Palmer was 1.36 seconds, and Player's was 1.60, while the recorded time for Nicklaus was 1.96 seconds, more than a half second slower than Palmer.

Jack's ability to produce a smooth swing nearly every time out assisted him in another important way. In addition to enabling him to hit many great shots, it prevented him from hitting too many bad ones. Rarely did Nicklaus ever break the cardinal rule of hitting two bad shots in a row. "Nicklaus had fewer double bogeys or worse than anybody." Phil Rodgers said, "He never made high scores." That was especially true in the fourth round of major tournaments when victory hung in the balance.

A great part of Nicklaus's success with tempo was patience. Chi Chi Rodriguez, Jack's competitor for more than thirty years, said, "I wish I'd had Jack's patience. If I made nine pars in a row, I'd be upset, but Jack was so patient that he waited for the birdies and eagles to come."

"Ghandi said patience is self-suffering," Gary Player said. "It takes a lot of work and time. The two best I ever saw were Arnold and Jack. Arnie used to sign autographs for hours. What patience he showed. Other players didn't like to sign them, but Arnold signed every one. And Jack—he could make seven on a par three and then make birdies on the next two holes. His patience was unbelievable. He never hurried anything."

Golf writer Dick Taylor described Nicklaus's emotional control. "At Augusta, I saw rounds where Jack played bad, hit incandescent shots, nothing was going right. By day's end, he'd have a 67. I'd say, 'Where'd that come from?' It was his patience. Jack is a very patient man on the golf course."

Senior Tour veteran Bob Murphy said that Jack's ability to mature as a player and become more patient was the difference in his new found success as a contender. "I looked up patience in the Irish dictionary and it's not there," he said. "[If] we had all been smarter in our younger days, we would have all watched Jack a little more closely than we did. I learned that guys [like Jack] made a lot of mistakes on Thursdays and Fridays, and yet on Sunday there they were, the great players . . . still vying for the tournament."

Nicklaus's ability to be patient on a golf course's easy holes, where a birdie or better was *expected*, impressed Chi Chi. "All of us get pumped up for the hard holes and concentrate and manage our game well on those holes," he said. "But Jack managed his game so well and was so patient on the easy holes, where other players would lose their concentration. It's like a fighter getting ready for an easy fight. They might slack off. But Jack never slacked off. He fought every hole the same way. Patience was his greatest virtue."

# CHAPTER 25

# Jack's Regiment

J ack Nicklaus's ability to play at a consistent level of competitiveness was no accident. He was the finest manager of his game that golf has ever known. Tour veteran Don Bies said Jack "started managing his game on the practice tee." That was true.

On the practice tee, Jack put many of the facets of his game to the test. Then he deciphered what elements of his game were in sync on a particular day and which ones might be suspect.

"What I'm attempting to do [on the practice tee] is to find out how much feel I have," Nicklaus observed. "Can I play a slow rising draw? Can I play a soft fade that doesn't tail off until the very end of its flight? Can I hit a low, boring, straight shot?"

The answer to those questions dictated Nicklaus's play, although he was the first to admit that some days practice shots varied greatly from those hit during the round. The point was that after carefully examining the golf course, and Nicklaus always arrived at courses earlier than anyone else to prepare, he was already practicing the shots he knew he needed during the subsequent round.

Nicklaus never had to guess at club selection. He always knew precise distances. "On my trips," he said in the early seventies, "I carry along a portable card file of the tournament courses—a separate card for every course. On each card I have noted, hole by hole, the distance to the green from various points."

He discussed his habit of keeping notes about courses in 1965, just after completing the Portland Open. "I have an accordion-type file with scorecards and notes on courses and a master sheet showing which course are recorded," Jack told *Golf Digest*. "When I checked the master sheet it showed [a card for this course], but then I couldn't find it. I had to make my calculations all over again in a practice round."

Of course, the meticulous Nicklaus would not have that problem again. "I'm going to have to get copies made of all the cards and keep a set at home. Then if I lose one, I can call my secretary and she can dictate the information to me."

From his practice sessions, Jack knew to the inch how far he hit various clubs. Nicklaus was studied and fully prepared when he hit his drive on the first tee. He knew the limitations he had that day and stayed within them. No wonder other golf professionals remember few times Nicklaus tried a shot that was beyond his capabilities. Jack always had a strategic game plan and stuck to it.

NBC's Gary Koch observed, "Mapping out a strategy of how to play the golf course and having the mental discipline to stick to that game plan, those were Jack's chief assets. Whether he was five under or five over or five ahead or five behind, he stuck to his game plan."

Angelo Argea echoed Koch's words when he said, "Jack was the consummate strategist, taking chances when the odds were in his favor, not taking chances when they were not."

The 1973 United States Open, won by Johnny Miller, featured a vivid example of the way Nicklaus prepared his mental game. In the opening round, Nicklaus was two over par facing play on the 322-yard, par-four seventeenth hole.

In an effort to prevent competitors from driving the green (many obstacles were positioned specifically for Jack during his career), twenty-five yards were added to the hole by tournament officials. They also placed tall trees on a crest just in front of the green to prohibit the competitors, namely Nicklaus, from attempting to drive the green.

Undaunted, Nicklaus practiced the tee shot and found that he could still drive the green. Needing something to ignite an otherwise lackluster round, Nicklaus chose the driver. Playing partner Bob Goalby believed the choice to be suspect, telling an official, "Boy, if that's not a dumb shot," when Nicklaus decided to go for the green.

Jack heard Goalby's comment. Even more determined, he launched a high floating shot that landed a few feet in front of the green. The ball bounced to within ten feet of the pin, and Nicklaus holed the putt for eagle. Goalby struggled to make par, causing Jack to joke as they left the green, "That's because you played a dumb shot from the tee."

What Nicklaus meant was that Goalby's shot was not high-risk. Needing a lift to get him into contention, Jack had gambled, but the gamble was far from reckless. It was an expertly calculated risk.

Phil Rodgers believed Nicklaus's resistance to altering his game plan was best exemplified at the eighteenth hole at Baltusrol in the

1967 United States Open. "Here Jack had a chance to break Hogan's record," Rodgers said. "He had the tournament won, so most players would have hit driver off the tee. But Jack's game plan said one-iron and that's what he hit. Arnold Palmer criticized him for doing so, but Jack's strategy worked."

After practicing the shots he expected to hit during a tournament round, Jack Nicklaus strode to the practice green. There his calculating mind-set was in order once again. "My stroke doesn't vary that much," he said. "What I practice is timing and feel. I'm after two things. I want the ball to feel right when I strike it, and I want to develop an instinctive sense of the speed of the greens on that particular course so that I have a feel for distance."

Nicklaus followed a specific routine when he took practice strokes before putting in competition. In his mind, he visualized the ball and the distance it had to cover, and then he took practice swings accordingly. "I try to tailor the practice stroke to the putt coming up," Jack said.

Some golfers who constantly rim the cup with putts believe their putting is solid, but Nicklaus disagreed with that philosophy. In fact, he was especially careful to take extra time to practice putting if he was rimming the ball out of the hole. "When you lip out several putts in a row," Jack said, "you should never think that means that you're putting well and that 'your shares' are about to start falling."

"The difference between 'in' and 'almost' is all in the [mind]." Jack further elaborated, "If you think the game is just a matter of getting it close and letting the law of averages do your work for you, you'll find a different way to miss every time. Your frame of reference must be exactly the width of the cup, not the general vicinity. When you're putting well, the only question is what part of the hole it's going to fall in, not if it's going in."

Nicklaus believed most missed putts were not a result of technique, but of the wrong frame of mind. "It doesn't take much technique to roll a 1.68-inch ball along a smooth, level surface into, or in the immediate vicinity of, a 4¹/4" hole," he said. On the other hand, he admitted that short putts could be killers. "A short putt—a 'makable' putt—is golf's 'last chance' shot," he observed. "There is always pressure on the short putts."

Nicklaus had three simple keys to good putting. He felt the superior putter needed to be confident about reading greens, aiming the ball, and striking the ball in a solid manner each and every time.

Those revelations were not newsworthy, but no one who made

as many putts as Jack could do so without being a master of the art of putting.

Nicklaus's expertise on the greens was due in part to his ability to adapt a wide variety of putting strokes to the surfaces he encountered. Ever meticulous, Nicklaus studied the greens on which he competed as a surgeon would examine a patient before a heart transplant.

"On the putting green," Jack said, "I can become a real chameleon, making small adjustments to some part of my set-up or stroke from hole to hole."

Jack had three basic approaches to stroking a putt. He could utilize a "square-to-square stroke" (the club face was swung with no turn to it), the "open-to-closed swing" (the putter moved back clockwise and then through the ball counter-clockwise), or the "closed-to-open" (the club face rotated counter-clockwise on the backswing and then clockwise through the ball).

The various techniques were chosen according to the conditions of the greens, especially when it came to speed.

If the putting surfaces were moderate, Nicklaus simply used the square-to-square method. Slow speeds meant he chose the open-to-closed stroke, in an effort to propel the ball at a faster speed. The closed-to-open stroke was implemented on fast greens, since it produced less speed at impact.

No better example of Nicklaus's game plan on greens, and his ability to vary from it when he had a "hunch," exists than the one he used during the 1972 season. On the hairy Bermuda greens at the Doral tournament, Nicklaus used the open-to-closed stroke. At the Masters, even though the greens were quick, he used the same putting stroke because he felt confident with it.

When Nicklaus competed at Pebble Beach in the United States Open, the greens were "Open" fast. He implemented the closed-to-open stroke, one that required a deft touch. That wasn't required at Muirfield in the British Open, where Nicklaus's observations dictated the square-to-square stroke would be best.

Nicklaus was never shy in sharing the secrets of his putting plan, but it was another matter to execute it to perfection the way he did. The key to his success involved two factors: his incredible confidence and a great pair of hands.

It is the latter that has received little notice over the years, but Jack Nicklaus's success, especially on the greens, would not have been possible without athletic hands. Small as they were, they permitted him to be a good baseball, football, and basketball player as a youngster and an excellent tennis player as an adult.

The "feel" Nicklaus had, especially on fast greens, allowed him to precisely swing the club as intended. Even when the pressure was enough to conquer pros with the most adamant mettle, Jack's steady hands enabled him to calmly swing the putter with the nonchalance of a Sunday pleasure golfer.

The significance of Nicklaus's hand action did not go unnoticed, however, by amateur great Bill Hyndman, who played in twenty United States Amateurs, ten Masters, and thirteen United States Open Championships. "Jack was a great putter. Nobody ever made as many putts as he did. The key was his great mind. And he had great hands. I saw that during the World Amateur Team Championship at Merion in 1961. He handled those fast greens like nobody I ever saw. What a touch."

With time spent on the practice tee and green and a true strategy in mind, Jack Nicklaus would confidently approach the first tee of a tournament round. He and the caddie would then check the club count. Jack would have already made certain the bag contained everything he could possibly need on the golf course.

Jack's golf bag was meticulously arranged. Besides tees and exactly twelve golf balls (first Slazenger, then MacGregor, then Ultra), Nicklaus carried an umbrella, rain jacket, pants, and a hat. In a larger compartment, he stored a sweater, a turtleneck dickey, a towel, spare golf gloves, a package of Band-Aids, a USGA rule book, and the rules sheet for the tournament in which he was playing. A metal ball ring to measure the size of the ball was also usually kept in the bag—at the height of his power, Nicklaus changed balls five or six times over eighteen holes because his hard swing knocked them from their true spherical shape.

Why he needed the metal ball ring is a mystery when one considers a story told by George Nichols, a former Nicklaus business associate. "Jack liked a ball with a compression of about 102," Nichols told USA Today. "When MacGregor engineers tested them, they'd try to trick Jack . . . [They'd] slip one in of 99 to see if he'd catch it. He'd hit a drive and say, 'I hit that one pretty good, it carried about 255, and that compression is about 99.'" These are the types of stories that contribute to the Nicklaus legend.

# CHAPTER 26

# Playing with Jack

Caddying for Jack Nicklaus was a unique experience. In the United States Open at Olympic in 1966, that task fell to Steve Nessier, a tall, young, bespectacled supermarket clerk who attended the tournament while on vacation.

"Nicklaus rarely fools around, even during practice," Nessier told *Golf Digest*. "He is very particular about pin placements, much more than the average pro. He also warned me, 'I might get mad and take it out on you because you're closest, but don't pay any attention to me.'"

Bagging for Jack left a lasting impression on Nessier. "Golfwise," the caddie said, "I was very impressed with his accuracy with the irons, with his determination and the way he works on every phase of his game during the practice rounds."

Although Nicklaus utilized various caddies during his career, the most common and recognizable was Angelo Argea, who worked for Jack into the nineties measuring distances on golf courses. During their more than twenty years together, Argea, whose celebrity status was similar to that of Rabbit Dyer, the caddie for Gary Player, saw every side of Nicklaus.

"Before the round," Argea said, "I gave Jack his glove, and he gave me his watch and money, which I put on my wrist and in my pocket. . . . At the practice tee, Jack would hit the ten-iron, eight, five, two, driver, then bunker and chip shots."

Nicklaus may not have been overly superstitious, but Argea noted his strict adherence to regiment. "One time I forgot to wish him good luck on the first hole," Argea said. "So I said it on the second. He played 'lights out' that day, and so I kept doing it from then on."

Over the years Argea—who dubbed himself "The Silver Greek" and was known by the press as the "Gold-Plated Caddie," "Cold Cash Caddie," and the "Rags-To-Riches Bag Carrier"—became as well known as some of the golfers Jack competed against. It was Jack, however, who ran things on the golf course. "I don't think a caddie can be a great asset in terms of shot making," Nicklaus said, "but he can be one heck of a detriment."

Regarding the "reading" of greens, Jack was boss. Argea tried it one time, was wrong, and never expressed his opinion again. As for club selection, Argea knew his place, saying, "Who am I to challenge his strategy? It would be like telling Michelangelo to use a different brush for that ceiling he was about to paint."

Argea was the brunt of harsh comments when things were not going well. "I'm his pressure valve out there," he said, "and I've absorbed a lot of steam." He added, "If [Jack] hit a bad shot, he'd turn and say 'Why did you let me pick that thing out of the bag?' I never took much from it. I knew he didn't mean it personally."

Unlike Arnold Palmer, Nicklaus was not one to watch the leader board, content to play the course and not the man. On occasion, he'd make Argea promise not to tell him who was doing what; then Jack would ask him and become upset when Angelo refused.

When he began caddying for Nicklaus, Argea initially earned $25 a day and five percent of Nicklaus's prize money. Argea was later doled out a bi-monthly salary that added up to less than $50,000 a year. He was also rewarded by a good Nicklaus finish. Argea received bonuses of $1,000 if Nicklaus won a regular Tour event and $2,000 if Jack was victorious in a major tournament. In the early years, Mark McCormack's IMG company also took a percentage of Jack's winnings, something they still do with their players today.

Argea earned his money. Besides carrying the bag, he tried to inspire his player. On occasion, Nicklaus was known to hum or sing a song while he was playing well. If Angelo noticed things going sour, he'd say to Jack, "Isn't it time for a little song?" Argea was also in charge of reminding Jack of certain thoughts to keep in mind during his rounds. "I'd mention extension, patience, swing putter head, and hands high at finish," Angelo observed.

Jack admitted Angelo helped him deal with distractions. While waiting for the group in front of them to clear, the two would stand on the tee and girl-watch. The goal was to find a date that evening for the bachelor caddie. Angelo would say, "I like that one over there," and Jack would reply, "No, no, this one over here is more your type."

Nicklaus was extremely punctual when it came to his starting time. Jack was almost late for a tee time in a junior tournament, and the lecture he'd gotten from the starter left a deep impression. Never again would he even come close to missing a starting time.

With caddie in tow, game plan prepared and memorized, and full knowledge of what the strengths and weaknesses of his game were on that particular day, Jack Nicklaus would ready himself to do what he did best—manage his golf game. That management hinged on his ability to place shots in certain advantageous positions on the golf course, where the next shot had the best chance for success. No guesswork entered into Nicklaus's game, enabling him to concentrate on the swing and nothing else.

Australian Graham Marsh, a successful Tour player in the seventies and now highly rated on the Senior Tour, commented, "When all is said and done, Jack's ability to manage himself and his game on the golf course was something he did better than anybody else ever did. Especially when it counted." He then added, "I can name a number of players who were equally as good in any one department [as Jack], but what made him a great player was the ability to bring it all together— manage it, if you will, in a tight situation."

Nicklaus's expertise in management made an impression on golf phenom Tiger Woods during his first few tournaments on Tour in 1996. When he astounded the golf world by winning the Walt Disney Classic for his second victory in five tournaments, Woods told *USA Today*, "I haven't had a great putting round yet, or a great ball-striking round, but I've managed my game really well. . . . Ask Jack Nicklaus how well he was playing when he won major championships, and he says he wasn't playing at his best, but he managed his game better than anybody."

NBC's Gary Koch credited Jack's management skill to his "mental approach." "Jack was not a whole lot better [than anyone else] with his short game. Length was an asset, but I don't think he was ever the longest." Koch added, "As for iron play, he was very good, but guys will say others were better. And I wouldn't consider him to be a great putter, but I watched him make a number of clutch putts. Jack was just great when he needed to be—brought it all together."

Raymond Floyd, an adversary of Nicklaus's for most of his career, also commented about the way Jack managed his game. "[He] has been the best that I ever seen at doing that," Floyd told reporters prior to the U.S. Senior Open. "Jack and I are only a couple of years apart, but . . . he was always way beyond his years when he started in the twenties. . . . He had the ability to be disciplined and play proper and play within himself and not do the wrong thing."

When Tour great Tom Kite recalled a round with Jack at the PGA

Championship at Kemper Lakes in 1989, he spoke of Nicklaus's patience. "Jack hit a good drive at number one," Kite said, "but at the fourth hole he duck-hooked the ball almost out of bounds. From that time on, the driver stayed in the bag. He hit three-wood and one-iron the rest of the way, even though the course was a long one. I couldn't believe how patient he was, how well he managed his game."

Although Nicklaus loved to hit the driver, he knew an iron off the tee was the better play, whether the hole was a par four or par five. Having made meticulous mental notes, he knew where the architect had placed the trouble. If for some reason a shot varied slightly from its intended flight, Nicklaus missed it in the right place. He kept chances for pars alive and rarely positioned himself where he had even the slightest chance for disaster.

"In short, Nicklaus never beat himself," observed television commentator Jack Whitaker, "the competition had to do that." Phil Rodgers agreed. "Other players beat themselves," Rogers said. "I knew I had to beat Jack."

Nicklaus's game plan meant bunker shots and chips were hit below the hole and onto the flattest part of the green. Likewise, long putts were lagged to precise locations where he had a tap in. Phil Mickelson, another in a long line of "the next Jack Nicklaus" candidates, said in 1996 that this element of Nicklaus's game is what impressed him most. "He's able to lag putts from forty, fifty feet to within a foot and just tap it in and never have to work very hard after his initial putts . . . and I could see that was a huge asset for him when it came major time because the greens were so much quicker, and he wasn't working on every hole to salvage par."

Nicklaus meticulously studied the landscape around the greens. He knew the architect played tricks with the golfer, placing obstacles in strategic, deceitful positions. Many times a gallery's enthusiasm deflated when he hit a seemingly errant shot into a bunker instead of on the other side of the green, where it appeared there was simply rough. Having examined the slope of the greens, Nicklaus knew he actually had an easier shot from the bunker, one that he could hit to an advantageous position below the hole. From the other side, a slippery slope chip might have too much variance to it, requiring guesswork for the shot. If Nicklaus had a weakness to his game, at least early in his career, it was his short game around the green, but he made up for it by almost always giving himself an easy recovery.

"That's where Nicklaus differed from someone like Greg Norman," observed Richard Hinds of the *Melbourne Age*, a longtime "Norman-watcher." "Greg has enormous talent, but he has a defect with thinking intelligently on the golf course. Nicklaus always put him-self in good position. Greg couldn't do that."

Nicklaus was also a master at managing his game from the rough. Instead of attempting impossible shots, Nicklaus always remained con-servative. He called his attempts an exercise in "mature recovery." "The rough does strange things to people," he said. "They stop think-ing. Even experienced club players try to pull off circus shots they would never dream of hitting from a fairway lie."

Nicklaus always tried to get the ball from a dastardly lie in the rough to safe ground, even if it meant foregoing the green. "That way," he said, "you have a relatively routine little pitch or pitch-and-run left, the kind of shot you can often stick in one-putt range."

Since Nicklaus didn't grow up in a windswept state, he also had to learn how to play when Mother Nature turned on the fan. Adaptation was even more difficult because he had learned to hit the ball so high.

To manage his golf ball in various types of windy conditions, Nicklaus pointed out that he "concentrated on staying behind the ball and on working under it. . . . I'd take one club less than the distance called for and hit it hard."

Against-the-wind shots, he said, "called for a boring shot flight, the kind on which the ball seems to peak out but keeps driving for-ward." To play such a shot he knew the ball could not have backspin, or it would rise in the head wind. To achieve that type of shot, Nicklaus observed, "I drop the ball back a little in my stroke and close the club face a shade." He played a near-equal shot when cross-winds were prevalent, preferring to play the ball into the wind with a slight draw or hook. The swing never varied, however, only the set-up and stance. Tempo was a constant, one reason it's difficult to remem-ber Nicklaus ever over-swinging or slashing at the ball during an important shot.

Using his ability to take most of the guesswork out of a sport that lends itself to chance, Jack Nicklaus was able to overpower the opposi-tion. That would not have been possible if he didn't possess a thought process second to none among the great players who have attempted to master the game of golf.

# CHAPTER 27

# Jack's Mind

When Jack Nicklaus was in his early thirties, famed artist LeRoy Neiman captured his essence with sketches he drew for *Golf Digest*. He also took time to describe the man he met:

> [He's] not revolutionary, he is the opposite of a Namath in lifestyle; nevertheless he resembles the controversial quarterback's mannerisms while in competition. Once on the green, he stalks to his ball with the same gait as Namath when he splits the huddle and advances to call signals. He has the same clean-cut seriousness and determined facial frown when slamming the ball as Tom Seaver has bearing down on a key pitch. When addressing the ball, his eyes fix on it with the same viciousness that Pancho Gonzales relates to the ball on his fierce big serve. He has the same set jaw of a decision-making executive such as his look-alike, Roone Arledge, chief of ABC Sports.

Neiman's description was accurate, but what the artist couldn't convey to the reader was a portrait of Nicklaus's mind. Although Jack possessed great physical skills, it was his intellect and superb ability to reason that helped him attain and maintain his lofty position in the golf world for over thirty-five years.

"An astonishing amount of golf, that is, good golf, is played between the ears," Bobby Jones said. Jack's ability to deal with the mental aspect of the game is the result of his upbringing and early teachings. His parents and Jack Grout not only taught him the power of "positive thinking" before that phrase was fashionable but also how to think before doing.

Nicklaus, the greatest final-round player who ever lived, was once asked his thoughts about controlling nerves during pressure-packed situations, such as when tournament championships were on the line.

"I say to myself," he responded, 'Okay, what are you frightened of? You obviously played well or you wouldn't be here. Go ahead and enjoy yourself. Play each shot one at a time and meet the challenge.'"

He followed his advice and in doing so, towered over the opposition. While it became white-knuckle time for his frenzied competitors, Jack "enjoyed himself."

Nicklaus's emotional make-up allowed him a control that was unlike any of his competitors. He had such a remarkable ability to compose himself and master concentration; he could block out any distractions that could ruin a perfect shot. Touring professional Frank Beard, a chief competitor of Nicklaus's during his prime, put it this way: "The mental side—Nicklaus is best in this department. His ability to organize himself and maintain his discipline, concentration, and composure is unparalleled. I've never seen Jack select the wrong club, hit a stupid shot, or lose his cool. If you put together a composite best golfer—the best driver, best putter, and so on—Nicklaus could give him two a side."

Legendary amateur champion Bill Campbell told *Golf Journal*, "Of all his talents, [Jack's] mind was his greatest strength. They write about Hogan's secret weapon as his fade or his grip or his swing. But Ben Hogan and Jack Nicklaus have the same secret weapon. I believe it is their minds, their thinking."

NBC commentator Gary Koch added, "He's the strongest mentally to ever play the game. Every single shot was hit with the same care and preparation . . . whether it was a two-foot putt or a 220-yard one-iron."

Nicklaus's ability to keep cool under pressure was apparent in nerve-wracking situations other than golf. Dick Fink, a sporting friend of Jack's, told *Golf Digest* in 1968:

> One day we got caught in a heavy ground sea off the coast [of Florida]. A huge roller came up behind us, about 30 feet high. I started to go down into the cabin for something, and Jack grabbed me by the shoulders and threw me back. Somehow, he got the boat turned into the wave. If I'd been below, and he hadn't gotten the boat straightened out, it would have been all over for me. That guy has nerves of steel. . . . He doesn't know what panic is all about.

In the early seventies, when he was playing golf at his best, Nicklaus expounded further on the importance of keeping emotions under control. He explained that the many golf experts who believed power was his chief weapon were wrong. "Where I believe my strongest suits lie are in the mind, not the body," he said. "I am a reasonably intelligent individual, and at golf I have almost always been able to apply my intelligence ahead of my emotions and my muscles.

"My intelligence told me that once you possess the shots, two factors above all others will determine your success in golf. One is the degree of reality you can apply to the game. The other is the degree of patience you can sustain, especially when you are under the pressure of either winning or losing something immensely important to you."

Obviously, Nicklaus practiced what he preached. The key was confidence, and his definition was a simple one: "[It's] feeling sure of your ability to do something. If I have it in my head that I'm going to do something, knowing I have the ability to do it is confidence."

He talked about how his positive attitude affected him in *Golf Week*. "I liked walking into a tournament and having everybody say, 'He's the guy who is going to win' and have everybody scared of you. . . . I've always been upset when I wasn't number 1."

Canadian PGA Tour Commissioner Dick Grimm told *Golf Journal*, "[Jack] always seems to do the right thing. I don't think I ever met a man who has as strong a positive attitude as [he] does or who has the observation qualities he has."

Deane Beman saw that firsthand at the Americas Cup in Canada. "On the fifth hole," Beman said "I found [team member] Charlie Coe's sand wedge in my bag. Jack was my partner and due to the penalty we were five down. But Jack wasn't the type to give up and neither was I. We battled back and tied them."

That type of confidence served Nicklaus well. He was a special player at thirteen, a tournament champion at fourteen. He was raised by loving parents, he had the perfect wife and the right business tutor in Mark McCormack (an association that brought him financial security), and he enjoyed instant success on the professional Tour. The only real bump in his career came when his self-admitted, pouty attitude and unpopular confrontations with Arnold Palmer resulted in a contentious relationship with golf fans.

But even that experience didn't affect his attitude on winning and losing. Many times observers interpreted this attitude as arrogance, but like other great champions in any sport, he simply felt he could win under any circumstances.

A fellow Tour professional put it this way. "Imagine that the mind is a quart jar. Nicklaus always makes certain the jar is full of positive thoughts—intentions of hitting good shots. . . . His mind is so permeated with the task at hand, there's no room for negatives."

Tom Weiskopf saw up-close how confidence made Nicklaus a winner during a match he and Jack had with Brian Barnes and Peter Butler in the 1973 Ryder Cup. "The alternate shot match was tighter than it should have been," Weiskopf recalled. "At sixteen, I hit a four-iron on the green. To my surprise, Jack said, 'C'mere.'"

Weiskopf was startled because Jack never asked anyone for advice on putting, club selection, on anything. "Angelo Argea never had to be a very good caddie," Tom said. "None of Jack's caddies did. He never used them for anything. He never asked yardages, or club choices, and he never had them read greens. He did it all himself. All he really needed was for fourteen clubs to follow him around."

After saying, "Who? Me?" to Jack, Weiskopf ambled over and looked at Jack's putt. "It breaks a bit to the right," Tom said. "That's what I thought," replied Nicklaus.

What happened next bordered on the unbelievable, according to Weiskopf. "Jack hit the putt and I can still see the ball in slow motion, the label turning over and over, as it headed toward the cup. The ball went in and then came out, made almost a 360 degree turn, and ended up on the front lip. The crowd started to give out a respectful roar, but then groaned."

Nicklaus stood watching in shock. "His piercing eyes stared at the ball," Weiskopf said. "Then I walked over and said 'Pardsy, I can't believe it, we'll get 'em.' Jack looked straight at me and replied, 'Tom, I made that putt. It just didn't go in.'"

On the way to the next tee, Weiskopf mulled over Nicklaus's comment. "It showed what confidence he had." Weiskopf said. "Jack had done nothing wrong. In his mind, he'd made the damn putt. On the next tee, Jack launched a ball so high and so far that the bunker on the left side of that hole was never in play. I had a three-iron into the green, put it on, and Jack holed the putt for eagle."

In the 1975 Ryder Cup matches, Weiskopf saw another sample of Jack's full-fledged confidence. While Nicklaus was lining up a fifteen-footer, Weiskopf posed the question, "You've never missed one of those in your life, have you, Jack?" Nicklaus replied, "Not in my mind."

Weiskopf also recalled the time in the 1973 Ryder Cup when Barbara, who was eight months pregnant, told Jack she didn't know if she could walk the entire match. "Don't worry," Jack told her, "it won't be a long walk." His confidence was legitimized on the first hole when Nicklaus faced a twenty-footer for birdie and Weiskopf had a ten-footer. "He told me to 'rack my cue,'" Weiskopf said. "I said 'What do you mean?' 'Pick it up,' said Jack. 'Oh, you mean mark it,' I said.

'No . . . Pick it up. There's no way in the world I'm going to miss this putt.' "And," Weiskopf added, "he didn't."

Perhaps the best example of Nicklaus's supreme confidence came when he decided to lose weight. Jack was so sure he could shed the excess baggage that he had a New York tailor fit him for clothes at the anticipated weight level Nicklaus intended to meet. Wife Barbara, seasoned to Jack's exploits, was nevertheless amazed. "Can you imagine anyone having such confidence in himself?" she asked.

Confidence was part of Nicklaus's make-up early in his Tour career. In his first Jackie Gleason Inverrary, he started his round, double bogey, bogey, double bogey. "I'll probably lose this tournament by one shot," he said to a playing companion. And he did. "Nicklaus is the only man on the Tour," a fellow player explained, "who can have two or three bad holes, then turn his day around with two or three birdies."

The confidence Jack had, Tour veteran Bob Murphy noted, made him realize he could come back from poor starts or a stretch of poor plays. "The game is seventy-two holes," he said, "and you must play all seventy-two holes and keep fighting."

Johnny Miller recognized that confidence. "[Jack] might be playing mediocre or have a bad start," he said, "but he's going to get his licks in there in seventy-two holes and finish right up there, somewhere in the top ten every time. He's the best at it I've ever seen. He can play just terrible, but I think he knows inside that if he just stays cool, it'll happen."

Nicklaus stresses the importance of a positive attitude when it came to holing putts under strenuous conditions. "Confidence has to be the golfer's greatest single weapon on the greens," Nicklaus observed. "If he believes he can get the ball into the hole, a lot of times he will, even if techniques appear unorthodox or even downright faulty. If he doesn't believe he can get the ball into the hole, most of the time he won't, even though his technique is flawless." Those words sound quite similar to ones propounded by Jack Grout, who said, "In the end, before you putt, you should clearly see in your mind's eye the ball rolling toward and into the cup."

A significant part of Nicklaus's confidence is a result of his even temperament. Controlled emotions have permitted him to ease his way through a round without becoming overly distraught or too excited with his play.

Nicklaus believes there are "three types of temperament in golfers: players who never learn to control emotions, ones who have little emotion at all, and others who have deep-seated fiery ones who use them to their advantage." He also said, "Outward demeanor is just a matter of the golfer's personality. Who would have ever thought a person like Bobby Jones, a man of remarkable composure, would have burned up so much inside fuel during one Open [championship] that he lost sixteen pounds."

Gary Player believes Nicklaus had the perfect mix of emotional attributes. "Jack is a marvel when it comes to temperament," Player said. "In fact, I think he has the most even disposition of any human being who's ever played golf. Even when Jack is hitting the ball poorly, I've seen him come off the course with a 68. The secret is his ability always to remain calm or on an even keel."

As he did with other facets of the game, Nicklaus loved to use Bobby Jones as an example when it came to curbing emotions. "When [Jones] was nineteen," Nicklaus said, "he tore up his scorecard in disgust during the 1921 British Open, and the shame he felt afterward gnawed so deeply into him that from that day on he proceeded to set a standard of conduct and sportsmanship that was matchless."

Nicklaus's thoughts about his contemporaries reflected his own set of standards. "Most of the fine professional golfers," he said, ". . . have acquired fine, stable temperaments. They keep themselves well under control and have a winning attitude. The very best have the capacity to keep working on a poor round, and often they end up with a respectable score through sheer doggedness."

Despite the tough outer crust, Nicklaus found time when playing competitively to exhibit moments of relaxation. Vinny Giles recalls playing with Jack in the 1973 United States Open at Oakmont, where Nicklaus tied for fourth. On the fifteenth hole in the second round, Giles recalls, "Jack drove the ball ten to fifteen yards in front of me. I hit a six-iron and the ball went into the hole for an eagle two. There was lots of noise as Nicklaus got ready to hit. Then he stopped, smiled, backed off, and plumb bobbed his seven-iron toward the hole. I said to myself, 'This guy's a little looser than I thought he was.'"

Nicklaus surprised Giles again on the eighteenth green of that round. Fighting to make the cut, Vinny had followed his eagle with two 3s and then faced a fifteen-footer in an attempt to finish the round 2, 3, 3, 3. When he scampered past Jack to the hole to pick his ball from the cup, Nicklaus peered over and said, "Excuse me. I didn't mean to get in your way."

The consensus is that most golfers enjoyed playing with Nicklaus. "He's the ideal pairing," Graham Marsh observed. "The thing that's so impressive about Jack is that he has this tremendous aura about him when he walks on a golf course—in the same way Palmer, Player, and Trevino do. But Jack never used it to intimidate—he was always fair and not trying to overpower the competition. It was a nice pairing—to be with a gentleman."

Bruce Crampton also saw the gentleman golfer in Nicklaus. "When we played in front of huge galleries, Jack always said, 'If you want to putt out first before the fans move, go ahead.' I appreciated that courtesy."

Gary Koch described a different experience playing with Jack. "I found it difficult the first time I played with him to keep my mind on what I should do," he observed. "I found myself spectating—watching what *he* was doing. After all, there I was a few feet away from the greatest golfer who ever lived. After the first time, I was more relaxed. Jack's fun to play with."

Donna Caponi also experienced some nervousness when playing with Nicklaus during a round on National Golf Day at Canterbury Golf Club in Cleveland. "I was a nervous wreck," Caponi said. "I felt like Jack was watching every part of my swing. I could barely take the club back because I knew he was watching how I swung every club."

Chi Chi Rodriguez welcomed the chance to play with Nicklaus. "They said he played slow, but that never bothered me," Chi Chi said. "Jack was just grinding on every shot. And I knew when to clown around with Jack, when I wasn't the show. I loved to play with him because he concentrated so well."

Rodriguez said he saw a different side of Nicklaus from time to time during competition. "At the Tournament of Champions one year, we were playing a 450-yard par four. The wind was behind, and I hit the ball about 330 yards. When we got to the fairway, Jack walked to the farthest ball. I stood back watching him. He looked at the ball and then turned around and walked back toward me. 'You little son of a gun,' he said smiling, 'you knew that was your ball.' I just laughed. The longest walk in life is having to walk back to your ball like that."

Senior Tour player Tom Wargo, the fairy-tale golfer who rose from driving range owner to PGA Seniors Champion, was paired with Nicklaus and Palmer his first year out on the Senior Tour. He had a dream round and beat them both. He said of Nicklaus, "I admire the man greatly. I've been around him when he's played miserably, but the personality is the same on the outside. I'm sure he was burning up on the inside, but it didn't affect the way he treated me. If you want to model after someone to play like, it's Nicklaus."

Despite his mental toughness, Nicklaus admitted pressure got to him on occasion. "[Good golfers] have the ability not to get frightened of their scores when things are going great," he said. "Beneath his sheath of outward calmness . . . a seasoned tournament player frequently experiences all sorts of qualms and tribulations, the same tortures that afflict the average player. . . ." Then he added a comment that should make all mortals feel better. "I know *I* have these spells of anxiety," he said.

After a victory in 1968, Nicklaus was asked whether he was nervous playing for a sky-high first place prize of $25,000. He told *Golf Digest*, "There are not degrees of nervousness. I'm as nervous over a $5 bet as over a tournament prize."

Nicklaus once told Dr. Bob Rotella, the noted author and sports psychologist, "I don't know how you play well unless you're nervous. . . . I don't get nervous unless I'm in a major and in a position to win. If I could only learn to concentrate when I'm not nervous, so I could get in position to win, then I'd be fine."

Nicklaus offered this advice for times of turmoil: "Instead of burning up with frustration on your bad days or becoming a bundle of nerves at the prospect of victory on your good ones," he wrote, "I would say . . . think of the wonderful challenge that golf provides and try to meet that challenge. That's where the real kick lies—not in being a lion in the locker room and a lamb on the links. Don't try to be foolishly heroic, to play way over your head. Keep your feet on the ground. Just try to do yourself justice. Accept the challenge and enjoy the challenge."

To find that mind-set, Nicklaus played fewer tournaments than his contemporaries and prepared himself mentally by freeing his mind of all distractions before a tournament began. His fine balance of career, family priorities, business matters, and other sporting activities helped take him away from golf, so that when he reentered the Tour he was fresh.

To get his mind off the game, Nicklaus played with his kids, fished, hunted, and participated in community activities near his home in North Palm Beach, Florida. On several occasions, he would compete the Saturday before a tournament in a friendly nine-hour decathlon session at home with his sons, kids in the neighborhood, and friends. They matched up in events at Nicklaus's practice green, tennis court, Ping-Pong table, basketball court, and swimming pool. Throwing and kicking a football and a forty-yard dash were added for good measure.

Although he was rarely crowned the winning decathlete—despite competing as if the events were part of the Olympic games—Nicklaus had fun and cleared his mind at the same time. Then it was time to go back to work and win another golf tournament.

# CHAPTER 28

# Jack the Anomaly

In the early years, Tour professionals recognized right away that Jack Nicklaus was a ball buster who was not only an extraordinary player but a thinking man as well. Above average intellect, solid judgment, and a good sense of right and wrong combined to create his strong, confident character.

Tour veteran Bruce Crampton said Nicklaus possessed great intelligence. "Jack is smart," he said. "It came from his upbringing. Jack was around a great many adults when he was growing up. And he traveled a great deal. Coming from Australia, that's how I learned, by traveling and meeting people. Jack was like that and he had good education as well."

Herbert Warren Wind has seen every great player who has picked up a club in the past half century. He first met Nicklaus in 1959 at the Walker Cup in Scotland. Some twenty-five years later in the mid-eighties, he made observations about the Golden Bear that are still appropriate today:

> In several respects, Nicklaus has undergone some noteworthy changes. He has expanded his vistas in many directions, developing a good mind, through exercise, into a great one. His memory can be astonishing. He has learned to understand people better, and has become more generous of spirit. All in all, he has matured very well—particularly when one takes into account how long he has been in the spotlight and the disruptive effect that this kind of thing has had on many celebrities.

The memory Wind spoke of has been a great Nicklaus asset. Being able to remember the layout of golf courses, the nuances of the greens, and nearly ever shot he ever hit provided Jack with a bank of

*When he was sixteen years old, Jack Nicklaus shot 64 en route to winning the Ohio State Open Championship.*

*Charlie Nicklaus was not only Jack's father but his best friend and inspiration, too. Here, he and Jack check out the eighteen-year-old Nicklaus's score of 66-70 that qualified him for the 1958 United States Open.*

*Jack Nicklaus, Billy Joe Patton, Deane Beman, Tommy Aaron, Ward Wettlaufer, Frank Taylor, and Harve Ward: members of the victorious 1959 United States Walker Cup Team.*

*Jack Nicklaus's individual performance at the 1960 World Amateur Championship shocked the golf world. He won by thirteen strokes, battering Ben Hogan's record at Merion Golf Club by eighteen.*

*The greatest rivalry in sports history—Arnold Palmer vs. Jack Nicklaus. Here the two foes pose after the twenty-year-old Nicklaus finished runner-up to Palmer in the 1960 United States Open.*

*Barbara Bash became Mrs. Jack Nicklaus on July 24, 1960. Golf champion Alice Dye called their romance "one of golf's greatest love stories."*

*Jack Nicklaus won his second United States Amateur Championship at Pebble Beach in 1961, beating Dudley Wysong 8 and 6 in the finals.*

*Jack Nicklaus's win at the 1962 United States Open was his first professional Tour victory*

*Sons Jackie, three-and-a-half years old, Steve, two years old, and their French Poodle, Nappy, join Jack and Barbara in a family photo in 1965, the year Nicklaus won his second Masters title.*

*Jack Nicklaus is awarded his third green jacket at the Masters in 1966. If he was in contention on the final day of competition, Jack would wear golf attire that didn't clash with green.*

*Jack Nicklaus, the course architect, poses here with his plans.*

*Though they were fierce rivals who had a prickly relationship, Arnold Palmer and Jack Nicklaus were unbeatable in partner competition. In 1971, they successfully defended their title in the PGA National Team Competition.*

*Tom Weiskopf said, "Lee Trevino had Jack's number." Here the Merry Mex walks off the eighteenth green at Merion in 1971 after defeating Nicklaus in a playoff for the United States Open crown.*

*Jack Nicklaus completes the swing of his famous one-iron shot to the seventeenth green at Pebble Beach in the 1972 United States Open. The ball rifled through the air and finished just inches from the cup, sealing Nicklaus's third Open title.*

*Jack shows his comic inclinations here with Bob Hope.*

This is Jack's favorite picture. After Nicklaus completed the second round of the 1973 PGA Championship at Canterbury, four-year-old Gary jumped into his arms on the eighteenth green. Nicklaus's win was his fourteenth major championship, breaking the record set by his boyhood idol Bobby Jones.

Jack Nicklaus and Pete Dye combined their talents to design Harbour Town Golf Links, one of the greatest courses in the world.

*Jack Nicklaus offers some friendly advice to Jackie Gleason, President Gerald Ford, and Bob Hope during the 1975 Jackie Gleason Inverrary Classic.*

*The Nicklaus clan in 1978. Barbara and Jack are surrounded by, from left to right, Steve, fourteen, Nan, twelve, Michael, four, Jackie, sixteen, and Gary, nine.*

*The miracle at the Masters in 1986. Jack Nicklaus fired eagle, birdie, birdie, and par on the last four holes to shoot 65 for his twentieth major championship victory.*

*Gary Player watches Jack Nicklaus's tee-shot during the 1991 Masters. Nicklaus admired Player's tenacity and valued his friendship. Gary, Jack's son, is named after Player.*

*Ashley Sutton, wife of PGA Champion Hal Sutton, called Barbara Nicklaus "the classiest woman in golf." Amateur great Dale Morey's wife said, "Barbara always kept Jack level."*

*Though Arnold Palmer and Jack Nicklaus bickered behind the scenes, they had tremendous respect for each other's skill. Here, Nicklaus gives Palmer a back rub prior to the Senior Skins game in Hawaii in 1995.*

*Four grand men of golf; Raymond Floyd, Arnold Palmer, and Tom Watson join Jack Nicklaus prior to the 1995 British Open at St. Andrews. Together, these players won thirty-six major professional championships.*

At the 1996 PGA Championship, Jack Nicklaus spars with the great Mohammed Ali. It was the first meeting of the two great champions.

Jack Nicklaus is flanked by his two sons Jack Jr. (left) and Gary prior to the 1996 British Open. At the age of fifty-six, Nicklaus astounded the golf world with opening rounds of 69-66.

*Jack Nicklaus believes Tiger Woods will break his record of twenty major championships. Here Woods receives the 1996 College Player of the Year Award from Jack, for whom the award is named.*

*Arnold Palmer and Jack Nicklaus must wish they were thirty years younger so they could challenge the "next Jack Nicklaus," Tiger Woods. Here they watch the young phenom drive the ball during a practice round at the Masters in 1996.*

information paramount to his ability to prepare for tournament competition. Numerous examples of the "Nicklaus memory" exist. Longtime business associate Tom Peterson recalls an executive of Uniden mentioning that he played basketball against Jack in high school. When Tom asked Jack about it, Nicklaus not only remembered the man but described him as a "gunner."

Oftentimes, during play on the golf course, Nicklaus would astound Angelo Argea with his memory. "Jack can remember shots he hit ten years ago," Argea said. "And the results."

"Jack's not as good as Barbara is when it comes to names of people," a close friend of the family said. "But he's close. And I know his business associates are careful, because Jack never forgets a thing. If you tell him something, he'll remember it the rest of his life."

"Having such a great memory has really helped Jack," amateur player Bill Hyndman said. "He has total recall. I love to listen to him march back in time and tell me what he hit on this hole or that. Jack's brilliant."

Touring professional Ed Sneed labeled Jack "Karnac" because he had an answer for everything, but one former associate has a different view of Jack's "intelligence." "Nicklaus is a know-it-all. He's an expert on everything. Hell, by the time he played four holes with banker David Rockefeller, Jack had convinced the man he was an expert on international monetary policy."

Nicklaus's tendency to be overbearing came from being insecure with private conversation. His shy, introspective nature (as Tom Weiskopf said, "Jack never liked the limelight, wasn't comfortable with it.") led him away from anything too personal, and he filled the gap by portraying himself as the expert. Nicklaus also wanted to be known as more than simply a golfer, especially during in his early years on Tour. Appearing to be worldly about all aspects of human life brought an approval Nicklaus desired.

Jack's favorite area to ponder was medicine. One would have thought he went to medical school and had practiced for years. He could diagnose any ailment, especially his own, a tendency that drove those close to him bonkers.

The expertise came in handy, since Nicklaus is a hypochondriac. He always seems to think something is wrong with him. He once told Tom Peterson, "My big toe is dead." After taking a moment to decide if his boss was serious, and deciding that he was, Tom said, "I've never heard of that." Nicklaus replied, "Oh, yes, it's quite common."

Over the years, Jack suffered from every ailment known to modern medicine. "He knew just enough from being the son of a pharmacist to be dangerous," a close friend said. Jack's dad put it another way. "It's either his ass or his elbow," he said. "Something's always hurting him."

Thomas Boswell, the fine writer for the *Washington Post*, wrote of another Nicklaus flaw. "All in all, it's probably good that Jack Nicklaus never completely lost his love handles, always had a squeaky voice, couldn't tell a joke, was color blind, couldn't resist raiding the refrigerator for ice cream, and had a lousy sand game. (Yes, and he backslid a thousand times on the damn cigarettes, too.)"

The cigarette habit is one that surprised many people. Jack started puffing away early on, quit a dozen times, then smoked again into his first days on the PGA Tour. He quit again after his victory in the '62 United States Open when he saw his unflattering presence on a film the USGA sent him. It showed Nicklaus during the playoff smoking as he stood on the thirteenth green surveying a putt. "I looked at that and said that's one of the worst examples for an athlete to send to youth that I could think of," he said. "And I've never smoked a cigarette on a golf course since then."

Even more astounding than knowing that the goody-two-shoes Nicklaus began smoking is knowing that he, with his incredible will power, couldn't give it up. Instead of dumping the habit, he simply restricted his smoking to off the course. Cameras never caught him with a cigarette hanging from his mouth in a tournament, but Jack didn't entirely quit smoking until 1982.

Another puzzling side of Nicklaus, seemingly the calmest competitor on the golf course when the pressure was intense, involved his propensity to faint at the sight of a newborn child. When Jackie was born, Nicklaus was away from Columbus playing in a match. He hurried home to the hospital. "A nurse carried my son out so that I could see him, and as I was walking forward," he said, "I sank to the floor and collapsed. Another nurse revived me with smelling salts."

"When Stevie was born," Nicklaus said of his second son, "I waited patiently at the hospital, and then when he was brought out, I collapsed. Another gutsy performance."

When their third child, Nan, was born, Jack had played in a bene-fit match at Scioto in Columbus with "Maverick" (James Garner), ol' ski-nose (Bob Hope), and Walker Inman, the club's fine professional. Immediately after a steak dinner at the Nicklaus home, Barbara gave the signal that a baby was imminent. Jack rushed her to the hospital, and Nan was born a little after midnight. When the nurses wheeled mother and daughter out to see the proud papa, Nicklaus promptly fainted *again*. With Nan's birth, Jack spent more time in the recovery room than Barbara.

The Nicklaus sense of humor is difficult to pinpoint. Although he has never been an outwardly funny man, he does possess a dry sense of humor and likes to play practical jokes.

One fan of Nicklaus's wit is writer Dick Taylor. "Jack likes to put people on," Taylor said. "I call it trolling, trout-fishing. He likes to see how long he can do it before the person catches on. All the while, Barbara is saying, 'He doesn't mean it, he doesn't mean it.'" Dick's wife, Lynne, added, "Jack likes to tease and be teased. He doesn't like pretentious people." Nicklaus's tendency to tease runs in the family. "My dad was the world's number one needler," Jack said, "and I come in a close second."

At times, Nicklaus's ability to put someone on could border on being cruel. Dick Taylor remembered one incident involving an executive of one of Jack's companies who came by the Nicklaus house while Taylor and his wife were house guests. "This poor fellow started talking about his Christmas bonus, and Jack kept saying, 'What bonus?' And the guy said, 'Like the one I got last year.' And Jack said, 'You didn't get one last year.' The poor guy was in a tizzy until Jack finally relented and told him he'd be getting a good bonus in his paycheck."

Other exercises of Nicklaus's biting humor have been at the expense of longtime friend John Montgomery, a tournament director who later sold his business to Jack's company, Golden Bear. On one occasion, Montgomery had positioned a donkey at the Nicklaus residence and it kicked Jack's car. Nicklaus never mentioned the incident, but soon thereafter, Montgomery found tons of horse shit dumped unceremoniously on his lawn.

Professional Mike Souchak said Nicklaus was "misunderstood like Hogan." He added, "Ben always said 'This is my office,' when he was playing. But off the course, he was fun to be with. Jack was the same way."

The testy side of Nicklaus was seldom seen, but there have been a few explosions that made front-page headlines. The disagreement with a rules official during the final round of the World Match Play tournament at Wentworth made international headlines. Two years later, Nicklaus took out his frustrations on a golf bag. He was in contention at Carnoustie, but at the sixth in the final round a duck-hook on the drive produced a ball out of bounds. Instantly, he vented his anger on his huge golf bag, held by his ally and caddie Jimmy Dickinson. A swift kick catapulted the bag from Dickinson's hands, and the gallery flinched at Nicklaus's childlike behavior.

Although Nicklaus had occasional slips like these, they are few and far between. It appears that he has been able to provide a command performance in virtually every area of his life. In some ways, this resiliency has made him suspect, and initially it caused friends and colleagues to question his priorities. Eventually though, it evolved into a respect for Nicklaus, the human being.

Tour contemporary Bruce Crampton observed, "Jack is super. He's been good to me in more ways than one. He's the consummate gentleman. Very respectful and a great family man. He and Barbara still send me a Christmas card. That means a lot to me."

Although there has been some scuttlebutt about a quick temper and a tendency to belittle others when he senses incompetence, Jack Nicklaus's demeanor seems to be "what you see is what you get." He genuinely loves life and has a deep respect for others. Above all, he has had the ability to prioritize his time: family, first and foremost; competitive golf, second; and architecture, third; followed by other business interests.

If signs of inner character, emotional stability, and perseverance in the face of diversity are indications, Nicklaus is more often than not a true champion. Nicklaus's superlative degree of mental health permitted him to wade through the unpopularity he felt when his skills allowed him to pull even with, and then pass, Arnold Palmer in the sixties. He was able to shake off the disappointing losses to Gary Player and Lee Trevino in the seventies, resurrect his career by winning the United States Open and PGA Championship in '80, overcome his own insecurity by winning the '86 Masters at age forty-six, and then compete as competently as he did in the British and United States Open in 1996 at age fifty-six.

His inner strength has been constant, but his outer appearance has always been in flux. He was lean as a teen; a chunky short-haired, intense golfer in his twenties; a less-serious, hairy Weight-Watchers devotee in his thirties; a middle-aged fashion plate in his forties; and a bit of a disheveled, grand old man after passing the mid point of his fifties. In the United States Open in 1996, he was competing against men *thirty-seven* years his junior, and on a few occasions he looked fresh and confident, while they appeared to be battered and bruised. Nicklaus has the heart of a young man, the smile of one at peace with himself, and the stubbornness of one who still thinks he can win a twenty-first major championship.

Nicklaus's longevity (thirty-four years on the PGA Tour through 1996) is understandable when one considers the state of his physical health. Although he has been characterized as a "worry-wart" because of his hypochondriac-like attention to health and carrying the infamous "Nicklaus dope kit" full of remedies for every conceivable medical problem, his innate optimism is reflected in the state of his body.

In many ways, Nicklaus is the Cal Ripken Jr. of golf, a man who has competed in tournament after tournament on a continuing basis since joining the Tour in 1962. Like Ripken, Jack has never missed a beat. Seldom has he withdrawn from an event, no matter how big or small. Jack has teed it up consistently, and, for more than twenty years on Tour, he was always the man to beat.

A book explaining how Nicklaus has sustained superior health would be a bestseller. Today, as he approaches his sixties, he is still athletically fit. Some wonder if he found the fountain of youth on one of his globe-trotting ventures to design golf courses. To be sure, the mid-nineties had a few notable exceptions where a short-tempered, slump-shouldered Nicklaus replaced the one who once walked sprightly down the fairway looking for birdie at every turn. But on the whole, the ever-smiling optimistic Jack Nicklaus still prevails.

Whether he can win a major again is a debatable question. The only golfer to win a PGA Tour event on the other side of fifty was Sam Snead, whose swing was crafted by God for longevity.

In 1974, at age sixty-two, Slammin' Sammy rekindled the old fire and finished third in the PGA Championship. Others of the mature generation who have challenged in a major include Ben Hogan, who was 54 when he shot 66 at Augusta in the 1967 Masters (finished tied for 10th); Tommy Bolt, who at fifty-two tied for third in the 1971 PGA; and Harry Vardon, fifty, who lost by one shot to Ted Ray in the 1920 U.S. Open.

The chief challenge for older players involves strength, Nicklaus's main weapon early on in his career. His powerful build put him a step ahead of other competitors, and that strength stayed with him most of his career. Only in the last few years has he been unable to bust the ball with all comers. One Senior Tour competitor said, "It's tough to watch Jack now. His strength is gone."

According to Nicklaus, his superiority in golf kept him from spending time pursuing excellence in other sports. In a 1979 *Sports Illustrated* article, he said, "I don't react very well. In tennis, my best shot is the serve . . . I respond terribly when I have to hit a ball *back*. In basketball, I was a really good shot [not long ago he sank eighty straight free throws on his home court], but I was poor at passing and at defense."

Inability to react also hindered Nicklaus in football, but he could handle being a placekicker. *Sports Illustrated*'s Frank DeFord noted that Jack spent hour upon hour kicking field goals, sometimes from as far out as forty yards.

Nicklaus's balancing act with his family and his careers, his uncanny ability to use good mental judgment 99 percent of the time both on and off the golf course, and a physical stamina that an Olympic athlete would envy have combined to make Jack one of the most remarkable athletes of this century.

# CHAPTER 29

# Blocking out the World

Jack Nicklaus is the greatest study in concentration the professional golf Tour has ever known. "He had those eyes, ones like Hogan's and Palmer's, too," Chi Chi Rodriguez observed. "Those magnificent eyes that told you he was in his own world."

Carol Peterson, wife of Tom Peterson, remembered Jack during a round in the PGA Championship in Florida. "Jack walked right up to Barbara and Tom and me, but he didn't really see us. Those eyes of his were focused on playing. Later, he said he didn't recall seeing us."

The stories about Nicklaus's ability to block out the world have become legendary. Phil Rodgers said, "Jack is so intense, so in a trance you could have the Long Beach State marching band there [on the tee], and he wouldn't have any idea." Recently, he added, "Jack has a rare personality. You can say something to him, and he won't answer. An hour later, he'll remember the question and answer it. He would put himself into a virtual state of oneness. Like Hogan, and these days, Nick Faldo."

Nicklaus could also block out pain while he was playing. After a heartbreaking loss to Tom Watson in the 1977 British Open, Jack retired to his hotel room. "While taking a shower," writer Dick Taylor recalled, "he noticed his bum had red marks all over it. Seems at eighteen, as he was hitting the superb second shot to the green, he did so while puncturing his back end by hitting the sharp little leaves on the close-by holly berry bush. He never even knew it, he was concentrating so hard."

During television commentator Jack Whitaker's first playing round with Nicklaus, he saw Jack and his caddie Angelo Argea huddled along the side of the tee on the second hole at Sawgrass in Florida. "I thought I'd get a glimpse of them planning strategy, so I walked over toward where they were standing. I hear Jack say, 'That green is in a terrible place. They ought to move that tree, and put it over there,' and so forth. He wasn't thinking about his golf game, but then when he got ready to hit the next shot he was focused again, and I could see the enormous concentration back with him."

At the 1996 PGA Championship, a meeting between Nicklaus and boxing legend Muhammad Ali was arranged beside the ninth hole at Valhalla, the site of the tournament. While reporters, photographers, and fans scurried about to gain a glimpse of Ali, Nicklaus faced a twelve-footer for par just a few yards from where Ali was seated in a golf cart. With all the commotion and crowd noise, Nicklaus calmly stepped up to the putt and holed it. Then he walked over to Ali, whom he had never met, and embraced the former champion.

Nicklaus has approached each shot as if to say, "This is the last shot I'm ever going to hit in my life, so I'd better hit it perfectly." His ability to concentrate solely on the shot was learned early on and has continued throughout his career. Keeping focused 100 percent of the time permitted him to out-think his opponents at nearly ever turn.

"I define concentration," he once said, "as the ability to make my body do what my mind wants it to do. When I'm able to think clearly about what I want to do and then make my body do it, that's when I'm concentrating."

Senior Tour veteran Tom Wargo says playing with Nicklaus has permitted him to see Jack's pattern of concentration up close. "You can't concentrate totally for four and a half hours," he said in 1996. "There have to be peaks and valleys, and Jack's the greatest at that. He can raise and lower his concentration level between shots. When he finally pulls the trigger, it's a great thing to watch."

Wargo then added, "I asked him once what he [concentrates] on when he practices putting. He said, 'Just on one thing, and when I get it done I'm out of here.' All the other players groove their golf swings. Jack grooves his mind."

Veteran player Bob Dickson said, "When Jack's on the golf course, I've never seen him without his game face. He's the eye-of-the-tiger. He separates all of the stuff out of his life and works on one shot. You can almost feel it." *Indianapolis Star* reporter Phil Richards added, "Jack never mailed it in like so many other golf professionals. He grinds on every shot. On the practice tee, the practice green, on the golf course."

LPGA great Donna Caponi agrees. "Jack has the ability to tune in and tune out," she said. "Many players get exhausted trying to concentrate for four and a half hours. Actually, you only need to do so for something like 105 minutes. Jack was the best at that. He'd visualize a shot and then execute the play."

Professional opinion of the Nicklaus mind-set is varied, but Dr. David Morley, a psychiatrist and acquaintance of Jack's, observed:

> He has tremendous ability to concentrate under conditions where most of our minds would be going a hundred ways at once. It has to be his single greatest asset. A primary factor is the continual application of intellect, rather than emotion, to the job confronting him. He controls every move to a very specific end. There are no false starts, no blank spots, no slipping into neutral gear. The clutch of his mind responds quickly without pause or hitch.

In the mid-seventies, Nicklaus further elaborated on his ability to focus. "I never hit a shot, even in practice, without having a very sharp, in-focus picture of it in my head. It's like a color movie," he said. "First I 'see' the ball where I want it to finish, nice and white and sitting up high on the bright green grass. Then the scene quickly changes, and I 'see' the ball going there: its path, trajectory, and shape, even its behavior on landing.

"Then," he continued, "there's a sort of fade-out, and the next scene shows me making the kind of swing that will turn the previous images into reality. Only at the end of this short, private, Hollywood spectacular do I select a club and step up to the ball."

Claude "Butch" Harmon was impressed with Nicklaus's ability to visualize his shots. "Jack Nicklaus is the best ever," he wrote in his fine book, *The Four Cornerstones of Winning Golf*, "at previewing a shot and then trusting his body and his senses to recreate those shots."

That ability to concentrate, Nicklaus admitted, was more difficult when he played with "talkers" like Chi Chi Rodriguez and Lee Trevino. Early on, Jack had weathered the storm of playing with Tommy Bolt, but Trevino was a new challenge. Tour player Bob Murphy loved to tell the story of Nicklaus walking up to Lee as they prepared to play the final round of the British Open. "'Lee,' [Jack] said, 'I really don't want to talk too much today.' 'Fine,' Trevino replied, 'you just listen, and I'll do all the talking.'" Trevino's rattle may have been responsible for Nicklaus's playoff loss in the '71 Open. Trevino's famous snake trick and non-stop chatter pierced even Nicklaus's tough outer crust. Later, Jack admitted he'd let himself get trapped in Trevino's web.

Trevino was the exception to the rule, for Nicklaus rarely let the play of opponents get to him. He was certainly aware of their presence, but when it came time to hit a shot, Jack slid into a vacuum and didn't reappear mentally until the shot was completed.

Jack Nicklaus's emotional control and ability to concentrate were amplified by his fierce competitive spirit. Whether it was a major or an office raffle, Nicklaus wanted to come out on top. "I do not like to lose," he has said on many occasions. "It's as simple as that. Pride is probably my greatest motivation, because I just refuse to get beat, I can't stand to get beat, and I hate to have someone come along and beat me."

The fine journalist William Price Fox pointed out that the term "Golden Bear" was a real misnomer for Nicklaus. It was pinned on Jack by an Australian journalist in the tradition of other great golf nicknames, such as "Moose" for Julius Boros, "The Hawk" for Ben Hogan, "Skippy" for Al Geiberger, "The Walrus" for Craig Stadler, "Big Momma" for Jo Anne Carner, "Digger" for course designer Pete Dye, "Gentle Ben" for Ben Crenshaw, "Smokey the Bear," for Mike Souchak, and "Buffalo Bill" for Billy Casper.

Because Nicklaus exuded the icy personality associated with killer instinct, Fox suggested Jack's nickname should be "El Tigre," Spanish for "the tiger." With "his yellow sweater and beltless blue double knits, his towhead catching the light," Fox said, "there can be no denying he is the predator."

Fox also compared Nicklaus's demeanor down the stretch to that of boxers Jack Dempsey and Joe Louis and golfers Bobby Jones and Ben Hogan. Others said Jack's respect for fine play permitted him to go for the jugular. "I don't mind losing, if a guy plays better than I do," he wrote. "That's one nice thing about golf, it's a humbling game. . . . The only thing that embarrasses me is not giving 100 percent. . . . If I give it all I have and I lose to somebody who plays better, then I don't mind losing so much."

Nicklaus is not the only sports figure to have a calculating mind that stayed cool in the home stretch. Sports greats such as quarterback Joe Montana, baseball player Ted Williams, basketball star Larry Bird, and tennis legend Billie Jean King all had reputations for being tough in the clutch. They all sought the pressure, wanted to be there when it was crunch time. For the most part they succeeded, but the fact that they were there and in contention separated them from their peers.

Nicklaus had this quality as well. Time and time again, he was there knocking at the door, contending for victory. He was first, second, or third *forty-four* times in 102 major events through 1986. That meant he was in contention for the title a remarkable 43 percent of the time.

That statistic is most impressive to current top Tour players who understand how difficult it is to be a factor come crunch time on

Sunday in the majors. "That's the key," 1996 British Open Champion Tom Lehman said, "getting to where you have the chance to win. I've had to learn how to do that. Winning just happens if you do it enough times. Nicklaus was superb at that."

Comparing Nicklaus to other players of international stature underscores the remarkable nature of his record. Nick Faldo, great golfer of the nineties, had contended eleven times in fifty-nine tries through 1996. Compared to Nicklaus this statistic is not that impressive. But Faldo has notched six major championships when in contention, a mark that approaches Nicklaus.

Discounting a few major tournaments where he may have shot a lights-out final round to pass other players, Nicklaus went to the well at least forty times with a chance to win and was victorious in nearly half. By contrast, through 1996 Greg Norman, an athlete of immense physical skill, found himself in a contending position twenty-six times in his career yet could convert only twice, both times in British Open Championships.

Comparisons between Nicklaus and Greg Norman have been inevitable over the years. *Melbourne Age* writer Richard Hinds, who has covered Norman for many years, said, "Years ago, Norman learned how to be a good loser. It costs him time and time again. When he blew the Masters ['96], he was still the friendly sort with the press. Unlike Nicklaus, he doesn't know how to perform under the pressure. It's a basic character flaw."

Interestingly enough, even though Greg Norman hasn't handled pressure like Jack, he plays well on Nicklaus's courses. Five times he has emerged victorious in tournaments played on Jack's designs, known for their "thinking man's philosophy."

Being nervous goes with the territory. European great Colin Montgomerie, when ask how he handles the pressure, replied, "It starts in the first round of a tournament when you birdie the first couple of holes. Then it gets worse after that. The good players know how to handle it. The others fade away."

After the third round of the 1996 PGA Championship, Tour veteran Kenny Perry said, "When I was near the lead, I felt like a statue. I was so nervous I couldn't raise my arms. I don't know how Jack did it so many times."

Three-time PGA Club Professional Champion and two-time PGA Senior Tour winner Larry Gilbert told *Senior Golfer Magazine*, "That's the reason I play the game, to get nervous. . . . You've got to get yourself in that position, and that's what you thrive on."

Jack Nicklaus has never been impoverished for pressure-filled situations, and he agreed that there is little or no difference in relative pressure at any level. "Sure, there's more [pressure] at a U.S. Open or a Masters because there's more tension to it," he said. "But that means your ability to focus and concentrate should be greater, too." He added, "The fun is to put yourself in that position and being nervous, being excited, being ready to have to do that. That's what's fun. I never look at it as pressure. I look at it as fun and excitement. That's why you're doing it."

Never would Nicklaus be more challenged to keep his wits about him and deal with pressure than on the back nine in the final round of the 1972 Masters.

Heading into Sunday's finale, Nicklaus had recorded rounds of 68, 67, and 73. He led by three over Tom Weiskopf and by four over Bruce Crampton and Bobby Mitchell.

His play in the final round required that he exercise self-control, exhibit extreme concentration, and show his adversaries he would not be deprived of his fourth green jacket. The three three-putt greens he had had late in the round disturbed him, but he kept plugging.

What saved his play were his iron shots to the greens, a result of hard practice after the third round. His desire to correct a perceived weakness in his game put him on the practice tee when the fifty-fourth hole was completed. "During the third round, [I] was not able to fly the ball as high as [I] wanted" he later explained. "I worked on using my legs more, driving them toward the target. That's what you have to do to hit the ball high."

His connection obviously worked. *Golf Digest* reported that in the final eighteen, "[Nicklaus's] iron shots threatened small aircraft take off and landings at a nearby airport."

Down the stretch, Nicklaus was superb. Augusta played tough and no one could mount a serious charge. None of the leaders broke 71, and Nicklaus's 74 shook off challenges from Bruce Crampton, Bobby Mitchell, and Tom Weiskopf, who tied for second at 289, three behind Nicklaus. Low amateur was a talented collegian named Ben Crenshaw.

"Augusta played hard that year. The scores were high," Crampton recalled. "The greens had a lot of poa annua [undesirable grass], and they were hard. There's really only a ten-foot radius to hit the ball in on those greens. You have to nip the ball off the fairway and hit a perfect shot. The condition of the course permits you to do that, but in '72 it was really difficult. I played well, but Jack was better."

Augusta's treacherous hole locations, marble-slick greens, and gusty winds had not permitted a single golfer other than Nicklaus to finish in red figures. But it was Nicklaus who had played the best by using his mental make-up to tame the field.

When Nicklaus left Augusta that Sunday evening, he had pocketed major number one for 1972. The United States Open at Pebble Beach was the second leg, and he was supremely confident that he was about to go two for two.

# BOOK V

# King of the Majors

❖ ❖ ❖

# CHAPTER 30

# Nicklaus and the PGA Championships

T he sky was ashen and the winds were gusting as Jack Nicklaus approached the seventeenth tee at Pebble Beach in the 1972 United States Open. On the course that *Golf Magazine* editor George Peper called "God's gift to golf," Nicklaus was attempting to add the Open crown to his April Master's victory.

The weather turned sour on Saturday and downright nasty on Sunday, June 18. Carmel Bay was tossing with white-capped waves, and a small craft advisory was in effect. The antagonizing elements, however, didn't deter the champions of golf from staging an epic struggle to determine who would be crowned the United States Open Champion.

"The greens got real glassy; they looked like they were dead," Nicklaus told *Golf Magazine* later. "It was the toughest conditions I can remember in the [United States]." Bruce Crampton echoed those thoughts, recalling that the greens were "wilting, gray, and players' foot marks could be seen all over them."

For three rounds and sixteen holes, Nicklaus fought back challenges from the best golf had to offer: Arnold Palmer, Lee Trevino, Johnny Miller, Tom Weiskopf, and Crampton. No one could escape the wrath of Pebble Beach and the weather, making par as slippery as the water-swept beach.

The shot that Nicklaus faced on seventeen required the ball to travel with a sling-shot trajectory 209 yards into the teeth of the wind. He debated between a four-wood and the one- and two-irons. Caddie Angelo Argea and Nicklaus finally settled on the one-iron, the iron with the least loft, and Jack took his position on the tee. He knew the tournament might very well be won or lost on that shot, since the seventeenth green abounded in disaster. With seven bunkers guarding the green like Cerberus at the gates of Hades, Carmel Bay cut into the hole a few paces to the left edge of the green. Any variance to that side would mean double bogey or worse.

Nicklaus, with twelve major championships to his credit, carried with him on that cloudy day the ghost of Bobby Jones. Just one more win in a major and he'd tie his god of golf. With two holes of challenging play ahead, Nicklaus knew that it was the one-iron shot that would determine victory or defeat.

The wind was unrelenting as he tried to steady himself over the ball. The swing would have to have perfect tempo he knew, otherwise he would unleash an uncontrollable shot headed for either the bunkers, the bay, or the deep, spiky rough that hugged the surface around the green.

Finally, Nicklaus cocked his head and drew back the thinly lofted club. The wind fought hard to alter the swing, but Jack forced the one-iron up to level position and then down and through the ball. When he came square to the ground and perched his right foot in vertical position, he looked up to watch the white sphere spiraling toward the green.

During his professional golf career, Jack Nicklaus won major tournaments at such meccas as Augusta, Oakmont, Baltusrol, Pebble Beach, Oak Hill, Muirfield, St. Andrews in Scotland, Firestone, Canterbury, and Broadmoor. He was a runner-up in majors at such fabled courses as Merion, Riviera, Hoylake, Carnoustie, Royal Birkdale, Turnberry, Laurel Valley, and Tanglewood.

In all, through 1996, Jack won twenty major tournaments: six Masters, four United States Opens, five PGAs, three British Opens, and two United States Amateur titles. He is the only man to have captured all four professional major championships three times.

Comparing Nicklaus's success in majors to the success of other athletes of his caliber reinforces just how special he is.

Certainly, Margaret Smith Court's twenty-four championships in Grand Slam tennis events comes close. Tennis star Billie Jean King's thirty-years-plus on Tour with thirty-nine Grand Slam titles (twelve as a singles player), A.J. Foyt's thirty-years-plus as a top race car driver (ran in thirty-five straight Indy 500s, winning four), and

"Mr. Hockey" Gordie Howe (thirty-two-year career, six-time MVP, more than one thousand goals) also parallel Nicklaus's marks. His domination of his profession in his prime is something future generations will find hard to believe. They will speak of Jack Nicklaus with reverence and awe, unable to comprehend how he could have achieved such feats.

Championship play is something golf's golden boy relished from day one. Tales of Bobby Jones filled his young mind, and the moment he turned professional, he was in hot pursuit of his idol's collection of trophies. His story might seem the stuff of fairy tales, yet it's an amazing reality.

Over the course of seventeen years, Jack Nicklaus won five PGA Championships. He finished second four times.

The PGA championship was conceived at precisely nine A.M. on October 10, 1916, at the Siwanoy Country Club in Bronxville, New York. Englishman "Long Jim" Barnes and Jock Hutchison, a native of St. Andrews, Scotland, met in the final. On the green of their thirty-sixth hole, both men faced five-footers. Hutchison, after a measurement, putted first. He missed but Barnes didn't, thereby becoming the first winner of the Wanamaker Trophy, named for Rodman Wanamaker, the department store magnet who helped to organize the PGA and provided the $2,580 purse for the first championship.

Five years later, Walter Hagen won his first PGA (beating Barnes 3 and 2), then four straight in the years 1924-27. The tournament was match play until 1958, when Dow Finsterwald won by shooting 276, Billy Casper finished second.

The fifth of Jack Nicklaus's wins in the PGA Championship came at Oak Hill, the famed Donald Ross course in Pittsford, New York, in 1980. Nicklaus was forty at the time and saw a different golf course than the ones that had hosted United States Opens in '56 and '68.

The latter year was the one in which Lee Trevino scrambled around the course to shoot 69-68-69-69. Nicklaus finished runner-up by four to Trevino. The galleries were mesmerized by the red-and-black clad Trevino, who sported a sunshine smile and a non-stop motor mouth.

Trevino's blitz of Oak Hill did not sit well with the USGA. Designers George and Tom Fazio were brought in to revitalize the course. Opinions were mixed regarding the results. No matter, Nicklaus scored a hole in one in a practice round in 1980 and felt confident entering the tournament.

Jack's attitude stemmed directly from a putting lesson administered by his son Jackie. After Nicklaus had shocked the golf world by winning the United States Open in June, his putting had gone south. Jackie had noticed the flaw in his dad's stroke on the short grass during a practice round at Muirfield Village.

The key was to hit on through the ball instead of using a stroke that now stopped at impact. Positive results were immediate, and Nicklaus approached the PGA believing his putting was back on track.

His putting was true during the first two rounds, and Nicklaus removed any lingering doubt at the thirty-seventh hole of the tournament. Faced with a fifty-footer on the first hole of the third round, he slammed the ball into the back of the cup.

Later, Nicklaus recalled the victory for *Golf Magazine*. "In contrast to the United States Open [that year], I did not play well [tee to green]. My son Jackie gave me a putting lesson the Sunday before about moving the heel of my putter through the ball. I went up there with that idea and holed it from everywhere. I can't remember ever putting that well in a major championship, and I won by seven strokes playing mediocre golf." That statement must have warmed the hearts of his fellow competitors.

Nicklaus's success on the greens left opponents in the dust. In spite of the USGA's attempt to toughen Ross's design, Jack shot 70-69-66-69 (274) to beat Trevino's 1968 total by one shot. Nicklaus's seven-stroke win over Andy Bean permitted him to tie (with five PGA Championships) the immortal Walter Hagen, described by one sportswriter as a "golfer with the guts of a burglar." The win was worth $60,000. Jack's margin of victory was the largest in PGA history.

The first of Nicklaus's PGA Championships came in 1963, his sophomore year on the Tour. The tournament was held at the Dallas Athletic Club, a 7,046-yard, par-71 course designed by Ralph Plummer, a one-time caddie at the same Glen Garden course in Texas where Nicklaus's mentor Jack Grout had apprenticed before going to Scioto.

Before the tournament, Nicklaus put on an intimidating display of power. Just twenty-three years old, he launched the ball 341 yards and 17 inches to win the long drive contest. He said later it was the longest measured drive of his career.

The win in Dallas was Nicklaus's fifth major championship, but it didn't come easy. The temperature hovered around 100 and then some, and Jack was reeling from his devastating loss in the British Open at Royal Lytham and St. Anne's the previous week. There, he had uncharacteristically lost by bogeying the last two holes.

The first three rounds produced little fanfare by Nicklaus. Battling the heat took its toll, and heading into the final round, Jack stood three shots behind Bruce Crampton.

Although Nicklaus had produced many late-round heroics to seal championship wins, the tee shot on the very first hole of round four proved pivotal. He knew early birdies were crucial to catching Crampton; thus, he concentrated on the opening tee shot as if it would decide the tournament.

Addressing the ball, he was consumed by one thought: achieving a full arc backswing to propel the ball a Texas-sized distance down the fairway of the 521-yard, par-five hole. Just one day after winning the long drive contest, that powerful swing produced a prodigious drive of equal length, leaving him just 170 yards from the green. A high, lofted five-iron placed the ball fifteen feet from the cup. When he drained a left-to-right curler, the eagle three put him back in the thick of the championship run. Bruce Crampton remembered the shot. "It was all downhill from there," he said. "Jack was unbeatable."

The eagle inspired Nicklaus and kept him at a fever pitch throughout the round. By the time he had completed seventeen holes, he led by two shots with just one hole to play. Then, he hit a gagged three-iron tee shot into deep rough short of a winding creek.

After using the wedge to get out of the rough, Nicklaus hit a nine-iron twenty-five feet from the hole. If he could hole out with two putts, he would win his first PGA championship. The first putt, however, scampered four feet by the hole. A challenging second putt faced him, but Nicklaus was unperturbed. He stroked the putt dead center to win by two shots over Dave Ragan.

Later, Nicklaus talked about winning the PGA Championship on the heels of losing the British Open. "I lost the one I thought for sure I was going to win, and I won the other before I had hardly realized it was in my grasp," he said. "I would also agree with the golfer who said . . . that while some championships are won, most of them are lost."

Nicklaus attributed his triumph that year to, among other things, club selection. He told reporters, "Using these cards [charts] removes any element of doubt for me. I know precisely how many steps I can hit every iron in my bag. If I have 181 steps to the green from a certain spot, all I do is pull out the club I can hit 181 steps." All golfers should be so lucky.

Although his ability to be precise was a significant factor in making Jack a champion, the fact that he slept ten hours a night during tournament week probably gave him another edge. In any event, the Wanamaker Trophy now had the name Jack Nicklaus engraved on it for the fifth time.

# CHAPTER 31

# Hollywood Jack

Although he didn't win the 1965 PGA Championship (he was runner-up to Dave Marr with rounds of 69-70-71-71 (281) at Laurel Valley), Nicklaus's relationship with the media during that tournament revealed another dimension of Jack's personality: He never knew a press conference he didn't like.

Charlie Nicklaus taught Jack from the beginning to be accessible to the media. On the golf course, Jack was singularly focused, to such a degree that some thought he was lost in space. But when the television lights glowed or a wired microphone was in the vicinity or a reporter started scribbling, Nicklaus became a star. He loved to talk, and his only regret was that the interviews often ended before he was finished outlining the details of each shot.

Some competitors mocked Nicklaus. One called him "Mr. Hollywood," an apt moniker indeed, for Nicklaus craved the limelight. His desire for media attention was best exemplified by his comment one year at the PGA Championship, "Thank goodness I made the last birdie," he said. "I was afraid I wouldn't get to be in the [press] tent."

Reporters appreciated his accessibility. ESPN's Jimmy Roberts said Nicklaus "always had time for people. At St. Andrew's in 1995, Jack took that ten out of the bunker. Yet after that horrendous experience, I saw him standing in the rain talking about it."

When asked why he enjoyed talking to the press when so many others abhorred it, Nicklaus replied, "[Interviews] help me unwind from the tension that accumulates during a tournament round. . . . I simply enjoy talking golf with a lively, interested audience, and the press fellows are that."

It wasn't always that way. Early in his career, Nicklaus learned important lessons. "As an amateur," he said, "I was so forthright that if

215

someone asked me how I was playing, it never occurred to me not to say, 'Just great' if I was playing that well. Sometimes this was interpreted as cockiness and brashness, when all it was in truth was delight. Today, if any young athlete were to ask my advice, I would counsel him not to be too slick, to be himself, and to try and temper honesty with tactfulness." Richard Hinds of the *Melbourne Age* recalled a time when Jack was asked his opinion of the revered Royal Melbourne course designed by Alister MacKenzie. "When Jack said it was a 'good member's course,' he meant that as a compliment, but the press had a field day with the remark."

Dick Taylor said that Nicklaus got along with the European press much better than the domestic press. "The Europeans asked better questions," he said. "Over there they have a small contingent of media who follow every tournament. Their questions are much more focused, and Jack liked that, liked the volley back and forth."

Although Nicklaus had a professional but distant relationship with most of the media, he was always fond of the quick-witted Taylor. At one press conference, Jack wasn't pleased with the questioning, so he looked over at Dick Taylor and said, "Why don't you show these fellows how to ask a good question?" Taylor, never at a loss for words, quickly replied, "I've always wanted to ask you, Jack. What flavor of ice cream cone did you choose between nines at the 1989 Open at Oak Hill?" After a good belly laugh, Nicklaus replied, "Pralines and cream. You probably would have had vanilla."

Dick Taylor has also been a favorite foil for Nicklaus. Once, the discussion at a news conference turned to American Frances Ouimet's defeat of British legends Harry Vardon and Ted Ray at the 1913 United States Open at The Country Club in Brookline, Massachusetts. When someone asked for details of the tournament, Nicklaus pointed to Taylor and quipped, "Why don't you ask Taylor, he covered it!"

Contemporary journalists still have a fascination with Nicklaus. The November 1994 issue of *Time* magazine, in a story entitled "All the Names Fit to Print," counted the number of times certain people appeared in the news from January to Labor Day. Nicklaus finished in fourth place (with 3,133 stories), behind President Bill Clinton (36,987), O.J. Simpson (10,866), and Michael Jordan (6,275). He joined the list just ahead of Jackie Onassis (2,491), John Daly (2,293), Arnold Palmer (2,073), and Beavis and Butt-head (1,336).

Even at age fifty-four, Jack maintained his relevancy. That's because Jack always was the proverbial "good interview." Journalist Thomas Boswell observed,

Bobby Jones was certainly golf's best player-writer, but Nicklaus may have been its best extemporaneous player-talker. He wasn't funny or colorful or charismatic. Instead, he seemed to have a rarer gift: simple, unadorned insight. He knew exactly what was on his mind and, whenever politic, he said exactly that. He spoke almost without spin, with no double meaning or hidden agenda. His words were a pane of glass that revealed an analytical, well-lit, and fairly guileless mind.

After his first PGA Championship victory in 1963 at twenty-three, Jack Nicklaus was absent from the tournament's winner's circle for eight years. The return came in the 1971 tournament held in February at the PGA National Golf Club in Palm Beach Gardens, Florida. The course was a short drive from the Nicklaus home at Lost Tree.

When play began in the tournament, Jack was in a severe majors drought. At thirty-one, he'd only won one (the 1970 British Open) in the past four years. Because a quirk in the Tour schedule put the PGA Championship first in 1971, Jack was determined to prove he was still tops in the world.

Prior to the tournament, Jack practiced more intensely on the greens in Florida, which were 100 percent Bermuda grass. He had never won on that type of putting surface. In a move that recalled son Jackie's tip at Oak Hill in 1980, friend and fellow professional Deane Beman advised Jack during a game of bridge that he needed to "complete his backstroke."

The tip came after Nicklaus shot 80 during a practice round with Beman. The future PGA Tour Commissioner told him he hadn't been finishing his backswing with the putting stroke. While other players, like Lee Trevino, preferred to correct problems on their own, Nicklaus wasn't that way. LPGA Tour great Carol Mann said, "Above all, Jack was very coachable. He wanted to learn. He knew it made him a better player."

In this instance, Nicklaus paid attention to Beman because he had never putted well on Bermuda greens. "Jack grew up on bent grass greens," Beman recalled. "I told him he needed to be a little less rushed with his stroke. When he didn't complete his backswing, that knocked the ball off line." During a session on the artificial turf behind Jack's house, Beman became the instructor. "Deane showed me how I had shortened my backswing. It was causing me to lift [the putter] and hit down on the ball," Jack said. "So I started thinking, 'finish your backswing,' and immediately I got the ball rolling better."

Nicklaus found another ally with his putting that week. "The other gimmick I used," he explained, "was to line up my putter by concentrating on the two lines across its top instead of the blade itself. I'd never done that in my life before, but it worked wonders for me."

The result of those revelations was an excellent first three rounds of putting, resulting in scores of 69, 69, and 70. Nicklaus led by four as the final eighteen holes began. Approaching the seventeenth tee, four bogeys and two birdies cut his lead to only two strokes over Billy Casper.

Despite the 588-yard length of the par five, Nicklaus knew a prestigious drive and ample second shot could reach the green. The question was whether he wanted to hit a driver or play cautiously with a three-wood off the tee.

The resulting choice showed Nicklaus as a champion who never threw away opportunities to win. Even though he realized Billy Casper, playing ahead of him, might birdie eighteen, Nicklaus dodged the temptation to go for broke on seventeen. Instead, he hit a precise three-wood off the tee. As he approached his second shot, he heard the roar of the crowd at eighteen. Casper had made birdie. Nonplussed, Nicklaus stuck to his strategy and hit a one-iron short of the bunkers that guarded the green. A superb pitching wedge shot rolled to within five feet of the hole. The putt was automatic for birdie. He then parred eighteen to seal the victory by two shots. Jack was back. Again.

Within the next four years, Nicklaus returned to his native state of Ohio to win his third and fourth PGA Championship crowns.

In 1973, Nicklaus sparkled in the PGA Championship at Canterbury Golf Club in Cleveland, designed in 1922 by Herbert Bertram Strong, a native of Sandwich, England.

Prior to Canterbury, called "one of the temples of golf" by former USGA President Sandy Tatum, Nicklaus had close calls in the Masters (tied for third), the U.S. Open (tied for fourth), and the British Open (fourth). For fourteen months Jack had tried without success to pass Bobby Jones's major championship mark of thirteen tournaments.

Nicklaus fired a 72 in the opening round, but back-to-back 68s gave him a one-shot lead over Mason Rudolph and Don Iverson with eighteen holes to play. In the final round, both challengers faded, and Nicklaus's lead grew two shots over playing companion Bruce Crampton.

The pivotal hole was the fourteenth, where Jack drove to the deep rough. Crampton was next to the out of bounds markers on the left, yet Nicklaus was no better off, since a dead tree blocked his path to the green. Hitting the ball over the obstacle was not an option, so Jack had to decide between hooking the ball around the right side or fading it just past the left side of the tree.

Realizing that due to lack of control hooking the ball from the long grass was the high-risk shot, Nicklaus opted for the fade. He set up in an open stance and positioned the ball back. Utilizing a firm left-hand grip, he exploded down through the ball. It leaped off to the left of the tree trunk, faded at just the correct angle, hit short of the green, and bounded to within thirty feet of the hole. Two putts later, Nicklaus owned par. The last four holes proved to be anticlimactic. Nicklaus was on a mission, one he completed in style with a four-stroke victory. Bruce Crampton was second, recalling, "Jack had the game that day, and I didn't."

The final-round 69 enabled Nicklaus to not only break Bobby Jones's mark but to surpass Walter Hagen, who had recorded eleven major victories. After the round, Nicklaus played down the significance of his achievement. "Fourteen [majors] is just a number," he said. "You have to wait for history to list the records."

Nicklaus's regard for the feat was more accurately revealed in a statement he'd made earlier about his longtime idol. He told *Golf Digest*, "Rocky Marciano once told me that when he started boxing, Joe Louis was his idol and always remained so. When the two met, Rocky wanted to win very badly but never felt so badly about a fight after he had won. That's how I feel about Bob Jones."

Later, Nicklaus wouldn't remember the win as much as a special moment during the tournament when son Jackie urged his younger brother, Gary, then all of four, to slip through the ropes and give his dad a hug. He did so on the eighteenth green. The picture of Gary in Jack's arms as he left the green is Nicklaus's favorite photo of all time.

"What a great moment that was," Tour player Don Bies said. "One never to forget."

Then, in 1975 the tournament was held in Nicklaus's old back-yard at the Robert Trent Jones-designed Firestone Country Club in Akron, Ohio. The way he played the sixteenth hole in the third round was more revealing than the eventual two-stroke victory he achieved over a frustrated Bruce Crampton, four times a runner-up to Nicklaus in major tournaments on the regular PGA Tour.

Nicklaus took the lead in that third round despite what he later called "one of the dumbest played holes of my life." Trouble began on the redoubtable 625-yard, par-five sixteenth. After play at the fifteenth, caddie Angelo Argea handed Nicklaus a driver and headed down the sixteenth fairway. When Jack stood at the tee markers, he realized they had been moved up twenty-five yards. That meant water on the left came into play. Instead of calling Argea back on the hot, sultry afternoon and changing to a three-wood, Nicklaus decided to stay with the driver. When Nicklaus bombed the drive, the ball took a swim. He was now hitting three after the drop. A safety shot exploded out of a fluffy lie and bounded into the rough, behind a huge forty-foot tree some 140 yards from a green protected in front by a lake.

After that spot, Nicklaus told *Golf Magazine*, "I remember hearing Bob Rosburg, the ABC commentator, say, 'He's dead here. He's got absolutely no chance at all.'"

Always one to prove the experts wrong, Jack surveyed the shot. The safe play was a wedge to the fairway, a short iron to the green, and one or two putts for bogey six or double-bogey seven.

Instead, what followed was a Nicklaus classic, a shot that in all its components demonstrated the uncommon ability of the Golden Bear. With little room for error, and intense pressure building as the third round came to a close, Nicklaus gambled with an open-faced nine-iron. Setting the ball far forward in his stance, he hit a towering shot that narrowly missed the tree. Seconds later, it plopped down soft as a mother's kiss, thirty feet from the hole. Naturally, Nicklaus holed the putt and then strutted off the green with a par that CBS golf commentator Gary McCord recently said "would be a felony in some states."

His spirits buoyed, Nicklaus finished the third round with 67. Coupled with earlier scores of 70 and 68, he enjoyed a four-shot lead going into the final round. A safe 71 brought home the victory, but for all practical purposes, the inimitable nine-iron shot at sixteen had made the difference.

Even in victory, Nicklaus was quick to illustrate how mightily different his record was from that of Jones's, who, in contrast to Jack, earned victories in the only recognized majors of his day, the Amateur and Open championships held in the United States and Great Britain. Moreover, Jones won his thirteen majors over a seven-year period—

competing essentially in his spare time, because he was either in school or starting his law practice. Nicklaus required thirteen years to win his titles, a period when he concentrated on little but golf. Among his victories were those in the PGA Championships and the Masters, fledgling tournaments when Jones was competing. Nicklaus played in an average of twenty tournaments each year over the thirteen year span. Out of characteristic respect for his idol and for the facts, Jack observed, "In my view, *both* totals are records, and each should stand independently until they are broken in the same tournaments and by comparable types of players."

As impressive as Nicklaus's record in the PGA Championship was, a total of seven shots kept him from at least a playoff for four more titles.

He had a near miss at the Columbus Golf Club in 1964, where he finished three shots behind Bobby Nichols. At Laural Valley in '65, he lost the championship to Dave Marr by two shots. He finished a shot behind winner Lee Trevino at Tanglewood and one behind Hal Sutton, touted then as the next "Heir Bear," at Riviera in L.A. in 1983.

At the 1983 PGA Championship, Nicklaus exposed the golf world to two miracle rounds. At forty-three years of age, he delivered a superb 65 on Friday and then nearly matched it with a 66 on Sunday. Unfortunately, a first-round 73, including a disastrous double bogey at eighteen, cost him the tournament.

The unlikely finish was caused by an errant shot not typical of Nicklaus. Faced with a six-iron distance from the right side of the fairway, Jack attempted to fade the ball around a eucalyptus tree that hovered over the right rough. Unfortunately, the ball started right, continued right, hit a branch, and bounded down. When Nicklaus made double bogey and shot 73, *Los Angeles Times* writer Jim Murray saw fit to write a column telling readers that Nicklaus was finished in the majors. Jack was not pleased with Murray's requiem, especially since he considered him a friend.

Nicklaus's overall record in the PGA Championship included five wins, four runner-ups, and three third-place finishes. He was in the top ten a total of fifteen times.

In the thirteen-year period between 1963 and 1975, Nicklaus finished either first or second seven times in the PGA Championship. Only Walter Hagen's performance in the tournament during the twenties comes close to matching the records the Golden Bear set in that championship.

# CHAPTER 32

# Nicklaus and the British Open

One hundred and six years before Jack Nicklaus won his first British Open, Musselburgh, Scotland, professional Willie Park captured the first one. The event took place at Prestwick Golf Club near Ayrshire, Scotland, on October 17, 1860. Park and seven other professionals played twelve devilish holes with such names as Stone Dike, Tunnel In, Sea He'therick, and Alps.

Willie and the other competitors toured the course three times that day. The Scot was victorious with 174-strokes, forty-two shots over the "estimated par." Old Tom Morris, Prestwick's designer, was second, two shots back.

Unfortunately, Jack Nicklaus never competed in the British Open at fabled Prestwick, aptly labeled "The Home of the Open Championship." It was unfairly deleted from the Open "rotation," with the last one held there in 1925.

The first British Open championship for Nicklaus is not a pleasant memory. It was held at Troon, a windswept course on the west coast of Scotland that tossed and turned the shots of the recently crowned 1962 United States Open Champion so sufficiently that he finished with an 80. A second-round 72 permitted him to make the cut. Rounds of 74 and 79 followed, and Jack lumbered home, unhappy with the set of new Slazenger golf clubs that he was using under an endorsement contract arranged by business manager, Mark McCormack.

During that time, Nicklaus was playing in various special events. In 1962, he appeared on *Shell's Wonderful World of Golf* and television viewers witnessed Nicklaus defeat Sam Snead with a birdie on the final hole at Pebble Beach. After that, McCormack (called "the father of specialty golf") arranged for a series called *Challenge Golf*. In the match held during 1962, Nicklaus and Phil Rodgers played Arnold

Palmer and Gary Player in a four-ball match at the Los Angeles Country Club, losing three to two.

"I never could figure out why Jack wanted me as a partner, because we got beat all the time," Rodgers remembered. "In that match Arnold chipped in all over the place and they sent us home early."

In 1963, Nicklaus made another appearance on *Challenge Golf*. He and Mike Souchak lost to Palmer and Player, also McCormack clients, two and one. "They beat our butts," Souchak recalled.

The next year, Nicklaus beat Palmer and Player in eight "Big Three" tournaments, four at the Firestone Country Club and four in Hawaii. Four more were held the next year.

Nicklaus's promotion wizard then brought the bigtop show to Europe. In 1966, McCormack made an agreement with the British Broadcasting Company for a program called *The Big Three in Britain*. Palmer, Player, and Nicklaus played two matches at Carnoustie and one each at Gleneagles and St. Andrews. When they tied, a playoff was held in Puerto Rico, where Palmer was the eventual winner.

The matches in Scotland were televised after the 1966 British Open. Days before the event, Nicklaus went head-to-head with Peter Allis as part of a series of matches dubbed by McCormack, "The USA against the World." Later, McCormack took the roadshow to Japan, where he made even more money for himself and his clients.

Jack Nicklaus's first British Open challenge came in 1963. That tournament was held at Lytham and St. Annes, and Nicklaus nearly pulled off a victory. Before the tournament, he was even more confident than usual. "From the start I felt I was going to win it," he said later.

Playing with that frame of mind, he took the lead in the fourth round. Then, he made an uncharacteristic mistake. When he birdied the sixteenth, he thought the margin was two strokes over Bob Charles and Phil Rodgers. Actually, it was one. When both Charles and Rodgers, playing behind Jack, birdied the sixteenth, they were dead even with Nicklaus, although he didn't realize it.

"Television was wrong with the scores," Rodgers remembered. "The scores were mixed up. But I knew where we stood. When Bob and I were on the eighteenth tee, I told Bob, 'This is between you and me.'"

The seventeenth had proven to be pivotal for Nicklaus. After a splendid drive, he was left with long-iron distance to the green on the 427-yard par-four that Bobby Jones made famous in 1926 when he hit a perfect mashie (five-iron) shot to the green on the way to his first British Open Championship.

The dilemma for Nicklaus involved whether to use a two- or three-iron. In the morning round (thirty-six holes were played on the last day), the three-iron, from ten yards less distance than he faced now, came up twenty feet short of the hole.

With that in mind, Nicklaus selected the two-iron. He addressed the ball with the hope of boring it toward the green and a potential birdie. But his adrenaline created too much power, and the shot landed well past the cup and bounded into thick rough. A poor chip caused a bogey.

At eighteen, Nicklaus made a second late-round mistake that cost him the championship. For the first time all week, he hit just a hint of a hook (he called it "The Nicklaus Special") off the tee, and the ball glanced the rough and bounded into a deep, highly-lipped bunker on the left. A side-saddle recovery was needed. Nicklaus wedged the ball back toward the fairway utilizing the club invented by Gene Sarazen. His third shot catapulted the ball to within twenty feet, but Nicklaus two-putted for bogey, believing that was all that was required to win his first British Open.

On the eighteenth, Charles and Rodgers both hit the green in regulation, but Phil had the advantage. "Bob had a seventy-footer, and I was fifteen feet away," he said. "His approach left him a putt of seven feet. I sniveled a putt up about two and a half feet short. Bob made his par putt, and then I gagged and vomited a putt that rimmed the hole and fell in."

One indication of how time can dull one's memory is evident in Bob Charles's version of the hole when compared to Rodgers's. "My putt was actually about forty-five feet," Charles said. "I hit it to within five. Then Phil hit a putt from fifteen feet that was wide and two feet short. He putted out. The ball caught the edge of the hole and spun around, then dropped. He heaved a sigh of relief, pulled off his cap, and put it over the hole. The reserved English gallery didn't know quite what to think. Then he removed the hat and gave me a view of the cup. I holed my putt to set up the playoff. That Phil is something."

Nicklaus's back-to-back, bogey-bogey finish meant he was short by a shot. In the thirty-six-hole playoff, Charles prevailed (140 to 148) and became the first left-hander ever to win a major championship. "I'm the only person to lose a major to a left-hander," Rodgers joked.

The 1963 British Open saw the start of a player-caddie relationship between Jack and Yorkshireman Jimmy Dickinson. Like Angelo Argea in America, Dickinson became a fixture with Nicklaus in

Europe, in spite of the fact that Nicklaus's strong personality made the caddie extremely nervous, causing him to have ulcers.

Nicklaus's thoughts about the British linksland courses were quite harsh and perhaps a bit pompous. "I don't much care for courses that represent the extreme in British linksland conditions—courses where the fairways and greens are so hard and fast that on every approach shot you must land the ball many yards short of the green and hope you have correctly estimated the amount of bound and run the ball will have. . . . This, as I see it, puts too much of a premium on luck and not enough on ball control."

At St. Andrews in 1964, the year Bill Campbell beat the talented amateur Ed Tutwiler in the finals of the United States Amateur, Nicklaus fell five shots short of win to popular "Champagne" Tony Lema. Jack couldn't catch the devil-may-care Lema, even though he set a final day thirty-six-hole record with rounds of 66 and 68.

Nicklaus dug himself too deep a hole with his first-round 76, recorded on a day when the 50 m.p.h. winds were gale force strength. But the 1964 tournament was dominated by Tony Lema, and although Arnold Palmer did not enter, his influence was strongly felt—Champagne Tony used a driver he borrowed from Arnie and employed the services of Tip Anderson, the stalwart caddie who had toiled for Arnie in three previous championships.

After his victory, the effervescent Lema joked with reporters about how he'd spend the prize money. "I'm only the third leading money winner in America," he said, "but I'm the leading money spender."

The year after Lema's win at St. Andrews, Nicklaus was twelfth at Royal Birkdale, where Peter Thomson won the last of his five Open Championships. That year, Nicklaus turned twenty-five. Barbara had a birthday party for him, complete with cake and candles. At the appropriate time, Jack huffed and puffed and tried to blow out the twenty-five candles. Try as he might, he couldn't blow them out (they were trick candles that kept relighting), prompting Arnold Palmer, sitting at a table nearby, to give Jack a new title, "The Bear with No Air."

Nicklaus began to wonder if he'd ever win the claret jug given to the British Open champion. In the early seventies, he admitted, "To earn a rating among the world's finest golfers, a man must win the British Open, and I had begun to get it into my head that, for one reason or another, the Open might always elude me."

Nicklaus's breakthrough win came in 1966 at his favorite British course, Muirfield. Seven years after he'd first played there in the Walker Cup, Nicklaus produced a win he later said he was "as proud of . . . as anything I've achieved in golf." That performance came after Nicklaus decided he needed a different mind-set for Scottish and British courses. He admitted his attitude was a dour one and intended to remedy the situation at Muirfield, an inland course much more to his liking. When he arrived at the course for practice, he was shocked by what he saw.

Muirfield had played host to nine British Opens by the time Nicklaus competed in 1966, the first being held in 1892. Through all the championship rounds played on the ancient course, it had never played with more difficulty than it did in 1966. The officials attempted to restrict the advantage of the long-hitting Americans by narrowing the fairways to twenty-five yards and permitting the rough to grow long enough that Doug Sanders exclaimed, "I wish I had the hay concession."

Nicklaus thought what the Royal and Ancient Golf Club had done to Muirfield was a sin, and he said so. His comments were not appreciated. Sometime after the initial shock and before the tournament started Jack got his head straight, and his play was exemplary. Later he would recall how he thought the course had been tricked up and what he had decided to do about it. "The fairways at Muirfield that year were certainly among the slenderest I have ever encountered, and the rough quite definitely the most penal I've ever experienced anywhere in the world," he observed. "[It] was waist high and waving at you like Kansas wheat on a majority of the holes."

Jack's frustration with the course could have either sent him reeling or inspired him. As it would most times in his career, the latter occurred.

Nicklaus's positive attitude gave him a convincing edge over the grouchy field. "I was able to look at the event not in terms of my hole-by-hole score or even my day-by-day score," he said, "but as a seventy-two hole contest within which there would inevitably be considerable fluctuation of fortune involved, including myself."

Nicklaus was in a great frame of mind on the eve of the tournament. "It was still Muirfield, and if anyone could handle it," he said, "I could. After all, I was an old Muirfield man."

Proving that to be true, Nicklaus was at the lead by three after two rounds, and by seven midway through the third. Using his driver sparingly, he kept the ball out of the rigorous rough and flushed out birdies with precision iron shots. A back nine collapse to 39 on Saturday, however, put him two shots behind Phil Rodgers, who'd closed his round with a remarkable 30 on the backside. Sunday saw Nicklaus return to form in blustery, westerly winds.

A birdie at the first hole was a fine beginning, and after 33 on the front side and a par at ten, Nicklaus led by three. Then a miss of a fifteen-inch tap-in at eleven sliced the lead, and Nicklaus began to play what he later called "jittery golf." The thirteenth proved pivotal with Nicklaus hitting a smoking duck hook toward the heavy heather. Luck was with him, because the ball was hit so far left it catapulted into lighter rough where the gallery had walked. Par resulted, then Nicklaus bogeyed the par-three thirteenth. Another bogey at fourteen, and Jack was now tied for the lead with four to play. Since Welshman Dave Thomas, who'd told a sportswriter he had his eye on a new Aston Martin if he won, and Doug Sanders had both finished at 283, Nicklaus would need four pars to win.

A superb two-putt par at fifteen from forty feet over the "Camel's Back" hump in the green brought the 198-yard, par-three sixteenth into view. There, with the wind howling behind him, Nicklaus hit the ball to within thirty feet and when he safely two-putted, two pars on the last two-holes would give him the championship.

Nicklaus's play was significant because many saw a "different" Jack in the final round of the '66 British Open. He somehow was able to fight off not only adverse feelings about the course set-up but also a downward trend toward bogeys by parring both the fifteenth and six-teenth holes to stay near the lead. Winning six majors by this time and being an established world class player, Nicklaus showed maturity in his play. He used every bit of physical strength and internal fortitude in fighting back the tendency to lose a championship he coveted as much as the one he had lost just three years earlier at Royal Lytham and St. Annes. There, his opening round of 83, the highest score he ever had in a major tournament, caused one British reporter to say, "I've always wanted to play like Jack Nicklaus, and now I do."

The battle in 1966 continued at the seventeenth. Later, he recalled his emotions on the hole. "I walked to the seventeenth tee full of confi-dence, a different man. I was no longer thinking about how I might lose the championship, I was thinking about how I might win it."

At the 528-yard, par-five seventeenth, which features a blind tee shot, Nicklaus drew out a three-iron and hit the fairway, some 240 yards from the green.

Nicklaus now faced an important decision. Normally he utilized a 1-iron from 240 yards, but the elements and his mental make-up made it imperative that he think through the shot choices very carefully. Exhibiting the ability to calculate with a clear mind under extreme pressure, he started with the normal club selection of a one-iron and worked backward. First, Jack took off one club since he was using the smaller British ball. The favorable wind caused him to subtract another one and one half clubs.

Another half club was taken off when he considered the adrenaline coursing through him. The correct club selection, Jack then deduced, was a four-iron. But hard ground in front of the green required yet another club reduction.

With a five-iron in hand, Nicklaus swung with confidence and great precision. The wind grasped the ball exactly as he visualized it would, sending it spiraling across the musky gray sky. It hit on a perfect hard spot just short of the green, bounding forward at just the right pace and finishing fifteen feet from the hole.

The huge Scottish crowd applauded the effort, and when Nicklaus barely missed an eagle attempt but made birdie, he knew bogey or better at the 430-yard, par-four eighteenth would give him his first British Open Championship. If he succeeded, he would join Harry Vardon, James Braid, and Gary Player, all of whom had captured their initial titles at Muirfield.

Nicklaus's razor-sharp one-iron split the eighteenth fairway, just 210 yards from the green. For his approach to the green, Jack first chose a four iron but then hit a slight left-to-right, high-flying three-iron that nestled twenty-five feet from the hole. Lagging putts of that distance was a Nicklaus specialty, and his effort stopped the ball eight inches from the hole. When he tapped the short putt in, Jack Nicklaus had won his first British Open Championship, one he thought he might never capture. Doug Sanders was stymied again, and Thomas canceled his order for the Aston Martin.

With Barbara at his side, Jack fought back tears at the presentation ceremony. "I hadn't been at all sure that I would ever be up there standing beside that trophy—a high-ball hitter like me who couldn't handle hard linksland fairways," he said later. Jack, the high-ball hitter, had learned a thing or two about how to play in Scotland, and some important things about himself as well.

Later Nicklaus talked about his new-found maturity and the winning experience. "I don't know what lay behind this stroke of intelligence, this sudden burst of maturity, but I think it must have been Muirfield itself," he observed. "The memory of the 1959 Walker Cup match was still fresh in my mind. That whole week at Muirfield . . . had personified sport at its best, people at their best, the world at its best."

## CHAPTER 33

# Classic Confrontations

The British Open victory at Muirfield was followed by second-place finishes at Hoylake and at Carnoustie. In 1967, Nicklaus finished two shots behind Robert DeVicenzo at Hoylake. At Carnoustie in 1969, Nicklaus's complaints about the shape of the terrain on one hole caused the membership to position a bunker on the exact spot where he could reach it. He and Bob Charles lost by two strokes to Gary Player. That was followed by a sixth-place showing at Royal Lytham, where Tony Jacklin triumphed.

In 1970 Nicklaus began play in the 105th British Open at St. Andrews. Home to twenty Opens prior to 1970, the storied course tested the might of such great international players as Lee Trevino, Tony Jacklin, Harold Henning, Doug Sanders, and Peter Thomson.

Nicklaus's passion to win at the "Old Course" was well known. Since his early years, he'd felt that no professional golfer could ever rest easy if they hadn't won at St. Andrews. He'd been runner-up to Tony Lema in 1964, but the five-stroke margin hadn't permitted him to sniff victory.

Prior to the tournament, Nicklaus glimpsed the rich history of the legendary Open when the Royal and Ancient Golf Club hosted a gathering of past champions. Rubbing elbows with Gene Sarazen, Bobby Locke, Henry Cotton, Arnold Palmer, Peter Thomas, Bob Charles, and Gary Player made Nicklaus even more determined to bring home a win.

Nicklaus opened with 68 and 69 to be positioned just one shot back of Lee Trevino. A third-round 73 dropped him another stroke back. The Merry Mex then skied to 77, leaving the door open for Nicklaus's 73 to nip him by a shot. Sanders actually had the tournament won, but after hitting the final green in regulation, he missed a slippery three-footer for par that caused one of the great "oohs" in St. Andrews gallery history.

That putt came as Nicklaus sat in the scorers' tent next to Tony Jacklin, who was beating himself up for not playing better. Jack was certain Sanders was going to make his putt, but Jacklin wasn't so sure. "I'll give you ten thousand pounds for your chance to win," he said to Nicklaus, making him laugh. Sanders then missed the putt.

Nicklaus dominated the playoff the following day until the last few holes. He led Sanders by four with five holes to play, but then the American with the rickety-rock, short backswing made his move. By the time they had played the 358-yard, par-four eighteenth, he'd closed to within one shot.

Determined to make birdie, Jack hit a thundering drive of more than 360 yards. It hit on the hard ground and scurried through the green into heavy rough halfway up the bank. When Sanders produced a superlative pitch and run shot to provide him a birdie opportunity from six feet, Nicklaus knew he had to get down in two to win the title outright.

Since the green at eighteen slopes down from back to front, Nicklaus knew a delicate shot was required. A scuff would leave the ball on the upper part of the green, a shot too hard and the ball would roll into the dreaded "Valley of Sin" set beyond the hole location at the front of the green.

Choosing a sand wedge for the critical shot, Nicklaus took several practice swings to capture the feel of the task facing him. He positioned the ball to the front part of an open stance and swung parallel to the downhill slope. The ball popped cleanly and rolled to within ten feet. When the putt found the bottom of the cup, Nicklaus hurled his putter skyward, nearly beaning the distraught Sanders, who, in spite of Nicklaus's ostentatious enthusiasm, was most gracious in defeat.

The win at St. Andrews in 1970 marked what many felt was the end of the first third of Nicklaus's career. At the ripe old age of thirty, he had collected *ten* major championships and twenty-four Tour victories.

At the start of 1971, Nicklaus began an incredibly consistent streak unmatched by any professional golfer before or since. In the next forty major tournaments he entered during the ten years that followed, Nicklaus won nine times and had twenty-two top-three finishes. He recorded six fourth-place finishes and was in the top ten a remarkable thirty-five times in thirty-six events.

Three victories apiece in the Tournament of Champions and the

Tournament Players' Championship, both just a step below the majors, added more luster to his stellar career.

At British Open championships, Nicklaus tied for fifth at Royal Birkdale in '71, was second at Muirfield in '72, fourth at Troon in '73, third at Royal Lytham in '74, tied for third at Carnoustie in '75 (despite confidence brought on by practice rounds of 67, 65, and 67), and tied for second at Royal Birkdale in '76.

That year Nicklaus actually lost the tournament at the 468-yard, par-four sixth hole in the final round. Although he started the Sunday finale three shots behind Johnny Miller, he birdied the third and fourth holes to threaten the leaders.

At the sixth, Nicklaus hit a darting one-iron short of the bunkers. He faced 240 yards to the green, which was set on an uphill incline entirely bordered by trees.

Even though one-iron shots had proved pivotal in many Nicklaus triumphs, the club bit him this time. On the downswing, he failed to stay behind the ball. The result was a pushed shot that landed in the brush—Jack never found the ball. A double-bogey six left him too far behind the leaders to catch up. Johnny Miller emerged as champion.

A year later, Nicklaus had his whirlwind confrontation with Tom Watson at Turnberry. Journalists have called the shoot-out in 1977 "golf at its best," "the most perfect championship ever played," and "the greatest golf match ever." It certainly was the finest of all Nicklaus man-to-man duels, even overshadowing the legendary ones with Arnold Palmer.

The site was the seaside links at Turnberry, a picturesque, celestial creation where time seems to stand still. In the forties famed journalist Henry Longhurst wrote about the legendary course: "In those long periods inseparable from wartime service where there is nothing to do but sit and think, I used to find myself sitting and thinking of the time when once again I might be playing golf at Turnberry."

Originally designed in 1909 by Willie Fernie, whose son Tom was Turnberry's first golf professional, the course sits above Turnberry Bay. It might be best described by golf course designer Pete Dye, who recalled, "I was dazzled to see beautiful vistas of the sea, the rolling sand dunes, the vast open areas where the holes were built, and the incredible rock formation that bordered the seaside holes at Turnberry."

The course was christened as a new home for the British Open in 1977. Although most of the finest players were there, it was Jack and Tom, two athletes whose first names were all sports fans needed to identify them, who brought high drama to center stage. After two rounds, they posted identical 68, 70 scores. Then they rocked the field with superlative 65s to lead their closest pursuers by three shots. Their tie meant they would be paired together for the first time in a final round of a major championship.

Nicklaus knew Watson was a formidable opponent. On the eve of the tournament, he told reporters, "If I'm playing Tom Watson, I know I have to win. With somebody else, you feel maybe they'll lose instead."

The fourth-round battle seemed destined for British Open folklore. A drought had made Turnberry play fast and furious, but Nicklaus and Watson were precision craftsmen, both at the pinnacle of their games.

Jack vaulted to the lead with two quick birdies and led by three. Watson countered with three birdies at the fifth, seventh, and eighth to pull even. A bogey at nine left him a shot behind Nicklaus.

At twelve, Jack led by two. In seventy-two appearances in major championships, Nicklaus had never lost when leading by two shots with six to play. Major number seventeen seemed all but in the bag for the Golden Bear, but Watson persevered.

Displaying the finest iron play of his career, Watson birdied thirteen from twelve feet. He scored another birdie at fifteen when he hit an astonishing sixty-foot putt from light rough that hit the flag stick and dove into the cup. Now the two were dead even. "Jack and Tom looked at each other," *Sports Illustrated*'s Dan Jenkins later wrote of the sixteenth tee. "The blonde and the redhead. Yesterday and today. Then and now. Dominguin and Ordonez."

"This is what it's all about," Tom said.

"You bet it is," Jack replied.

The Stanford Cardinal had made up three shots in five holes to nose ahead by one with one hole remaining when Nicklaus uncharacteristically missed a four-footer on seventeen for birdie to match the birdie Watson had holed.

The final hole, a 431-yard, par four now tested the two warriors. Watson, driving first, hit a winner one-iron straight and true, but Nicklaus under extended and hit a right-to-right shot that drove into devilish rough a millimeter from an ugly gorse bush.

Sensing victory, Watson paced the fairway as Jack evaluated his chances. Tom had 180 yards to the flag stick. He first chose a six-iron, then reconsidered. Pulling a seven-iron from the bag, Watson then hit the shot of a lifetime, an arching beauty that wafted softly onto the green and trickled to within twenty-four inches of the cup. Dan Jenkins later called the shot as one that "stuck to the flag like an arrow in the ribs of the bear." The enthusiastic crowd drowned the countryside with cheers. Watson had sealed the door; Jack would surely take heed and surrender.

Somehow, through pure resolve and fighting spirit, Nicklaus dislodged his ball from its nasty spot and sped it toward the green. It bounded on, thirty feet from the cup.

True to tradition, the Scottish gallerys rushed to where Nicklaus had hit the shot. They dropped two-penny and six-penny coins on the exact spot where Jack had torn away the turf. The pile of coins was meant to ensure success with the birdie putt. Success at that moment meant making the long birdie putt, even if Nicklaus couldn't win the Open.

On the way to the green, Watson told his caddie he expected Nicklaus to make the putt.

Even though the length of Watson's putt made it a near-gimme, Nicklaus never stopped hoping. Facing almost certain defeat, he rammed the birdie straight into the cup. The Scots who had dropped the coins went wild. The legend, its seemed, was indeed true. Tom Watson just smiled and then went to work. Nothing Nicklaus did surprised him. He carefully lined up the two-footer and hit it straight and true. The crowd went "potty," according to writer David Davies of the *Guardian*.

Watson's 268 topped the field by eleven shots: Nicklaus's 269 outdistanced Hubert Green by ten shots. Spectators and an international television audience were held spellbound by the supernal play of the two.

After the round, Dan Jenkins said Nicklaus, with longtime American caddie Angelo Argea beside him, had the expression of an aging gunfighter. "I just couldn't shake him," Nicklaus said of Watson.

By all accounts, Nicklaus should have been a picture of disappointment. Barbara certainly was—she cried, the first time any of the observers had ever seen her do that.

When asked by his long-time friend and collaborator Ken Bowden if he wanted to cancel their dinner plans, Jack, ever the gallant sportsman, put his hand on Bowden's shoulder and said, "What's the matter, Kenny. It's only a game."

One year after that memorable event, Nicklaus returned to St. Andrews in search of his third British Open championship.

The 1978 tournament at St. Andrews would be remembered as one in which Lanny Wadkins recorded two eights at fourteen, Arnold Palmer made two sevens on the famed "Road Hole" seventeenth, and

Japan's Tommy Nakajima became infamous after a round-three escapade in the left greenside bunker at seventeen. He kept flapping away at the ball and ended up with a nine that dropped him out of contention. Thereafter, the bunker became known as the "Sands of Nakajima."

For this tournament, Nicklaus had a new weapon, a steel-shaft, wooded-head driver that measured 43½ inches. For years, he had used one that was 1⅜ inches shorter. The new one also had a little less loft, and the combination permitted him to draw the ball better than before.

Nicklaus's careful preparation for the British Open in 1978 paid off. While other contenders chose to sightsee and play other courses in the area, Nicklaus practiced at the Old Course. He was thirty-eight years old at the time and knew there wouldn't be many more chances to win at St. Andrews. In search of his eighteenth major championship in sixteen years, he played the extra practice round with the wind 180 degrees opposite its usual course. That meant the opening holes played into the wind while the homebound holes would play with it.

Nicklaus couldn't match America's Ben Crenshaw and Tom Kite, Britain's Pete Oosterhuis, or Japan's Isao Aoki for thirty-six holes, but a third-round 69 catapulted him into contention. On the morning of the last round, the wind conditions were just as Nicklaus had experienced during his extra practice round.

With no major victories in nearly thirty-six months, Nicklaus wanted this British Open desperately. By the time he approached the legendary "Road Hole" seventeenth, a 461-yard par four where the tee shot is hit directly over the corner of the Old Course Hotel, the championship edged within his grasp.

When Nicklaus made birdie and playing companion Simon Owen, a native of New Zealand, bogeyed at sixteen, the lead dropped to one stroke. At seventeen, Jack placed a three-wood tee shot dead center in the fairway. Owen ended his chance to win by duck-hooking a drive and then hitting his second across the road and out of bounds.

Only Englishman Pete Oosterhuis lurked behind Nicklaus. Jack knew a third British Open title was his if he could par the "Road Hole," which Ben Crenshaw labeled a "tough par four because it's a par five." Deliberation as to what strategy provided the greatest chance to make par told Nicklaus that a mid-iron intended to land the ball anywhere close to the flag stick, set back and left, was risky. If the shot was short to the left, Jack knew the deep pot bunker would devour it. If long, out of bounds might be the result, since the distance between the front of the green beyond the bunker and the back was only a few paces, and the wall bordering the road lurked just a few more paces from there.

Exhibiting his ability to think clearly in pressure situations and to never beat himself, Nicklaus chose the safer play, a six-iron that headed for the depression in front of the green and to the right of the pot bunker where John Daly hit his electrifying shot en route to winning the 1995 British Open.

True to his plan, the six-iron produced a ball that ended up in the hollow. A superb lag putt that yielded par proved fatal to the competition, and Nicklaus's 69 beat Simon Owen, Ray Floyd, Crenshaw, and Kite by two strokes.

Television commentator and journalist Jack Whitaker remembers vividly the moment Nicklaus walked up the eighteenth fairway toward the green. "It remains for me," he said recently, "the finest ovation I've ever seen anybody get—actor, politician, athlete, anyone—because of the nature of the applause, where it was, who was giving it, and to whom it was being given. It was almost stately. It wasn't a cheering and yelling, there was a warmth to it as if the crowd was saying 'You are so good, you are the very best from the Scots themselves.'"

Nicklaus had earned his third British Open Crown. More importantly, he had become the only golfer to record three wins in each of the four professional Grand Slam events.

The three wins, along with seven second-place and three third-place finishes, made Jack Nicklaus one of the most decorated golfers in British Open history. The achievement was no surprise to W. J. Ferguson, the wily English golf professional at the Harrogate Golf Club in Yorkshire, England and the coach for European champion Colin Montgomerie. "I watched Nicklaus play many times," Ferguson said, "and he had the greatest will to win of any golfer I ever saw."

# CHAPTER 34

# Nicklaus and the Masters

CBS broadcaster Jim Nantz said it best in a prelude to the 1996 Masters. "It's easy to feel like you're suspended in time at Augusta," he told his audience, unaware that he had just described Jack Nicklaus's play over a span of thirty-four years and counting.

The Golden Bear's record at the Masters, a bona fide American institution like the Rose Bowl, the Kentucky Derby, and the Indianapolis 500, is unparalleled. Six times he won the revered green jacket, more than any other golfer. On four other occasions, Jack was a bridesmaid. His championships were scattered over twenty-three years, and he is the oldest man ever to win a major championship, having done so in storybook fashion in 1986 at the age of forty-six.

What had been known as the Bobby Jones Invitational, in 1954, became the Masters. Twenty champions had been crowned by then, including Horton Smith, Gene Sarazen, Byron Nelson, Jimmy Demaret, Sam Snead, and Ben Hogan. Of equal importance was Dwight Eisenhower's presence in the White House that year. The President had been a member of Augusta National, located near Atlanta, Georgia, for six years. His golf score was a source of great speculation, often competing with hard news for front page attention.

Amateur Billy Joe Patton helped popularize the Masters that same year by coming within a single shot of beating Sam Snead and Ben Hogan, the two best players in the world at that time. Television emerged two years later; the Masters, with its alluring azaleas and lush, verdant greens and fairways stirring the passions of still-snowbound northerners, was an instant success with viewers. Jack Burke Jr. beat Ken Venturi in the '56 tournament. Golf journalist and historian Charles Price pointed out that Augusta is a major championship "in spite of the fact that it is actually not the championship of a country or a state or anything." It was simply the Masters, held on a majestic course that Bobby Jones and Alister MacKenzie crafted from a 365-acre nursery known as Fruitlands.

Over the years, the Masters achieved "event" status. Although the United States Open remained the most prestigious tournament, an invitation to the Masters induced a whoop and holler among golfers. After they'd competed at Augusta, the thought of not doing so devastated them. Amateur Bill Hyndman, who competed ten times, said his wife Ginny told him, "You aren't fit to live with when you miss one."

Jack Nicklaus first played in the Masters, which is by invitation only, as an amateur in 1959. He failed to make the cut, but it wasn't a total loss. The food was great, and he and fellow amateur Phil Rodgers ate well. Abusing a privilege that permitted them to "sign" for everything, the two gobbled down two steaks and two shrimp cocktails at every dinner until they were reprimanded by club officials. "They changed the rules on us," Rodgers said. "I guess ordering chateaubriand for two did the trick."

Nicklaus's golf score was 150, putting him on the sidelines for the final thirty-six holes. He hit thirty-one of thirty-six greens in regulation but was so baffled by Augusta's greens that he three-putted eight times. Despite those woes, Nicklaus progressively worked his way to the top, from a tie for thirteenth as low amateur in 1960 to ties for seventh and fifteenth in 1961 and 1962 before contending in 1963.

Golf fans in Georgia weren't quite sure what to make of the Ohio strongboy. At five-feet, ten-inches and 210 pounds, the label "Fat Jack" had been pinned on him. His chubby face sported a double chin, and next to the rangy Arnold Palmer, his paunch made him appear to be a twenty-three-year-old kid who had been chained to the dinner table.

The gallery at Augusta was still angry at Jack for sweeping Palmer aside in the '62 Open at Oakmont. Although Palmer did not contend at the 1963 Masters, another fan favorite, the ageless Sam Snead, replaced him. When Nicklaus defeated Snead, he became the villain once again.

The West Virginia native was fifty-one at the time, but his sweet swing and "Aw shucks" persona still electrified the crowd. When the final round began, Slammin' Sammy was just three shots behind Nicklaus, whose 74, 66, and 74 led the tournament after three rounds.

Nicklaus began to hear catcalls from the gallery on the back nine. When Jack bogeyed, a huge cheer went up from the gallery, who knew that Snead had just birdied to come ever closer to Nicklaus. "Obviously, [that] hurt," Jack said later, "a lot more than I hope I ever showed."

With seven holes to play, Nicklaus was one ahead of Snead, who was playing in front of him. While Sam birdied the fourteenth, Nicklaus was playing the par-three twelfth, the second of three holes dubbed "Amen Corner" after the old jazz classic "Shouting at Amen Corner." The phrase was coined in 1957 by golf historian Herbert Warren Wind in *Sports Illustrated*.

On thirteen, Jack hit a thin seven-iron that barely crossed Rae's Creek. A bunker shot from soggy sand jumped over the green, described as being as "big as a Des Moines phone book" by Rick Reilly of *Sports Illustrated*, leaving a downhill curler that Nicklaus hit too boldly. Now the twenty-three year old faced a difficult ten-footer, a must putt to make under tough conditions. With double bogey looming, Nicklaus stepped up to the challenge and sunk the putt for bogey. It was the turning point of the tournament. Jack had averted disaster and trailed by but one.

As fortune would have it, the big hitter now faced two par fives in the next three holes. Steadying himself, he birdied the thirteenth from four feet, then parred fourteen.

At fifteen, the 500-yard par five with a pond interceding between fairway and green, Nicklaus faced another of the make-or-break shots that visited nearly ever major tournament in which he competed. His task here was even more difficult. While his tee shot was long and true, the ball rolled into a divot that had been left unattended.

Although many players would have let that bad break shake them, Nicklaus remained composed. "I see a lot of bad temper and self-pity on Tour," he observed, "especially on difficult courses. . . . But even if anger or self-pity are excusable, I still dislike them intensely, in myself more than in others. The reason is that they are crutches, cop-outs."

That attitude prevented Nicklaus from becoming upset. "You face a situation that you fear you cannot cope with," he said, "so you give yourself an excuse for possible failure by getting mad at the course or the injustice you've suffered."

Nicklaus impressed Tom Weiskopf with his ability to ignore adversity. "Jack never complained," he said. "There were never any excuses. If he played bad, he admitted it. There was 'no winning through whining,' as I call it."

Though Nicklaus was in the proper frame of mine, he was still one-down to Sam Snead and knew he needed birdie. Since his wedge play was suspect, laying up was an undesirable option. His normal choice of club would have been the one-iron, but Nicklaus instead chose a three-wood. Because he wanted to produce a high fade that would land the ball softly on the green, he turned to an open stance.

Although Nicklaus's cerebral game was on target, his swing was not. The result was a low-level hook that headed over the left portion of the green toward the water at the sixteenth hole. For one of the few times in his career, Nicklaus had seemingly failed to produce the right shot at the right time.

Luck changed all that when the ball hit on soft turf and pulled up just a few feet from the water on sixteen. From there, Nicklaus hit a deft chip shot to within four feet. A canned putt meant he could escape with a birdie instead of a bogey or double bogey, but for the second time in less than ten minutes, Nicklaus faltered, missing the short putt.

The muff meant Nicklaus settled for par, but Sam Snead cooperated by bogeying the par-three sixteenth. The young challenger and the wily veteran were now tied.

Down the stretch, the twenty-three-year-old Nicklaus was rock steady while the others, including Snead, faded. Jack birdied the par-three sixteenth from fourteen feet, then parred the seventeenth. All he needed at eighteen was a par to win. A hooked drive provided dramatics, coming to rest on a muddied area that had been trampled by the gallery. Relief was given from "casual water," and then Nicklaus hit a high mid-iron onto the green. A lengthy putt and a curling three-footer provided a final-round 72, making him the champion, $20,000 richer, and the owner of a size 44 long green jacket. Tony Lema, who closed with 70, finished second behind Nicklaus's four-round score of 286. Snead tied for third with Julius Boros.

Nicklaus said later that the 1963 Masters taught him a lesson that he would take with him in future major tournaments.

During the third round, Jack was paired with Mike Souchak, the muscleman with Hollywood looks who still holds the all-time PGA Tour scoring record at 27 under par. Heavy rains had left Augusta gasping, and when the two golfers approached the thirteenth hole, a portion of the fairway was under water. Nicklaus said Souchak remarked that the round would surely be called and nonchalantly proceeded to play his way to a 79 that included a seven on the thirteenth.

Souchak confirmed Nicklaus's remarks. "I was upset that they didn't call the round off," he said. "The course was under water, unplayable. I lost my concentration and got angry. Jack didn't. He showed a lot of character. Whether he was shooting 65 or 75, Jack just kept grinding away. I couldn't do that."

Nicklaus could have packed it in as well, but he battled the elements to record a 74 that kept him near the top of the leader board. The lesson learned, he said, was "that most golf tournaments are not so much 'won' by optimistic play as not lost when opportunity presents itself. It's a great realization for breeding patience and perseverance."

Two other notes about Nicklaus's first win at Augusta are worth mentioning. Comments he made later regarding how he felt when he walked toward the eighteenth, needing two putts for victory, are a ready glimpse into the incredible composure of a man who was just twenty-three (the youngest champion in history). "I suddenly started thinking and worrying about how I should react after I'd holed out [and won]. Perhaps people talking and writing about me being so cold and controlling was what prompted the thought. . . . After some deliberation . . . , I decided that I'd throw my hat, *even got to thinking about the mechanics of how I'd throw it.*"

And throw it he did, but only after narrowly escaping a three-putt that would have sent him to a playoff. Later, defending champion Arnold Palmer helped him pull on his green jacket. Nicklaus had his second Masters victory and his fourth major championship.

Nicklaus also remembered to heed a suggestion from Ralph Hutchinson, the announcer at the eighteenth hole. Although incomprehensible with the championship still in doubt, when Jack approached the green after his second shot, Hutchinson said, "If you win Jack, save the ball so that you can give it to Bob Jones at the presentation ceremony."

After two-putting for the win, Nicklaus kept the ball and then gave it to his boyhood idol. "I shall never forget the look in his eyes," he remembered later, "He was so delighted for me."

Since Nicklaus had now won three tournaments (Tournament of Champions, Palm Springs Classic, and Masters) of the five he'd played in and the three were those that Palmer had won the previous year, *Time Magazine* wrote, "Whatever Arnie wants, Jack gets." Doug Sanders put it this way: "Baby Beef is doing to Arnie what Palmer did to the rest of us." Palmer wasn't ready to concede the dawn of a new era quite yet. "When I started, Sam Snead was beating me all the time," Palmer remarked, "and I turned the tables. Right now, it's just that I happened to lose three big tournaments that Nicklaus happened to win. He's a wonderful player, but he's still got a long way to go."

# CHAPTER 35

# Thrills and Spills at Augusta

In 1964, Jack Nicklaus assisted Arnold Palmer, who was dominant in the "even" years of the 60s, with the green jacket honors at the Masters. Arnold won by shooting 69, 68, 69, and 70, becoming the first four-time champion of the event that is more closely associated with him than any other major tournament. No wonder. Between 1958 and 1968, Palmer won the Masters four times, was second twice, third once, and fourth twice.

Nicklaus shot 282, six behind Palmer, despite an injury, something he managed to escape throughout most of his career.

The problem was tension in his right wrist and forearm. It restricted his backswing because he could not cock his wrist at the top. A shank at the twelfth hole during the third round was a direct result of the frozen hand action. Nicklaus later cured the problem by moving his right hand down on the base of the club, a bit more to the right.

Domination of the Masters by the so-called "Big Three" in the early 1960s reminded golf aficionados of Hogan and Snead in the '50s. Arnold Palmer won in '60, Player in '61, Palmer again in '62, Nicklaus in '63, and then Palmer in '64, the year the total purse of $129,800 made the tournament the richest in history until the Carling Open paid $200,000 later that year.

As if to outshine Palmer's six-shot victory in 1964, Nicklaus shot 67, 71, 64, and 69 in 1965, winning by nine shots in the most lopsided Masters of all time. Jack's playing companion, lawyer-turned-golfer Dan Sikes Jr., called the 64 "the best round I've ever seen." It included eight birdies, not a single bogey, and nothing more than four on the scorecard.

The four-round total was achieved despite Nicklaus's pretournament concerns regarding a draw that became a wayward hook. Jack Grout helped Jack correct the problem, and the hook disappeared for a time, but then Nicklaus (who had his caddie wear the same

241

number 90 he wore during his first triumph at Augusta in 1963) started hitting wild tee shots that bombarded Augusta's trees. Practice playing partner Deane Beman spotted the trouble, telling Nicklaus, "Your feet are square to the target, but your shoulders and hips are aimed to the right of it. This is something you never did before."

(Beman later admitted that his advice to Nicklaus wasn't from someone who studied the golf swing. "If what I told Jack was prior to 1968, it was just a stab in the dark," he since recalled. "After 1968 I learned more about the golf swing, but back then I'm not sure I knew what I was talking about." Based on the result Nicklaus disagreed.)

The leader after the first round of the '65 Masters was Gary Player, who told the press, "I'm playing so well I can't believe it." That led to a 65, with Player admitting his reading that week of Norman Vincent Peale's *The Power of Positive Thinking* and a new putter purchased in Japan for $50 led the way to a two-stroke lead over the field. By day's end, thirty-three golfers were in red numbers, causing an Atlanta paper to exclaim in next morning's headline, "The Scoreboard Dripped Blood."

After the round, Player discussed a new weight and exercise program, which included strengthening golf muscles by swinging an iron bar from a set of barbells. His program added length to his game and demonstrated an understanding of the importance of fitness that was profoundly visionary. "It's amazing what you can do with your body," he said, "I predict within five years most players will be doing some sort of exercise along these lines. Jack and Arnie kid me a lot about my muscle building, but let me tell you, they wouldn't if they shrunk to five feet seven and had to stand on a tee with me. Then we'd see who outhit who."

Nicklaus entered the '65 Masters buoyed by seven straight practice rounds under 70. Before Augusta, Jack discovered that his sore right hip and back were a result of his right hip being a half-inch lower than the left. He corrected the problem with a Dr. Scholl's foot pad. The foot pad, together with Beman's tip, produced a five-under first round.

Although Player led, he kept an eye on Jack. "There's no such thing as a par five on this course for Jack," Palmer said. "He can reach any green in two. Not only that, he has a great touch. I predict that if the weather is good, Jack will break the tournament record."

After that opening round, Arnold Palmer's wife, Winnie, compared her husband's game with Jack's. "The big difference between Jack and Arnie right now is confidence," she said. "It does not occur to Jack that he can miss a putt."

In the second round, Augusta stiffened. Raymond Floyd shot 83, Frank Beard, 77. The only score in red belonged to Palmer, who shot 68.

The 64 Nicklaus fired in round three was a gem, tying the eighteen-hole record set by Lloyd Mangrum. With hard fairways, soft greens, and little wind, Augusta was defenseless and Nicklaus showed no mercy. During the round, Nicklaus wore a floppy pork-pie hat with the brim turned up in back, causing one journalist to observe that he looked like a "German trolley car operator." Later in his career, he changed to the visor, then occasionally to a baseball cap that looked off-center and out of place. It also made him look somehow "older," the consensus of nearly everyone.

The third round contained enough memorable shots to fill a scrapbook. At the first hole, Nicklaus made par from fifty feet with a trademark long-putt lag to six inches. The par-five second was the trigger hole for the round. Despite a poor right-to-right drive, Nicklaus threaded a three-iron through an opening in the pines just short of the green. A fair wedge shot positioned the ball within twenty-five feet of the hole. The putt was dead center and the birdie placed him at one under.

By the time he reached the seventh hole, Nicklaus had collected four more birdies, coming at four, five, six, and seven. Behind him, Palmer heard the roars and admitted later, "I started pressing."

A front-nine 31, accompanied by thunderous ovations, ignited Nicklaus's competitive fire. In the gallery, Barbara noticed a change in how her husband was being greeted, a far cry from the days when he was the PGA black sheep.

Both she and Jack said later this was the day their love affair with Augusta began. The spectators were responding to superlative golf—not to a threat to Palmer's hegemony. Thus, they cheered Jack as never before.

Pars at ten, eleven, and twelve, two-putt birdies at the par-five thirteenth and fifteenth, and a nine-foot birdie at sixteen put Jack at eight under. Lloyd Mangrum's record of 64 was in jeopardy, but par at seventeen and a miss from twenty-five feet at eighteen for birdie left Jack even with Mangrum's 64.

The record-tying score furnished Nicklaus a five-shot lead over Gary Player. Having tied Mangrum's record, he took dead aim at Ben Hogan's 1953 four-round total of 274. He needed 71 to break it.

Nicklaus's ability to preserve a five-shot lead entering the final round in 1965 later proved to be a foil to Greg Norman, who was unable to hold a six-shot lead in the fourth round of the 1996

Masters. Perhaps "The Shark" needed to heed the words of the Golden Bear, who said years later, "Even when you're holding as comfortable a margin as five strokes, as I was, setting the pace on the last day of a tournament creates pressures and problems." Jack added, "The worst error you can make is to play too cautiously, too defensively, for pars can slip into bogeys only too easily, and then if someone gets hot, you're in trouble."

At the 1965 Masters, there would be no trouble for Nicklaus. The hole that highlighted Jack's round was the twelfth, the dastardly 155-yard par three across Rae's Creek. With his huge lead, Nicklaus could hit a safe shot to the heart of the green. Demonstrating the concentration of someone who needed to make up a bushel of strokes, he stood on the tee with an eight-iron. Ever deliberate, he took two practice swings and then dawdled over the ball for what seemed an hour. With the gallery holding their collective exhalations, Nicklaus hit a high shot with just a touch of cut to within twenty-five feet of the hole. Once again, he had produced a safe, calculated shot when the circumstances called for one, but he holed the twenty-five-foot putt for birdie as a bonus.

By the sixteenth hole, Jack was ahead by eight. He coasted in, shot 69, and beat Hogan's mark by three. Bobby Jones then inaugurated Jack's mythical status by uttering, "Jack Nicklaus plays a game with which I am not familiar."

"Obviously, I played some of the best golf of my life that week," Nicklaus recalled. "I could have shot three or four shots better." Arnold Palmer and Gary Player, his "Big Three" rivals at the time, must have choked when they heard that.

But Jack was right. Especially in relation to his putting performance. In posting a record score that included nineteen birdies, Nicklaus had putted an inordinate 123 times (32, 31, 30, 30) in the four rounds.

Nicklaus later added, "I have never consistently hit my drives as far and as straight or my irons as accurately over seventy-two holes as I did in that Masters." He told *Golf Magazine*, "[That Masters] is probably the easiest tournament I ever won, because I was totally in control of what I was doing." He also called the final round at the time, "the most enjoyable of my life." No wonder, he reached eleven of the greens in regulations using a wedge.

Just a few days after the Augusta victory, Nicklaus's third child, Nancy Jean, to be called "Nan," was born. True to form, the new Masters Champion, the one who had just conquered the pressures of high-test tournament golf, fainted outside the delivery room!

# CHAPTER 36

# Two in a Row

J ack Nicklaus released his first book, *My Fifty-Five Ways to Lower Your Golf Score*, in 1965. The book included instructional tips for the amateur player. Its sales were robust; subsequent books would sell just as well. *Fifty-Five Ways*, *Golf My Way* and *Golf, The Greatest Game*—all published more than two decades ago—remain popular with golf fans and players. Jack's pending autobiography, *Jack Nicklaus, My Story*, written with Ken Bowden, will run almost five hundred pages, and cover Nicklaus's life from birth to the last shot he hit before deadline. Jack the writer is as meticulous as Jack the golfer. He and Bowden, a superb journalist, have been collaborating on the book for twelve years.

What the reader will be reminded of is that in 1966, Nicklaus became the first golfer to win back-to-back Masters. The ability to defend a title became a Nicklaus trademark, prompting United States Open champion Hale Irwin to call Jack, "the best defender who ever played."

Jack won the 1966 Masters in spite of a personal tragedy on the eve of the tournament when a close friend from Columbus died in the crash of a private plane while traveling to Augusta. He considered withdrawing, but at the insistence of Barbara, he played on. In memory of his departed friend, Jack and Barbara set up a trust fund.

When tournament play began, an opening 68 was followed by an undistinguished 76 (Nicklaus admitted he was playing poorly) and a 72.

The turning point in round four came as it had and would so many times, at the par-five, 500-yard fifteenth. At that stage, Nicklaus was three strokes behind Gay Brewer and two behind Tommy Jacobs.

As before, fifteen thus became a must-birdie hole. Nicklaus made his task even more formidable by hitting the tee shot directly behind two pine trees down the left side of the fairway. Seeking to defend his Masters championship, Jack faced two options, both risky. He could hit a faded long iron around the left side of the trees or draw a two-iron to the right of the pines to curve the ball back toward the green.

Nicklaus was forced to choose between these dangerous options because a birdie was a must. Studying the angles, he finally chose to draw a two-iron. With uncanny accuracy, the ball barely missed the trees, curved at just the right angle, and plopped softly onto the green. A birdie four was the reward.

Though he ended up in a playoff with Brewer Jr. and Jacobs, Nicklaus nearly won the tournament outright, but a disloyal three-footer for birdie at seventeen ignored the hole. Later, Jack rationalized the poor stroke by saying he had problems with alignment. "My head was bent so far over that my eyes were positioned *beyond* the ball, outside the target line," he said. "By aligning the putter to the line my eyes saw, I had given myself no chance of making that putt." Close observers believed he simply mishit the putt.

The debacle at seventeen was followed at eighteen by what Nicklaus called, "The best putt I ever hit that didn't go into the hole." It was caressed from the upper level of the greenside hill toward the cup forty feet away and appeared dead center until it veered a human hair to the left.

In the playoff, Nicklaus shot 70, besting Jacobs (72) and Brewer (78), who had missed a six-footer on the eighteenth hole during the fourth round that would have won the tournament outright.

Regarding the 1966 tournament, Nicklaus told *Golf Magazine*, "After we shot lights out the year before, it appeared as though they [officials] weren't going to let that happen again. The grass on the fairways was long enough that you couldn't put any spin on the ball, and the greens were as hard as a rock."

The back-to-back victories sent an unperishable message to those who doubted Nicklaus deserved mention among the greats of the game. "The wins were the beginning of my awareness that Jack had become a complete, all-around player," television commentator Jack Whitaker said. "He had such a presence. He was more than a guy who could hit a long ball."

Nicklaus had now won three of the last four Masters. When he did not contend in 1967 (he didn't even make the cut), it was a disorienting event for not only Nicklaus but for many in the golf world. Gay Brewer won his first Masters with 280 in a year when a third-round 66 by Ben Hogan nearly stole the show.

Three more subpar performances at Augusta followed 1967. The slump ended, finally, in 1971 when Jack finished only two shots behind Charles Coody.

The 1970 Masters had been a rough one emotionally for Nicklaus. It was the first tournament he played at Augusta without his father, Charlie Nicklaus, at his side. Charlie had died of cancer of the pancreas and liver in February of that year.

In 1972, Nicklaus won a fourth Masters, even though Augusta appeared the real winner that year over a disgruntled field (see pages 145 and 204).

A year later, Nicklaus produced a second-round 77 that all but eliminated him. On Saturday, however, he was a different player, and by the end of fourteen holes he had rebounded to be one-under par for the round and one-over par for the tournament.

The fifteenth, the 500-yard par five that is a key hole in nearly every Masters produced an unusual Nicklaus moment. His drive was a long one, but the ball stopped on the side of a mound located down the right side of the fairway. He faced a thorny dilemma: lay-up short of the pond in front of the green or attempt to hit a three-wood from an uphill lie 245 yards over the water. Because previous attempts to charge at fifteen had been successful, Nicklaus never considered laying up in front of the pond.

Jack's occasional high-risk choices caused reporters to debate whether he was as conservative as most thought. The word "gamble" and Jack Nicklaus seemed illogical partners, but former United States and British Amateur champion Vinny Giles, famous for holing out from the road on the "Road Hole" seventeenth at St. Andrews and beating British Walker Cup player Michael Bonallack in the 1971 matches, agreed with those who said that Nicklaus was far more daring than perceived. "I think he was a risk-taker," Giles said. "Some people thought he was calculating, playing by the percentages, but I never saw him look like he was playing very safe."

Tom Weiskopf saw Nicklaus's strategy another way. "Jack was a very conservative, methodical player until he knew it was time to strike," Weiskopf said. "Then, he'd roll the dice. He was the best I ever saw at doing so. His gambles paid off."

Sensing it was time to strike, Nicklaus chose the three-wood, but an uncomfortable stance and awkward ball position produced a poor swing that caused him to deposit the ball in the water. Matters were made worse when a he hit a wedge shot fat, causing another ball to go kerplunk. The result was a snowman eight, and even a final-round 66 couldn't right the wrong of a bad decision made on fifteen in the third round.

In 1975, Nicklaus exploded toward the top of the leader board in the Masters and stayed there to the very end.

The tournament was a sensational one. Nicklaus's 135 total at thirty-six holes looked unbeatable, but a third-round 73, while paired with Arnold Palmer, brought Jack back to the field.

Nicklaus said that playing with Arnie did neither of them any good. In spite of efforts by each to compete against the course and not one another, it was impossible not to become drawn into the crowd's predilection for choosing sides. In the third round in '75, Nicklaus was fortunate to shoot 73, and Palmer knocked himself completely out of the tournament with erratic play.

In the third round, Johnny Miller, the 1973 United States Open champion, blazed to a 65. Even before the tournament started, it was clear that he was a man in pursuit of a goal. "I had a good year last year," Miller said, "but I was lousy in the majors. This time I'm determined to prove I'm not a dog in the big ones." He made his point. His razor-sharp irons produced pinpoint shots and low, very low, scores. He had been eleven shots down to Nicklaus after thirty-six holes, but the 65 closed the gap by eight.

"It was fun, we were all making birdies," Nicklaus later told *Golf Magazine*. "It was probably the most exciting Masters we played."

For Nicklaus, the most memorable shot in the final round was, of course, the second at the fifteenth, the 500-yard par five.

After bogeying fourteen, Nicklaus was tied with Tom Weiskopf for the lead. His drive left him 240 yards from the green. Most players, recalling the error made a year earlier, might have considered laying up. Not Jack.

Without hesitation, he and caddie Willie Peterson debated club selection, and Jack almost pulled out the three-wood. Further thought produced the selection of the one-iron, Nicklaus's favorite club. Keeping in mind that he needed to "complete the backswing," a mantra he'd focused on the entire week, Jack hit a towering shot that positioned the ball thirty feet from the flagstick. Two putts later, Nicklaus had birdie.

Jack then hit a nonchalant five-iron onto the front of the green at the par-three, water-laden sixteenth. Tom Weiskopf, whose 66 in the third round had put him one ahead of Jack, was now dead even with Nicklaus. Johnny Miller lurked just two shots behind.

The position of Nicklaus's ball at sixteen was precarious, just short of a sloping terrace that crisscrossed the green. With the pin in its usual Sunday back-left position, a golfer needed a superb tee shot with little margin of error. Nicklaus's shot, a lackluster one under the circumstances, left him looking at a likely three-putt.

Since playing companion Tom Watson had hit his ball into the water and had to take a drop before playing his third shot, Nicklaus stood and watched Weiskopf and Miller on the nearby fifteenth green. Both made birdie. Nicklaus now trailed Weiskopf by one.

Nicklaus got a break when Watson's third shot fell just outside his but on the same line. Jack watched Watson's line, then began another inspection of the forty-foot curler.

Later, drawing on his incomparable memory, Nicklaus said, "Realizing then that I couldn't simply lag the ball, I started thinking about similar putts I'd made from the same general area of the sixteenth green. Suddenly I had the feeling that this putt was makeable too."

After examining the situation with his customary precision, Nicklaus hovered over the ball for his customary lengthy inspection.

Finally, his putter head hit the ball and it scampered across the green, up and over the terrace, curving ever left toward the hole, which was ten paces from the water hazard. As the ball drew closer, Nicklaus raised his putter, and when it dropped in, he pranced backwards and then sideways in unrestrained, childlike glee. Caddie Willie Anderson joined in the frivolity causing *Sports Illustrated*'s Dan Jenkins to remark that he and Nicklaus resembled Ginger Rodgers and Fred Astaire. The putt was another golden moment for the great Golden Bear—the perfect shot at the perfect time.

The gallery's roar in appreciation of the most dramatic putt Nicklaus ever holed spread through the Georgia Pines like thunder. The fracas stunned his competitors, especially the often-nervous Weiskopf, who three-putted the same sixteenth minutes later. He and Miller, who later said he had to putt across "Bear tracks" on sixteen, would finish one shot short of Jack, who posted 276, twelve under par.

After putting on his fifth green jacket, Nicklaus said, "Thinking . . . about the pressure all of us were under in this incredibly close and hard-fought finish, people are often surprised when I talk about how much sheer fun it was . . . the tougher and closer the competition, the more I enjoy golf. Winning by easy margins may offer other kinds of satisfaction, but it's nowhere nearly as *enjoyable* as battling it out shot-by-shot, right down to the wire."

# CHAPTER 37

# Jack the Imperfect

Following his Masters win in 1975, Nicklaus had two more excellent opportunities to don the green jacket in the 1970s. But both times he failed to execute at a critical juncture, proving that even he was human.

The first came in the 1977 Masters. Tom Watson's play in the tournament was superb, and it appeared that Nicklaus had little chance, trailing by four shots with nine holes to play. Then Jack electrified the gallery by birdieing the tenth, twelfth, thirteenth, and fifteenth holes. The explosion put him even with Watson, who was playing in the group behind Jack.

But then the mistake. He selected a six-iron for the approach shot to the eighteenth hole, a 405-yard par four. With the six-iron in his hand, he heard the crowd from seventeen erupt, which signaled to him that Watson had made birdie. He now needed a birdie to tie Watson and force a playoff. The pressure led to indecision. He first switched to a seven-iron, then backtracked to the six, deciding to hit the ball softly. The indecision led to a miscue, as he dumped the ball into the front bunker. Bogey five meant the end of his chances. Watson won by two shots.

Two years later, Nicklaus faced a pivotal second shot at seventeen, the 400-yard par four. Fighting from eight shots behind when the round began, Nicklaus believed a 67 might catch the leaders napping. After a birdie at sixteen, a birdie and a par would reach that score.

Nicklaus calculated that it was 150 yards to the pin and 137 yards to clear the bunker in front of the green. Jack again had to decide between two clubs: a hard-hit nine-iron or a smooth eight. He first chose the eight-iron, then switched to the nine, then back to the eight. Again indecision proved costly, but unlike 1977, when his second shot at eighteen came up short, this time the eight-iron was too much club. The result was a ball that bounded through the green and down the bank. A wedge shot couldn't save the day, and the resulting bogey made Nicklaus miss the playoff, where Tom Watson and Ed Sneed lost to funnyman Fuzzy Zoeller.

When Jack Nicklaus arrived at Augusta in April of 1986 for his 97th major championship, it had been eleven years since his last triumph at the Masters. The year 1975 had also been Nicklaus's last "best" year on Tour. Counting the Masters victory, he had racked up five wins, finished second once, and third three times.

Although Nicklaus won the United States Open at Baltusrol and the PGA Championship at Oak Hill in 1980 for his eighteenth and nineteenth major Tournament victories, he won only one Tour event (1982 Colonial Invitational) in the early '80s. The sun was beginning to set on a golden career, and his dream of winning a twentieth major championship seemed as if it were riding off into the sunset.

The years 1984 and 1985 had been especially difficult for Nicklaus. He was an aging golfer in his mid-forties, trying to compete head on with the Tour's young limber-backs. Greg Norman, Tom Kite, Seve Ballesteros, Nick Price, and Payne Stewart, all of whom aspired to be the next Jack Nicklaus, were regularly listed as favorites by the media to win the significant events. Jack's name hadn't been on that list for a while.

A tie for sixth at Augusta in 1985 was by far Nicklaus's best finish in a major two years running. He had only broken into the top twenty in one major in '84, missing the cut in two majors in '85, something he'd only done four times since turning professional in 1963.

The early months of 1986 were sour ones for Nicklaus as well. He missed the cuts at the Crosby, the Honda, and the Tournament Players Championship, then withdrew at New Orleans when Barbara's mother died. Ties for thirty-ninth in Hawaii, forty-seventh at Doral, and sixtieth at Phoenix followed. It had now been months since he'd played well in any tournament (Jack was 160th on the money list) and six long years since he'd won a major.

The 1986 Masters, the fiftieth, marked the return of Nicklaus's mother, Helen, to Augusta. Now seventy-eight, she had not been in the pines of Georgia to see her son play since 1959, when Jack teed it up in his first Masters. "I always wanted to come back and see the course again," she told the *Los Angeles Times*. "I'm a flower lover. The dogwoods, the redwoods, the azaleas. . . . I think I wanted to see all that more than golf."

Jack's mother also commented on a little-known fact about her son's singing ability. When asked, "Can Jack sing?" by the *Times*, referring to Jack's performance in the ceremonial sing-along the family had the night before the third round, she replied, "No, but he tries."

When Jack began play in the 1986 Masters, the record book listed him nineteen times in the slot reserved for winners of major tournaments, both amateur and professional. His name was also listed as the second-place finisher nineteen times and the third-place finisher nine times. In all, he enjoyed sixty-six finishes in the top ten.

Records were important to Nicklaus, but he was most proud of his consistency over a lengthy career. "Basically, the majors are the only comparisons over time . . . played on the same courses for generations," he told writer Thomas Boswell. "All the best players are always there. But I'm just as proud of the whole way I've managed my career, the longevity of it. . . . You only have so much juice. You try to keep what you've got left so you can use it when it means the most."

As was often the case before a major championship in which Nicklaus provided memorable dramatics, Jack was tinkering with his golf game as he approached the start date for the '86 Masters. He believed three areas required immediate improvement: his swing tempo, his chipping, and his putting stroke. While other players were honing their game for the tournament, Nicklaus was about to reinvent his—again.

The first order of business was to see his mentor Jack Grout, who was recovering from heart surgery. "I was hitting [the ball] all over the world, especially with my irons," Nicklaus told Thomas Boswell. "When I played well, I was very quiet at the top and very quiet in the finish. I had been too violent with my hands going through the hitting area."

Grout told Nicklaus, "We're going to solve this [swing] problem." Then he explained to Boswell what the two men discussed. "You have to play with feel," Jack said. "If you don't, you're wasting your time. When you have to make five or six yards of difference in a club, you have to feel it. And that old touch started returning."

As a by-product of learning to "take his hands out of the swing," Nicklaus began hitting the ball with more gusto, something he needed at Augusta. The resurgence of power, Jack told Boswell, came as a result of hitting the ball "with more full body force." The writer pointed out that this was "lucky [for Jack] because he had more body—190 pounds—than he had allowed himself in years."

The chipping tips he received on the eve of the 1986 Masters came from son Jackie, who has been significant in helping Jack improve his game over the years. After seeking to improve his own short game with visits to Chi Chi Rodriguez, Jackie passed on that wisdom to Jack. "He went from the worst short game I've ever seen to being very, very good," Nicklaus told Boswell, "So, I had him teach me what Chi Chi had taught him—take the wrists out of the chipping as much as possible."

Regarding his sick putting stroke, Nicklaus was his own toughest critic. "As I've gotten older," he told Boswell, "I've fallen into the habit of decelerating the putter head at the moment of impact, instead of accelerating." Boswell made his own observation about Jack's comment. "[That's a] polite way to say that, as your nerves go, so do your guts," the veteran reporter said. "You just can't make yourself hit the ball anymore."

The answer, Nicklaus felt, wasn't in his stroke but in the putter he was using. "I wanted something with the largest possible moment of inertia and the smallest dispersion factor," he told Boswell in language better suited to an M.I.T. engineering graduate student. What Jack meant was that he wanted a perfectly weighted putter that he could stroke completely through the ball.

The result of his analysis was a putter that Boswell said "looked more like a war club." Tom Watson took one look at the oversized black beauty (Nicklaus's company later sold 125,000 of them in the few months following the Masters) and told Jack, "Looks like you're going out to kill something for dinner."

With the right "feel" back in his swing, Jackie's short game help, and the new putter, Jack was reborn. After a good practice round, he felt recharged, telling Barbara, "I think I found that fellow out there I used to know."

The opening rounds of 74 and 71 by Nicklaus in 1986 at Augusta were acceptable but hardly newsworthy. A third-round 69, blemished by a bogey at thirteen when a cranky one-iron shot landed the ball on the bank dropping it into a hazard, put Jack at 214, four behind Greg Norman. Nick Price, who broke the course record with 63, Donnie Hammond, Bernhard Langer, and Ballesteros were at 211. Tom Kite, Tom Watson, and Tommy Nakajima sat at 212.

Asked about Nicklaus's chances that year, writer Herbert Warren Wind said, "I thought that if he made the thirty-six hole cut in a major tournament, his extraordinary ability to compete may enable him to fight his way into contention, and if the fourth round turned into one of those grim afternoons in which there was a general falling away of the men close to the lead, Nicklaus, with his stubborn resolution, might hold on and win."

Golf analyst Ken Venturi was less optimistic. In the context of a sport where the press sparingly criticizes, Venturi told *USA Today* it was time for the Golden Bear to "start thinking about retirement." Tom McCollister, a reporter for the *Atlanta Journal*, seconded those thoughts. "Nicklaus is done," he said. "He's gone." For inspiration, Nicklaus taped McCollister's comments to the refrigerator in the kitchen where he was staying.

Thirty-seven-year-old Tom Kite, two shots ahead of a man nine years his junior, doubted Nicklaus's chances as well. "I don't think Jack can win another Masters," he told reporters. "I don't think he can win another golf tournament."

But Jack, dubbed a "forty-six-year-old antique" by *Sports Illustrated's* Rick Reilly, was always ready for Augusta. He was so ready and confident, in fact, that he wore a shirt and pants during the Sunday final round that wouldn't clash with the green jacket presented to the winner, something he did traditionally whenever he thought there was a sliver of a chance he coul win.

"There are fewer players who can win [at Augusta] because they can't handle the greens," Nicklaus told reporters on one occasion, "and my enthusiasm is always there."

When Sunday dawned at Augusta, Nicklaus, who had beefed himself up to 190 pounds because he felt he "wasn't strong enough to compete at 170," was well aware that most believed he was over-the-hill. However, with his son Jackie by his side as caddie, Nicklaus strode to the first tee with youthful confidence.

Before the final round, Nicklaus told his son Steve that it would take 65 to win the golf tournament. Eight years earlier, Gary Player had scorched the field in the final round with 64 to win. Nobody had ever shot 65 on Sunday.

Sportswriters clamored for Nicklaus's prediction about what score would be required to win on Sunday in major tournaments.

"Jack had the uncanny ability to choose a number that would win," said Phil Richards of the *Indianapolis Star*. "If reporters wanted a prediction, they'd just ask Jack. Most days he was right. Many times it was he who posted that score and won."

His playing companion on the final day was the Scot Sandy Lyle, who two years later would be fitted for his own green jacket. Behind them came Watson and Nakajima, Kite and Ballesteros, Hammond and Langer, and then the featured twosome Norman and Price.

The leader board would teeter totter on the opening nine holes.

During the first eight holes, Nicklaus missed birdie opportunities from twenty, eighteen, five, twenty-two, and ten. Time was running out. Just when Jack's game needed to shift into overdrive, it was grinding to a halt.

As Nicklaus stood on the ninth green scrutinizing a ten-footer for birdie, he heard back-to-back roars from the gallery at the eighth hole. Both Tom Kite and Seve Ballesteros had holed field shots from the fairway for eagle. The Golden Bear knew if he was to have any chance of contending down the stretch, he needed to drain a putt that neither he nor Jackie could read.

Standing even par for the day, Nicklaus peered over the birdie try at nine. Jackie told him to play it toward the left edge of the hole. His father thought just the opposite, that the putt would break slightly left, meaning he should play it to the right edge. "Let's split the difference," Jack said as both men laughed. After great deliberation crouched over the putt, Nicklaus eyed the line. He knew it was time to will a putt into the hole. His magnificent hands drew back the putter, his follow through was pure, and the ball sped off toward the cup. It appeared to veer left, but then it fell from sight into the hole. To the delight of the gallery, Jack made the turn at 35. It would take a heaven-sent 30 on the back nine, termed the "tournament within a tournament," to match Nicklaus's predicted score of 65.

# CHAPTER 38

# The Miracle

The thunderous applause from the crowd for the birdie three at the ninth hole brought a smile to Nicklaus's face. The tribute was a far cry from the disgraceful way Nicklaus had been treated thirteen years earlier during his duel with Arnold Palmer. Nicklaus later said the crowd noise down the stretch "was deafening . . . I couldn't hear anything. I mean nothing."

As he played the eleventh hole in his twenty-seventh Masters, Nicklaus was back in the hunt just three shots behind Ballesteros. He remained three back after making a nifty twenty-five foot birdie at the tenth, carrying him to two-under for the day and four-under for the tournament.

When a twenty-footer hit bottom after a delicious eight-iron at eleven, the crowd roared and television viewers all over the world started watching more closely. The Bear was on the prowl in a major for the first time in years.

Nicklaus's son Jackie sensed the drama as well. One writer said he jumped straight up in the air after the putt at the eleventh where "Amen Corner" began, "as if the bent grass under him were a trampoline."

His adrenaline pumping, Nicklaus now faced the unpredictable twelfth across Rae's Creek. Earlier he'd called it "the toughest tournament hole in golf."

Reverting to his play of recent times, he turned over on a seven-iron and missed the green to the left. A rickety chip and a missed seven-foot downhill putt resulted in a bogey four. The "oohs" of the crowd echoed Nicklaus's disappointment. Jack had played conservative golf as a Donnie Hammond would, and he was certainly no Donnie Hammond.

Nicklaus's whole body seemed to slump when the putt went awry.

The gallery shook their heads. Only those believing in destiny thought Jack had any chance to win.

Later, Nicklaus said that the bogey actually spurred him on, making him realize conservative play the remainder of the round would produce no results. That may have been a convenient memory, one symbolic of Nicklaus's desire to put the proper spin on a missed opportunity when the need arose. To hear Jack, there were few times in his career when something positive didn't occur from what others deemed a disaster. And although his comments seem unrealistic—even delusional—this facility for remembering only the positive moments from his career no doubt contributed to his rosy view of life in general. It surely contributed to his success in competition, for Jack rarely got down on himself.

On this day, Jack's positive attitude contributed to a birdie at thirteen that put him back at three-under for the day. Unfortunately, five-under for the tournament didn't rekindle much hope for victory. Nicklaus still trailed the foreign contingent, Norman and Ballesteros, by three with only five holes to play.

At fourteen, Nicklaus made par. He had only four holes to make his move. At two-under for the round, there was no indication that lightening might strike.

Nicklaus's good buddy, the 500-yard, par-five fifteenth, awaited him. He crushed a drive, sending it down the right side of the fairway to the area where the chocolate drop humps were located.

Jack and Jackie determined it was 214 yards to the hole. "How far do you think an eagle would go?" Nicklaus asked his son, knowing full well the answer to his rhetorical question. "Let's see it," Jackie replied.

Discussion of club selection led to a four-iron. After completing the familiar waggle, Nicklaus began the backswing. Extending the iron to level position at the top, he then pulled down and through the ball with perfect tempo. The club face lifted the ball off the fairway grass toward the green where Gene Sarazen's double eagle in the 1935 Masters had astonished the golf world. The ball fluttered just slightly left to right, landed like a marshmallow within a few feet of the flag stick, and stopped less than fifteen feet away. Because Jack was not only colorblind, which made reading the red and black leader board difficult, but also couldn't see the finish of the shot from such a distance, the huge ovation from the gallery was necessary to let him know that he had a winner. Jackie then told him the exact distance his ball was from the hole.

The Nicklaus smile swept Jack's face as he pumped both fists in the air. He had hit a great shot at a key time for what seemed like the thousandth time in his career.

There was never any question Jack Nicklaus would make the putt. From the moment he speared the four-iron, destiny took over.

The putt had a nasty break, but it made no difference. Later, he said he had hit the same putt too easy and missed it eleven years earlier. Again, that steel-trap Nicklaus memory. He probably remembered what he was wearing that day as well.

On this occasion, the putting stroke was firm and steady and the ball dropped squarely into the hole. The eagle three brought him to five-under for the day and seven-under for the tournament. Perhaps the 65 he sought wasn't an illusion after all, but to obtain that score he needed to birdie two of the three finishing holes.

At the fourteenth, Greg Norman and Nick Price were unsettled by the decibel level of the roar they heard at fifteen. "All Greg and I knew," Price said later, "was something astonishing was happening . . . "

The 170-yard sixteenth was special to Nicklaus. He'd always played the par three as if he owned it. In forty-one tries between 1977 and 1987, he played the hole with thirty pars and eleven birdies. The famous forty-footer he'd holed for two in 1975 had spearheaded his march to victory that year.

Now, with the crowd circling the hole in search of heroics, Jackie pinched a six-iron out of the bag for his dad. Nicklaus sent a towering, majestic shot toward the flagstick, which was cut in its usual Sunday position on the left side of the green, precariously close to the water hazard.

Just as the stomachs of Norman and Price had settled after fourteen, their ears were inundated with yet another outburst. Nicklaus hit a precision iron shot that flew near the flagstick and then rolled tantalizingly toward the hole for what was nearly an ace. It missed by inches, but the ensuing birdie dropped Nicklaus to six-under par for the day and eight-under for the tournament. The shot rang out like Reggie Jackson hitting a homer in the ninth in the World Series or Joe Montana tossing "The Catch" to Dwight Clark in the Super Bowl. Jack had once again played to the drama of the moment.

Besides his stellar play, Nicklaus received some help in his quest. Spaniard Seve Ballesteros still had a two-shot lead as he played fifteen. If he birdied, the green jacket was most assuredly his, but he duck-hooked a four-iron second shot into the pond. His bogey meant that he, Nicklaus, and Tom Kite all stood at eight-under.

At seventeen, the 400-yard par four, Nicklaus had to step away from his stance on the tee. Overcome with emotion, he had tears in his eyes. It took a few moments for him to regain his composure. When Jack finally addressed the ball, he attempted to position the tee shot down the left hand side of the fairway. He came over the shot a bit and ended up on hard ground beneath two huge pines. Surveying the shot, he concluded that a low boring, 120-yard wedge was necessary. He positioned the ball back in his stance and powered through the downswing. The result was a Nicklaus special, a low trajectory recovery shot that backed up the ball to within ten feet of the hole. Once again, the great champion had invented a shot for a special occasion.

The putt involved a tricky double-breaker, but by that point an angel was perched on Nicklaus's shoulder. "The putt was impossible to read," Nicklaus said later, "so I just hit it at the hole. It wiggled left, wiggled right and went in the center." The crowd nearly fainted when the ball disappeared. Jack Nicklaus was seven under par on his final round and leading the tournament at nine-under. Even *he* was awestruck. He rolled his eyes toward the heavens as if to say, "Thank you, Lord."

On the eighteenth hole, where the bunkers positioned down the left side were built specifically to catch his long tee shots, Nicklaus drove with a three-wood down the chute and then hit a five-iron from 180 yards to within forty feet. It was a conservative play and he knew it. It was also a smart one. "Come get me," he was saying, somehow aware once again what the winning score should be.

The forty-footer he hit came close to dropping (stopping four inches away), but he wouldn't need it. Tom Kite and Greg Norman, who had always credited two books his mother gave him, *Fifty-five Ways To Play Golf* and *Golf My Way* (both by Jack Nicklaus) for his golf success, could do no better than eight-under. Seve had busted his balloon with bogey at fifteen.

For Norman, the crushing blow was a pushed four-iron that resulted in a bogey at eighteen. "It was the first time all week I conceded to my ego," he said later. "I, let [the four-iron] get the better of me and tried to rifle it at the flag."

When the dust cleared, Nicklaus's twentieth major, his sixth one at Augusta in a twenty-three-year span, was in the record books. Take that, Venturi, Jack's smile seemed to say. You, too, Kite. And Mr. Sportswriter McCollister. The Bear is back and as fierce as ever. He'd shot 35 and 30–65, one of the greatest finishing rounds in the history of Augusta. When he approached the eighteenth green, *USA Today*'s Steve Hershey said, "I've never heard a sound, a roar like that."

The handshake with Sandy Lyle set the stage for a warm hug from son Jackie. It was a tear-filled Kodak moment, one both father and son will never forget. "Watching you play today was the thrill of my life," Jackie told his father.

"Coming down the stretch was an experience I'll never forget." Jack told *Golf Magazine*, "The last ten holes [seven-under] was probably the most enjoyable stretch of golf I've ever played." Later he added, "What came over me was that my golf game got fifteen years younger in a ten-hole period."

Nicklaus, taking home $144,000 for his victory, told the press that on three or four occasions besides the one on the seventeenth tee he had to wipe away tears because of the overwhelming crowd reaction. Golf fans everywhere probably wiped away a few of their own tears. Many consider this victory, perhaps the capstone of an illustrious career, as an epic achievement, a victory as impressive as any in the history of sports.

The win, according to Ben Crenshaw, "was something out of this world. It was magicial." Chi Chi Rodriguez said, "It was the greatest thing I ever saw in sports. I thought about how it would have been to have hugged my dad like that after a victory. I had tears in my eyes the whole time."

The win at Augusta marked the end of a revolution for Nicklaus's golf swing. He had exploded out of the gate in his twenties with the high arc, remolded his golf swing radically after losing weight during the late 60s, retooled it once again when he passed thirty-five, and then used that new swing, a remodeled short game and a new brood-flanged putter to achieve the victory in the '86 Masters. Nicklaus certainly didn't re-invent his game; he just kept changing with the times, leaving the results to speak for themselves.

Thomas Boswell was right on target when he said, "By craft and canniness, [Jack] discovered a succession of temporary blockages against age and self-doubt—almost against mortality itself. . . . Repeatedly, he prevailed with dignity. With easy good grace. With many of the qualities that seem to lose their substance unless some special person can live them out, embody them on his own terms."

Yes, Jack Nicklaus was special. Yes, he had the swing, retooled as it was on many occasion. And he had a superior mental attitude, one permitting him to focus clearly when the chips were down. And he had confidence and faith in himself, two traits that helped him persevere when others could not.

But the 1986 Masters victory underscored Jack's finest character-istic: his heart. Through victory and defeat, personal humiliation and triumph, Jack Nicklaus never conceded, never gave anything less than full effort.

And what did Nicklaus think of his fairy-tale feat in the 1986 Masters? "For a guy who won $4,000 this year, not a bad victory," he told a worshipping band of reporters.

# CHAPTER 39

# Nicklaus and the United States Open Championship

J ack Nicklaus made birdie on the very first hole he ever played in the United States Open Championship as a young amateur of seventeen. The year was 1957, the sixty-second anniversary of the Open.

The United States Open was first won at the Newport Golf Club in 1895 by Horace Rawlins with a thirty-six-hole score of 173. Five years later, Britain's Harry Vardon won the "turn of the century" Open championship, defeating his countryman J.H. Taylor by two shots at the Chicago Golf Club.

Through the years, the greatest professional golfers in the history of the game have had their names engraved on the United States Open Championship Cup. Francis Ouimet, Jerome D. Travers, Charles (Chick) Evans, Bobby Jones, and John Goodman are the only amateurs to succeed, with Ouimet's miracle victory over Harry Vardon and Ted Ray in 1913 one of the most storied moments in tournament play.

Three years after Nicklaus's debut in 1957, Jack almost won the tournament, but Arnold Palmer's final-round heroics busted him to second at Cherry Hills in Denver. After a fourth-place finish in 1961, he traveled to famed Oakmont, built on a plateau above the Allegheny River outside Pittsburgh, for the 1962 Open.

Palmer was as thin as a rail that year at age thirty-two while the twenty-two-year-old Nicklaus was a disheveled, two-hundred pounder who *Sport's Illustrated*'s Dan Jenkins said "could win first prize at a livestock contest." If anything, despite his baby face, Nicklaus looked older than his chief competitor.

In golf, the smaller, tougher breeds have always been heroes. Ben Hogan, Lanny Wadkins, Tom Watson, Lee Trevino, Ian Woosnam, Tom

Kite, Gary Player, and most recently Corey Pavin, all fighters, have been the darlings of the crowds. Modern-day players such as Ernie Els, Tiger Woods, and John Daly hit the ball a long way, but that advantage must be accompanied by their ability to have golf fans *relate* to them. Daly's antics work for him and Tiger and Els's boyish smiles are plusses, but to be embraced by the fans, they'll have to develop a rapport with the galleries that follow them.

Early, as mentioned, Nicklaus was not a crowd pleaser, and it cost him. His defeat of Palmer in the playoff 71 to 74 for the 1962 Open Crown was one of the most unpopular wins in the history of golf. The gallery didn't warm to a player who boasted, "[Oakmont] is a big sucker of a course, but I decided I could control it. I decided to hit everything just as hard as I could, because it was easier to go over the trouble spots than to go around them."

Nor did they take to one who had the audacity to say, "To me, in those early pro days Arnold Palmer was just someone in my way, just another guy to beat on the road to where I wanted to go. It wasn't until several years later that I started to think about what Arnold really had achieved and came to mean to the game of golf." He also added, "Then as now, I respected Arnold greatly as a golfer and as a man. . . . What I didn't see was why any of those feelings should stop me from trying to beat him on the golf course."

For his part, Palmer's choice of words regarding the Open playoff in 1962 were curious ones. "I wish I were playing anybody but that strong, happy dude," he told reporters, causing one to question whether Palmer sensed the inevitability of what was about to occur. Later Palmer recalled how tough a win the Open had been for Nicklaus in view of the rowdiness of the fans. "At times it must have seemed to Jack as though the whole world was against him," he said. "I don't know how he stood up to it. A lesser person surely would have crumbled."

Once Nicklaus's victory in the 1962 Open was assured, experts suspected that, as the age of Hogan before it, the age of Palmer could be entering its twilight. Jack Nicklaus had entered golf front and center when he earned his first professional victory in the United States Open.

Nicklaus's string of victories in the majors occurred on courses that read like a bible of golfing meccas, and none is more cherished by him than the win in the United States Open at Baltusrol in 1967.

This win came two years after the Golden Bear's fabled victory in the 1965 Masters and Bobby Jones's pronouncement that "Nicklaus plays a game with which I am not familiar." If Jones loved that performance, Nicklaus's heroics at Baltusrol in '67 must have sent his head spinning.

Baltusrol is the only golf course in the world named after a murdered man. When wealthy New Yorker Louis Keller decided to build a golf club near Spring, New Jersey, in the 1890s, he picked that name in memory of a local man, Baltus Roll. Roll's murder, which had "crime of the century" magnitude, came at the hands of killers trying to rob him of gold and silver coins.

Englishman David Hunter designed the mystical layout, which attracted the United States Women's Amateur Championship in 1901. Through the years, Baltusrol hosted a record number of United States Open Championships, including ones with victors Willie Anderson (1903), Jerry Travers (1915), Tony Manero (1936), and Ed Furgol (1954).

That tournament was played, as was the one in '54, on a new golf course (The Lower One), designed in the 1920s by A.W. Tillinghast. He was a dashing local figure, smitten by golf after a trip to St. Andrews. Later, he became known as "Tillie the Terror," a nickname based on the killer courses he designed at Baltusrol, Winged Foot, and the San Francisco Golf Club, among others.

The course Nicklaus faced in 1967 was par 70 (34-36) and played at 7,076-yards. One hundred twenty-six bunkers dotted the layout. The 1954 Open Champion Ed Furgol described Baltusrol's Lower Course, "like Augusta, only sixty percent tighter off the tees."

Four contenders for the '67 Open emerged as the tournament entered its final phase. They were an unlikely group: Nicklaus, Palmer, Billy Casper, and a twenty-three-year-old Texas amateur named Marty Fleckman, whose drop-dead good looks and whiplash swing earned him many admirers.

Nicklaus was coming off a stretch of play marked by confusion and disappointment. He had won only a little over $31,000 in the early months of the '67 season and not one tournament in five months. His last major victory had been the 1966 British Open.

"I've been learning to do things the way they're supposed to be done, instead of the way I do them naturally," he told *Time* magazine prior to the tournament. "From now on, I'm going to play my own way."

That meant returning to the left-to-right fade that had, to that point, produced eight major championships. No more draws or hooks, which he could not control.

Nicklaus's putting stroke also needed surgery. Advice from "experts" had somehow persuaded him to replace his short, tempo-driven stroke with a long, conventional one. At Baltusrol, he returned to the old short putting stroke while using a new white, wide-flanged Bulls-Eye putter he borrowed from Fred Mueller, a friend of Deane Beman's. It was named "White Fang."

"I had that putter in my bag," Deane Beman remembered. "I tried it but it didn't work for me. Jack saw it and that was that."

"I seem to get a better line with it," Nicklaus told *Golf Digest*. "I changed my putting stroke too. Now I'm taking a shorter stroke and hitting harder through the ball. I had been taking a longer stroke and hitting it easier."

The putter and the shorter stroke had been suggested by Gordon Jones, an Ohio friend. The improvements helped Jack shoot a 62 (with a par-par finish on two par fives) in a practice round, a sign to Nicklaus that his game was ship-shape.

Despite that round, which required only twenty-seven putts, Nicklaus reverted to his previous putting woes on the first eighteen-holes at Baltusrol with thirty-five putts. The balky putter threatened to shove him out of contention. "White Fang" was sentenced to probation. One more poor putting round and it faced extinction.

Although he was better known for his putting heroics in later rounds of championships, a putt at the 194-yard, par-three fourth hole in the second round proved critical.

At that point in the round, Nicklaus stood at two over par. His tee shot found the rough to the left of the green and a poor chip shot caused him to face a ten-footer for par. With everyone else in the field heading to higher numbers in red figures, Nicklaus knew another bogey might position him too far behind to catch up.

Recalling Beman's tip, he hovered over the putt with a single thought: Keep the stroke short and hit the ball firmly. The result was a confident pass at the ball that produced par. Heartened by the effort, he putted well the rest of the round, recording five birdies, which placed him in the thick of the tournament. "White Fang" had earned a reprieve.

Marty Fleckman stole the headlines during the first three days. The son of a lumber dealer fired 67-73-69 (209) and led by one stroke over Palmer, Casper, and Nicklaus. Lee Trevino, someone Nicklaus later swore he'd never heard of at that time, was four shots back at 213.

A *Time* magazine reporter wrote that he could have picked the winner at the first tee of the final round. "Fleckman was visibly nervous," he wrote. "Arnie was intent, Casper trance-like . . . gazing vacantly at the sky, and Nicklaus was smiling and strutting around like a sergeant major."

The final eighteen holes of the tournament were played on a day with ninety-degree temperatures, high humidity, and little wind. The conditions produced wayward tee shots by Casper (72), missed birdie opportunities by Palmer (69), and a "do not pass go" 80 from the bedeviled Fleckman, whose career as a professional was as short as Doug Sanders's backswing.

All the while, the dancing bear was annihilating Baltusrol with a birdie barrage. This despite placards placed by the bunkers that read "Right here, Jack" and a "Miss it, Jack" yelled by a detractor in the gallery at the second hole just before Nicklaus missed a short effort to complete a three-putt.

Despite the remarks, Nicklaus canned a twelve-footer at three, a four-footer at four, a fourteen-footer at five, a twenty-footer at seven, and a four-footer at eight. Combined with two bogeys, Jack had finished the front nine with 31.

When Jack came to eighteen, birdies at thirteen and fourteen and one bogey put him at four-under. The only suspense left was whether Nicklaus could make yet another birdie and break Ben Hogan's Open record of 276.

Although Nicklaus was clearly the best fourth-round player who ever lived (through 1988, he had shot 70 or better fifty-one times in the final round of major tournaments), he was also the finest eighteenth hole player as well. Jack manufactured birdie on the final hole so many times it was news only when he didn't.

In fact, Nicklaus's play down-the-stretch in nearly every round was exemplary. That ability to finish well, whatever round of the tournament he was playing, left Jack in a great frame of mind for the next eighteen holes or the next tournament. Rarely did Nicklaus botch up holes fifteen through eighteen.

No better evidence of the dominance Nicklaus exhibited on the final hole exists than his performance at Baltusrol in 1967.

Nicklaus later recounted for reporters from *Golf Digest* what was going through his mind as he approached the eighteenth. "I had a four-shot lead, and I figured if I made a seven and Arnold a three we would tie. All I was trying to do was win, so I decided to use an iron from the tee and play safe. I remembered that Dick Mayer made a seven here in the last round in 1954 and lost his chance for the title."

Despite the decision to "play safe," the attempt at birdie to set the record got a shaky start when Nicklaus, playing with Palmer, drove to the right in deep rough with a one-iron on the 542-yard par five. Watching on television, Hogan must have felt a sense of relief when he saw Jack punch an eight-iron to a position short of the creek that criss-crossed the fairway. Now he faced a distance of more than 230 yards. His chances at birdie had vanished; par was now the goal.

With Palmer next to the green in two, Nicklaus studied the shot, uphill and against the wind. He first considered a three-wood, then decided on a one-iron, a club Gary Player said Jack "could hit so high it would stop on concrete."

The key to the shot was to carry the sand bunker guarding the front portion of the green. With his usual diligence, Nicklaus decided to cut the ball just a hair, and a slight outside-in swing produced a high, spiraling ball that hit just over the bunker and short of the green. Despite the intense pressure, the superbly hit long iron dropped the ball twenty feet from the hole. Hogan must have slumped in his seat in front of the television.

Although there must have been doubters, Nicklaus mavens expected the putt to drop. Like few before or after him, Jack rarely spoiled the drama.

Sure enough, "White Fang" cooperated by holing the putt. Nicklaus had won his second United States Open crown (the electronic scoreboard at eighteen read "Jack is Back") and in doing so broke Hogan's record. Arnold Palmer stood on the green just as he had five years earlier at Oakmont. His face betrayed disbelief, even shock. At forty-seven, he knew time was running out for him. Nicklaus had stolen yet another Open Championship he wanted so desperately to win. Home in Texas, Ben Hogan smiled and shook his head. One more record erased by the Golden Bear.

Nicklaus's thoughts at the time were in character: "Records are just bonuses—the cherry on the sundae," he said, playing down the triumph.

Ironically, the skies darkened and rain came pouring down in buckets shortly after Nicklaus finished. Perhaps the gods decided that Baltusrol needed a thorough cleansing so it could start fresh after the thrashing Jack had given it.

# CHAPTER 40

# Jack under Pressure

The United States Open golf championship is the most nerve-wracking, pressure-packed, professional event in the world of individual sports. Tour professional Corey Pavin said his 1995 triumph at Shinnecock put him under "the most pressure I've ever felt."

If a golfer wins the title once, the pressure increases the next time. Walter Hagen agreed, "Any player can win a U.S. Open, but it takes a hell of a player to win two."

Words such as patience, perseverance, resilience, and the term "mentally tough" are often used to describe what it takes to win the United States Open, the national championship of United States golf. Why is this ancient tournament the ultimate test of nerves? It's not as if life or death is in the balance, but it always seems as if it is. The surreal atmosphere begins weeks before the tournament, intensifies during the practice rounds, elevates to another level with the very first tee shot on Thursday, escalates through every shot during the first sixty-three holes, and then grips the throats of the competitors as they approach the perilous final holes.

"I could barely breathe the last few holes," 1996 Open winner Steve Jones said. When the players walk the final holes, it's hold-your-breath, bite-your-nails, grind-your-teeth time. The last-second plays in the Super Bowl and the NBA finals may have their moments, but sports fans across the world ride a different emotional roller coaster with the golfer who somehow tries to get a grip and win the Open on a hot Sunday in June.

And it's the United States Golf Association, the watchdog of golf, who has made it that way. Former official Sandy Tatum, when asked by a reporter why the USGA was trying to embarrass the best players, said, "We're not trying to embarrass them, we're trying to identify them."

Tour veteran Bruce Crampton sees playing in the Open as a singular challenge. "The USGA doesn't care about the scores," he said. "They want a champion worthy of the crown, someone who can confront adversity and be tested to every nook and cranny of their ability."

Jack Nicklaus was in that position more times than not. In the forty Open championships in which he had played through 1996, he collected four victories ('62, '67, '72, '80), four second-place finishes ('60, '68, '71, '82), and one third-place finish ('66). In all, he's recorded thirteen top-ten finishes in the Open.

Four of Nicklaus's greatest disappointments in golf involve Open losses. They include his second-place finish to Palmer at Cherry Hills in 1960, a four-shot loss to Lee Trevino at Oak Hill in 1968, and two other second-place finishes, one to Trevino at Merion in 1971 and the other to Tom Watson at Pebble Beach in 1982.

At Merion, Nicklaus had a chance to win only because he recovered from a disastrous bout with the 370-yard, par-four eleventh hole in the second round. When he hit his tee shot, Jack was one stroke off the lead, but a right-to-right shot positioned the ball into the heavy rough. A fat second shot moved the ball well short of the green, just over a winding creek and short of the trees that border the right side of the hole. A poorly played wedge missed the green to the left, and a sculled chip shot sent the ball scurrying over the green, down a bank, and nearly into the creek behind the green.

Nicklaus was looking at perhaps a double-bogey six and, more likely, a triple-bogey seven. Surveying the shot, he realized a poor chip might mean he'd do something he rarely did—produce a score that would send him out of contention early.

Gathering himself, Nicklaus took sand wedge to ball, and the resulting pitch shot left him four feet from the hole. A successful putt meant a six, but a saving shot at eleven in the second round proved critical to his chances of winning.

By the time Nicklaus stepped up to a fourteen-foot putt on the final hole, his tenacious play had put him in a position to win. His chance to do so occurred when a young boy removed a sign nailed to a tree near the eighteenth green, causing enough distraction that Trevino pulled a six-footer left of the hole for bogey. Nicklaus, however, missed his putt, necessitating a playoff.

Nicklaus was only in that position because of several short putts he had made down the stretch. NBC's Gary Koch remembered being impressed. "He knew he had to par in to tie," Koch said, "and each time he had to putt, he stood over the ball, and stood over the ball, and stooped over it. He wasn't going to pull the putter back until he knew he could knock the ball in the hole. He just made them boom, boom, boom. It was amazing."

Before the playoff, Trevino told the press, "My chances are just as good as Jack's. . . . The pressure is on him. He's the best ever, the odds-on favorite. If I lose, people expect it. If he loses, it makes me look like a hero."

Despite his bravado, Trevino admitted later that he was shaking when both combatants stood at the first tee. "I was nervous. We had five minutes until tee time and my glove was soaked with sweat."

Before the first shot was hit, Trevino livened up the proceedings. Reaching into his golf bag for a new glove, he found a rubber snake he'd bought for his daughter. "I had pulled it out on the eighteenth green at Colonial and scared Miller Barber's caddie, Herman Mitchell, so bad that he damn near ran into Crampton's Lake," Trevino said.

According to the Merry Mex's' version of the story, he held up the snake for all to see. The gallery was amused and so was Jack. "Toss it over here," Nicklaus said. Trevino obliged and Jack surveyed the rubbery toy. Seeing the straight-laced Nicklaus hold the snake made the gallery laugh. Jack shook his head and then threw it back to Lee.

Despite the frivolity with the snake, the first hole produced true-to-form play by the two competitors. Nicklaus spanked a drive dead center in the fairway, plopped an approach shot within fifteen feet of the hole, and two-putted for par. The less experienced Trevino, only five years removed from a state of oblivion, and winner of only one major championship, pushed a nine-iron second shot into a greenside bunker and made bogey.

After one hole, the mental edge Nicklaus enjoyed had Trevino on the ropes. The commanding presence of Nicklaus loomed large. If he could overwhelm Trevino on holes two and three, an early knockout punch could be delivered.

But Jack's tee shot on the second hole produced just the opposite result. Later, Trevino said, "On the next two holes he hooked his ball into the left bunkers and hit some poor shots, trying to get out. I parred both holes and took a one-shot lead. But more important, I realized he was nervous, too."

Jack's shaky play calmed Trevino. After Nicklaus pulled even at six, Lee nailed an iron shot to within seven inches of the hole. The resulting birdie put him in the lead—one he never relinquished. Putting with the touch of a gifted sculptor, Trevino holed twenty-five-foot and thirty-five-foot birdie putts at the twelfth and fifteenth holes, then nearly rammed home a seventy-foot putt for another birdie at sixteen.

When Nicklaus bogeyed seventeen, Trevino led the Golden Bear by three strokes. Trevino played eighteen in par, and the resulting 68 provided him with a three-shot victory and his second United States Open championship.

"Jack was very gracious when he congratulated me," Trevino said. "He told me, 'you played absolutely fantastic.'"

Later, Trevino was philosophic. "That playoff taught me something else. The Good Lord doesn't give you everything. He kept one thing from Jack Nicklaus: his sand wedge. He's a poor wedge player, out of the fairway and out of the bunker. If he had been a good wedge player, I sure wouldn't have beaten him that day at Merion. He left his ball in two bunkers and chili-dipped two wedges."

He added, "I got lucky today and won . . . against a guy I consider to be the greatest player on the Tour today—Jack Nicklaus. I didn't beat Merion. I just compromised with her, like a wife, trying not to let her have her way too often."

Later, Nicklaus reflected in *Golf Digest* about his poor play in the bunkers. On the second hole, he said, he was afraid the ball would move if he took a normal stance. "I was in an awkward lie. I wasn't set up right and took a bad swing." At the third, Nicklaus admitted, "I tried to hit well under the ball and pop it up softly on the lip so it would run down. . . . I just missed it."

Proving he had an all-around bad day around the green, Nicklaus also discussed a chip shot he muffed at the tenth. "I wanted to carry the ball over a ridge on the green and stop it short of the hole. Then I hit it fat. That shot ate me up inside."

To be sure, playing badly didn't set well with Nicklaus. If he played his best and lost, so be it. But to play poorly left an incredibly bad taste in Jack's mouth.

An equally memorable United States Open runner-up finish came for Nicklaus at Pebble Beach in 1982. By then, Tom Watson had risen to the top of the contender board, having won thirty tournaments, including three British Opens and two Masters. The Kansan had also led the money list and had been PGA Player of the Year four years running.

Despite Watson's prowess, he still wasn't a United States Open Champion and it gnawed at him. On two occasions, at Winged Foot in 1974 and a year later at Medinah, experts said Tom choked down the stretch. Head-to-head wins against Nicklaus in 1977 at the Masters and Turnberry in the British Open brought new acclaim to his game, but Watson needed a United States Open crown to mark his place in history.

Before the tournament, Watson made his thoughts clear. "To be a complete golfer," he told reporters, "you have to win the Open, you just have to."

Bruce Devlin led both Watson and Nicklaus by two shots after the first and second rounds at Pebble Beach. The Aussie faltered with 75 in the third round, and Watson's 68 put him in a tie for the lead with willowy Bill Rogers. Nicklaus, at 71, was three back.

Five consecutive birdies for Nicklaus on the front side (including one that was nearly a hole-in-one at the par-three fifth hole) offset two early bogey fives, and he vaulted past Watson. He was now in a tie with Rogers, who was playing with Watson two holes behind him.

At the eighth hole, a 431-yard par four, Nicklaus experienced a turn of events that were a portent. A well-positioned three-wood shot set him up perfectly for a six-iron second shot to a cup set middle green.

The resulting swing made Nicklaus think a sixth straight birdie was possible, but at the top of its flight, the ball began to waver to the right. Suddenly, Jack's mindset changed, for he knew that unless that ball righted itself, it was headed either for the bunker to the right of the green or, worse, the heavy, coarse grass surrounding the bunker.

The rough had been a source of irritation to Nicklaus all week. He openly criticized USGA officials for its penal nature, but his words and those of the other players fell on deaf ears.

When Nicklaus located his ball, it was barely visible. A sand wedge plopped the ball to within eight feet, but a misread putt caused a bogey five. The bogey halted Nicklaus's momentum, and his play down the stretch was uninspired.

Despite the miscue, Watson and Nicklaus were square at nine, with Jack still spying his magical twentieth major win and fifth Open crown. By the time Watson walked to the thirteenth, Nicklaus birdied fifteen. The birdie offset a three-putt bogey at eleven. The two men were tied.

Nicklaus recorded three pars on the home holes. Watson made a forty-footer for birdie at fourteen to open up a one-shot lead, which promptly disappeared when he botched a tee shot at sixteen and bogeyed.

As Nicklaus watched on television from the scorers' tent behind the eighteenth green, Watson played the seventeenth. When Watson overplayed his tee ball into the ratty rough a few feet off the green just to the left of the pin, Nicklaus's chances improved. But fate took over and Watson popped a wedge shot that feathered onto the green and directly into the hole. While the crowd cheered his birdie putt, Watson pranced across the landscape. "Did that go in?" Jack asked Tom Meeks of the United States Golf Association. "Yes, it did, Jack," Tom reported to the startled Nicklaus. "Yes, it did."

The result was good-bye to Jack's twentieth major and hello to Watson's first United States Open victory. Tom even curled in a twenty-footer at eighteen to put the cork in the bottle of a two-shot victory. Later, Watson said of his historical shot, "I couldn't have written a script better. That was the best shot of my life. [It] had more meaning to me than any other shot of my career."

Despite the crushing defeat, Nicklaus stayed around and hugged Watson after his play on the final hole. "That's the Jack Nicklaus I know," Tom Meeks said. "The ultimate good sport."

# CHAPTER 41

# Fireworks at Baltusrol

A
lthough none of Jack's championships may match Ken Venturi's warriorlike, last-gasp victory in 1964, 1980 produced a scintillating one when Jack Nicklaus and Japan's Isao Aoki battled vigorously for the Open championship.

Coming into the tournament that year at Baltusrol, Nicklaus's doubters were in full force. In five years, Jack had only won a single major, the 1978 British Open at St. Andrews. In 1979, Nicklaus's play was a yawning nonevent, showing him seventy-first on the official Tour money list; a fourth had been his previous worst.

The leader board would be dotted with players such as Hale Irwin, Tom Watson, and Tom Weiskopf, but Nicklaus attempted to assume command of the championship when he threw at the field a seven-under 63 on opening day. Weiskopf matched it but then faltered. By the end of fifty-four holes, Aoki had tied Jack and set the stage for a tussle.

Nicklaus led by one after eight, two after nine. Every time the Japanese native threw a punch, Nicklaus counter-punched. Aoki's main weapon was his tin-colored Acushnet putter, which he tipped up on the putting surface in a most unusual, but highly effective, manner.

Aoki's technique stemmed from the propitious fact that his first set of clubs had been too long for him. To adapt, he crouched low over the ball, hands knee level. That caused the tip of the toe of the putter to stick up. Despite the unorthodox nature of it all, when Aoki gave the ball a sharp rap with the right hand, the results were astounding. His smooth stroke in the Open resulted in only fifty putts over the first thirty-six holes, and even the ones he missed barely slid by.

Attempting to become the first Japanese-born golfer to win a major, Aoki kept things tight with a competitor who, at age forty, was outdriving him forty yards. This despite the observation from British commentator Peter Allis, who said of Aoki, "I don't think I've ever seen a worse swing from a player at this level of golf."

An article in the Open program that year carried the headline "Jack Will Be Back." Thirteen years earlier, "Jack Was Back" had been the creed. Now Nicklaus was on the verge of proving the article right, holding a two-shot lead with two to play.

The turning point came at the par-five seventeenth. Nicklaus unleashed a 275-yard tee shot, but since the hole played 630 yards (the longest in major championship history), it was a three-shot experience.

After Nicklaus hit an iron to level ground just short of an incline, Aoki deposited his third shot onto the green just five feet away. The way the deft Asian putted, Nicklaus knew he'd make birdie.

Jack figured he had ninety yards to the pin. He also realized, as he had many times before in majors, that this was the moment for the kill, the time to put his opponent away. Just as the slender golfer from Asia saw the door open slightly, Nicklaus wanted to slam it shut by hitting what Angelo Argea described as a "that's-a-wrap shot."

When he faced these difficult shots, Nicklaus prided himself on never rushing anything, prompting Arnold Palmer to say, "Jack's approach to a shot reminds me of an airline pilot doing an exhaustive cockpit check."

True to form, Nicklaus first chose the spot on the green where he wanted to position the ball. Trouble lurked in the left greenside bunkers, so Jack decided to play to the right side and attempt to keep the ball under the hole.

Club selection dictated either a pitching or sand wedge. He chose the latter, but there was mental work to do before hitting the shot.

All week long, Nicklaus had been "coming off" the ball on his short-iron shots. Before he hit, Angelo Argea reminded him to keep his head still.

With that thought in mind, Nicklaus's subsequent swing placed the ball twenty-five feet below the cup. Later he would tell *Golf Digest*, "It was my biggest pressure shot of the year." He also paid tribute to his improvement with the wedge by saying, "I don't use a single shot around the green that I used the first thirty-nine years of my life."

As Jack stalked the putt like a tiger, his face showed the strain of his day-long duel with the challenger. Finally, Jack hunched down over the ball and eyed the left-to-right breaking putt. Carefully he stroked the ball near, near, and into the cup. Nicklaus raised his putter toward the sky, imitating dancer Gene Kelly. The joyous expression not only was on the front page of every sports section in America the next day, but it would also appear on the cover of several golf books in the future.

Aoki finished second. Both broke Nicklaus's eighteen-hole Open record. Aoki joined the ever-growing ranks of professionals who had experienced the frustration of finishing behind the great champion in a major championship.

Due to his Open victory and the one in the PGA Championship, Nicklaus earned another honor: He was named *Golf Digest*'s Comeback Player of the Year.

Nicklaus was just twenty-two years old when he won his first United States Open, in 1962, forty when he was victorious at Baltusrol. Combined with the victories in 1967 and 1972, that meant Jack had won championships in his twenties, thirties, and forties.

Through 1996, Jack Nicklaus's performance in United States Open competition was staggering. His remarkable play had produced four championships, nine finishes in the top three, eleven in the top five, eighteen in the top ten, and twenty-two in the top twenty-five.

In forty starts, Nicklaus made the cut thirty-three times. Over one hundred and forty-eight rounds, the most by any golfer in history, Jack produced twenty-nine scores in the sixties, and thirty-seven rounds under par.

That record impressed Gene Littler more than any other. "You wouldn't think Jack Nicklaus would have a great Open record. Normally the champion was someone who hit the ball dead straight and Jack wasn't like that. But his power overcame that weakness. And he used his cunning to outthink everybody."

Littler saw another reason for Nicklaus's success in the Open. "Jack is the greatest putter I ever saw inside six feet. Especially on fast greens, which are typical of the Open. He didn't make a lot of long ones, but up close, under pressure, he was deadly."

The sixteenth United States Open in which Nicklaus played was at Pebble Beach in 1972. When he hit the vaunted one-iron at seventeen, two-up with two holes to play, Jack had weathered the storm of uneven play over the back nine.

Prior to Pebble Beach, Nicklaus had discussed his chances in *Golf Digest* and his thoughts about the seaside course as compared to Augusta National. "Augusta is a placement course for your second shot. Pebble is a placement course for your second shot. At Augusta, where it's usually calm, you have to hit it high. But at Pebble, where it can be rainy and windy and the ball stops better on the greens, you have to hit a lot of low, knockdown fades and hooks."

Nicklaus then added, "Pebble is the best thinking man's course in this country—probably in the world. Being a seaside course, you can get all different conditions. In the wind it can be the toughest course we play." Asked to assess his chances at the Grand Slam with one leg up (Masters), Nicklaus said, "It's possible. You would have a much better chance, though, if the tournaments were played four weeks in a row."

An astounding 4,196 golfers applied to play in the '72 championship. Qualifying rounds had pared that number sufficiently. First prize was $30,000 from a total purse of $200,000.

As if the pressure of the Open and the severity of Pebble Beach weren't enough, competitors faced another stiff challenge in 1972: breathing. Northern California in June had produced pollen and fog and inconsistent cold-hot conditions that drove noses crazy. Among the casualties was Orville Moody, who wore what *Golf World* journalist Dick Taylor called a "Ben Casey mask." Lanny Wadkins was making daily visits to the doctor's office for allergy shots, Ben Crenshaw had "itchy eyes," Bob Rosburg suffered from a bad cold, and Doug Sanders had a viral condition that left him ten pounds off his playing weight.

The most severely afflicted of the group was Lee Trevino, the defending Open champion who played despite doctor's orders to the contrary. A flu virus had weakened him to the point where he couldn't hit a drive more than 250 yards. "I feel like hell," he told reporters. "I should have stayed in bed." As for his medicinal assistance, Trevino told *Golf World*, "I've got all kinds of pills, I tell you. I got some that make you walk on water, some that let you swim, and some that make you fly. . . . But, hell, man, this is like the Indy 500, once a year, and if the engine blows, get a new one. I've got to give it a try."

Jack Nicklaus's play in the first round had been tolerable, though his putting was disappointing. He opened with 71, one-under, but missed five times from inside twelve feet, one for eagle, four for birdies. Meanwhile, Pebble served notice of tough days ahead. Frank Beard wrote a column criticizing the course as being too easy; then the golf gods got him and he shot 41-44-85. Professional Jim Jamison fired 41-41-82. His playing group also included 85 and 85, prompting him to ask the USGA's Frank Hannigan, "Can we turn in a best ball?"

Round two saw Nicklaus produce a lackluster 73. Two under par at thirteen, he'd knocked a ball out-of-bounds at fifteen. Two more bogeys squandered the makings of a good round.

The day belonged to Arnold Palmer. He carried out a 68 with six birdies and two bogeys. Despite the fine score, he missed nine putts under twenty feet, including a dinky one at eighteen. Dick Taylor wrote about Palmer's performance, "It must be awful to be putting like a human being after all those godly years."

Lanny Wadkins matched Palmer's 68. A first-round 76 had put him at 144 and earned him a six-way tie for the lead with Nicklaus, Bruce Crampton, Cesar Sanudo, Homero Blancos, and Kermit Zarley. Prospects of a shoot-out at tournament's end prompted *San Francisco Chronicle* journalist Art Spander to say, "It may be the first time the USGA started a play-off with a shotgun start."

Amazingly enough Lee Trevino, carting his portable medicine cabinet, was still a factor after three rounds. A 71 added to 74 and 72 left him one away from Nicklaus, who stood at 216. Zarley and Crampton were with Trevino at 217, Palmer (third-round 72) and Crampton at 218.

The wind had fluffed about inconsistently in the first three rounds of the '72 Open, but it rose to a vigorous gust in round four. Besides the difficulty of gauging club selection, another factor influenced fourth-round play: the state of the greens. Killer *Poa annua* had weakened them. Billy Casper commented about the wind and the condition of the greens to *Golf World*, "You had to absolutely plan the perfect shot, shot after shot, then execute the perfect shot, then be lucky . . . "

Jack Nicklaus later echoed those thoughts. "I can't recall a day like this when we were almost not playing golf," he told *Golf World*. "Golfing skills were almost eliminated. Half the greens were dead. I don't think the USGA was looking for this much wind the last day and rolled the greens the night before. If you made a putt, it was luck, not skill."

Lee Trevino's six at the second hole (en route to 78) eased Nicklaus's worries about him, but Jack was erratic as well. Bogeys at four and six presaged troubles, but Nicklaus recovered with two birdies, one coming at the seventh when a twenty-five-footer bobbed into the hole after a schizophrenic ride across the bumpy green. All the while, contenders were falling back. Putting dimmed Palmer's chances and Johnny Miller and Kermit Zarley were hacking their way to 79s.

The tournament was now Nicklaus's to lose. He led by four with nine to play, but it was far from over. Jack promptly opened the door when a gust of wind caused him to knock his tee ball on ten over the cliff on the right side. Later, he'd say, "The shot was about ten yards off line. But unfortunately there was no fairway in those ten yards and it landed on the beach."

Nicklaus's miscue threw the Open up for grabs. He made it even more so when after parring eleven, he rifled a three-iron too hot to handle over the 205-yard par three into heavy rough. The ball was barely visible and a slashing wedge moved it only a few feet. The new lie was a bit more manageable, permitting a recovery shot to within seven feet of the hole.

Up ahead at fourteen, Arnold Palmer faced a similar seven-footer for birdie. At the exact same moment in time, both tapped their putts. If Nicklaus missed and Palmer made, they would be dead even.

Even though he was visibly upset with his sloppy play, Nicklaus surveyed his putt with icy resolve. He knew any chance to win the tournament was on the line, since a double bogey at this late stage of the Open meant curtains.

After deliberate calculation, Nicklaus decided the putt moved just a hair from right to left. Calming his emotions, he crouched down over the ball. Time seemed to stand still as Jack took what felt as if it were five minutes to get his mind right to hit the ball. When the voice inside him finally said, "It's time," he drew back the putter and carefully stroked the ball toward the cup.

When it dropped and Palmer missed, Nicklaus kept his lead. Palmer proceeded to bogey the next two holes and finally finished four strokes back.

The putt Nicklaus holed was a corker. It was a classic chokepoint putt, the kind he faced time and again under the gun in major championships. "That seven footer I made was the most important all day," he told *Golf World*. "I would have gotten a little excited had I missed."

He also observed "I don't take things as seriously as I used to. After the tenth hole [double bogey], I simply thought, well, I had made my one big mistake of the round, everyone else was making at least one like that, maybe more, and refused to worry."

Nicklaus parred the thirteenth and fourteenth and then made a convincing birdie from twelve feet at the fifteenth. Sixteen was a routine par, and then Jack came to seventeen, the pivotal par three.

Bruce Crampton, fighting Nicklaus stroke-for-stroke, also double bogeyed the tenth. "I had been doing a good job of surviving all day even though play was tough. I nailed a good drive at ten, into the wind, but it was hit too far and I ended up in the bunker. I made six. Then I saw Jack had doubled the hole too. I thought I still had a chance."

His round of 75 completed, Bruce Crampton stood behind the eighteenth green and assessed Nicklaus's chances. "The seventeenth was playing so difficult with the wind and all," the Aussie said. "Since Jack hit the ball so high I thought he might knock it in the ocean."

Wishful thinking, Bruce, since the one-iron Jack hit there never wavered. It was bored low toward the pin, hitting just six inches or so directly in front of the cup and perfection. Its bounce flirted with going in, and then settled less than a foot from the cup. Point, set, match, tournament over.

"I heard the roar," Crampton said. "I knew Jack had done something special."

Nicklaus's description of the miracle shot was revealing. He explained that he was very aware of the threat to the left of the green. Guarding against a pull or hook, he dragged the club back inside of its intended route.

Realizing the continued pattern would produce a right-to-right shot, Nicklaus was able to adjust the effort on the downswing. The compensation factor worked perfectly. "The result, a very slight 'blocking' of the shot, produced a nice low, drilling-type flight dead on the stick," Jack later said.

Of course, no one but Jack knew he'd blocked the shot. To the thousands of spectators and millions of television viewers, it was just another memorable precision effort under pressure by Nicklaus. The fact that it was a one-iron on the seventy-first hole of a major championship catapulted it into the "unforgettable shot list."

Even a three-putt bogey at eighteen couldn't dampen the victory. Nicklaus's 274 was three shots better than Bruce Crampton, who had also finished second at the Masters, prompting him to tell *Golf World*, "I'm working on my own Slam, runner-up in all four major events in one year."

Nicklaus now had the Masters and the Open Championship in his pocket in 1972. Asked for his thoughts about equaling Bobby Jones's major wins record and his chances at the Grand Slam, he told Dick Taylor, "It's a funny feeling. I'm proud to be in his company. But to tell the truth, despite all the talk about the Slam, and thirteen majors, my only goal to this point was to win the first two major events of the year. I have never been able to do that before."

With the United States Open victory in 1972, Nicklaus was halfway home toward the Slam. Two down and two to go, the British Open and the PGA Championship.

# BOOK VI

# Nicklaus, The Renaissance Man

❖ ❖ ❖

# CHAPTER 42

# The 1972 British Open, Westchester, U.S. Pro Match Play

Midway through his career as a professional golfer, Jack Nicklaus decided he had better look for work. In other words, get a real job, one that would sustain itself when his playing days on the PGA Tour were over.

He was only twenty-five at the time, but thoughts of "retirement" were already filling his head. When someone pointed out that rival Arnold Palmer was thirty-five, Jack told friends he'd never be playing professional golf at *that* advanced age.

Nicklaus's sentiment was not unusual for a Tour player. His comment came long before anyone dreamed of the Senior Tour, and most professionals believed their playing days were numbered when they reached the age of thirty.

By 1972, Nicklaus had been pondering a career as a golf course architect for several years, and casting an ever increasing critical eye on the designs of courses. One such course was Westchester Country Club, home of the Westchester Classic in August of '72. There Jack was playing yet another fabled golf course, one rich in the heritage of legendary course designers.

Scores of 65, 67, and 70 propelled Nicklaus to the third-round lead at Westchester, designed by Aussie Walter Travis in 1916. Jack's chief pursuers were Jim Colbert, Homero Blancas, ex-Dallas fireman Dwight Nevil (a Tour rabbit who won the Monday Qualifier), and George Archer.

Heading into the final day at Westchester in 1972, Nicklaus led by two over Nevil. The final round saw charges by Jim Colbert, who fired a 65 that included a hole-in-one, and Homero Blancas, who also shot 65, but Nicklaus was never seriously threatened. He followed a career-long pattern by sealing the victory with birdies at the final two holes. He won by three over Colbert and five over Nevil, who closed with an uneventful 75.

Westchester followed by two months his stunning win at the United States Open and the recent unforgettable trip to Muirfield in Gullane, Scotland. Winning the second leg of the Grand Slam at Pebble Beach added additional credence to the notion that Jack could match Bobby Jones's 1932 achievement, and it sent him off to the British Open at Muirfield brimming with confidence.

No wonder golf fans liked his chances. Nicklaus's game was at a fever pitch, and the British Open was being played on his second favorite course in the world, one where glorious champions such as Harry Vardon, James Braid, and Ted Ray had won championships. Nicklaus had won there, too, galloping home with the British Open Crown in 1966 when he shot 70, 67, 75, and 70.

The 1972 British Open, billed "The Grand Slam Open," riveted the sporting world. Nicklaus arrived early and prepped by playing seven practice rounds. His chief rival appeared to be Trevino, the defending champion, who told reporters, "I didn't come to Scotland to help Nicklaus win the British Open. If I played golf with my wife, I'd try my best to beat the daylights out of her."

Trevino's low-level collection of shots were perfect for Muirfield, and, not surprisingly, he opened with 71, 70, and 66 to take a one-shot lead after fifty-four holes. The 66 was especially impressive because Trevino made birdies on the last five holes. Two of them came from a sand bunker hole out at sixteen and a chip-in at eighteen.

British favorite Tony Jacklin shot 67 in the third round and was a stroke back. Nicklaus stood six shots back after mundane rounds of 70, 72, and 71.

The final round was a dogfight between Trevino and Jacklin, but Nicklaus made it interesting.

Upset with his conservative play during the first fifty-four holes, Nicklaus produced an early birdie barrage and then two more at nine and ten. The result was a tie for the lead. Another birdie at eleven not only put Jack ahead but caused Barbara to later say she was moved to tears by the eruptions of the crowd.

Nicklaus missed four makeable birdie putts, however, on the next four holes. By the time he approached the sixteenth, a 188-yard par three, the lead remained a precarious single shot. If he parred sixteen, a birdie at the par-five seventeenth and par at eighteen (the same 3-4-4 finish he had in 1966), might very well mean a championship.

Ready for the challenge, Nicklaus hit a savvy four-iron. The ball pulled slightly, and an unlucky bounce left it in thick grass. The subsequent chip shot produced a seven-foot test, and Nicklaus hit his downhill right-to-left breaking putt a touch too hard. The resulting bogey put a clamp on the optimistic round. A poor drive at the seventeenth prevented any chance at birdie, and when Nicklaus parred eighteen, he finished 4, 5, 4, two-strokes worse than expected.

Meanwhile, Trevino and Jacklin moved to the seventeenth, which features a second shot landing area that *Golf Magazine* editor George Peper called "the most extraordinary terrain in golf, a one-hundred-yard expanse of humps, hollows, dips, and ridges containing three enormous bunkers."

At seventeen, the career of one golfer took a forward bound while another took a body blow that virtually ended his days as a contender in major championships. While Jackin played three fine shots to within fifteen feet of the cup and a potential birdie, Trevino was hacking his way all over the seventeenth. He finally faced a devious down hill pitch shot from a heavy lie laying four, prompting Jacklin to later say that he thought Trevino was resolved to making bogey or worse. Surely, the Brit had the tournament win within his grasp, that is, until Trevino holed the chip and Jacklin, dazed as a staggering boxer, three-putted for bogey.

In one of the great turnarounds in major tournament history, the diminutive Jacklin had made bogey instead of birdie, and he'd lost a shot to boot. Later, he said, "By tenfold, that was the worst shock I've ever had on a golf course."

In spite of Nicklaus's course-record 66, Trevino's par on the final hole made him the victor. The 3, 4, 4 finish Jack had desired would have won the tournament, but instead of winning by one, he lost by the same number. His chance for the Grand Slam in 1972 had ended, causing Nicklaus to lament, "Golf can be a heartbreaking game, and this was my number one heartbreak."

How Nicklaus would respond to the narrow loss was the question every golf fan asked himself. To lose by one shot after four grueling rounds must have weighed heavily on Nicklaus whether he would admit it or not. He had been so close. If just one of the 279 shots hit during the tournament had been saved, he would have been in a playoff for the third leg of the Grand Slam. If he had saved only two, whether from ten inches or 300 yards, he would have made the third turn in his race for history.

Instead, the euphoria surrounding Jack's shot at the Grand Slam ended. Part of any furor Nicklaus possessed was left on a Scottish tennis court that evening. By the next day Jack appeared to have shrugged off the defeat.

Nicklaus's ability to recover from such a loss was indicative of his strong character but was bolstered by a dose of Barbara's sound advice. Shortly after the British Open was over, she explained to *Golf Digest* her thoughts about her husband.

"Jack no longer goes into a major tournament feeling he *must* win," she explained. "He doesn't have a defeatist attitude if he doesn't win a big title. And he really doesn't think much about the Grand Slam. That's a concept that others have manufactured. It really hasn't changed him."

Barbara then went on to talk about the past. "After he lost the '71 Masters [Charles Coody won], he was really down. He had played well but lost. He wanted to pull out of the Tournament of Champions," she admitted, "but I told him he'd look like a crybaby if he did, so he played and won. . . . I think that incident made him realize that, though he'd lost [the Masters], he really hadn't lost his life. I really think it helped him mature both as a golfer and as a person."

In the article, Barbara also shed light on what winning meant to Jack. "Five years ago [1967] he really wasn't enjoying golf," she said. "He had this great talent and he was winning, but winning wasn't completely satisfying. Then when his father died [1970]—they were great buddies—it was the first real tragedy of Jack's life. He felt that he'd let his dad down; that he'd wasted the last three years of his golfing life. . . . Jack now has more desire to play than ever before."

Jack Nicklaus's thoughts in the same article supported Barbara's words regarding his refreshed attitude about golf and life in general. After the British Open defeat, reporters asked him about the potential for a Grand Slam in the future. A smiling Nicklaus joked, "I guess I'd have to say the odds have gone up a bit."

Nicklaus did have words of praise for the better man at the British Open, a trait his dad had instilled in him at an early age. "I told Barbara before the [final] round I thought a 65 would win. . . . I simply did my best [66], but got beat by the best around. That Lee Trevino is some good player."

Barbara and Jack's thoughts aside, his comment that the loss at

Muirfield was "heartbreaking" seems more in tune with his mindset. Never one to reveal inner emotions, he exhibited the tough exterior that was to become a Nicklaus trademark. Like the turtle who withdraws into its shell when besieged, Jack felt uncomfortable exposing any sign of weakness.

Privately Nicklaus stewed about the loss in Scotland and viewed it as a profound setback. He thought the victory was his and his only. How many more chances would he have at the Grand Slam, the one record he coveted most of all?

His bravado notwithstanding, Nicklaus appeared to go through the motions at the PGA Championship at Oakland Hills. His play was lifeless, at least until the last few holes when, in true Nicklaus fashion, he resurrected the spirit of a champion.

Playing companion Dan Sikes saw the Nicklaus drive. "He came to the fifteenth hole several shots behind," Sikes told *Golf Digest*. "Those [at Oakland Hills] are four of the toughest finishing holes in golf, and do you know what he said? He said that if he could birdie in he still might win. He just never gives up."

Many blamed an injured finger for Jack's flat play at the PGA; the more likely cause was Muirfield and the scars it left.

Prior to the PGA, Bruce Crampton had been listed by *Golf Digest* as the odds-on favorite at six to one. Tom Weiskopf and Nicklaus were next at seven to one, followed by Lee Trevino, George Archer, and Bob Murphy at eight to one. Gary Player was listed as ten to one to win.

It was Player who emerged victorious in the PGA Championship, beating Tommy Aaron and Jim Jamison by two shots. Ageless wonder Sam Snead finished in a tie for fourth at age sixty.

Nicklaus would have liked to borrow some of Player's magic that year but rounds of 72, 75, 68, and 72 placed him thirteenth. Experts wondered whether Nicklaus would fold his tent for the year and simply play out the schedule, which included competition at Westchester, the Liggett and Myers U.S. Match Play Tournament, the Kaiser International, the Sahara Invitational, and the Walt Disney Open.

The PGA tournament at Westchester again demonstrated that Nicklaus played the course, not his fellow players. Sizing up Walter Travis's famed layout, he found elements of the design that were appealing to him and stored them away in his memory bank.

Nicklaus's fascination with course architecture was his bridge to the business world. Through the years, Mark McCormack had counseled him regarding business affairs and lined his pockets with cash from endorsements, investments, and other business transactions. Finally, in 1970, Jack decided to go solo.

Ventures in golf club design, golf schools, golf centers, and licensed products came later, but Nicklaus's early fascination away from competition was golf course architecture. Alice Dye, designer Pete's better half, remembers Jack's enchantment with course design in the late sixties.

"He told Pete he was looking for something to do after golf," Alice recalls. "He was only twenty-seven or twenty-eight at the time, but back then professional golfers thought they wouldn't play much past thirty."

Pete Dye remembers his early talks with Jack. "He came out to The Golf Club, a course I was building near New Albany, Ohio. It was in its early stages then, but he liked what we were doing. He and I walked the course and he gave me several good suggestions. Years later, that memory like an elephant he has allowed him to remember every hole and exactly the comment he'd made the first day he saw the course. It was truly remarkable."

In the early seventies, Nicklaus said, "I chose to work with Pete . . . because he tries to make it a rule never to be involved in more than three courses simultaneously. He believes the architect must be present during the building of a course and personally direct his crew in shaping the greens, the hazards, and the rest. This is the way I feel that you must go about constructing a course." Although those may have been his thoughts at the time, he later modified them when he formed his own architectural firm.

Nicklaus's main intent in the mid-sixties was still to win every golf tournament in which he competed, but he prepared for the future by becoming associated with Dye's budding design company. That led to a collaboration of sorts, which produced one of America's finest golf courses, Harbour Town Golf Links.

The shot-makers paradise was the result of a joint effort between Nicklaus and Charles Fraser, the visionary developer who turned a desolate island without a bridge near Hilton Head, South Carolina, into a first class international resort. Fraser had already built two courses on the island but wanted an "old-fashioned" look for a new one to be located on four hundred acres of low-lying land.

Wanting a "name" attached to the design, Fraser phoned Nicklaus, who put him in touch with Pete Dye. The opportunity to build the seaside links course with the famed lighthouse on the eighteenth hole was the break of a lifetime for both men in terms of their respective architectural careers.

How much each man contributed to the actual design of Harbour Town is subject to opinion. Although Nicklaus was designated a co-designer, respected golf journalist Charles Price guessed Jack's contribution was a scant "one percent." That crosses hairs with Dan Jenkins's headline in an article he wrote for *Sports Illustrated* immediately after Arnold Palmer's victory in the first Heritage Classic that read, "Jack's Course Is Arnie's Too."

In the article, Jenkins labels Harbour Town, "Pebble Beach East," but the course had a distinctive character and was revolutionary in design. Tedious holes as those designed by Robert Trent Jones featured long, flat fairways and large greens. At Harbour Town, they were replaced by short- and medium-length holes featuring undulating fairways, long waste areas, pot bunkers, and railroad ties abutting many of the hazards. The Scottish tradition that impressed Pete and Alice Dye during a trip to the old country in the sixties now was to be a part of their American course design forever. Their innovative designs—as those of Alister MacKenzie, Seth Raynor, Donald Ross, and Robert Trent Jones before them as well as Nicklaus, Tom Fazio, and others of note later—dictated the "look" of golf in the twentieth century.

Pete Dye was quick to point out Nicklaus's contributions at Harbour Town (Jack made numerous site visits), as well as that of others. "What I built there," he wrote in his autobiography, *Bury Me in a Pot Bunker*, "is a Pete Dye, Alice Dye, Jack Nicklaus, George Cobb, (initial routings) Charles Price (the writer made several suggestions) course. Nicklaus was especially helpful in an area that one might not expect. In spite of being a long hitter," Pete wrote, "Jack had a real sensitivity for what I wanted to do with the shorter yardage holes at Harbour Town."

Nicklaus also surprised Dye with suggestions about the size of the greens, in particular on the par-five fifteenth. "We then walked to the pint-sized green site, where Jack surprised me by suggesting it be half the size I had in mind."

Whatever the relationship or individual contribution, Harbour Town was an instant success when it opened in 1969. The achievement boosted Dye's career, and he paid tribute to Jack for bringing him in on the project. Nicklaus also benefited from the experience. Fewer than four years later, at age thirty-four, he started his own design firm. Today, he lists Harbour Town in his corporate brochure as one of his four courses included in *Golf Magazine's* list of "World's Greatest

Courses," although taking sole credit for it seems an exaggeration at the very least.

Regardless of who did what at Harbour Town, the two giants of their respective professions have remained good friends throughout the years, although Nicklaus takes a teasing about Harbour Town from time to time. At the 1996 convention of the prestigious American Society of Golf Course Architects, Nicklaus and Dye shared the forum at a symposium on course design.

Jack was the first speaker and took the opportunity to detail the marvelous design of Pinehurst number 2, which was near the conference. After astounding the audience with a detailed hole-by-hole analysis of the Donald Ross gem and each shot he had ever hit there, Nicklaus introduced Dye by saying, "Here's Pete Dye. I first worked with him at Harbour Town. The reason I remember is that he got paid, and I didn't."

After the audience finished laughing, Pete took his shot. "And that's exactly what you were worth," he said, while Nicklaus howled with the rest of the group. No one was sure how Jack really felt about the remark. Nicklaus could be thin-skinned and has, at times, resented not being fully accepted by his design peers for the outstanding work he feels he has accomplished. That made it difficult for him to gain entrance into the Society of Golf Course Architects because many felt he wasn't qualified.

Over the years, Nicklaus courted that acceptance and respect for his design ideas. At first, many thought he might be another in a long line of golf professionals who charged a fat fee for simply lending their name to a course. These interlopers would make a visit when ground was broken, again when the course opened, and then be on their merry way. Nicklaus never did things that way, though. He became a hands-on designer who was genuinely interested in course architecture.

# CHAPTER 43

# Jack the Golf Course Designer

Jack Nicklaus knew early on that he wanted to design golf courses. "It has been said that every golfer is a golf course architect," he observed in the late sixties. "While I'm not an especially artistic or creative person, even when I was a boy making my first visits to new courses something inside of me responded instinctively whenever I came upon a hole that appeared to have exceptional golf quality."

By the time Nicklaus decided to become a golf course architect, he had played nearly all of the great courses in the world. From one end of the globe to the other, he had experienced the wonders of Pebble Beach, Augusta National, Pine Valley, Merion, Oakmont, Prairie Dunes, Oakland Hills, Pinehurst #2, Muirfield, Turnberry, and St. Andrews. He kept mental notes of the positives and negatives of each course and began to glean whatever knowledge he could regarding other aspects of golf course architecture.

Just as he had learned to play golf from Jack Grout, a master craftsman, Nicklaus sought instruction on course architecture from Pete Dye. Ever the traditionalist, Dye had followed in the steps of Donald Ross (the wunderkind of designers who gave the world Pinehurst and Seminole) and Seth Raynor (a disciple of Charles Blair McDonald, designer of the great course Camargo in Cincinnati). "Jack always wanted to learn," Pete said.

Nicklaus also looked to the designs of Desmond Muirhead, a Cambridge-educated Englishman whose ideas were deemed radical by some. Later, when the two collaborated on several designs, *Links Magazine* dubbed them "Ying and Yang."

Based on conversations with Dye and Muirhead, and his own observations, Jack caught the designer bug. His mind like a sponge, Jack never forgot a hole. Finally, it was time to act. "The experience [of working with Dye] has proved to be so stimulating," Jack said, "that it has confirmed my long-range intentions to spend more and more time in that field as I cut down on the amount of competitive golf I play."

When Jack said this, his golf game was ailing. The years from 1967 through 1970 were disappointing ones. Until he won the British Open in 1970, he'd endured a drought of major victories dating back to the 1967 United States Open.

Nicklaus was thus apt and eager to learn all he could about his new profession. It was then that he laid the groundwork for what turned out to be a second passion with the game he loved so much. By doing so, he followed in the footsteps of golfers such as McDonald, a national amateur champion, and Ross, a professional, who had successfully pursued golf course architecture as a profession. Through the years, Bruce Devlin, Tom Watson, Gary Player, Arnold Palmer, Tom Weiskopf, Ben Crenshaw, Hale Irwin, and Raymond Floyd, among others, would try their hand at design as well.

How much Nicklaus studied the techniques of past masters is an unanswerable question. During an interview in 1994 with he and Pete Dye, Jack was asked about a collection of books on a nearby office shelf that included those written by Donald Ross, Alister MacKenzie, George Thomas Jr., Charles Blair McDonald, and others of note. "I see you have the same set of books that Pete has in his home," the interviewer observed. "Yeah," Jack said, "but he's read them and I haven't."

Whether Nicklaus was being flippant or not (business associate Tom Peterson said Jack read them and also told his son Jackie to do so), his ideas about course design in his early years reflected a traditional view. "All first class golf courses," he explained, "and all outstanding golf holes have one thing in common to the golfer's eye: They look absolutely natural, as if the terrain had always been that way, waiting to be discovered for golf." He also added, "This is where the golf architect comes in as he visualizes and stakes out his holes. His job is to make the best possible use of the natural features of the terrain, then to use his modern earth-moving equipment with taste and imagination in shaping the supporting features that his holes need."

The specific holes that Jack said impressed him at that time included the par-five thirteenth at Augusta and the par-four third at Pebble Beach. For Jack, they were prime examples of holes where the player needed to make one great shot for birdie. The fourteenth at Augusta, which exemplified Bobby Jones's concept of "intrinsically long par-four-and-one-halfs," and the extremely difficult "drive and pitch" 378-yard eleventh at Merion, called the "Baffling Brook" hole (a creek cuts in front of the green and then continues along the right side), were also high on Nicklaus's favorite-holes list. Examples of "strong, assertive finishing holes" included the eighteenth at Pebble Beach, Carnoustie, Merion, Muirfield (Scotland), Hoylake, and Baltusrol.

In effect, Nicklaus wanted to build golf holes that had no trick to them and were devoid of gimmicks an props. Though he admired Pete Dye, famous for pot bunkers, railroad ties, and gyrating mounds, as well as Desmond Muirhead, later to build courses with holes shaped like mermaids and tomahawks and bunkers resembling animals, Nicklaus went his own way. And his courses reflected his perfectionist tendencies.

That philosophy was in Jack's mind for an early course he wanted to design and build near his hometown of Columbus, Ohio. Later, Nicklaus was to tell *Golf Digest* that the idea for the course came to him during play in the 1966 Masters. At the time, he was sitting on the veranda at the clubhouse with Igor Young, a close friend from Ohio. "I thought the Masters was a great thing for golf, and I'd like to do the same thing in Columbus," Jack told *Golf Digest*. "I wanted the finest course we could have to house a major tournament and to be of service to the game. I told Igor to go back and buy some land."

That "land" turned out to be acres of farmland in Dublin, northwest of Columbus. Jack and his partners not only envisioned a golf course of distinction but also an entire community of homes and shopping areas. It would take nearly eight years for Nicklaus to break ground, but Muirfield was worth the wait.

With Desmond Muirhead working with him as co-designer, Jack incorporated all of his favorite architectural ideas into Muirfield. Over a period of twenty years, he revised it considerably. "No great golf course is ever right at the start," he said, ". . . golf courses aren't built . . . they evolve." Muirfield, named after the famed course in Scotland, was a masterpiece from the first day, however. Located among beautiful rolling hills in deep woods, the course sat like a brave warrior, awaiting a challenge. The trouble was laid directly in front of the golfer, with deep-set, stately bunkers pockmarking the course.

Nicklaus's imaginative routing ideas and the diversity of the hole lengths challenged the player at every turn. Despite spring rains that threatened to devour it on occasion, the course was kept in perfect condition, with nary a blade of grass out of place.

Nicklaus treated Muirfield as a pampered child, and its reputation grew steadily through the years. Jack drew on his knowledge as a player to set up a practice area that the professionals deem the finest on Tour. "Muirfield's a great course," said Tom Watson. "Jack's done himself proud."

In 1975, Muirfield became the home for the PGA event The Memorial. The tournament is dedicated each year to an individual, living or dead, who has played or served the game with conspicuous honor. The first to be honored was, predictably, Robert T. Jones Jr. Other honorees include Gene Sarazen, Tom Morris Sr., Tom Morris Jr., Patty Berg, Tommy Armour, and Mickey Wright. Ben Hogan has been invited several times but has refused to attend. In 1993, Jack and his colleagues honored Arnold Palmer, signaling further proof of Jack's respect for his bygone adversary.

A distinguished advisory group also exists at Muirfield under the banner "The Captains Club." Members include a diverse array of personalities, including golf author and historian Herbert Warren Wind, entertainer Bob Hope, 1965 PGA champion and television golf analyst Dave Marr, and Academy Award winning actor Sean Connery. Each year a captain of Muirfield Village Golf Club is honored for his or her support of the tournament. The 1996 winner was none other than Barbara Nicklaus.

Two years after completing Muirfield, Nicklaus designed Glen Abbey in Oakville, Ontario, Canada, significant because it was the first public golf course to be designed for major tournaments with the spectator in mind.

"The theory of Glen Abbey was that spectators could stand in the central core and see the greater part of play on fifteen of the eighteen holes," Nicklaus said. "I then designed a mid-core where the golf fan could come closer to the competitors and really feel like they were part of the action."

The course served as a springboard to future Nicklaus "spectator-friendly golf courses."

"When we began to work on the Tournament Players course at Ponte Vedra, Florida," Alice Dye said, "Commissioner Deane Beman said we needed to go look at Glen Abbey. We flew up there and Pete looked at the spectator mounds. Jack was the first to do that."

Although Muirfield may be Nicklaus's legacy as an architect, the course that catapulted him toward the top of the profession was Desert Highlands, completed in 1984. Just as Pete Dye had revolutionized design, Jack Nicklaus's fine work in the deserts of Arizona provided a model for other designers. Ron Whitton, golf course-design aficionado and respected author of *The Architects of Golf*, described the course this way: "Desert Highlands didn't prove that golf could be successfully integrated into the desert. . . . What [it] did was mesh the game into a desert better than anyone else had done before." The key, Whitton wrote, was "the use of 'transition areas,' a buffer between manicured turf and native desert of unplayable pebbles and course rock. The transition areas were wide troughs of native sand . . . on each side of the fairway. These troughs collected errant shots, prevented balls from bounding out into unplayable lies and afforded opportunities to hit decent recovery shots."

Ron Whitton and others also noted the exquisite look of Nicklaus-designed courses. "Nicklaus wanted his courses to look almost perfect," Whitton wrote. "No expense was spared." That meant many areas had to be hand mowed, since machines couldn't traverse the uneven terrain. High construction and maintenance costs, added to Nicklaus's million-dollar fees, forced course owners to have deep pockets.

Over the years, Nicklaus's Golden Bear Company diversified into areas of business besides golf course design: personal endorsement, golf club design, and an assorted array of opportunities unrelated to golf. At the center of it all was Jack, who retained his high visibility with continued great performances on Tour and around the world.

Nicklaus's ability to stir interest in his persona with product endorsements reflected a strong ability on his part to self-promote. His decision to do so came at just the right time.

In the 1960s, Nicklaus's unattractive appearance and aloof nature brought few product endorsement offers. In a decade known for its unrest, others, like boxer Cassius Clay, were more in tune with the times. As journalist Jimmy Cannon told the *Washington Post*, "It is as though [Clay] was created to represent [the sixties].

With the dawning of the seventies, however, companies were looking for a different personality, one who conveyed stability and reason. The "new," svelte Nicklaus was the perfect choice.

The sports figures who competed against Jack for endorsements were notable, but even the likes of Fran Tarkington, O.J. Simpson, Richard Petty, Kareem Abdul-Jabbar, and A.J. Foyt couldn't muster just the right image. Nicklaus did. He had carefully cultivated it over the first part of the decade when he lost weight and let his hair grow.

Soon, the more attractive Jack was seen everywhere. Ken Denlinger of the *Washington Post* observed, "Off the course, [Nicklaus] can scarcely escape you. He pitches cars and clothes, lawnmowers, airlines and entire golf courses. He smacks wedges from enormous dirt movers. Dash to the kitchen and you bump into his wife's picture on an oven ad."

Like other opportunities he pursued, Nicklaus exhaustively prepared himself for the endorsement area. He and Barbara both took acting lessons, though Jack was self-effacing about his abilities.

At the time, Nicklaus's business acumen was just beginning to flower. "I've always had a third motivation [besides family and golf]," he said, "which is the sheer enjoyment of exercising and stretching my mind in a field completely removed from golf."

That said, Jack laid out the Nicklaus standard of excellence in business. For him to join a venture, no matter how potentially lucrative it might be, a rigid set of criteria had to be met: The product had to be a "credible one he believed in"; an association could be made "over the long haul" (it wasn't a get-rich-quick scheme); he could fully commit himself "regarding his ideas, expertise, interest, and time"; and the business arrangement was one that worked equally well for all the parties, in both "human and financial terms."

Nicklaus endorsed American Express, Magic Chef, and Uniden (Extend-a-phone). The visibility made him a familiar face even to those who knew nothing about his golf ability.

LPGA Tour veteran Carol Mann applauded Nicklaus's desire to build solid relationships of long duration. "Many players just took the money and signed their names to the contracts," she said. "They didn't care who they represented. Jack was a great role model. He wanted quality relationships with products, like Pontiac, that he used himself."

Nicklaus believed his involvement in the business world was actually good for his golf game. "The truth is that if I didn't have something to exercise and stretch my mind beyond hitting a golf ball, I'd go nuts." Then he added, "Within the scheme of things, business, by taking me more completely away from golf than any other activity, is actually what most keeps me hungry to get back in it."

During this time, Nicklaus's mug was everywhere, and he continued to expand his diverse business dealings off the golf course. His interests included deals with Toro (irrigation), Kaiser-Roth (shoes), MacGregor Golf, Hathaway (shirts), Firestone, Eastern Air Lines, Pontiac, Murray (lawnmowers), and Hart, Schaffner, and Marx (clothing).

Many early opportunities were rejected when associates found difficulty persuading Jack to cooperate with potential endorsement opportunities. "Jack's basically shy," a former associate said. "And he didn't really like to dress up and go hob-nob with the corporate set. Later on, he got better at it."

Even overtures from the White House were ignored. He received several invitations to visit but turned them all down. It didn't matter whether the request came from a Democratic or Republican president. "Jack was never much into politics," the associate said. "He's probably more inclined toward the Republican way of thinking, but that's about it."

In addition to his success with endorsements, Nicklaus was making huge strides with fees as a course designer.

Putt Pierman, whose loss of forty pounds served to inspire Nicklaus's weight loss, was responsible for bringing Jack together with Desmond Muirhead. Pierman then helped negotiate a one million dollar design fee for the two in Japan, the highest ever paid for architectural work at that time.

Nicklaus's price tag, in turn, elevated the fees charged by other architects. Some were jealous of Jack's compensation figures and criticized them, but they all benefited from his success.

Nicklaus's decision to leave IMG (International Marketing Group) and Mark McCormack as a management client in 1970 was intriguing. One thing is certain. At the time McCormack was bitter, later calling Nicklaus a "fat kid with a golden spoon in his mouth." McCormack felt he was responsible for Nicklaus's success and that the "kid" was unappreciative and unreasonably jealous of Arnold Palmer's relationship with him.

Another view of the split came from Pierman, the successful businessman from Ohio, who teamed up with Nicklaus after he left IMG. "Jack was not well-apprised of his financial situation—for someone who earned as much as he had, he had grave problems," Pierman told *Golf Digest*. "The McCormack stable grew too fast, probably faster than Mark realized. At the time, Jack was a programmed second-stringer in the McCormack stable."

Whether Nicklaus perceived it that way or not, he parted company with McCormack, just as Greg Norman would do years later after he had signed with IMG. Time seems to have healed many of the wounds between Nicklaus and the Cleveland-based lawyer and agent. At least McCormack wants the public to believe that's so. In IMG's 1996 publication, "Guide to Sports Marketing," a picture is prominently displayed of a smiling Jack and Barbara beside McCormack. Still, no one seems comfortable when the two men are in the same room.

Carol Mann saw the Nicklaus-McCormack split as significant. "Jack's leaving IMG made a point," Mann said. "He was the first one to go out on his own and his decision made some skeptical of IMG. I admired him for doing it."

Deane Beman said, "Mark was very good for Jack, removing early financial burdens. But then Nicklaus decided he had his own agenda."

The company Jack Nicklaus started in 1970 was small in size and stature. He had a staff of two, Ester Fink, his bookkeeper, and Tom Peterson, a successful former banker served as treasurer. Putt Pierman, described as a visionary by some and an out-of-control whirling dervish by others, joined the company until 1975.

In 1976, Chuck Perry, the former president of Florida International (college), was added. Two years later, the company expanded its executive staff, adding noted writer Ken Bowden to handle the Nicklaus publishing interests and Larry O'Brien, a highly respected journalist, to handle public relations. Larry launched the annual "State of the Union" address that Nicklaus gave every winter when golf writers from around the country were invited to Jack's business lair.

Bill Sansing, another Nicklaus executive, established the annual "Partnership Meetings," at which Jack met with corporate executives with whom he had endorsement contracts. All the while, Chuck Perry permitted Golden Bear, Inc., to drift into oil and gas development, real estate, and insurance. During that time, the company acquired MacGregor Golf, a brand Nicklaus had used since his first days as a golfer.

Through the seventies, the Nicklaus business boom continued as he cultivated relationships with large corporations. His interest in such matters increased to the point where even fishing took a back seat. He told *Golf World*, "It is a beautiful arrangement I have with my business associates. I can be as involved or uninvolved as I wish. I choose to be involved. This means no more fishing, but I enjoy this much more."

The business grew steadily through the eighties, until a dark cloud appeared over Nicklaus's kingdom. With Perry's input, Nicklaus's company found itself 90-percent owners of two golf course projects—one at Bear Creek Golf Club in Murietta, California, the other at St. Andrews Golf Club in Hastings-on-Hudson, New York. Both projects experienced severe financial problems when the real estate developers operating the facilities miscalculated. Membership campaigns and accompanying real estate developments bordering the courses fell short of expectations. When the dust settled, each development was swimming in debt of six million dollars. Nicklaus was forced to come up with twelve million dollars out of his own pocket to plug the dike.

Predictably, Chuck Perry, who, one former associate said, had "Nicklaus in the palm of his hand," was relieved of his duties. He took the fall for the golf course investment debacle even though design fees for Nicklaus skyrocketed from $75,000 to one million dollars during his tenure. Later, Perry told *USA Today,* "Jack's a good guy to work for and to work with . . . [but] he has a couple of flaws. He listens to the last guy who talks to him. I used to say, 'Jack, if the guy pumpin' gas told you to change the design on your golf shirt, you'd change it.'" Nicklaus saw it differently, saying, "Chuck worked very hard for me . . . but he wanted to build an empire . . . But I don't want an empire . . . I've got five kids, a beautiful wife, and I'm hoping on some grandchildren. That's what I care about."

The twelve-million-dollar hit, which answered concerns that the company would file for Chapter 13 bankruptcy, caused not only Perry's exit but also a reorganization of the company in the mid-eighties. Just as he'd done with a golf game gone sour in the late sixties, Jack took charge, brought in new associates, sold off assets including condominiums and other real estate, and began to slowly pull the company from its doldrums.

"It was Jack's finest hour," Tom Peterson says. "He was a bit like his mother, a wonderful lady, but one who had a negative side. He always had a glum attitude, especially when it came to business. That made it tough for people to deal with him in the early days. But when he lost all that money on the golf courses, Jack really showed his stuff. He said, 'OK, let's turn this around.' Jack, Dick Bellinger, the CEO of the company now, George Chane, David Sherman, and I, all members of the executive committee, came up with a game plan. In less than four years, the company was back in the black."

There is no doubt that Jack Nicklaus actively ruled each division of Golden Bear, especially after the golf course development fiasco. Although he encouraged associates to exercise independent thinking and gave them responsibility, Jack was and still is the boss.

Those who have gone head-to-head with him in business report the same intensity that Nicklaus exhibits on the golf course. "He's been taken advantage of on occasion," one associate said, "but those instances have been few and far between." Tom Peterson said, "Jack's fair with everyone but those who try to bullshit him. He has the great ability to sort through the wheat from the chaff. The worst thing to try to do is bullshit Jack."

As a negotiator, Jack is fair but firm. "He truly seems to want a deal that is fair for everyone," commented one businessman who has dealt with Jack through the years. Even so, Clark Johnson and George Nichols, two former associates, told *USA Today* that "like most professional athletes, Jack is self-centered, which can be both good and bad in business."

Their comment seems at odds with others who have worked with Jack. Certainly he enjoyed his celebrity status, but no one could accuse Nicklaus of being pompous.

And he is exceedingly loyal to those who are loyal to him, especially employees. When former Scioto friend Hugh "Sockeye" Davis, who worked for Jack for years, retired, Nicklaus paid him a full salary for as long as he lived.

His loyalties extend to friends and business associates. Gary Player said, "Jack is as loyal as they come. If I asked him to come to South Africa and play, and he committed, he'd be there. No questions. Other pros would phone the week before and skip out. Not Jack. If he said he'd do it, he'd do it. We've been friends for more than forty years. I love the man."

According to Tom Weiskopf, Nicklaus was loyal to the point of harming his golf game. "Most people don't realize," Weiskopf said, "that Jack played the game during his prime with an inferior golf ball and horrible clubs. At the time, he was linked up with MacGregor. Their golf ball was awful, much inferior to the Titliest, which was the only good ball."

Nicklaus also played the MacGregor irons. "They made bad irons, especially the eight, nine and pitching wedge," Weiskopf said. "In effect, Jack played with a handicap. I know because I played with the damn clubs too under an endorsement deal. But Jack wouldn't switch. He was loyal as hell to MacGregor."

# CHAPTER 44

# Jack at Work

The Nicklaus/Golden Bear conglomerate is located along United States Highway One in North Palm Beach, Florida, not far from Jack's home at Lost Tree. The interior is a blend of gold and green, the atmosphere resembling a corporate locker room.

There are eight divisions in the company: Golden Bear, Inc., Jack Nicklaus Marketing Services, Nicklaus Design, Jack Nicklaus Golf Operations, Nicklaus/Flick Golf Schools, Nicklaus Sierra Development Company, and Nicklaus Publishing. Nearly 140 employees work for the company. Yearly revenues run between fifty and sixty million dollars.

Jack is not a nine-to-five man. He juggles his hours of work between a schedule that takes him around the globe in Air Bear, his Gulfstream jet.

The jet serves as Nicklaus's office away from the office. In May of 1991, he embarked on a two and a half day global tour of all his golf courses, taking off and landing like Canadian geese looking for scattered corn.

Nicklaus's corporate office on the fifth floor at Golden Bear (design takes up the fourth) is unpretentious. It is also immaculate. His huge desk sets at one end. Two couches at the other. Cabinets and bookshelves line the walls. There is little hint of Jack the golfer.

The desk is never littered with work. Jack the businessman is as meticulous with his office as he is on the golf course.

Nicklaus's longtime secretary Marilyn Keough, a fastidiously organized woman with a lovely smile, keeps his imposing schedule in check. Jack is the only one who spends much time on the links, telling employees, "I'm the only guy in this company who gets paid to play golf."

Although most of Nicklaus's business endeavors have been pleasant ones over the last few years, he experienced two disappointments in the mid-nineties. First, the hometown folk in Dublin, Ohio, rejected plans regarding the site of a proposed Jack Nicklaus Museum. Still searching for a site, Jack felt betrayed by the decision, but as usual, kept his thoughts to himself.

Nicklaus was also rebuffed in his efforts to raise private venture capital to expand the company. Instead, a public offering was initiated in August of 1996, with 1.8 million shares being offered at $14 to $16. Unrest plagued Golden Bear International for months before the offering, with faithful employees unsure of the impact of dividing up the Nicklaus empire. For years, profit in the design area of the business (sixteen million dollars in 1996) had counterbalanced losses in the other divisions, including Executive Sports, a management company Jack bought from friend John Montgomery. Employees wondered what the result of the offering would be because the unprofitable divisions plus ten percent of the design division were being included in the deal.

When the nearly half-inch thick prospectus offering 2,160,000 shares of Golden Bear, Inc., hit the NASDAQ stock exchange, it featured a large imprint of the Golden Bear logo on the cover. Inside, prestigious stockbrokers lauded the Nicklaus name, and the pages were dotted with color photos of a Golden Bear Golf Center, The Jack Nicklaus Coaching Studio, and Jack Nicklaus licensed apparel. The chief entity, Golden Bear, Inc., included three divisions: Golf (licensing, ownership, and operation of golf practice and instruction facilities), construction (technical construction services in connection with construction and renovation of golf courses), and marketing (licenses Nicklaus, Jack Nicklaus, and Golden Bear branded consumer products, as well as operates Nicklaus/Flick Golf Schools). Not included in the offering was the remaining 90 percent of the Nicklaus design business and Nicklaus Golf Equipment, the latter a partnership Jack shared with former publishing magnet Nelson Doubleday.

In sum and substance, the offering's effect on Golden Bear, Inc., was to provide more than thirty million dollars worth of operating capital. Financial gain to Jack, Barbara, and the five children meant millions on paper through their stock options. The offering was fully funded, with the stock opening at $16, rising to $22½, and then leveling off in the $18 to $19 range.

The success of the venture was not surprising since Nicklaus's name recognition was still producing whopping endorsement revenues in 1996. In a poll conducted by *Sports Marketing Letter*, Jack's endorsement level was pegged at $14.5 million a year, a figure ranking him just behind Michael Jordan ($38 million), Shaquille O'Neal ($23 million), Arnold Palmer ($16 million), and Andre Agassi ($15.8 million).

All of his business ventures have been important to Nicklaus, but it is the golf course design division that he is most proud of. In the company brochure, he observed, "Designing golf courses is my legacy. They will be here for players to enjoy long after I am gone."

Nicklaus's superb reputation and name value allowed him to command million-dollar fees for course design and construction all over the world. He tentacles stretch into every corner of the globe: Solbiate, Italy; Jakarta, Indonesia; Zongshan, China; and Boffemont, France. By 1995, 124 Nicklaus courses worldwide were open for play in twenty-one states and twenty-four countries, with twenty-eight more under construction.

Nicklaus has brought into his architectural firm several young, talented designers, such as Lee Schmidt, who apprenticed with Pete Dye. Like Dye, who tutored many aspiring designers, Nicklaus was responsible for the evolution of the multi-talented Bob Cupp, and Jay Moorish, who later associated himself with Tom Weiskopf.

Although Nicklaus's controlling nature and power-broker propensities have caused turmoil between him and his apprentices from time to time, most who have worked for him speak more positively than negatively.

"Jack has always shown great respect to Lee," one of Nicklaus's close friends said. "In some ways, other than Jack, Lee *is* the design department. Jack may differ with him about his style with bunkers and so forth, but there's a definite mutual respect there."

The designers working for Jack walk a tightrope. "Jack is very opinionated, always has to be right," one former associate said. "He criticizes people in front of others and can be quite rude. That alienates him to a lot of people. It's the reason he doesn't have any real close friends. But the designers who work for him like doing so, and Jack also has a generous side that is very appealing."

The associate added, "He's not like Palmer, who spent little time at some of the courses that bore his name. Jack's not like that, he's totally involved, especially with courses in the States. He gives his designers latitude, but wants them to tell him before they do anything drastic to change a hole. If they mess up, and get on Jack's bad side, it's tough to reverse that feeling." In fact, it's virtually impossible.

Another designer who has worked with Jack talked about recognizing how to size up Nicklaus from day to day. "I wouldn't call him moody, but there are days when he *is* a bear. He comes to the office in shorts, a golf shirt, and Rockport Shoes nearly every day, but I watch his reaction to the first question I ask or what he brings up. If he's in a bad mood, I stay away, but in the last couple of years he's been pleasant since the company is doing well."

When Nicklaus is disgusted or downright mad, he is not one to normally produce a verbal barrage. Instead colleagues talk about the "Nicklaus Look." Many have described it, but the best description may have come from caddie Angelo Argea.

The incident that precipitated his comments resulted when Angelo overslept during a round of the Sahara Invitational in Las Vegas. A night-owl itinerant gambler, Argea failed to show for Jack's tee time. Since Angelo had Nicklaus's clubs, the Golden Bear became the Angry Bear when he had to buy new clubs at the pro shop prior to his round.

"The clubs Jack bought had aluminum shafts," Tom Peterson recalls. "And he'd never played with those shafts before. I could never figure out why he bought them, but he played awful."

Argea's faux pas nearly ended his relationship with Nicklaus. Jack penalized the caddie for months before permitting him to tote the bag again. Reflecting on the incident, Argea said, "Jack doesn't get rattled easily, but when he does get angry, you just know it. He doesn't have to say a word. He simply looks at you in a certain way. . . . He casts those steely blues on you. . . . I've always referred to it as 'The Look.'"

Maybe that's why meeting Jack Nicklaus for the first time can be intimidating. Though he's not large in stature, the "Nicklaus persona" can be overpowering.

LPGA veteran Carol Mann noticed this when she met Jack at the 1961 Walker Cup in Seattle. "I was struck by his eyes," she recalled. "And the fact that he seemed to stare right through me like he was measuring everything. Jack puts everyone in his 270-degree perspective. I've never seen anyone with such a burning stare."

Nicklaus's employees operate on "Jack's time." "Mentally, Jack's always got his clock going," one former worker said. "Schedules are set up for site visits and so forth and he keeps to them. I don't know how he does it, but Jack gets through everything. He also has the greatest sense of recall I've ever seen. Jack can visit a course site, approve the routines for the hole, and then be away for a year or so. When he comes back, the holes better be as he designed or it'll be a dark day for whoever screwed up."

Although there are those who denounce his lavish spending on construction and maintenance and his excessively high fees, Nicklaus has gained respect from his peers. His courses, especially those constructed in the last ten years, have popped up on lists of the great courses of the world. Muirfield, Shoal Creek, and Cabo del Sol (Los Cabos, Mexico) made *Golf Digest*'s Top 100 Courses in the world.

His present state of mind about golf course architecture was reflected in a recent interview he had with Pete Dobereiner in *The World of Golf*:

> Power in golf has become totally out of proportion. This is a game of precision, not strength. . . . Where is the challenge in just beating at the ball? Any idiot can do that. Length is only one factor, and if everyone is to enjoy golf, the course must be within his capabilities. Golf should make you think, and use your eyes, your intelligence, and your imagination. Then, if you hit your best shots, you should be rewarded. To me, variety and precision are more important than power and length.

Nicklaus also wrote in a Golden Bear International brochure, "I like golfers to think their way around the course, and I like to take them through different emotions when playing. The elements of risk and reward are important." Later, he added, "In essence, we are trying to design holes that are striking as well as challenging."

Chi Chi Rodriguez is an admirer of Nicklaus's courses. "I've always liked them because they make me concentrate on every hole. You can't let up on a Nicklaus course. I've always played well on them because he builds holes than make you work on every shot."

Nicklaus can be blunt and dismissive toward those who criticize his designs. He told *Golf Magazine*, "I'm not concerned about some guy who comes off the Tour and is an instant expert. Those guys comprise the biggest part of the critics. It's very easy to criticize something when they don't have a clue. . . ."

As Rodriguez had alluded to, Nicklaus believed that, whether a designer or player, "golf should make you think." Tom Weiskopf, himself a designer, said, "Jack's courses reflected his thoughts on the game. If you look at where he won major championships, they were ones that required preparation, planning, and strategy. And the need for highly accurate shots. On Jack Nicklaus courses, the golfer had to make a decision, accept the challenge like Jack would. Some golfers couldn't handle that, but Jack stayed with his design philosophy."

Bruce Crampton, a usual advocate of Nicklaus courses, had a beef with one in Michigan. "There was a blind shot on one hole, and I asked Jack about it since I don't like them," Crampton said. "I got a most uncharacteristic Nicklaus response. He said, 'I want to punish the golfer if they can't figure out the shot.' I was surprised he said that because Jack seems very sensitive to the golfer's needs."

Regardless of the comments of others, Jack Nicklaus understood where course design fit in with his competitive record. He told *Sports Illustrated*'s Frank DeFord, "My golf game can only go on so long, but what I've learned can be put into a piece of ground to last beyond me. I'll always be a part of golf because I'll have the courses. Building a golf course is my total expression."

# CHAPTER 45

# Jack the Creative

B obby Jones wrote in his autobiography, "Just because you're a good player doesn't give you a license to build golf courses." From day one, Jack Nicklaus was soundly committed to his new profession of golf course design. Like Pete Dye, however, he didn't hesitate to turn down opportunities, which other designers would have snapped up, if the topography of the land or other crucial factors didn't pass muster.

Over four decades and counting, Jack Nicklaus has endeavored to build a collection of courses around the world that will one day make him nearly as famous as a course designer as he has been as a professional golfer. Jack's willingness to listen makes this a strong possibility.

His attentiveness has resulted in a variety of golf courses that have reflected different aspects of Jack's personality as he progressed as a designer. The nature of the changes caused author Ron Whitton to observe, "Jack has had more transformations than Bill Clinton."

Bobby Weed, a protégé of Dye's and a rising star in the design field, collaborated with Nicklaus on the TPC course in Dearborn, Michigan. "We toured the layout, and I noticed Jack's soldiers were reluctant to speak up. I felt there were long-term maintenance problems in a few places, and I said so. I felt the heat on the back of my neck as I awaited his response. The other guys froze in their tracks, but Jack said he agreed with my observations and told his colleagues to make the changes."

In the earlier days of design, Nicklaus's courses were often criticized for being too difficult. The reviews were spotty, especially when it came to discussions of the greens he built. "Jack had the uncanny ability to play the high floating left-to-right shot," Weed says. "His early work reflected a belief that the average golfer could do that, and they wanted them cut short almost to the bone. Since he's the greatest 'fast greens' putter who ever lived, that was understandable."

Ron Whitton believes the severity of the courses Nicklaus initially designed was in tune with his personality. "When Jack started out," Whitton said, "he wanted not only to be the greatest golfer who ever lived, but the greatest golf course architect who ever lived. He built ball-busting courses that absolutely overwhelmed the average golfer."

In effect, Nicklaus was designing courses with shot requirements that were impossible for anyone but him. "You must remember," Whitton observed, "that Nicklaus was playing at such a superior level that he produced golf shots we could only imagine. Like his early idol, designer Dick Wilson [Bay Hill, NCR, La Costa], Jack built holes that could be played only one way: with high floating, left-to-right shots. Those were the Nicklaus trademark, but no one else could hit them."

Throughout the seventies and eighties, Nicklaus courses maintained their reputation as being too severe, something he shared with Pete Dye. Forced carry shots (over water, ravines, etc.) were prominent as were Scottish type rolls around the greens and undulating slopes and rolls on the greens. Later, Nicklaus called the era his "humpty dumpy design mode."

Despite the criticism, Whitton says Nicklaus was enhancing the visibility of golf. "One of Jack's contributions to the game was the development of residential communities around golf courses. Through his efforts, the reputation of the design profession was elevated. He became the marquee architect and drew interest in developing the residential property. Developers flocked to him because his name was magic."

Entire communities were born through development of Nicklaus golf courses. One of the finest examples of his work is at Shoal Creek outside Birmingham, Alabama. The time frame within which he worked on the course also showed his ability to juggle his professional golf career with his new vocation in golf course design.

Nicklaus was brought into the Shoal Creek project in an unusual way. One of the developers asked Clifford Roberts, of Masters fame, whom he would hire as an architect if he were going to redesign Augusta National. Roberts's answer was quick in coming. "Jack Nicklaus," he said, respectful of Nicklaus's influence on the design of Harbour Town.

Since this was 1974, Roberts's answer may have been surprising to many. Not only was Nicklaus a bit of a novice in the design profession, but he also had a full-time job that was producing rather remarkable results on the PGA Tour.

While working on Shoal Creek from 1975 through 1977, Nicklaus found time to win the Masters, the United States Open, and the PGA Championship, as well as numerous other titles. He was also in the early stages of operating Golden Bear International and its business ventures, handling millions of dollars worth of endorsement opportunities, taking time to fish, hunt, and pursue other hobbies, as well as be a faithful and loving husband and the father of five children. Jack's balancing act caused Chi Chi Rodriguez to observe, "Nicklaus is a legend in his spare time."

The mindset of Jack Nicklaus the professional golfer segued seamlessly into Jack Nicklaus the designer. At Shoal Creek, Hall Thompson, the force behind the course, cut paths out to indicate routings the holes might follow.

"One day, after we walked about the three 'holes,'" Thompson told *Golf Magazine*, "Nicklaus stopped and said, 'We're going the wrong way.'" They turned around and Thompson saw that the holes now had more of a downhill nature to them, perfect for Nicklaus to design greens and hazards visible from the tee, with no blind shots, his trademark design philosophy.

Later, Nicklaus said of Shoal Creek, "My design ideas change with every course I do, but I believe all my thinking came together at Shoal Creek." He then added, somewhat surprisingly in view of his love for his course at Muirfield Village in Ohio, "It's better balanced than Muirfield. . . . There are more options on approach shots and less penal results on missed shots."

When the world's finest professionals came to Shoal Creek in 1984 for the PGA Championship, the course played tough but true. A superb shotmaker, Lee Trevino, was crowned champion. Nicklaus could only muster 77, 70, 71, and 69 (287) to finish in a tie for twenty-fifth.

When that same championship returned in 1990, the professionals were bedeviled with high, rough, hardpan greens. Commenting on the firmness of the greens, Tour professional Tim Simpson said, "You couldn't dent some of these greens with a shot-put." Fuzzy Zoeller added, "This is the hardest golf course I've ever played in my life."

At the end of four days of play, Australian Wayne Grady finally emerged champion. He was six under par, but the course had left its mark.

Commenting on the architectural value of Shoal Creek, George Peper said, "It was a propitious marriage, Shoal Creek and Nicklaus, for the site fits his vision." He pointed out that Nicklaus had said, "Watching the flight of the ball is at the heart of golf's appeal. . . . I don't like blind shots." Peper then added, "The ideal Jack Nicklaus course would play downhill from the first tee to the eighteenth green. That's never possible, but with each property that is his idea."

In 1996, a course with those same Nicklaus design characteristics played host to the PGA Championship. This time the venue was Valhalla, an idyllic course named after the great hall in Greek mythology where Odin received the souls of fallen heroes of battle.

Located outside Louisville, Kentucky, Valhalla is a beautiful portrait of Americana. Standing behind the ninth green and looking back toward the tee, the view is lush countryside, heavy forests, towering tension wires, and an occasional train puffing along the tracks that border the course.

Valhalla was built by Nicklaus on 430 rolling acres that he told owner Dwight Gahm, a noted kitchen cabinet maker, was "perfect for a golf course." Then, Gahm told television commentator Bob Rosburg, "Jack proceeded to move 50,000 cubic feet worth of dirt."

The course was emblematic of Nicklaus's designs in the mid-eighties. Tom Watson described it as "a typical Nicklaus style [in that] it's pretty generous in the fairways but the greens are narrow in the scope where you have to hit the ball straight to get to the greens." Tom Kite added, "[Valhalla] is one of Nicklaus's trademark designs. Very, very wide fairways, and then he penalizes you to the greens. . . . The targets are small. The hazards are deep and very penalizing."

Fuzzy Zoeller was asked what Nicklaus design imprint he saw with the course and said, "[He] kind of closes things down at the greens. It caters to a high ball hitter."

Comparisons to Muirfield were typical of the other opinions of the professionals. Two of Europe's finest players agreed they liked the Nicklaus design. Colin Montgomerie called Valhalla "one of the best new courses I've ever played. It's a second-shot course, lot of left-to-right shots."

Six-time major champion Nick Faldo saw further evidence of Nicklaus's philosophy in the course design. "[Jack] will make you think. There's always a way of playing a Nicklaus hole. He's thought it out and he's thought about the strategy and that's good."

The competitors at the PGA Championship also pointed to the grassy knolls and hollows surrounding the greens. To some, there was definitely a wrong side of the green from which to play with chip shots and often times the golfer was better in the bunker than imbedded in the scraggly blue grass of the deep rough. "Manage your game," Jack was saying in the design. "Manage your game."

CBS broadcaster Ken Venturi compared the rough to "barbed wire." His fellow broadcaster, Gary McCord, warned the competitors before the championship, "The bluegrass is so thick and long, you can do one of two things. Sharpen the edge of your multi-faceted deep-grooved cutting tool sand wedge or buy a Kentucky thoroughbred and let him feed on the rough."

The 1996 PGA Championship, played for the third time on a Nicklaus-designed golf course (Shoal Creek in 1984 and 1990), proved a winner for everyone involved. Experts thought the professionals might tear the course apart, but Texan Mark Brooks sported just eleven under par and then took a playoff win from unheralded Kenny Perry to gain his first professional victory.

Beginning with Colleton River, a beautiful South Carolina course Nicklaus built in the early nineties, the design experts saw a "newer, softer Nicklaus." "There will always be a tremendous emphasis placed by Jack on the greens," Bobby Weed says, "but beginning with Colleton, I saw him taking a less severe approach."

Ron Whitton believes Nicklaus's shift to tone down the severity of his courses was a reflection of Jack's perception of himself. "Nicklaus finally realized he was never going to be perceived as the greatest golf architect of all time. History just wasn't going to elevate him to that level, so he decided every course he built didn't have to be a blockbuster. He became much more realistic, listened to others better, and shared credit for ideas that impacted his designs. Colleton River was the first of his courses that didn't demand the high degree of skill for the unskilled laborers who play from the forward tees."

Dick Taylor liked Colleton River so much he let Nicklaus know right away. "I knew enough to know this was a gem. I faxed Jack a note. 'Colleton River is your best, so why don't you retire?'" Later Taylor dubbed the course, "a user friendly venue for all. The first nine is Pinehurst with moss, and the second is a junior Turnberry."

The veteran writer was also enamored of Nicklaus's later designs at the Paris International Golf Club, where the green on the thirteenth hole is surrounded by a reflecting pool and the backdrop for the hole is a beautiful French country manor. He also enjoyed Palmilla and Cabo San Lucas, two Nicklaus courses on the Baja Peninsula in Mexico, and Mount Juliet, near Dublin, Ireland. Nicklaus christened Mount Juliet with a foursome that included actor Sean Connery, race driver Jackie Steward, and Prince Andrew.

Taylor's comments about Nicklaus the designer included recollections of what he told him in the early part of the nineties. "He had advanced," Taylor said, ". . . from being the Picasso of architects to Rembrandt." When Jack inquired as to what he meant, Taylor said, "I didn't always understand his early courses, as I didn't understand modern art, but that I thought his designs of the past five years could be classified among the works of the old masters."

Taylor's remarks are in sync with other experts in the field. "Like Pete Dye in the seventies, Jack revolutionized design in the eighties," Bobby Weed said. "He's a damn nice guy. A true professional. There's lots of respect out there now for Jack."

As for Nicklaus's contribution to the game as a designer, Weed believes the Golden Bear is responsible for upgrading the maintenance level for golf courses. "Over the last thirty years," he said, "Jack has made everybody aware of the importance of maintenance. His relentless pursuit of perfection, to make playing conditions better, easier for the golfer, is his legacy.

*USA Today* golf writer Jerry Potter says he can spot a Nicklaus course from a mile away. Prior to the 1996 Senior Players Championship, played at PGA National, another of Nicklaus's courses, he wrote that the design characteristics are "long, forced carries over marshes and lakes, deep bunkers, fast greens." Raymond Floyd was quoted as saying, "I can tell one of Jack's courses in a heartbeat. In art, if you know Gauguin, you'll know another the next time you see one."

Just where Nicklaus's collection of courses, scattered as they are around the world, fits in with the greats of golf course architecture is the subject of much debate. Perhaps the most objective view of Jack's position in history comes from Dick Taylor. In 1996, Taylor wrote in *Senior Golfer*, "[Jack] has [finally] been accepted as a world-class architect by his peers, but it has never been as easy as it looks."

Taylor, and others like him, professed no real appreciation for what Nicklaus was trying to do with his early courses. Just as was the case when he first bounded onto the golf scene in the sixties, many doubted his ability to play the game at a highly skilled level. Even though he possessed a formidable record as an amateur, struggles through the first months of the 1962 Tour events brought a swarm of skeptics. Many Tour professional hoped Jack would fall on his face. It was only when Jack won at Oakmont, proceeded to win twice more on Tour, and then win the first of four World Series of Golf titles did the pundits say, "Okay, this guy can really play."

Taylor pointed out that a similar pattern followed when Nicklaus became a designer. "As an inveterate Nicklaus watcher," he wrote, "I have felt that in both of his careers [golf and architecture], he has had to stoically quiet detractors with his talents." Taylor then added, "It can't be easy being number one with everyone wanting to knock you off . . . he suffered the same outrageous slings and arrows of his early playing days."

There's little doubt that when Nicklaus played in the Westchester Classic in 1972, he was stowing away design ideas utilized there by Walter Travis, also known to many as the "Grand Old Man." Unlike Jack, Travis took up the game not as a youngster, but at thirty-five. In spite of his tardy entrance into golf, he was a formidable player within a few years. He won four national championships (United States Amateur three times, British Amateur once) and was a runner-up in the United States Open.

During his final round at Westchester in 1972, Nicklaus played with gutsy determination. The opening-round 65, which included an eagle and five birdies, was a signal to his fellow competitors that the devastating loss at the British Open and a lackluster performance in the PGA were behind him. Second and third round scores of 67 and 70 put him into position to win. Now he needed to apply the finishing touch, a fourth-round hammerlock. This would remind everyone that he was still the premiere player in the game.

In addition to winning the tournament, Nicklaus had another goal. He wanted to become the first man on Tour to win $300,000 in a single season. "I'd like to do it this year," he told *Golf World*. "I feel I'm a better player than I've ever been in my life."

First prize at Westchester was $50,000. A win there would mean his 1972 total would hit $240,490, putting him within striking distance.

Using money earnings as a goal was nothing new for Nicklaus. Sure, he'd lost the chance at the Grand Slam, but now he needed to look ahead, to find something to motivate him.

The ability to find that factor was a true Nicklaus blessing. Despite disappointment, he looked at what could be accomplished next. That attitude prevailed whether he was trying to save par on a particular hole with a sixty-footer, break 70 or 80 in a single round, make the cut, win a Tour tournament, or win a first or twenty-first major title. Like no other before him, Jack motivated himself. It is the single most important reason he could be a champion at age fourteen and a champion well into his fifties.

No better evidence of that attitude exists than by recalling Nicklaus's supreme effort to make the cut at the 1996 PGA Championship (also see Introduction). After he fell on his face with an opening-round 77, which he characterized as "hacking around," Nicklaus created another goal, that of "making the cut." He knew that at age fifty-six, he'd played all four rounds in the Masters, United States Open, British Open, making the cut in each start. When he began the second round of the PGA, the idea was to play well enough to make the cut and be the only golfer ever to play all four rounds of the Majors in one year at that age.

Paired with defending champion Steve Elkington, who told reporters, "It helps me concentrate when I play with [Jack] because he has the right attitude when he plays in majors," Nicklaus bounced out of the gate with an eagle two at the second hole. With the thirty-six-hole cut projected at one-under, Jack knew he needed to play the final sixteen-holes at two-under. Fighting relentlessly all day, he came to seventeen and eighteen needing one more birdie. A ten-footer at seventeen didn't drop, but two strong wood shots and a delicate wedge put him within the same distance at eighteen.

Grinding along, if only for the pride of making the cut, Nicklaus surveyed the putt from all four angles. Later, Jack said he read it to break a hair left, and when it didn't, par left him with 77 and 69 (146), missing the cut by a shot. Nevertheless, Jack had shown the world once again what *USA Today* writer Steve Hershey called "the work ethic of a champion."

# BOOK VII

# Nicklaus's Legacy

❖ ❖ ❖

# CHAPTER 46

# Disney World Open—1972

Jack Nicklaus's courageous 1972 season ended on December 3 at the Walt Disney World Open in Orlando, Florida. Chi Chi Rodriguez had blasted out of the pack in the first round with 65, but Nicklaus shot two 68s that gave him a one-stroke lead after thirty-six holes over George Archer.

When Nicklaus fired a 67 in the third round, he found himself one shot up on long-hitting Jim Dent and two over Archer. Other contenders included Frank Beard, Bob Goalby, Bobby Mitchell, Bert Yancey, and Sam Snead, who would close with a 65 at age sixty.

Nicklaus was seeking his seventh win of 1972. In August he picked up number six when he added the Liggett and Myers U.S. Pro Match Championship to victories at the Crosby, Doral, the Masters, the United States Open, and Westchester.

Just as was the case before he played at Westchester, Nicklaus was attempting to find the competitive spirit that had been drained from him under the rigors of golf in 1972. "Deep down, I didn't want to play [at Westchester]," he said later.

To overcome his lack of resolve, Nicklaus once again manufactured a challenge. This time he focused on the fact that he had been beaten the year before in the first round of the tournament.

The 1971 Liggett & Myers U.S. Pro Match had been played at the Country Club of North Carolina at Pinehurst, a course designed by former United States Army Corps of Engineer William C. Byrd. The '72 tournament returned to that venue.

The format chosen by the PGA Tour produced a golf doubleheader. The U.S. Match Play crown would be decided between sixteen players, eight "stars" of the Tour and eight who qualified by being at the top of the heap after thirty-six holes of the Liggett and Myers Open, a seventy-two-hole event being played simultaneously with the Match Play tournament.

That half of the field was led by Bob Barbarasso, who shot 66 and 70. Fellow qualifiers were Deane Beman, Lanny Wadkins, Babe Hiskey, Dave Stockton, Leonard Thompson, Don Bies, and Paul Moran. Those professionals joined Nicklaus, Arnold Palmer, Lee Trevino, Frank Beard, Jerry Heard, defending champion DeWitt Weaver, Miller Barber, and George Archer as contenders for the Match Play title's winning purse of $40,000.

A surprising first-round loser was forty-two-year-old Arnold Palmer, who succumbed to Don Bies, five and four. "It was one of the highlights of my career," Bies said. A dejected Palmer talked about his putting to *Golf World*. "What I really need is to quit and start over . . ." he said. "I don't know whether it's not enough concentration or too much concentration. I just can't get [the ball] rolling toward the hole."

Other first round losers were Miller Barber, two and one to Lanny Wadkins; Jerry Heard, one-down to Leonard Thompson; DeWitt Weaver, two and one to Lee Trevino; Paul Moran, one-down to Frank Beard; George Archer, one-down to Babe Hiskey; and Bob Barbarrasso, one-down in nineteen holes to Dave Stockton.

In round one, Nicklaus defeated Deane Beman, one-up, although he nearly blew a lead of five-up.

"In my mind, I didn't lose," Beman said. "I just ran out of holes."

Trevino, Thompson, and Stockton faded in round two, but Nicklaus pounded out a five and three win over Lanny Wadkins. Wadkins told *Golf World*, "Jack just kept hitting great shot after great shot, and I forgot about my own game. . . . I guess it's admiration more than anything else. You're standing so close to greatness and that's what you're working toward, and you just start watching him."

The semifinal matches produced predictable results. Nicklaus beat Bies two and one, robbing the young professional of the chance to beat Palmer and Nicklaus in the space of three days. Frank Beard ended Hiskey's hopes with a one-up victory.

Writer Ron Coffman summed up the finals for *Golf World*. "[It] provided a sharp contrast, Nicklaus hitting those long, high floaters from left to right, and enjoying himself, versus Beard, everything loose and right to left and not caring much at all for match play."

After the match, Nicklaus told reporters neither he nor Beard played that well. "The whole match was a big defensive battle," he said. "Neither of us could get anything going."

Beard had taken an early lead with a birdie at one. Nicklaus tied him with a winning par at six, lost the seventh when he three-putted from fifty feet, and then squared the match at nine.

Later, after the two and one victory, Jack said the turning point was the thirty-footer he had made at nine. "That putt was awfully big," he said. "It gave me a lift. I wasn't able to get my concentration going until I made that one, and I started to play better after that."

His "better play" resulted in a win at the par-five twelfth, but Beard drained a forty-footer at fourteen to get square. Bogeys from tee shots in the rough at fifteen and seventeen (Beard missed a par putt from four feet) doomed his chances, and Nicklaus waltzed to victory.

Nicklaus told *Golf World* he had used the pursuit of the Grand Slam to spur him on to victory at the Match Play. "I got a lot out of my game during that period," he said. "And it's bound to carry over. I worked hard for the Grand Slam and it was a great experience. I think everybody should have a chance to go through it."

The win at the U.S. Match Play was worth $40,000 and upped his earnings in '72 to more than $280,000 for the year. Nicklaus was on target to surpass the $300,000 mark.

The win at the U.S. Pro Match Play didn't seem to help Nicklaus in the first round of the thirty-six hole World Series of Golf. There, squared up with Gay Brewer, Lee Trevino, and Gary Player at Firestone in Akron, Ohio, he opened with a 75 that put him dead last, four shots behind Player. He sliced two from that lead with a 69 the next day, but Player used a strong short game to beat Nicklaus and Trevino by two and Gay Brewer by three.

Nicklaus's performance left him in an ugly mood. "At Akron, I tried to bear down," he said later, "but it didn't work out. I'd had it. I was burned out. I couldn't force myself to concentrate. The more tense I became the more diabolical the shots I hit. . . . It got so bad in the end that it affected not only my own game but, I felt, my opponents' as well."

Recognizing that his behavior was objectionable to his fellow competitors was rarely ever evidenced with his play, but during the World Series in 1972, Jack saw it for what it was. "I believe I have a good relationship with my fellow pros," he observed. "It's something I cherish and want to keep. But on the sixteenth hole in the second round I began to really feel concerned about my behavior that weekend."

Later, Gary Player, Lee Trevino, and Gay Brewer said they were surprised at Nicklaus's comments but appreciated his courtesy. Jack's apology was succinct but weighty: "Fellows, . . . I've been nasty, mean and irritable, and I've offended you," he said. "I'm sorry. It won't happen again."

After the World Series championship, Nicklaus had two October events in Northern California and Nevada. At the Kaiser International

Open at Silverado near Napa, George Knudson emerged victorious with a seventeen-under 271 to win by three strokes over Bobby Nichols and Hale Irwin. Nicklaus fired 69, 71, 68, and 72, ten shots behind the bespectacled Canadian.

In Las Vegas a week later, Lanny Wadkins won the Sahara International with a total of 273 including an opening 65. Arnold Palmer delivered a matching 65 that day as well, and the two professionals with whiplike swings then proceeded to battle down the stretch. Wadkins finally beat the legend by one stroke to win $27,000. Nicklaus was only a shot back after thirty-six holes with 66 and 69, but a third-round 73 doomed his chances. A final-round 68 put him at 276, three behind the winner and tied for fifth with Bob Eastwood.

Heading into the Walt Disney World Open, Nicklaus had put together a remarkable string of rounds since the PGA Championship. Beginning at Westchester, he shot 65, 67, 70, 68, followed by scores of 69, 71, 69, 72, 66, 69, 73, 68 at the Kaiser and the Sahara. Only one of the rounds was over par, and combined, he shot a total of 37 under par. In between, he played superbly and won the U.S. Match Play. Six tournament wins, including two Major championships, made the year an unforgettable one, but Jack Nicklaus wasn't through yet.

# CHAPTER 47

# The Best of the Best

Superb years of competition such as the one Jack Nicklaus enjoyed in 1972 add fuel to the often heated debates about who is the greatest golfer who ever lived. Even though such men as Lee Trevino, Johnny Miller, Hale Irwin, Nick Faldo, Seve Ballesteros, Tom Kite, Ben Crenshaw, Greg Norman, and Tiger Woods enjoyed outstanding performances in the seventies, eighties, and nineties, the main contenders for the title of "best ever" come from an elite though unmistakably subjective list that includes the likes of Harry Vardon, Walter Hagen, Bobby Jones, Byron Nelson, Ben Hogan, Sam Snead, Arnold Palmer, Mickey Wright, Gary Player, Tom Watson, and Jack Nicklaus.

Pundits have compared these chosen few with such measuring sticks as swing quality, number of PGA and international tournament wins, and scoring averages. Although these factors are important, far better indications come from major tournament victories, head-to-head competition against the "best of the best" during a particular era, and perhaps surprisingly, a total look at the golfer in terms of physical ability, mental make-up, and chosen lifestyle, all of which affect his or her competency as a great player.

Before assessing Jack Nicklaus's record in the majors and his head-to-head performance against the greatest players of all time, it is imperative that consideration be given to the private side of the Golden Bear. Then and only then can one compare him to others who have risen to the top of the game. Nicklaus's life away from the golf course reveals a great deal about his ability to compete at such a high level for so many years.

Jack's upbringing, his tutelage from Jack Grout in his early days as an amateur, his years as a PGA professional, and his pursuit of a career as a golf course designer and businessman have been well documented, but Nicklaus's relationship with his family merits close attention as well.

Any discussion must begin with Jack's relationship with wife, Barbara. If there was ever a perfect match, it was the one conceived when the two met the first week Jack attended Ohio State University.

Barbara knew little about golf then. The first time she watched Jack compete was at the 1958 Rubber City Open at Firestone. On the way back to Columbus, Jack asked her about his second shot on the thirteenth hole. Later she said, "I'm thinking, I don't even remember the thirteenth hole. How am I going to remember the second shot? And then I thought, this is never going to work. I'm never going to be able to talk golf with him."

But that was not the case. Not only did she become knowledgeable about the game, but she also began to play more after reading the book *Advanced Golf*. It was given to her by their Florida neighbor and golfer-turned-author Cary Middlecoff, whose famed eighty-two-foot putt for eagle on the thirteenth hole at Augusta led the way to the 1955 Masters championship. Middlecoff, called a "voluntarily unemployed dentist" by Bobby Jones, inscribed it, "Happy Birthday, Barbara. I know he [Jack] won't tell you the secrets, here they are."

Two insightful glimpses into the persona of Barbara Nicklaus come from Herbert Warren Wind, who co-authored with Nicklaus the fine book *The Greatest Game of All*.

> When Barbara is at a tournament (which has been 99 percent of the time), she walks the full eighteen holes each day in her husband's gallery. She knows golf, she knows Jack's game inside out, she knows the state of the tournament at every moment, and she knows which golfers are playing really well, and even why they are. Barbara Nicklaus is as exceptional in her way as Jack is in his. She is one of those people who, with no apparent effort, can keep a great many balls in the air at the same time.

Wind also noted the incredible respect Barbara enjoyed from professional golfers on the Tour. "Whenever the wives of young golfers have begun to attend tournaments, it has been standard practice for their husbands to tell them, 'Just watch Barbara Nicklaus and you'll know exactly what to do.'"

That sentiment is as true today as it was in 1985. In 1996, Barbara was elected the Captain of the 1996 Memorial Tournament, a tribute to her years of hard work at Muirfield. "She's the type of person who thinks of the little things nobody else thinks of," Hale Irwin's wife Sally commented. "She has an impeccable sense for what's right." That statement echoed one made by Ashley Sutton, wife of PGA champion Hal Sutton, who told *Sports Illustrated,* "Barbara's the classiest woman in golf."

Barbara's influence on other wives of Tour players stretches beyond being a role model. "Stick with your husband. Don't send him off alone," she told Johnny Miller's new wife Linda. "Remember he doesn't have to look for women. They'll find him."

Others away from Muirfield respect Barbara as well. In 1990, the World Series of Golf bestowed upon her their Ambassador of Golf Award. She's also been lauded for her efforts on behalf of the golf tournament she oversees every year at Loxahatchee, Florida. It benefits the Fellowship of Christian Athletes. Honorees have included former Dallas Cowboys head football coach Tom Landry.

Jack has commented on his wife for thirty-five years, but the crux of the message has always been the same: He realizes he's been one of the luckiest men on the face of the earth to have found her. He would probably agree with Phil Rodgers, who, when asked how a guy like him found a wonderful woman like his wife, answered, "[Tour players] are all overmarried."

Jack's observation in the early seventies, after some twelve years of marriage, caught the spirit of his feelings at the time. "I've never had much of a problem saying no to people," Jack said. "Barb's the opposite. She can't say no to anyone, ever. Wherever we go and whatever we do, she has to spend time making sure everyone else is happy, often to the point of exhausting herself." Then he added, "She forever puts others ahead of herself, is forever thoughtful. In fact, it sometimes gets to my conscience how many darn things she does exactly right in life."

Jack was also envious of Barbara's ability to remember names. Carol Peterson, wife of Tom Peterson, says, "Barbara has an amazing recall of names. She never forgets one. I don't know how she does it."

In the early years of their marriage, Jack called Barbara "the most organized person you ever met. Her folks have always kidded her about this trait."

Twenty years later, his praise was just as vocal. "As my wife, she has contributed to everything I've been involved in over the years," he said. "She's been right in the middle and helped me. . . . She's been amazing. But she's never been out front. She's always in the background. That's her way."

*Sports Illustrated* sized up Barbara and Jack's relationship this way: "[W]hat is crucial to understanding Nicklaus and his success is that the former Barbara Bash is his only partner. More than that, she is really the only lasting contemporary in his life." Martha Morey, wife of noted amateur Dale Morey said, "She always kept Jack level," noting that Barbara was the one who encouraged her husband and helped him through the rough spots, especially during his early years on Tour.

"Barbara was always there for Jack," Carol Peterson said. "She's the best."

Barbara and Jack have been married for more than thirty years, and there has never been a hint that Jack has been unfaithful. Chi Chi Rodriguez says he knows the reason. "Jack's a guy of his word. A man you can trust. I could leave my wife in a room with Jack for a year and he'd never cross the line."

Together the Nicklauses have raised five children, but it was Jack who wanted the big family. Alice Dye recalls a dinner with Jack and Barbara in the early seventies. "They already had two kids and with all their commitments, I wondered whether they had time for more. But Jack wanted lots of kids."

Friends say times were tough for Barbara because the kids were unruly at times and she had to take care of them while Jack was away. When he came home, Jack wouldn't discipline them, and that upset her. But she handled it.

The inability to be a disciplinarian with his children is a Jack Nicklaus characteristic. "Jack loves his kids," a close friend said, "And he never could be tough with them. He's got a soft heart. One time when Nan was flying up to see her fiancee every weekend and charging the tickets to the company, Jack was asked to say something to her about the expense. 'Oh, no, not me,' he said, 'No, sir.' Jack wasn't about to scold his only daughter."

There was no question that Jack's golf was his priority, and everything had to fall in behind that. Barbara dealt with Cub and Girl Scouts, YMCA, gymnastics, PTA, and Little League, among other things.

Barbara was calm in crisis. When Jack was away on a hunting trip, four-year-old Jackie cut his finger off in a blender. Ever the cool one, Barbara wrapped his hand in a towel and rushed to a nearby hospital. A plastic surgeon worked diligently to reattach the finger. Jackie and Barbara stayed the night. When Jack called to tell his wife about the great duck hunting he and his buddies enjoyed, Barbara interrupted to explain what happened to Jackie. There was dead silence on the other end of the phone. Jack had fainted.

Barbara followed her husband during nearly every one of his Tournament rounds over the years. Of the majors, she missed only the 1963 Masters. While other touring professionals' wives cheered and nervously paced the sidelines, Barbara seemed calm and somewhat detached. A fellow wife said Barbara "acts like she's at a tea instead of a golf tournament." Jack even scolded her on one occasion for not showing any emotion.

Barbara's calm demeanor didn't mean she wasn't behind her husband. Ever superstitious, Barbara wore a lucky Golden Bear pin whenever she followed Jack.

Evidence that the romantic flame still burns brightly between Jack and Barbara, described by a writer in the seventies as a "superhomemaker with a sunny disposition and a chatty, easy way about her," comes from writer Thomas Boswell. In his wonderful 1991 article, Boswell recalls, "Once, in the late seventies, I stepped into a hotel elevator and caught the old married Nicklauses doing a little necking between floors." Writer Dick Taylor's wife Lynne recalls Jack kissing Barbara on the neck while she was hard at work cooking a dinner for twelve. "They're very loving to one another," Lynne says, "very affectionate. Jack loves to tease and be teased."

The Nicklaus kids are, in order, Jackie, Stevie, Nan, Gary, and Michael. As of June 1996, there were eight grandchildren in the Nicklaus clan.

Early on, the kids had varied interests. Jackie loved golf, Steve baseball, and Nan T-ball. Gary was a toddler who followed Jackie around, and Michael at ten months loved to drink the family dog's water from the bowl. Later Jackie would attend the University of North Carolina on a golf scholarship. Steve attended Florida State on a football free ride (he was known as "Arnie" to schoolmates), Nan went to Georgia on a volleyball scholarship, and Gary to Ohio State on a golf scholarship. Michael currently studies engineering at Georgia Tech.

Of the group, many consider Nan to have had the greatest potential as a golfer. "She's the most natural athlete of the Nicklaus kids," a family friend said. "But she never wanted to pursue golf as a career."

Being a son or daughter of Jack Nicklaus was not without incident. In addition to dealing with their celebrity status, Jack and Barbara faced the same problems other parents have encountered throughout the years. By all accounts, they have provided their children a home with the atmosphere of *Father Knows Best*, and the children remain extremely close to their parents.

To date, no scandal of any consequence has hit the Nicklaus household, but Jack and Barbara realize that the family has suffered by being in the spotlight. In an interview with the *Elementary School Journal* in 1991, Barbara said, "I think no matter what they had, no matter where they were, no matter even what sport they played, their name was Nicklaus, and they are always compared to their dad no matter what they did." Jack added, "They had to perform 200 percent to get credit for 75. I think they all understood that, and I think they all handled it well."

Jack realized the pressure on the family during his whirlwind year of 1972 when he challenged for the Grand Slam. "Life off the course for much of that year had been rugged," he recalled. "Not only for me but for Barbara and the kids and other members of our family and our close friends. . . . I may want to win more golf championships than anyone else, but I have no yen for the pomp and circumstance of kingship, especially if it filters into my own home where Barbara and I are trying to bring up five kids who will be just like everybody else's kids."

Although Nicklaus has had a professional life filled with glory, he told *The New York Times* in 1981, "The thing I'm most proud of in my life . . . is that being away as much as I am, that my kids are good kids. They don't seem to have any problems because of me. No ego problems. No identity problems. And to have good kids is the most important thing that Barbara and I can have."

Although Nicklaus has rarely used his prominence on the professional golf Tour for favors, he did so to the chagrin of some when it came to his golfing sons. Both Jack Jr. and Gary have pursued professional golf careers, and like any doting father, Jack wanted to assist his boys.

If resentment exists against Nicklaus with fellow professionals and tournament officials, it is a result of his willingness to play in certain tournaments only if his sons were granted exemptions. Seldom would Nicklaus's requests be denied, for his name meant a great deal to the prestige and attendance figures of a tournament.

The demands Nicklaus made were commonplace with other sons or relatives of famous players, but Jack apparently made such a habit of it that it wore thin. In fact, at the Doral tournament one year, when both boys played, one caddie spoke of a telling nightmare the Nicklaus clan had produced. "I dreamed Nicklaus had 155 sons," the caddie lamented, "and no one that wasn't named Nicklaus was in the tournament."

These and other instances have occured during the years, but they seem simply due to a father who wants to see his sons advance as professional players. Critics, however, have wondered what effect Jack's guiding interest in his sons' careers will have on them in the future. As one colleague of Jack's put it, "He's paving the road for the kids, but they need to find their own way."

Although those sentiments abound, there are those who refuse to criticize Nicklaus's attempts to help his boys. "Such a quality is admirable," a close friend of the Jack's said. "He's just being a dad."

If they had parted company with their father and sought occupations away from Jack and Golden Bear, few journalists would have given them ink. But Jack, especially in recent years, has sought to meld three of his sons (Jack II, Steve, and Gary) into his golf course design business, and that has made his sons vulnerable to close scrutiny.

In a Golden Bear newsletter sent to Nicklaus courses and business interests in the mid-nineties, Jack and his three sons are pictured together on the front page. The first line from the ensuing article read, "From the Philippines to Florida, and from England to Italy, the Nicklaus name is hard at work." The story then detailed each of Jackie, Steve, and Gary's latest golf course design projects, while Jack, the father, beamed in the accompanying photo.

The decision to add the boys to his design entourage has not set well with his experienced designers because many question their devotion to the design profession. Jack's wisdom in involving them in the Golden Bear design team remains to be seen. While he commands as much as two million dollars in design fees, the plan has been for Jack Jr., Steve, and Gary to be hired by developers at considerably less money. How substitution of the sons for the father will set with golf course developers depends on how important the developers consider Jack Sr.'s involvement to be. Pete Dye encountered the same challenge with sons Perry and P.B. Though both are talented, their attempt to be recognized for their own work was not easy.

Nicklaus's attempts to assist Gary's progress with his professional career were never more evident than at the Fred Meyer Challenge, Tour player Peter Jacobsen's two-day tournament in Oregon in August of 1996. There, Jack paired himself with Gary, a player without a PGA card or sufficient credentials to warrant an invitation on his own. While other teams included such tested professionals as Greg Norman and Brad Faxon, Mark O'Meara and John Cook, and Nick Faldo and Tom Watson, Jack put Gary in a position where his participation was an embarrassment. "[Jack] shouldn't do that to Gary," one player said, "He needs to make it on his own. Other players resent Jack doing that. It's making it tougher on Gary."

An incident at the tournament pointed out Nicklaus's tendency to "over-father" his sons. On the first day, Jack duck hooked his second shot into a creek on a par four. Gary promptly airmailed his second shot over the green on a slope where he was permitted a free drop. Instead of allowing Gary to figure out where to drop the ball, Jack stood hovering over his son and pointed low to the ground showing him the exact spot where the ball was to be placed. "Jack wants to help Gary," the same player said. "But he's got to leave him alone. Gary's a big boy."

# CHAPTER 48

# The Bear's Lair

Home for Barbara and Jack Nicklaus is Lost Tree Village, a North Palm Beach, Florida, real estate development built around a golf course. Jack and Barbara first came there in the mid-sixties and finally moved from Columbus on a full-time basis in 1965.

By all accounts the home is a comfortable one, the atmosphere unpretentious. "Little formality exists," Lynne Taylor said. "When Dick and I arrived on one occasion, there was Barbara at the front door in bare feet holding a dish towel. She even carried our bags up two flights of stairs in the guest house. Later, when we had dinner, we ate in the kitchen. Barbara does the cooking."

A 1978 *Sports Illustrated* article described the Nicklaus household. "[The house] is large but not ostentatious," the article said. "The climate is controlled. The rooms are attractive, and so perfectly stylized that they appear to be sets for a situation-comedy family, an athletic Brady Bunch."

The spacious homesite has all the amenities of a birthday wish-list: swimming pool, grass tennis courts, weight room, trampoline, basketball court, and a putting green (the Nicklauses bought the lot next door and put in the putting green and sand bunker). Two golden retrievers currently roam the property. The Nicklauses have always been animal lovers.

The yard is teaming with palm and citrus trees, tropical plants, and exotic flowers. Those who witness the vast variety of vegetation realize that Jack truly has a green thumb. "He bought all these exotic trees from the son of Senator Symington," a close friend said. "And then Jack spread them all over the three acres or so. Over the years, he's got every species known to man."

Phil Rodgers, a house guest of the Nicklaus family in 1980 when he was assisting Jack with his short game, called the Nicklaus estate "a

Seven Star Mobil Hotel." "You eat stone crab. And there's two tennis courts, boats, a bunker, a putting green. Jack and Barbara have it all. They made me feel like one of the kids."

Lake Worth borders the property, permitting easy access to Nicklaus's favorite passion besides golf and tennis: fishing. Evidence of his prowess is the mounted girth of the gigantic black Marlin (1,358 pounds) hanging above the fireplace, caught along the Australian coast after a six-hour struggle. Other trophies garnered from hunting and fishing trips fill a room in the guest house. Lynne Taylor says there are elephant tusks, bear skins, every sort of wildlife from Jack's adventures. The highlight may be a lamp made from an elephant's snout.

Nicklaus's golf trophies and other memorabilia have not been banned from the house by Barbara, as were the animal relics. Jack's championship hardware is displayed in a glassed in case in the hallway by the den.

Exceptional insight into Jack Nicklaus was never more evident than in the *Sports Illustrated* article in 1979, the year he was named Sportsman of the Year. Journalist Frank DeFord captured the essence of the Golden Bear, sizing him up from one end of his life to the other.

Regarding Nicklaus's dedication to all sports, DeFord wrote: "When not practicing on the golf course, he devotes himself to every conceivable athletic activity: tennis, skiing, basketball, hunting, bicycling, fishing, . . . weight lifting, touch football. You've heard of the girl next door. Jack Nicklaus is the jock next door. . . ."

There is no question Jack Nicklaus is devoted to his kids. "[He's] an especially good father," Herbert Warren Wind wrote. "He expects his children to come up to certain standards of conduct, but he loves their company, and he is endlessly encouraging about their individual pursuits." Dan Jenkins of *Sports Illustrated* preferred to go one step further and anoint Nicklaus sainthood. He wrote, "Nicklaus loves his wife and kids, is loyal to his friends; he is kind to his animals, and he can recite the Preamble [to the Constitution]."

Son Jackie told the *Los Angeles Times*, "My dad has been so successful, he has tried to keep us out of the spotlight. I see Jack Nicklaus not as a great golfer, but as a great father."

The gratitude is mutual. In 1986, after the special moment he and Jackie shared when Jack won the Masters, Nicklaus said, "My kids keep me playing golf. They are always after me to take the clubs out of the closet and get on the course."

Early on, Nicklaus cut back his tournament time to spend more time at home. By playing fewer events, he also kept himself fresh. But that wasn't the chief reason for staying away from the professional circuit more than any of his contemporaries.

Besides an agreement with Barbara that he'd try never to be away more than two weeks at a time, Nicklaus always made it a priority to attend as many school events as possible. When both Jackie and Steve played football and basketball in high school, Nicklaus missed only four games. Being financially able to travel in his own plane helped him balance his time, but Jack's responsibility to his family was always a priority. Even in the midst of the whirlwind of the Grand Slam possibility after he won the 1972 United States Open, he flew home to Florida the same night to watch Steve play in a Little League All-Star game.

There is no doubt that balancing his family activities with his work as a professional golfer, architect, and businessman actually made Nicklaus a better golfer. By cutting back on the number of tournaments in which he played and having interests away from golf, Jack was ready to go when the bell rang at tournament time. "I paced myself very well throughout my career," he told *Golf Magazine*. "So I've always been as fresh at the end of the year as at the beginning. I could have won a lot more tournaments when I was young. But if I had, I might not be playing today."

To gain a well-rounded perspective of Jack Nicklaus, it's important to consider the type of people with whom he has surrounded himself. If the adage is true that you can tell a great deal about a person by his friends, Nicklaus is a sure winner.

Although Nicklaus has made many new acquaintances over the years, both personal and professional, he has remained extremely close to two men from Columbus, Ohio.

The first of those is businessman Bob Hoag, ten years Nicklaus's senior. His name is familiar to golf fans who have watched the Crosby Clambake on television since Bob was Jack's partner in the Pro-Am for years. Though they had little success in the early years, despite the fact that Hoag was a fine player, Jack appreciated Bob's honesty and cherished their friendship.

Nicklaus loves to tell the story of when he and Hoag took on Arnold Palmer and a friend of his at Indian Wells in 1965. In spite of Jack's good play (eleven pars and seven birdies for 65), he and Hoag lost every hole and $180 in the process. Then the foursome played bridge at night. Whoever lost had to buy dinner. Jack and Bob bought every one. "Bob said I played rotten golf and worse bridge, and that he had been flawless," Nicklaus said later. "He said he just got bad lies and bad cards."

The second of Nicklaus's lifelong friends is Pandel Savic, a Yugoslav whose prowess at football made him the quarterback at Ohio State where he led OSU to a Rose Bowl victory in 1950. He met Nicklaus at Charlie Nicklaus's drug store where he saw young Jack stuffing his pockets with candy.

Savic, who is the General Chairman of Jack's Memorial Tournament, perhaps more than anyone else, is Jack's most trusted friend.

Although Jack's friends have appreciated their relationships with him, it was Savic who finally had to put Jack in his place during a vacation one year at Cabo San Lucas, a resort on the Baja Peninsula. Since there was no golf course available, Hoag, Nicklaus, and Savic, all highly competitive, played tennis, paddle tennis, and croquet. Despite their efforts, Savic and Hoag lost every time to Nicklaus.

Finally, the three turned to Marlin fishing, where Nicklaus caught the biggest fish. By this time, both men had had it with Nicklaus's egotism. When Savic hooked a whopper of a Marlin, and Jack castigated him by yelling at him to reel it in, Pandel finally screamed, "La Boca Grande, Old Big Mouth, shut up and let me catch my fish." To this day, when Nicklaus gets out of line with his friends, he's hit with "La Boca Grande."

There are numerous stories of Nicklaus's strong relationships with friends and fellow competitors, but one told by Savic reveals a side of Jack few may be aware of.

Just after Jack and Barbara moved in next door to Savic on Elmwood Avenue in Columbus, he told *Golf Journal*:

> None of us had much money then. Jack took me to the old American Pro-Am in Cincinnati in 1962. We took our wives and had a good time. We shot 63 and won. Jack took care of the hotel and had money left over from the winnings. Then a week later he went hunting and came over to the house with a bag of pheasants. After Jack left, I pulled the birds out of the bag and down there at the bottom of the bag there were three $100 bills Jack left for me. Jack's like that.

In addition to his friends from Columbus, Nicklaus has fostered ties with Mickey Neal, a high school coach and athletic director near Jack's home in Florida; Tom Peterson, his trusted ally and financial associate for over twenty years; and Joe Dey and Deane Beman, two former PGA commissioners. He formed few close friendships on Tour (save perhaps the ones with Gary Player and Phil Rodgers), preferring to stay at arm's length with his chief competitors.

Besides his relationship with friends (a close friend dubbed Jack's inner circle the "Eggheads") and fellow competitors, Nicklaus's partnership with his fans has definitely improved over the years. Some question his sincerity at times, but two accounts, one told by his son Jackie and the other by USGA committeeman Joe Luigs, portray a man who cared about the legions who watched him play.

Jackie recalled caddying for Jack at the Memorial tournament. "We came up to 18, and Dad was out of the tournament," he said. "The gallery was standing and going crazy. You couldn't hear yourself think. It was the most deafening roar you can imagine. I couldn't believe it. I got all choked up, and tears started running down my face. I was a little embarrassed about that until I looked over and saw Dad crying too. He said, 'Son, this is what it's all about.'"

Joe Luigs remembered an incident at the Western Open in the early eighties. He had heard about Jack's pouty behavior at times and that he was hard to work with. But he also knew Nicklaus's presence was worth at least ten thousand additional fans a day.

The incident with Nicklaus occurred on the practice tee, which was positioned on the polo field, a good distance from the course. "Because of the huge throng of fans," Luigs recalled, "we provided station wagons to take popular players like Nicklaus through the crowd. When he'd finished practicing, I ask him if he wanted to ride so wouldn't have to be badgered while walking along. He looked over his shoulder, and then said, 'What did these fans pay to get in here? I thought a minute and said 'seventeen dollars.' He smiled and told me 'Let's take a walk.'"

# CHAPTER 49

# Vardon and Hagen

Matching up Jack Nicklaus with the best players who ever lived requires a patient search, one on and off the golf course.

The first prominent golfer in history with whom comparisons can be made is Harry Vardon. In the late nineteenth and early twentieth centuries, he was the standard of excellence. To have one's swing compared with the grace and fluidity of Vardon was the ultimate compliment, something Nicklaus never enjoyed.

During his era, Vardon's record was unparalleled. He won the British Open a record six times (three more than Nicklaus) and was runner-up on four more occasions. He also won the British PGA Championship in 1912.

Vardon's first British Open victory came at age twenty-six, the last at age forty-four. He won on such prestigious courses as Royal St. George's, Prestwick, and Muirfield. He also won the United States Open in 1900 during a tour he was making on behalf of Spaulding. The ball he promoted during those exhibition matches was known as the Vardon Flyer.

Vardon, a gardener by trade who first arrived in England from the Channel Islands in November 1890 at the age of twenty, learned to play with the most rudimentary of equipment. His first rounds as a child were played with clubs he made himself. Blackthorn was used for shafts and bent oak roots became the club heads. The two were knotted together with nails and string.

Despite the use of the crude equipment, Vardon, like Jack Nicklaus, became proficient at golf at an early age. By the time he hit twenty, he began to compete in an era when the competition was stout. Not only did Vardon match wits with J.H. Taylor (four British Open wins), James Braid (five British Open wins), the other members of what were known as the famed "Triumvirate," but he also competed against such formidable golfers as Willie Park Jr., Walter Travis, Willie Anderson, Walter Hagen, Jerome Travers, Francis Ouimet, and Jock Hutchison.

Using the famous overlapping grip later dubbed the "Vardon Grip," although it was not he who invented it, Vardon was a master fairway woods player. He hit sensational brassie shots (two-wood) low into a stiff wind with such precision that author Michael McDonwell wrote, "Vardon developed a peerless degree of striking skill and could play brassie shots within five feet of a flag stick and even nominate which side he intended the ball to land."

Vardon, who always wore knickerbockers and a very light jacket on the course no matter what the weather, could hit the tee ball long and straight, a Nicklaus characteristic. He was so much straighter off the tee than any of his adversaries that experts conducted experiments to determine how he did it. Some said he was the closest thing to a mechanical golfer there ever had been, a label that would one day be pinned on other great golfers like Bobby Jones and Ben Hogan.

J.H. Taylor, coming off an eight and seven pounding from Vardon, surmised:

> In his early days, Harry Vardon had a most ungainly style. A lift in his back-swing violated the principle of accepted orthodoxy. One expected to see as a result the ball slung away far to the right or sharply around to the left but nothing of the sort happened. True, as the days went on, Vardon's lift became embodied in a style that was as graceful and perfect as any golf swing one is ever likely to see, which resulted in the perfect golfing machine.

The only flaw in Vardon's superb all-around game was his putting, which was often described to be worse than it actually was. "Ah, a grand golfer but Vardon could not putt," was a familiar cry, but as authors Charles Mortimer and Red Lighon recalled in the fifties, "If Vardon would have been a consistently weak putter, the known facts of his career would have been sheer impossibilities."

Those authors also observed that "during his greatest years, at the end of the century, Vardon had very nearly reduced golf to an exact science . . . " an accolade Nicklaus would enjoy seventy years later. Regarding his place in history, they surmised, "It is not much good asking how any good champion would have fared if he had lived in another period—or what Vardon would have [done] if he had only known the modern ball and the modern links."

In all, Harry Vardon, a quiet, placid man, won sixty-two events in his career, fourteen of them in a row. A tribute to his splendid play was memorialized by the PGA Tour, honoring him by calling the award for lowest scoring average for the year the "Vardon Trophy," which ironically Jack Nicklaus never won since he had too few Tour appearances to qualify.

Unlike Nicklaus, the chubby-faced, mustachioed Vardon, dubbed "The Greyhound" by an opponent he kept overtaking in tournaments, was dogged by ill-health when his playing prowess was at its peak. Nevertheless, his seven major championship wins place him tied for tenth on the all-time list with Sam Snead, Gene Sarazen, and Harold Hilton and just one behind Arnold Palmer, Tom Watson, and Mickey Wright.

When one is in search of the greatest player who ever lived, Walter Charles Hagen, the first giant of American golf, must be a contender. Although he was not, like Jack Nicklaus, blessed with the finest swing of the day (most said he took too wide a stance and swayed perceptively), he was, with all due respect to Lee Trevino, Chi Chi Rodriguez, Jimmy Demaret, and Doug Sanders, without doubt the most colorful man to have ever played the game.

The flamboyant Hagen was a polar opposite of Nicklaus. "At a time when golf pros were still dressing in sack coats and brogues," *Golf Digest* reported, "the Haig began wearing silk shirts, florid cravats, alpaca sweaters, screaming argyles, and black and white shoes at $100 a pair." His sartorial splendor and a penchant for the lifestyle of a Hollywood movie star (Hagen once said, "I don't want to be a millionaire, I just want to live like one.") belied a great talent as a true professional. He won eleven major championships and over seventy titles all over the world in addition to being the first man to win a million dollars in the sport. "He made more money than Babe Ruth," one fellow professional commented, "and spent more than the whole Yankee outfield."

Ben Hogan said of Hagen, "There was something extraordinary about the man, something grandiose about the way he refused to do anything the way anyone else might."

The Haig, a master of recovery, was born in December of 1892, and by 1914, at the age of twenty-two, he had won his first major championship, the United States Open. He won a second Open five years later, then assaulted the golfing world with four British Open Championships and five PGA Crowns, the last four consecutively (1921-1927). In addition to the three members of the great Triumvirate, Hagen competed against Gene Sarazen and Bobby Jones. His total of eleven major triumphs ranks him third behind Jack Nicklaus and Bobby Jones.

Whereas Jack Nicklaus never played mind games with fellow competitors, Walter Hagen simply wore down opponents with his incessant prattle and uncanny ability to pull a great recovery shot out of his hat when he needed it.

One man who loved to watch The Haig play was professional golfer Errie Ball, still a fine teaching professional at eighty-seven. Ball's grand-uncle was John Ball, the great Englishman who won the British Amateur eight times and the British Open once. While just a young sprout, Errie Ball saw Hagen play in the British Amateur and then watched the colorful American when he came to the States in the late 1920s.

Ball, who won the prestigious 1931 Southeastern PGA Championship, said, "Hagen made a big dramatic production out of all his shots. At Pinehurst, I played behind him. He hit his tee shot to the right in a swale behind a clump of trees. I watched him pace off the shot from every angle—must have taken five minutes. Then Hagen hit the ball on the green to great roaring applause from the spectators. Right after that, I drove the ball to that same spot. When I got there I saw Walter had a hole as big as a house to go through."

In the mid-thirties, Errie Ball experienced Hagen's wit firsthand during the PGA. "We were playing at Hershey [Pennsylvania] and Walter was having lunch at the table next to mine," Ball recalled. "His match play opponent Vic Ghezzi, came up and said, 'C'mon, Walter, we're on the tee.' Hagen looked up and replied, 'You go on ahead. I'll catch up after two holes.'"

Ball described Hagen as a stout man with a ready smile, swept back black hair, and "long, lean, and strong hands like a pianist with a twelve note spread." He recalled that Hagen made a big deal out of lining up putts on the sand greens. "He would fiddle around like he was trying to read the break. Of course there wasn't any on those flat greens, but Walter had many of his opponents convinced they needed to 'read' the green."

Bill Hyndman the 1983 United States Senior Amateur champion, remembered the first time he saw Hagen. "He was putting right-handed with a left-handed putter," Hyndman said. "The concave edge gave the ball overspin. I tried it, but I was awful."

"Hagen liked people," the legendary Gene Sarazen said. "If he didn't see a crowd following him, he wouldn't break 80." Sarazen also loved Hagen's sense of humor. "Few people know that there was a little extra pressure on the shot I ended up hitting for the double-eagle in the Masters. Before I hit it, Hagen, my playing partner says, 'Hurry up, will ya. I got a date tonight.'"

Walter Hagen, like Jack Nicklaus, was a supremely confident player. Standing with Harry Vardon as Sandy Herd was about to play out of a bunker that meant a win or loss, Walter calmly whispered, "If Herd knew as much about that shot as I do, he would win."

Authors Charles G. Mortimer and Fred Pignon observed that although Hagen was dubbed "The Showman of Golf," he was truly a superb player. "[Hagen] had a cool and cunning brain and no doubt at times he could stage things effectively. . . . He was at once happy-go-lucky and casual, and yet shrewd, observant, and resolute. . . . He was a teaser." Sound familiar?

None other than Bobby Jones learned of Hagen's prowess, losing once to the Haig in an exhibition match in 1926, twelve and eleven in seventy-two holes. Hagen won $7,500 for the victory but promptly spent $1,800 buying diamond cufflinks for Jones.

Like Jones, Nelson, and Nicklaus ahead of him, Walter Hagen was the favorite nearly every time he teed it up during his prime. Like Nicklaus, too, he was a great putter under pressure and possessed the ability to play championship-caliber golf even when his game was far from first rate.

Perhaps it was Arnold Palmer who best summarized Hagen's impact on the game, his ability to upgrade the sport and elevate the image of players. At a dinner honoring Hagen in 1969, Palmer said, "If it were not for you, Walter, this dinner would be downstairs in the pro shop and not in the ballroom."

# CHAPTER 50

# Jones, Nelson, and Snead

J ack Nicklaus's idol Robert (Bobby) Tyre Jones was born to be a champion. He won thirteen major championships, second only to Nicklaus, including the Grand Slam (British and United States Opens and British and United States Amateurs), or the "impregnable quadrilateral," as one writer dubbed it, in 1930.

That year British Open bookies made him 120 to 1 to win. Fellow competitor Bobby Cruickshank sent $500 to his father-in-law in Britain and took the odds. He won $60,000. The tournament was also noteworthy because Jones used a "concave wedge," a heavy club with a large flange and concave face that shoveled the ball out of bunkers. The next year the club was banned, but three years later Wilson introduced Gene Sarazen's new "R-99" sand wedge.

Unlike Nicklaus, Jones, with slicked-back hair, a handsome face, and eyes the color of the gray sky before a storm, was not an imposing physical specimen. He stood 5' 8" inches tall and weighed 180 pounds. Like Nicklaus, he had strong, thick legs. That strength enabled Jones to pivot correctly, causing the gifted writer Bernard Darwin to write, "Sit on the edge of the teeing-ground, and listen for the thrust of the hips as Jones pivots."

As Jack Nicklaus had found a mentor in Jack Grout, Jones found a teacher in Scottish professional Stewart Maiden, who taught him the simple mechanics of the correct way to play the game. Though he had suffered as a frail and sickly child, Jones's will to live and love for golf made him a threat on the national scene by the time he was fourteen. It took but a few short years for him to threaten the best players of the day, and then in 1923, he won the United States Open. From then on, Jones reigned.

Bobby Jones's triumphs came during an era described as "Jones against the field." They included one British Amateur at St. Andrews, five United States Amateurs at such courses as Merion (twice) and Oakmont, four United States Opens (Inwood, Scioto, Winged Foot, and Interlachen), and three British Opens (Royal Lytham, St. Andrews, and Hoylake). He accomplished all that over the short period of seven bountiful years.

Comparing Jones, the man who invented the Masters, to Harry Vardon, Bernard Darwin once said, "Harry Vardon and Bobby Jones combine exquisiteness of art with utterly relentless precision in a way not quite given to any other golfers."

Jones's competitive spirit was embodied in a comment made by biographer Dick Miller: "At the start of a match, Jones would approach his opponent, look at him straight in the eyes, shake his hand, and offer a quizzical smile that implied good luck. If the opponent looked at the smile long enough, however, its meaning became clearer. It said: Good luck, you're going to need it because I'm going to beat the hell out of you today."

And the whipping wouldn't take long, that was if Jones had anything to say about it. He played the game as if he had to catch a train. Unlike Nicklaus, he never sought advice from his caddie, never hesitated over club selection, and struck his ball without pausing to check his grip or adjust his feet. Jones played a hole in the time it took Jack to survey a putt.

It was Bobby Jones, a left-hander playing right, who encouraged the young Errie Ball to come to the United States. "Until Snead, Jones had the best swing I ever saw," Ball said. "Snead used steel shafts, Jones the hickory ones; and they had a lot of torque in them. You had to time it just right and wait for the club head to come around."

Ball was impressed with Jones for another reason. "He never played golf during the winter months. To train, he played Ping Pong. Then he'd come out in the spring and play. I know I've hit thousands and thousands of more balls than Jones ever hit on the practice tee."

Veteran Amateur Bill Hyndman said, "Jones had a full, fluid, graceful, picture swing." He was a master technician and his approach to the game was one Nicklaus admired. So did others. In the early thirties, Jones made a series of short teaching films that were shown in movie theaters around the country.

Despite his engaging persona, Jones, like Nicklaus, was a shy man. "Hogan, like Jones, was a brilliant player," Gene Sarazen told *Golf Digest*. "They were both wonderful strategists, great generals of the game. They were both brilliant thinkers, even though Hogan never had much formal education, and Jones got a law degree from Harvard. Neither liked people very much. That was their drawback. People got on their nerves. Both would go quickly off the eighteenth green and into the clubhouse."

Bobby Jones, the private person, was first and foremost a family man similar to Nicklaus. He married his high school sweetheart, Mary Malone, the daughter of a second-generation Irishman. When asked to explain where golf fit in his life, he said, "First come my wife and children. Next comes my profession—the law . . . Finally, and never as a life in itself, comes golf."

Although golf ranked low in his pecking order, it was a passion for Jones. Head-to-head, he was the master. Even though Gene Sarazen beat him soundly in their famous match, Jones played the best of his day when the chips were down. Worthy opponents such Bobby Cruickshank, Joe Turnesa, Tommy Armour, Johnny Farrell, and Walter Hagen tried their best to topple Jones.

Even in his later years when a crippling disease confined him to a wheel chair, Jones was stout. "He never complained," Bill Hyndman said. "He was a great gentleman."

To understand fully Bob Jones's impact not only on golf but also sports in general, he was named the fifth greatest athlete in the first half of the twentieth century in an Associated Press poll. He was ranked behind Jim Thorpe, Babe Ruth, Jack Dempsey, and Ty Cobb and ahead of Joe Louis, Red Grange, Jesse Owens, Lou Gehrig, and Bronco Nagursky. Perhaps more important than that honor was Jones's influence on the game of golf. As author Will Trombly wrote in *200 Years of Sports in America*, "He [Jones] gave golf a stature in the country that it never had before; he made it a major sport."

The philosophy of John Byron Nelson Jr. was simple: "Keep your woods in the bag, and the irons will put gold in your pocket." That creed permitted Byron, who learned the game as a caddie at age ten, to win nineteen PGA tournaments, exactly half of those played, in the year 1945. Eleven of those victories came in succession, and for the seventeen stroke play wins he recorded, he averaged an astonishing twelve under par.

Lord Byron, as he was called, played for nearly twenty-five years. He was the winner of five major championships, including the 1937 Masters, the 1939 United States Open at the Philadelphia Country Club, the 1940 PGA (beating Sam Snead in finals), the 1942 Masters (over second-place Ben Hogan), and the 1945 PGA. Only a British Open title escaped him.

Named Athlete of the Year twice (1944 and 1945), Nelson was never what one would call flamboyant. "[He] was not an electric personality," one writer ventured. "He was tall, expressionless, usually wore a white tennis visor, and always wore plain clothes."

Comparisons between Nelson and Jack Nicklaus involve their respective ability to think like champions under pressure conditions. Nelson, though not blessed with the finest swing of the day, was an effective player who maximized his chances to win. Like Jack, Nelson rarely beat himself, and took advantage of his opponent's mistakes.

Most experts agree that Byron Nelson is the finest iron player to have ever competed. His trademark was the piercing iron shot that produced razor-sharp results. Most times the ball stopped past the pin, for Nelson was a bold player who believed Bobby Jones's teacher Stewart Maiden when he said, "Never say 'Good Shot' if the ball's not past the pin."

Jack Nicklaus never competed against Nelson, but he remembered watching him in a 1954 exhibition in Los Angeles where, as Nicklaus later said, "His straightness was literally incredible. Certainly no one I've ever played with has hit the ball as consistently straight as he did that day."

Nicklaus also respected Nelson as a person. "One thing I've always admired about Byron is how he has handled himself as a top player," Jack said. "You'll never meet a more straightforward and unassuming man."

Of Nelson's ability, Bobby Jones said, "At my best, I never came close to the golf Byron Nelson plays." Teaching professional Errie Ball observed, "Nelson's one of the five or six greatest players who ever lived, despite a swing where he dipped into the ball. . . . The amazing thing is how well he played with the type of golf balls we had. Back then, we didn't know the compressions like they do today. When I got a good ball, I'd hide it for days and save it for short par fives. We used the Spaulding Dot. We wanted a ball that flew like hell. I can't even imagine what Byron could do with today's golf ball. He was flawless back then with every shot."

Though the war years took many of Nelson's competitors away, he beat the best the game had to offer with consistency. That included Hogan, Snead, Lloyd Mangrum, Cary Middlecoff, Gene Sarazen, Craig Wood, Lawson Little, and Henry Picard. When they went up against the tough Texan, they faced a scoring machine to whom par was a dirty word.

Born seventy-seven days before Ben Hogan was Samuel Jackson Snead, the Hot Springs, Virginia, legend with the swing any golfer would die for. He and Jack Nicklaus crossed paths when Nicklaus was a kid, playing in an exhibition in Ohio in 1956.

Sam Snead's career began at age twenty-five when he startled the PGA Tour with a win in the 1937 Oakland Open. He enjoyed a long and illustrious career, one that spanned five decades filled with superior play. A losing bout with the putter finally put strain on his game, but he was still highly competitive in the seventies when he was in his early sixties.

Sam Snead, a tall, willowy Southerner with an apple-cheeks face and Southern drawl, won more PGA Tour events than anyone in history: eighty-two. Nicklaus is second with seventy-one. Although he never secured a United States Open crown (Bill Hyndman said he "tried too hard"), Snead was victorious in seven major events, tying with Harold Hilton, Harry Vardon, and Gene Sarazen for tenth place on the all-time list. He won the Masters three times (1949, 1952, 1954), the PGA three times (1942, 1949, 1951), and the British Open (1946).

Snead once shot 59, a round that included eleven birdies, an eagle, and six pars. He was also the oldest man ever to win a regular PGA Tour event, doing so at fifty-two years, ten months. Watching him hit practice balls, one writer observed, "was like seeing fish practice swimming."

Gene Sarazen told *Golf Digest*, "Snead is a great athlete. He has about the finest golf swing I've ever seen." That sweet swing made the game look easy for him, but he had veins of ice and was a great finisher. His slow, methodical ways produced a golf game that, like Jack Nicklaus's, was paced on tempo.

Snead learned the game as a youngster when he outfoxed opponents who figured they could beat a shoeless kid who played them with a stick he found in the woods. They were wrong. As for his swing, Sam simply said, "I try to feel oily." That produced a swing Bill Hyndman said was "so good it was hard to believe. He could hit a one-iron straighter than I hit the eight." Hyndman added Snead "had a lot of stomach like Nicklaus."

Nicklaus's comments about Snead in the early seventies were generous. "Sam Snead, I would imagine, has ripped out more long, straight drives and covered the pin with more approaches than any golfer in the game's long history," he observed.

Regarding Snead's swing, Nicklaus added, "No one has a better position at the top of the backswing; the arms are fully extended, the hands fully cocked. He has great control of his legs during his swing, and he is still awfully strong. Though he plays all the shots well, I have always been particularly impressed by the accuracy of his seven-iron and eight-iron approaches and by the precision of his bunker play."

Nicklaus added, "[He] is the perfect illustration of the old adage that a swinger will last long after a hands-player has had to pack it up." And last he did, causing former United States and British Amateur Champion Vinny Giles to say that Snead, who was still able to play good golf in his eighties, was "the best athlete who ever lived."

Snead, who said, "Thinking instead of acting is the number one golf disease," faced head-to-head competition from Ben Hogan, whom he defeated in all three playoffs between the two men, and all the great players for four decades.

In 1974, at age sixty-two, Snead told the *San Francisco Chronicle*, "I still have the desire to play. They say I've worn out five bunches of golfers, from Sarazen to Hogan. I didn't. They just lost their desire. I play five rounds of golf a week when I'm home . . . . I've been known to play twelve to thirteen rounds, if can find some pigeons."

As for the state of his swing, Snead remarked, "The swing is about the same as it's always been, and my legs still feel good. But the putting stroke. It's got a few ripples, or as the British say, twitches. People tell me just to put the putter down and putt, but that's like telling a guy to go stand still by a rattlesnake—easier said than done."

Of all the players he competed against, Snead admired Jack Nicklaus's prowess on the greens. "If I putted like Jack," he told *Golf Digest*, "I'd have won a thousand tournaments."

Shortly after the 1967 United States Open at Baltusrol, Lee Trevino was paired with Snead at The Diplomat in Hollywood, Florida. During the round, he witnessed a shot he believed symbolic of Snead's ability to move the ball around.

The hole being played was a long par four. Trevino was forced to play a three-wood for his second shot. Snead then took out a driver and hit a high hooking ball that curled in twelve feet from the hole. "I knew I was going to have to go to practicing, and practice hard," Trevino later said, "because I knew I was completely out of my league."

Trevino added, "That probably helped me more than anything, to see that shot. I could never do it. I could have stood there till today, twenty-nine years later, and still wouldn't be able to hit that shot. Absolutely gorgeous the way he manipulated the ball."

His ability to invent shots will be Snead's legacy. During one match with Ben Hogan, he curved a three-iron shot around a tree at a forty-five degree angle, causing one sportswriter to observe, "Snead played the game like he's a race driver and needed to make a sharp left turn."

# CHAPTER 51

# Palmer, Wright, and Watson

O f Arnold Palmer Gene Littler said, "When he hits the ball, the earth shakes." Palmer, the greatest go-for-broke player in professional golf history, must be included with Vardon, Hagen, Jones, Hogan, and Snead when comparing the greats with Jack Nicklaus. Wearing his emotions on his shirt sleeves, Palmer single-handedly raised exposure of golf, like Walter Hagen before him, to new levels. He became the gallery favorite and general of "Arnie's Army" from day one, and his charging style and devil-may-care attitude on the golf course made his legend grow to colossal proportions.

Palmer captured eight major victories in his great career, including the United States Amateur title he won in 1954. He was victorious in four Masters ('58, '60, '62, and '64), one United States Open (Cherry Hills, '60), and two British Opens (back to back wins in '61 and '62 at Royal Burkdale and Troon). Although the PGA Championship eluded him, his eight wins tie him with Mickey Wright and Tom Watson for seventh place on the all-time list.

Unlike Nicklaus and Jones, Palmer, the native of Latrobe, Pennsylvania, never had an early teacher, save the tutelage of his father. At first glance, his swing seemed out of kilter and too jerky, but when he came through the ball the power generated was enormous.

In contrast with Jack Nicklaus, he was bold to a fault, whether it be with a fairway iron, a wedge shot, or a twenty-foot putt. If Nicklaus was known for feathering the ball, Palmer was known for attacking it with startling vengeance. Former caddie Nathaniel Avery said, "For Arnold Palmer, it's let it go or let it blow—all or nothing. This man just doesn't know when to play safe."

Television and a sportswriter named Bob Drumm greatly aided Palmer's popularity. Palmer had muscular, chiseled looks and a ready smile that appealed to every golf fan. "Television was made for Arnie, but Bob invented Palmer," writer Dick Taylor said of the legendary

"Drummer." Early in his career Arnie would get his bogeys and birdies and then come into the press tent and not say much. Reporters would flock to Drumm and he'd make up something. Later, *Sports Illustrated* wrote an article about Drumm entitled, "The Man Who Invented Palmer."

As for Palmer's game, Taylor made these observations. "I'm not sure he was ever a great player. He made it the hard way—with that swing of his. But he could really putt—how that man could putt." Errie Ball believed Palmer's biggest asset was his confidence, "Right before the last round of the '60 Open at Cherry Hills I saw Arnold," Ball said. "He looked nervous, but ready. I knew something big was gonna happen."

Asked about Palmer's buggy-whip swing, Ball observed, "He didn't look good swinging—but if you took a slow-motion look at impact—he was great. I also liked the way he kept his head still at impact."

Of all the competitors who could be considered as the greatest player who ever lived, Palmer may have had the greatest confidence level. Writer Will Grimley said, "Palmer walks to the first tee unlike any other pro. He doesn't walk on to it as much as climb into it, almost as though it was a prize ring." Gene Sarazen observed, "Arnold's most dangerous when he's on the ropes, ready to be counted out." Amateur Bill Hyndman, who at age eighty-one has seen nearly every great player in this century, said Palmer "was the greatest fighting tiger of them all."

That confidence enabled Palmer to earn an enviable record in match-play situations with the great players he faced in his prime. He took them all on, and bested them with a relaxed manner of concentration that belied his fire. Still competing regularly as he nears his seventieth birthday, Palmer continues to excite golf fans around the world with a style of play that defines the word "aggressive."

But it is Palmer's contributions to the game that will be his legacy. And his fellow players will never forget it. Perhaps Chi Chi Rodriguez said it best when he told *USA Today*'s Steve Hershey, "If it wasn't for Arnold, I'd be back in Puerto Rico cleaning clubs."

"Mickey Wright had the finest golf swing I ever saw, man or woman," Ben Hogan observed. "What a golf swing."

Although noteworthy women professionals such as Joyce Wethered, Babe Zaharias, Patty Berg, Kathy Whitworth, and Nancy

Lopez deserve strong consideration as the greatest golfer who ever played the game, the finest of them all was Mary Kathryn "Mickey" Wright.

The San Diego, California, native, born in 1935, was an over-powering, dynamic player who dominated the women's professional Tour in the late fifties and early sixties. Between 1961 and 1964, Mickey Wright, who turned professional in 1955 at the age of nineteen, won forty-four tournaments, thirteen in one season.

With eighty-two LPGA victories (one-fourth of all those she entered), she had one more victory than Sam Snead and just six less than Kathy Whitworth, who called Wright the "finest golfer in the history of the game." "We could all see she was just so far superior to anyone else," Whitworth said, "People just don't remember how good she was," a comment similar to one made about Jack Nicklaus. Feisty rival Carol Mann, the 1965 United States Women's Open Champion, who once described her height as being 5' 15" rather than 6' 3", said Wright had "a beautiful flowing swing. I'd rate Hogan number one and Mickey two."

LPGA Tour legend Betsy Rawls said, "Mickey set a standard of shot-making that will probably never be equaled. . . . [Her] swing was as flawless as a golf swing can be: smooth, efficient, powerful, rhythmical, and beautiful."

Like Jack Nicklaus, Mickey Wright had the ability to hit the ball high, especially with the long iron. "She was a spectacular golfer to watch," Rawls said. "Her shots were always high, with tremendous carry." Carol Mann echoed those thoughts. "She was, like her counterpart Jack Nicklaus for the men, the first women golfer to hit the ball that high," Mann said. "I was very envious. Mickey made hazards on the course obsolete. She just knocked the ball right over them."

Carol Mann drew another comparison between Mickey Wright and Jack Nicklaus. "Like Jack," she said, "Mickey was the one everyone wanted to beat. In 1967, I had a two-shot lead over Mickey heading into the final round at the Tall City Open. I hurt my back before the final round and had to go to the hospital for injections to stop the pain. I returned to the course on crutches and used them on the first five holes. Mickey thought she'd beat me, but I putted great and beat her by two shots. What a victory."

Rhonda Glenn, author of *The Illustrated History of Women's Golf*, called Mickey "Golf's Golden Girl." "She was a fine athlete and could generate great power," Glenn wrote. "Her shots had a long soaring beauty and a distinctive sound. Even with her irons she produced a loud crack at impact, a sound that only the best men generate."

Most professionals, man or woman, would have given their first-born for a swing like Mickey Wright. "She had the perfect swing," says Donna Caponi, herself a two-time United States Women's Open winner. "Over the years, everyone continues to marvel at Mickey's fluid motion. She's the best who ever lived."

All told, Mickey Wright, touted as the new "Babe" when she joined the Tour, won eight major championships to tie with Arnold Palmer and Tom Watson for seventh place on the all-time list. The wins included four United States Women's Open crowns, the first in 1958 when she was just twenty-three, as well as wins in 1959, 1961, and 1964.

Mickey Wright also claimed four LPGA titles and won the Western Open and the Titleholders Championships, recognized as "near-majors" in her era. All her wins were against such stiff competition as Patty Berg, Betsy Rawls, Sandra Haynie, and Carol Mann, equal to the type of world class players Jack Nicklaus faced when he competed.

Mickey Wright's record is even more impressive when one considers she played most of her career in poor health. She continually suffered from ulcers, arthritis in her wrists, skin problems due to a sun sensitivity, and difficulties with her feet.

Off the course, Mickey Wright was a loner, very guarded, almost, as one competitor said, to the point of being "scary." Through it all, she persevered. She was strikingly beautiful and had a smile that lit up the room. Of comparisons to Babe Zaharias, Mickey said, "Mrs. Zaharias was in a class by herself. I prefer just being Mickey Wright, and I want to be the best woman golfer in the world."

The latter comment evokes memories of Jack Nicklaus's similar statement when he joined the professional Tour. Like Nicklaus, Mickey Wright possessed a mental attitude that was superior to her fellow competitors. "I hate to lose," she said, "The perfectionist bit in golf doesn't have as much to do with doing it perfectly as the total rejection and horror of doing it badly." Carol Mann said Mickey was "a gracious loser when you played well and she did too. But if she played badly, she hated it."

That mental attitude gave Wright great confidence when she entered competition. "Winning really never crossed my mind that much," she observed. "It's trite, but I knew that if I did as well as I could, I would win."

Her picture-perfect swing, superior mental attitude, and undying confidence helped make Mickey Wright the dominant player of her era. Acclaimed British writer Pat Ward-Thomas said it best: "She set standards of achievement that have not been surpassed, the most lasting contribution any player can give to the game, especially when, as with Mickey Wright, it was gracefully done."

While top Tour players such as Jack Nicklaus, Bob Murphy, Ben Crenshaw, Tom Kite, and Phil Mickelson had impressive wins in collegiate tournaments when they joined the Tour, Huckleberry Finn look-a-like Tom Watson's collegiate record was undistinguished. He played number-one man on the golf team at Stanford, but his fortunes in the NCAA and amateur tournaments around the country did not forecast the superb play Watson would produce in the coming years.

In 1972, while Jack Nicklaus was making mincemeat of competition by winning seven tour events, Watson slipped in at seventy-ninth on the money list with $31,081. A second-place finish in the Quad Cities Open to Deane Beman was his only highlight.

Watson, dubbed "almost as great as Jack" by writer Dick Taylor, stepped up to the PGA challenge in 1973, but three back-nine collapses at the Hawaiian Open (75 last round), the World Open (an eye-opening 62 at storied Pinehurst #2 preceded a final-round collapse), and the United States Open at Winged Foot (led by one after three rounds only to sky to 79 in the final round) made experts wonder whether Tom had the mettle of a champion.

Although Watson came from six strokes back to earn his first professional victory in 1974 at the Western Open, final rounds of 78 and 77 at Medinah that year wiped out a 67, 68 start that tied the Open thirty-six-hole record. The poor final rounds further fueled his reputation as "Watson the Choker."

That label was put to rest when Watson, a great "thinker" on the golf course like Nicklaus, captured his first major victory, the British Open in 1975. Two years later, Watson had his finest year, winning twice in California before triumphant wins at the Masters and the British Open, both times defeating Jack Nicklaus down the stretch. Watson's mastery over Nicklaus was on exhibit again at the '81 Masters and at Pebble Beach a year later when he won with a miraculous chip shot on seventeen.

Tom Watson's swing was a classic, dependable one, repeatable on cue, but his intellect was perhaps his foremost trait. Like Nicklaus, he found harmony in a manner of playing that permitted him to be a champion at twenty-seven when he won the Western Open and again at forty-seven when he captured Nicklaus's Memorial Tournament in 1996.

Amateur Bill Hyndman calls Watson one of the great "leg players" of all time. "After the World Cup one year, I saw Tom," he said. "He told me, 'I can't play at all. Can you help me?' I watched him hit a few shots and said, 'You need to learn how to play with your legs. You need to see Byron Nelson. He's the best at not getting stuck on his left foot, which is what causes the hook.'"

Heeding Hyndman's advice, Watson partnered up with Nelson. Whatever Byron told him worked. He played well, so well that from 1977 through 1980, Watson dominated the Tour by winning the money title and receiving the PGA Player of the Year Award for four consecutive years. He averaged five victories a year during that span and won the Vardon Trophy for low scoring average three times. The wins became less frequent after 1980, but through 1996 he compiled thirty-three career victories, ranking him ninth on the all-time list.

Watson's eight major championships as a professional are surpassed only by Nicklaus (twenty), Walter Hagen (eleven), Ben Hogan (nine), and Gary Player (nine). He owns five British Open titles (1975, 1977, 1980, 1982, 1983); only Harry Vardon, with six, won more. Watson won his Masters titles in 1977 and 1981. In head-to-head play with the greats of his day, Watson had an enviable record. His wins over Nicklaus in two United States Opens and a British Open proved his zeal in competing with his chief adversary.

Former Tour professional Jim Ferriell believed that Tom Watson's best asset was his agressiveness. "Watson was the gutsiest putter I ever saw," he said. "Casper may have rolled the ball better, and Tom Kite was the best I ever saw from three feet in, but Watson had the most guts when Sunday came."

Despite his trademark bold approach to golf, and the ability to carve out championships by defeating the world's greatest players, a supreme love for the game and its challenge will be Watson's legacy. Asked about his dream round of the future, he replied: "I want to get to the day when everything will fall into place; when everything makes sense, when every swing is with confidence, and every shot is exactly what I want. I know it can be done. I've been close enough to smell it a few times, but I'd like to touch it, to feel it. I know it's been touched. Hogan touched it. Byron touched it. I want to touch it. Then, I think I'd be satisfied. Then, and only then, I think I could walk away from the game truly satisfied."

# CHAPTER 52

# Player and Hogan

Narrowing the field of eligible candidates for the distinction of "best ever" requires elimination of Walter Hagen, Byron Nelson, Sam Snead, Arnold Palmer, Mickey Wright, and Tom Watson. Based on the purely subjective criteria of major championship victories, playing ability, and competitive records, the consensus of experts places these fine players just a step behind Harry Vardon, Bobby Jones, Ben Hogan, Gary Player, and Jack Nicklaus.

To sort out number one from among "the best of the best," it is necessary to set aside Harry Vardon and Bobby Jones.

In Vardon's case, it has nothing to do with his exemplary record, which includes six championships, four second-place finishes in the British Open, one United States Open victory and second-place finish. Vardon won those titles over a period of eighteen years and was so fundamentally sound that his tee to green game was unmatched. Like Hogan, it was said that Vardon couldn't play the same course on successive days because he'd play the second day from the divots he made on the first.

Despite his record, it is difficult to strongly consider Vardon as the greatest player who ever lived since he never was tested in either the Masters or the PGA Championship. In addition, he played the game in such a different era that it is difficult to assess his true skill accurately. With other great players like J.H. Taylor and James Braid around, he never dominated the game like Hogan, Jones, and Nicklaus.

Because he decided to retire at an early age, Bobby Jones must be eliminated, too. Uncontestedly, his record over the course of an abbreviated career is astounding. His thirteen major championships rank second only to Nicklaus, and he clearly was the dominant player, perhaps like no other, during his seven years on the Tour.

Although Ben Hogan and Harry Vardon are often compared, it is Nicklaus with whom Jones must be contrasted. The similarities are amazing. Both were fine players at an early age who worked with skilled teachers. Each came from families who financed their play in national tournaments. Though there were physical differences in stature, each possessed extremely powerful legs.

Both men were meticulous planners and great organizers. Each had a goal and a definite plan to achieve what they wanted. More than anything, both revered the game itself, its traditions and purity. And most importantly, each knew how to win. It is no wonder they became close friends even though Nicklaus would erase many of Jones's marks.

Because he won the Grand Slam in 1930, Bobby Jones will be eternally engraved in history. He is the greatest amateur who ever lived, a step ahead of Nicklaus, whose record as an amateur in professional tournaments was remarkable, and the upstart Tiger Woods, winner of six USGA tournaments but never a contender in a professional tournament until he shed his amateur status.

Bobby Jones might well have been the greatest golfer, but he waived any claim by failing to turn professional or continue his amateur career so he could compete longer against the best of the best in the early thirties, a formidable group that included Gene Sarazen and Byron Nelson.

With Harry Vardon and Bobby Jones on the sidelines, three men, Ben Hogan, Gary Player, and Jack Nicklaus, remain to be considered as the greatest golfer of all time.

If ever there were an omen for the world of golf, it happened at the 1958 Kentucky Derby Open. There, a twenty-three-year-old competitor from South Africa named Gary Jim Player won his first tournament on United States soil. Like a race horse, Player blazed out of the starting gates. When he was through, the slight man with the hard-boiled face had put together a slate of national and international victories unsurpassed in golf history.

For more than twenty years, Gary Player globetrotted around the world collecting trophies as no one had done before him, even Jack Nicklaus. He won nine majors, including one United States Open (Bellerive '65), three Masters ('61, '74, '78), three British Opens ('59 at Muirfield, '68 at Carnoustie, '74 at Royal Lytham), and two PGA championships ('62 and '72). By winning all four Majors, Player joined Gene Sarazen, Ben Hogan, and Nicklaus in that exclusive club. His nine Major wins tied him for fourth along with John Ball and Ben Hogan.

The best "never-give-up" golfer ever to compete, Player's mindset was reflected in a comment he made to playing partner Seve Ballesteros in the 1980 Masters. He trailed by seven shots after fifty-four holes, and at age forty-five, he was not expected to be a contender.

With ten holes to play and little change in the stroke discrepancy between him and the leaders, Player told Seve, "These people don't think I can win. I'll show 'em." With that he birdied seven of the last ten holes at Augusta on Sunday, shot 64, and won by a stroke.

Like Nicklaus, the 5' 7" Player, called a "bulldog from start to finish" by ESPN commentator Jim Kelly, loved golf from an early age. He made up for lack of size through vigorous training and a style that literally seemed to walk the ball through his downswing. Often dressed in black, he was a two-fisted competitor ready for a fight. The golf course was the enemy, and he defied it to beat him.

Nicklaus and others admired his tenacity and fed off it. Player worked hard on every shot. Even when he described his shots to the media, they sounded urgent. Player was always in a war, intense, serious about the challenge. Writer Dick Taylor said he was that way with people too. "Gary was very sincere," he said, "and strong with his feelings."

In the early seventies, Nicklaus commented on Player's swing. "To compensate for his lack of size and to produce bigger and more powerful swings, Gary thrusts himself into many artificial positions, but he's such an exceptional athlete and has such great coordination that he can get away with it. . . . Sometimes Gary falls off the ball on his follow through, but when he's playing well, he doesn't." Bill Hyndman agreed. "Gary looks like he's jumping at the ball," Hyndman said. "But he stays in back of it. That's the key."

Top amateur player Vinny Giles also called Player a "bulldog." "One of the greatest competitors who ever lived," Giles said. "He got a lot of mileage out of just a good golf game." Errie Ball echoed those thoughts, saying, "When he first came over, I could outdrive him. Then he lifted weights, did push ups, got himself in great shape. Next thing I knew I was twenty yards behind. Gary made himself into a great player."

Off the course, Gary Player was the consummate gentleman. Nicklaus called him "a wonderful sportsman, a good winner, and a good loser, a real charmer." Although a devoted family man like Jack (he and his wife, Vivienne, have five children), his life was consumed by golf. He cut back play in the early seventies to less than twenty tournaments a year, but his search for victory took him to the far ends of the globe.

Player's record in match play was unparalleled. He won the Picadilly World Match Play tournament five times, defeating, among others, Nicklaus, Palmer, Casper, Johnny Miller, Dave Marr, Tony Lema, and Frank Beard.

The South African won his major championships over a span of nineteen years (from 1959 to 1978). Between '65 and '74, Player won five of his nine majors and five World Match Play titles, including two in which he beat Nicklaus. In comparison, Nicklaus won nine majors and one World Match Play title during that time.

Player can easily lay claim to being the greatest international player who ever lived, having won not only the British Open three times but also the Australian Open and Australian PGA, as well as significant titles in Japan, Chile, South Africa (twelve times Open champion, five in succession), Ireland, Egypt, Scotland (Dunlop Masters), and Brazil. Nobody has had more victories in more countries, the mark of a true champion.

The record impressed writer Dick Taylor. "I don't know how he did it," Taylor said. "Two to three weeks someplace. A week home. Then about again. All I know is that he told me there was one time a stewardess couldn't wake him on a plane. She thought he was dead."

Player had an attitude like the Energizer Bunny but a swing that was more compact and powerful. One European writer provided a glimpse of his early potential: "He came to Britain [in the fifties] with a four-knuckle grip, a backswing that shot straight in the air, and a movement back towards the ball that threatened to do him a permanent mischief. . . . [He] openly declared that [he] wanted to be the best golfer in the world at a time when there was little evidence to suggest it would happen."

The young Player's confidence level bordered on arrogance, but it was his "you can't beat me" attitude, like that of Nicklaus, that propelled him to the top of his profession. He was a long driver in spite of his small size, a superb iron player who manipulated the ball with the best of them, the best sand bunker player who ever lived, and a putter who made every important putt he needed.

Player's record against Jack Nicklaus was enviable. In 1966, when he was in his prime and Nicklaus perhaps just a bit shy of his, they met in the final of the Picadilly World Match Play Championship at Wentworth, England. Player dominated Jack that day, cruising to a 6 and 4 win.

Player's nine major titles match Hogan's number, and his World Match Play and international record is on a par with Nicklaus's. In the final analysis, however, he seems better suited to place third in the ranking of the best player of all time, perhaps because he was never seen as a golfer whose abilities completely dominated those challengers who competed against him.

Two who clearly did dominate during the peak years of their eras were Ben Hogan and Jack Nicklaus. Their rises to fame, however, took far different paths. While Nicklaus would rather be compared to his idol Bobby Jones, it is Hogan against whom he ultimately will be judged.

Any comparisons of great players must include William Benjamin Hogan, the gutsiest player who ever lived. There are many golfers who have triumphed over personal tragedy, but no one ever rose from the deathbed and came back to be a champion like Hogan.

When Jack Nicklaus took up golf at age ten in 1950, Hogan was just beginning his journey from automobile accident victim to champion. Hogan won six of his nine major titles after devastating injuries to his legs.

Hogan's nine major tournament triumphs tie him with John Ball and Gary Player behind Nicklaus, Jones, and Walter Hagen. They came four times in the United States Open ('48, '50, '51, and '53), twice at the Masters ('51, '53), twice at the PGA ('46, '48), and once at the British Open ('53). Hogan was never defeated in Ryder Cup play and won the Vardon Trophy for Tour scoring average four times.

The most prolific practice player in history (Mark McCormack called him the "man who invented practice"), Hogan possessed the same intensive nature as Nicklaus did in his early days as a professional. Some mistook Hogan for a grouch, but golf was more than a sport to him; it was a way of life.

Hogan concentrated like none other. Nicklaus could turn on and off his focus many times during a round. Hogan bore down on the first hole and never let go. Amateur Bill Hyndman said Hogan once apologized to him before a round about his anticipated silent play. "I played with Hogan a great deal. He said, 'Well, if I've got to play with an amateur, it might as well be Hyndman.' Then he proceeded to talk all through the round. Sportswriters were in shock. They said, 'What'd he say, what'd he say?' I told 'em we discussed fishing."

The intensity Hogan possessed made others squirm, whether it was on the golf course or simply in his presence.

Women's amateur champion Alice Dye remembers how silky smooth Hogan's swing was.

"Pete and I had a young woman with us who was a good player," Dye recalled. "We watched Hogan hit some shots on a private practice tee at Seminole. Then we headed toward the regular practice tee and there were Bruce Lietzke and Ben Crenshaw. The woman with us said, 'I didn't realize how jerky Crenshaw's swing was.' I laughed because it wasn't jerky. He had a beautiful swing. It was that she was comparing it to Hogan's swing."

Ageless professional Errie Ball, witness to nearly all of the great players of the twentieth century, said, "Back in the 1940s, there were a lot of different ideas about how to get to the ball. And Hogan knew a great deal about the swing. All the pros used to sit around and pick each other's brains—Nelson, George Fazio, Hogan, Snead—that doesn't happen anymore."

Ball remembers that first time he saw Hogan. "It was at Thomasville, Georgia. Henry Picard pointed him out to me. He was thin as a rail—looked like a one-iron. I watched him swing and frankly wasn't too impressed, but Henry was. 'You better watch this man,' Henry says. He was right."

Jack Nicklaus was obviously influenced by Hogan's swing. "When I played with him, it seemed like the next week I was playing Hogan's swing," he told reporters. "I remember making sure that my swing got a little flatter for some reason, and I always made sure that my right never would catch my left. I always remembered the back of my hand would lead everything through and up high."

Bill Hyndman said Hogan was very critical of others golfers. "One time we were playing in the U. S. Open," Hyndman recalled. "He looked up at the scoreboard and saw a certain name. 'He can't play a lick,' Hogan said in disgust."

One significant moment that embodied other professionals' feelings about Hogan's perception of the swing occurred in the late eighties when George Peper and *Golf Magazine* honored the centennial of golf in America. There, one hundred heroes of American golf gathered for a dinner, including Hogan, Nicklaus, and Palmer.

The program for the evening featured a silhouette of the fabled amateur Frances Ouimet swinging a golf club. When it was Hogan's time to speak, he remarked that Ouimet's elbow position was quite correct.

After Hogan spoke, Nicklaus ascended to the podium. He started out by saying, "Arnold and I have our speeches ready, but we've both been sitting here checking out the position of Ouimet's elbow."

During that dinner, Hogan had brought many of the honorees to tears when he said, "I love this game, I *really, really* love his game."

Experts noted that of the tournaments he entered during his career, Hogan finished in the top ten a remarkable 82 percent of the time. Even more stunning was that he finished in the top three in over 40 percent of the tournaments entered.

Hogan, who was fond of saying, "Every day you don't hit balls is one day longer it takes you to get better," faced head-to-head competition from Byron Nelson, Jimmy Demaret, Julius Boros, Jackie Burke Jr., Tommy "Thunder" Bolt, Arnold Palmer, E.J. "Dutch" Harrison, Sam Snead, and even the young Jack Nicklaus. It's fair to say just the mention of Hogan's name gave all of them the willies. No one wanted to challenge the Wee Ice Mon in his prime.

In the mid-70s, Jack Nicklaus spoke in awe of Hogan. "I grew up in the era of Hogan," Jack said. "Everything I saw of him and read of him and heard of him indicated that he had achieved utter mechanical perfection in the striking of a golf ball. Perfect reputation. Flawless automation. This was my dream . . ."

Like Nicklaus, Hogan was long off the tee when he first joined the Tour. He muscled the ball around with his hooker's grip and strong forearms, outlasting any course with brute play. Later, he abandoned the strong grip, and then, and only then, did he begin to hit the famous Hogan fade that made him a champion.

When he won the Masters in 1953 with fourteen-under par 274, a tournament record that stood until Nicklaus broke it twelve years later, Hogan said the tournament was "the best I have ever played for four rounds." Gene Sarazen called Hogan's performance "the greatest four scoring rounds ever."

The '53 Open, played at Oakmont, followed the Masters, and Hogan opened with 67. He finished with 287, beating rival Sam Snead by six strokes. He also sailed to Scotland and famed Carnoustie, where the Scots treated him like their long-lost child. He invented Hogan's Alley and delighted the fans with his piercing into-the-wind long irons, winning by four.

Only the PGA Championship evaded Hogan in 1953. Because of a schedule that conflicted with the British Open, he could not play in the PGA. Hogan was denied the opportunity to win the Grand Slam but is the only man to have entered and won three Majors in a year.

In all, Hogan won fifty-two tournaments. One writer called him "a Colossus of modern golf." Gary Player said, "I believe that Ben Hogan knows more about golf than any other man has ever known." Bob Charles added, "Ben Hogan came as close to perfection with control of the golf ball as anyone whoever played the game."

Whatever the tagline, Hogan was an anomaly to many, a crusty veteran of the wars who battled golf courses like a mechanical banshee. He teased reporters and fans with the famous "secret" of his game and laughed at a sporting world who never could figure him out.

To this day, those close to him say it's that bedevilment that he enjoyed the most. Surely, the world will never see another Ben Hogan, the second-greatest golfer who ever lived.

# CHAPTER 53

# Number One

Ben Hogan's place in history is cemented behind Jack Nicklaus, although there is certainly argument in the opposite direction. Tour veteran Tommy Bolt, for one, would not agree, having once said, "People are always wondering who's better, Hogan or Nicklaus. Well, I've seen Jack Nicklaus watch Ben practice, but I've never seen Ben watch anybody else practice. What's that tell you?"

Regardless of that observation, when all the facts of their respective games and the records Nicklaus and Hogan leave behind are compared, it is Jack Nicklaus who prevails as number one.

The great British player J.H. Taylor, when asked to give his definition of the best nearly a century ago, said, "He is one who over a length of years has played fewer bad or indifferent shots than any other aspirant, and in addition has shown during [a] period of time consistent brilliancy."

By Taylor's first standard, Jack Nicklaus should not be judged as the best. Although he was a consistent ballstriker whose accuracy was outstanding, wayward tee shots and poor approach on occasion wavered from the fairways and greens, placing him in disparaging positions from where it was difficult to recover. Nicklaus's short game, long an Achilles heel, also produced bad or indifferent shots that would have made Taylor cringe.

The second half of Taylor's definition of the best, however, fits Nicklaus perfectly. No one golfer in the history of the game has shown "consistent brilliancy" like the Golden Bear.

Suffice it to say that Nicklaus was a champion at fourteen and is still a champion at fifty-seven years old. That span of excellence, forty-three years, is rivaled only by the legendary Sam Snead, who competed at a high level into his sixties. Though others have tried, noted amateur

Kent Frandsen may have put it best when he observed, "I don't know how Jack sustained the competitive mental edge for thirty years. Most players tire of competition, but Jack tried as hard as he could on every shot over that time. It's remarkable since his talent wasn't any better than Trevino or Watson or others. I guess Jack just wanted it more."

Nicklaus's record portrays a man who was a dominant force as an amateur in the late fifties, a touring professional in the sixties, seventies, and early eighties, and a champion on the Senior Tour in the nineties. Even at age fifty-six, he still mastered rounds of 72, 74, 69, and 72 to tie for twenty-seventh at the 1996 United States Open and took the fans' breath away with a miracle 66 in the second round of the British Open the same year.

The span of brilliant play exhibited by Nicklaus is what separates him from Ben Hogan. Physical restrictions prevented the Texan from lengthening his career, but Nicklaus has sustained superb play through the terms of eight presidents (Kennedy, Johnson, Nixon, Ford, Carter, Reagan, Bush, and Clinton) and many of the finest golfers (Hogan, Palmer, Player, Miller, Trevino, Watson, and Norman) who ever took club to ball. Tour contemporary Bruce Crampton believed Nicklaus did so because of pride. "Jack never wanted to accept mediocrity," Crampton said. "He always wanted to be the best. That's what kept him going."

Gary Player believed Nicklaus's longevity went deeper. "Jack played so well because he was not a punch drunk athlete who forgot about other things in life," Player said. "He had his wife and kids and business interests. An old battery can't start a car. It needs to be recharged. Same way with a golfer. They've got to have another love in life, a diversion. Jack needed refreshing and his family and other interests provided that. That relieved the pressure. That's why he played so well for so long."

To accurately assess Nicklaus's greatness, one must start with the majors he has won: twenty, *seven* more than his nearest competitor Bobby Jones and eleven more than Hogan. Jack's records are a quantum leap beyond what any other golfer has ever achieved in the game and remind one of Babe Ruth's baseball records in the twenties, Wilt Chamberlain's scoring records in basketball in the sixties, and Wayne Gretzky's phenomenal scoring records in hockey in the eighties and nineties.

In the eight years between the British Open wins in 1970 and 1978, Nicklaus, who was named Athlete of the Decade for the seventies, only missed the top ten twice. During that span, he played in thirty-three majors, won seven, finished second six times, third five times, and fourth four times. He was second in major events a record nineteen times.

In his first twelve years on the Tour, Nicklaus won fifty-one times in 276 starts, nearly 20 percent of the time, and he finished in the top ten in over 65 percent of the tournaments he entered. New golf club technology that equalizes good and great players will probably rob golf fans of ever seeing a dominant player able to sustain high efficiency over a sufficient number of years; thus, in all likelihood, Nicklaus's record of twenty major championships will never be broken. Of the modern players, only Phil Mickelson, who at twenty-four has shown signs of prominence but has yet to win a major, and twenty-year-old Tiger Woods, with three United States Amateur crowns, are primed to challenge Jack.

Besides his successes in the majors, Nicklaus has captured a total of fifty-two PGA Tour events, six Australian Opens, and various other international events. This variety of victories proves that Nicklaus could play under conditions at any location in the world. In the nineties, Jack has added ten Senior Tour victories, including two wins in the United States Senior Open ('90, '93), three Tradition victories, and the Ford Senior Players Championship. Nicklaus's great play in the Tradition inspired Hale Irwin to say, "He was chipping and putting at a barrel, and all of us were going to a pinhead." The wife of one Senior Tour veteran observed, "Jack just comes out and wins anytime he wants to. Just like he used to do on the regular Tour."

The legendary Gene Sarazen, whose brusque style of play and compact swing contrasted significantly with Nicklaus's, assessed Jack during his 1972 season. "The class of the field today," he told *Golf Digest*, "is Jack Nicklaus. He's the greatest long hitter I've ever seen and the greatest putter. That's a combination that never went hand in hand before. The most impressive thing about Nicklaus is his concentration."

Dr. Cary Middlecoff echoed Sarazen's remarks. "He adds an awful lot of dignity to the game. I don't see how anyone can say he isn't the greatest golfer of all time. In his best days, Ben Hogan is like Jack Nicklaus is now."

Seven years later, Gene Sarazen told *Sports Illustrated*, "I never thought anyone would ever put Hogan in the shadows, but [Jack] did. Nicklaus has the remarkable combination of power and finesse, and he is one of the smartest guys ever to walk the fairways. And he has been an extraordinary leader. What more is there to say? Jack Nicklaus is the greatest competitor of them all."

Lee Trevino, who along with Tom Watson had more success against Nicklaus than any other players, said, "He can be beaten, but no one can say he's in Jack's class. . . . If [Jack] prepared for it [major tournament], he would win it. He's the only man I ever knew who was that way."

George Peper observed, "Nicklaus has outlasted Palmer, Player, Miller, Trevino, Weiskopf, and Watson. . . . The simplest way to put it is this: Nicklaus has won more major tournaments against much better competition over a long period of time than any other player in the history of the game."

Herman Mitchell, Lee Trevino's longtime caddie, was once quoted in *Sports Illustrated* as telling an exasperated Trevino, "The only way we're going to beat this guy is if he signs the wrong scorecard." J.C. Snead added, "When you go head-to-head with Nicklaus, he knows he's going to beat you, you know he's going to beat you, and he knows you know he's going to beat you." Tom Weiskopf added, "There will never be another Jack Nicklaus. Nobody can play golf like that guy can. *Nobody*." He added, "Jack *is* the record book."

In 1975, when Johnny Miller was at his best, he said, "Jack is better than I am. He has more capability and more experience.. . . . If Jack were at his best, I wouldn't want to play him." After the Masters, which Nicklaus won that year, Jim Murray wrote, "You can now if you will, go to the blackboard and write one hundred times 'Jack Nicklaus is the greatest golfer in the world.'"

*Golf Digest*, upon naming Nicklaus Player of the Year in 1975, wrote, "maybe next year we should start naming the second best player of the year. Nicklaus doesn't need the exposure anymore." *Columbus Citizen-Journal* writer Kaye Kessler once said, after picking Nicklaus to win the 1977 Masters, "Given a choice against the field, I'll take Jack Nicklaus every time and twice on Sundays, even if it's a Minnesota wheat field and the rest of the guys in it are driving John Deere's."

Dan Jenkins, in selecting Nicklaus as number-one player in history in a *Sports Illustrated* article, said, "Hard to argue with twenty majors, including the Masters six times, a whopping nineteen seconds in majors, and ninety-eight [now one hundred] victories overall. Winning his majors over four decades, Jack won them fat, thin, young, middle-aged, crew-cut, fluff dry, and never met a critical putt he didn't like. Might be the greatest winner in the complete history of sports, folks."

Accolades for Nicklaus are unending, but one of the most observant was written by author Stephen Goodvein. "Spiritually," he said, "Jack Nicklaus was the defending champion in *every* major event that was played. It is a slight exaggeration, but only slight, to say you had to beat the Golden Bear in order to win a major tournament."

That aspect of Nicklaus's play provided the inspiration for Thomas Boswell of the *Washington Post* to remark, "Few careers in any walk of life have started so spectacularly, then continued steadily upward, almost without interruption, for so long."

Obviously, others agreed with Boswell. At the gala celebration in New York City to commemorate the centennial of golf in America, the one hundred heroes of the game were honored. Among them were Arnold Palmer, Mickey Wright, Byron Nelson, Nancy Lopez, Jack Nicklaus, Patty Berg, Sam Snead, Kathy Whitworth, and Tom Watson.

At the same ceremony, Nicklaus was named Player of the Century. Based on nearly forty years of superb play, he was most deserving.

Going into the final round of the Walt Disney World Open, Nicklaus enjoyed a five-shot lead over his nearest competitors. Later, Nicklaus told reporters he played that round with sore feet, which he acquired by walking around the Magic Kingdom the night before with his two sons. Sore feet or not, Nicklaus, the family man, played like a Disney super hero bent on annihilating the enemy.

Under partly cloudy, warm conditions, Nicklaus simply left the field in the dust. Bobby Mitchell closed with 66 to finish in a tie with Jim Dent (71) and Larry Wood (67), nine shots behind Jack who swamped the field with an eight-under-par 64. Combined with earlier rounds of 68, 68, and 67, Jack finished twenty-one under par for the tournament.

Jim Dent claimed he was responsible for Nicklaus's fantastic play. "In those days, they played one, three, and five together the last day, so I was in the group ahead of Jack. I eagled the fourth hole to get even with him. Unfortunately, that really woke him up. He threw a little 32 and 32 at us and that was that. We never had a chance. As Lee Trevino said, 'Let the Bear hibernate. Let him sleep. Don't wake him up.'"

*Golf World* called the triumph "the most convincing victory since Richard Nixon sank George McGovern. "Next year we're going to let Jack play three extra holes to even things up," Disney President Cardon Walker told reporters.

The twenty-one under total was one shy of what Kermit Zarley and Babe Hiskey posted *together* in the National Team Championship. The nine-stroke victory margin was the biggest since Arnold Palmer, suffering the first winless year of his career, won the Phoenix Open ten years earlier.

The win made 1972 close as it had opened, with a Nicklaus triumph. He had emerged triumphant at the Crosby, on top at Doral, peppered the field at the Masters and the United States Open, and was the winner at both Westchester and the U.S. Match Play.

All told in 1972, Nicklaus won seven times to go along with three second-place finishes. He was in the top ten fourteen of nineteen events. His third United States Open title was his thirteenth major, tying him with the immortal Mr. Jones. He also achieved his goal of becoming the first Tour player ever to win $300,000 in a year, pulling in $320,542, which converted to a 1995 amount of $1,803,363.

Those winnings made him the all-time career money champion. His scoring average of 70.23 was the lowest on Tour, making Jack a four-time leader in that category.

The PGA named Nicklaus Player of the Year and *Golf Digest* presented him with its Byron Nelson Award for capturing the most wins. Lee Trevino was next with three and finished more than one hundred thousand dollars behind Nicklaus's money total. Jack also won *Golf Digest*'s Performance Average Championship (measurement of a player's achievement in official events in compared to that of his rivals) at .801.

Later, Nicklaus looked back at 1972. "It was a great year, certainly," he told *Golf World*, "Like any great year by anyone there were some near misses, always something you didn't expect. . . . I felt I paced myself well . . . how could I be more pleased with a year? What can I say?"

As for the future, Nicklaus turned philosophical. "I'll never stop learning," he said. "Hope I never do. I'll still be learning till the day I retire."

More than the titles, more than the money, more than the Player of the Year honors, or the low scoring average, Jack Nicklaus proved that year that he could rebound from a devastating, heart-breaking defeat in the British Open that crushed his chances for the Grand Slam. He came back to dominate the Tour in its final months.

Nicklaus's legacy will be his resiliency. Author Pat Ward-Thomas wrote: "Nicklaus accepts victory simply as the natural outcome of the event. His manner shows less of joy and relief than that of other men, and conversely, failure never disturbs his remarkable equilibrium and self-assurance. Obviously, he hates losing; there never was a worthwhile champion who did not, but the only effect is to harden his determination; there is no self deception in the philosophy of Nicklaus."

Writer Thomas Boswell wrote, "[Jack] remains a man who is inspired by failure, or even the thought of failure. Defeat always prodded his bearish nature into slow, inexorable, productive action."

That ability to define failure and continue the quest to learn made Boswell's final words on the subject especially apropos. "Because he never feared failure or experimentation, Nicklaus seemed especially suited to golf, the game of perpetual humiliation and embarrassment. Nicklaus approached his whole game, perhaps his whole life, the same way he lined up a putt—slowly, confidently, and from every angle."

Those abilities carried him far, but Nicklaus's success is an enigma even to him. Asked by *Sports Illustrated* to explain the keys to being a champion of golf for such an incredibly long period of time, Jack paused and then said, "If you look at the PGA figures, you'll see that the guy with the best average is usually less than a stroke under the guy back in thirtieth place. So you're talking about a fifth of a stroke a day between winning and thirtieth, and, Jiminy Christmas, you can't tell me there's that much difference in our swings. The difference is something else. I was fortunate in a lot of ways. I was fortunate to have a good father, who helped me get into this. I was fortunate to have a pretty good head. A lot of it's her [a nod to Barbara], a gal who's been understanding. There's all that. I know I've won with something besides the shots, but I don't know for sure what that something is."

Whatever that "something" is, time and time again Jack Nicklaus has shown the resiliency of a champion, one symbolic of the greatest golfer in the history of the game.

# Epilogue

J ack Nicklaus's will to win has not changed since the first day he teed it up in a golf tournament. The eternal optimist, he always believes that the next championship is right around the corner.

Never was that attitude more evident that at the 1996 PGA Championship played at Valhalla near Louisville, Kentucky. August had brought with it sweltering temperatures, bathing competitors in perspiration. Yet there was the fifty-six-year-old Nicklaus, practicing rigorously for a championship as if it were his first.

While Jack was out on the course playing with Scott Hoch and Billy Andrade, the talented European player Colin Montgomerie, still attempting to win his first major after several close calls, arrived at the press tent. When asked how he assessed his game, he proceeded to tell reporters that he had made a definite decision about that. "I plan to practice more," he said, "give it 100 percent," which apparently meant he hadn't done so in the past. Most reporters shook their heads at that comment, wondering what level of commitment Montgomerie, whose rounds of 71 and 78 left him without a Saturday tee time, really had for the game.

The morning paper that day contained a quote from Nick Price, in a slump since his resounding seasons in 1993 and 1994. "As long as I have two practice rounds, that should be sufficient," he told *USA Today*. "We're professional golfers. We should be able to figure it [the course] out in about nine holes." In the tournament, Price contended, and then fell back in the fourth round.

Just after Montgomerie had finished his interview and Price's comment was making the rounds with the reporters, Jack Nicklaus arrived at the press tent. While others much younger than him had either just practiced or played nine holes, the elder statesman had played the entire eighteen holes in August's choking heat.

As he sat and answered questions from reporters, Nicklaus braced his head with his right hand. He was dog-tired, flushed in the face, and badly in need of a good helping of bottled water. Yet the great champion patiently assessed the course, his game, the competition, and even his passion for a rule restricting the distance a golf ball can be hit.

It was unfortunate that players like Montgomerie, suddenly deciding he was going to give his game 100 percent, and Price, believing somehow that he could prepare for a major championship with two practice rounds, couldn't sit and listen to Nicklaus talk about the game he loves. Maybe they would better understand what championship golf is if they saw it through the eyes of one who has dedicated himself to the game for nearly fifty years.

When Nicklaus does win again, and he will, the championship will come in spite of the fact that for all practical purposes he should put his clubs in the closet and retire. He has nothing left to prove, and except for instances of brilliance shown in the '96 United States Open, in the '96 British Open, or on the Senior Tour, where he is competitive but seems sadly out of place, his tournament performance level has dropped off considerably.

Based on his performances, the time seems right for Nicklaus to heed the words he first uttered to writer Thomas Boswell. "I've wondered if I should still be playing this silly game," he said, "You see guys who have been winners who get to the point where they ought to get out of the game. They are the last to know. They make themselves seem pathetic. It hurts to think that is you. . . ." Nicklaus then added, "Once time is past, it's past. I'll never be 215 pounds, hit it so far, or have my hair so short again. . . . You can never return. I've lost the sixties and seventies. We all have. I'm not the same. I have to look to the future. I have to see what skills I now have. I have to find out what is in store for Jack Nicklaus in the eighties. I can't look backwards, because that man doesn't exist anymore."

In 1994, Jack told *Golf Digest*, "I've always said once I stop being able to compete and being able to enjoy what I'm doing, then I'll stop playing." In February 1996, Jack summed up his current feelings. "I have always felt there's a certain time in all of our lives when it's time for the younger fellas to have their turn. It's time for me to pass the baton."

A chance to do so with dignity was passed up at the 1996 United States Open Championship at Oakland Hills. When the tournament talk should have been about the eventual champion, the real story was Nicklaus's fortieth Open appearance. From the first day, television announcers and other media reporters seemed to ask only three questions: Will Nicklaus make the cut? Where will he finish? Will this be his last Open? When he did make the cut and finished in a respectable tie for twenty-seventh, it would have been wonderful for him to have acknowledged the roaring cheers at eighteen, closed with the chip close to the hole for par and a final-round 72, and then politely announce to his adoring fans and the television viewers that he was retiring from tournament golf. That act of courage would have been the perfect way to go out, but the desire within Nicklaus simply won't permit him to quit.

Why does Jack Nicklaus keep playing? When confronted with the question, he normally says it's because he loves the competition or believes he owes it to the game to allow golf fans to see him play.

At the heart of the matter, however, is a fierce desire to extend his records so that no one will ever break them. While potential challengers such as Nick Faldo, Greg Norman, Ernie Els, or Phil Mickelson loom on the horizon, none of these men will ever approach his mark of winning twenty major championships.

That doesn't mean that the present day field of golfers is void of a future champion who can challenge Jack's records. In this day and age of technical advances with golf balls and clubs, Nicklaus knows there is one man, twenty-one-year-old Tiger Woods, who is taking very accurate aim at him.

Many similarities exist between Nicklaus and Woods. Each took up the game at an early age, and each at the insistence of their fathers, who would guide their careers through the early years. Like Nicklaus, who had Jack Grout to tutor him, Tiger Woods became a pupil of Butch Harman, former teacher of Greg Norman.

Both Jack Nicklaus and Tiger Woods began to play competitively in their early teens with instant success. Aside from Bobby Jones, they possess the two greatest performance records as amateur players the game has ever seen, though Woods's three consecutive United States Amateur Championships outshine Jack's ability to garner two in the space of three years.

Nicklaus was twenty-two when he turned professional, Woods just twenty. Tiger had multimillion-dollar endorsement contracts with Nike and Titleist and a book publishing deal to assure him financial freedom, Nicklaus had a clothing endorsement and book deal when he began to ease the financial burden. Like Nicklaus, Tiger Woods turned to Mark McCormack and IMG for representation.

The physical skill level Tiger Woods has achieved entering his first year on Tour is as solid as that of Nicklaus at a similar age. When Jack joined the Tour, he hit the ball twenty to thirty yards farther than any of his competitors. Woods enjoys a similar advantage.

Certainly Jack has seen the spectacle of Woods, having played with him and admired his ability. Ever ready to put as much pressure on a challenger as possible, Jack told *USA Today*, "Tiger will win more majors than Arnold and me combined." He followed up that comment with one to Rick Reilly of *Sports Illustrated*, which may not have endeared him to the likes of Nick Faldo, Greg Norman, or other top players of the late eighties and early nineties. "I don't think we've had a whole lot happen in what, ten years," Jack said. "I mean, some guys have come on and won a few tournaments, but nobody as sustained and dominated. I think we might have somebody now."

Tiger Woods will not match Jack's record of recording a United State Open win as his first professional victory. In October of 1996, Wood's overwhelmed the field in the Las Vegas Invitational by shooting 70, 63, 68, 67, and 64.

The twenty-seven under score (twenty-six under for the last four rounds) tied Woods with Davis Love III, who promptly handed Tiger a victory by botching the first playoff hole. Later, Woods won the Disney World Open. He finished the year twenty-fifth on the PGA money earnings list with more than $700,000.

Woods's superb play qualified him for the Tour Championship at Southern Hills in Tulsa. In his only confrontration with the elite of the game, Ernie Els, Tom Lehman, Greg Norman, Fred Couples, Nick Faldo, among others, Tiger proved human. He opened with 70, but a second round 78 eliminated him from contention. It came after Woods learned that his father had been hospitalized with chest pains brought on by a bout with bronchitis. Earl Woods recovered, but Tiger finished far down the leader board despite a final-round 68.

Prior to that tournament, the plaudits for Woods had pressed him toward sainthood. In a preview of things to come, ESPN's Andy North, a two-time United States Open champion, prefaced an interview with Woods by saying, "This is the greatest sports story since Nicklaus's win in the '86 Masters."

As Tiger Woods continues his march toward fame and fortune, more comparisons will be made with Nicklaus. Jack played in eighteen professional events before he won, Tiger just five. Woods achieved two Tour victories in his two few months on Tour. It took Jack several before he won, but he totaled four the first year, including the United States Open.

When Tiger Woods tees it up for the 1997 Tour, he will start seventeen major victories behind Jack. No one doubts his potential to challenge that mark just as it was clear that Nicklaus had the potential to surpass Bobby Jones's record of thirteen major wins when Jack first appeared on Tour in 1962.

Since he continues to pursue another major victory, it seems Jack has a hunch that, while twenty major championship won't be enough, twenty-one might be. He should relax. Neither Tigers Woods nor any golfer in the future will ever match Nicklaus's marks in the majors. Jack simply played too well for too long a time. As Tour veteran Mike Souchak said, "There's about as much chance of someone breaking Nicklaus's majors record as there is somebody winning eleven tournaments in a row like Byron Nelson did." Amateur great Bill Hyndman agreed. "Nobody's ever gonna catch Jack," he said.

Despite those observations, the beat will go on, for Nicklaus truly believes he can win just one more significant event. That belief will propel him to tee it up for the one-hundredth Open at Pebble Beach in the year 2000. One only hopes the course he loves will not turn on him.

By year's end in 1996, Nicklaus had played in his 140th consecutive major tournament, his 148th appearance overall. To attain 150, Jack would compete in the 1997 Masters and then tee it up at Congressional for the 1997 United States Open.

When Jack Nicklaus does call it quits, he will leave a game that has been much the better for having him play it. The legacy of the Golden Bear has imprinted itself on golf in more ways than any human being who has ever competed.

For one, he has set records that will challenge all comers to the fullest extent of their capabilities. Whether it is Tiger Woods or not, the "new Jack Nicklaus" of the world will know that he or she must compete over a wide spectrum of time, and do so at the very highest level in order to come close to dominating the game as Nicklaus has. As writer Dick Taylor said, "All the challengers came along, and Jack shot down each one." Whether anyone will ever shoot down his records is subject to conjecture, but to do so they will have to have the physical presence, a fire in the heart, and something close to Jack's mental capability in order to even approach his performance level.

The only athlete in the modern era who rivals Nicklaus is Michael Jordan. In November of 1996, I watched Jordan and his defending champion Chicago Bulls compete against the Charlotte Hornets. For three quarters, Michael completely dominated play. During one sequence, he hit a three-pointer with a defender in his face, drained a turn-around jumper from the key, dunked from the right side, batted the ball to teammate Scottie Pippen for a lay-in, and then hit a fall-away with one tick left on the shot clock. The superb play confirmed how much better he was than any of the other athletes.

All the while, Jordan had a smirk on his face. After the impossible fall-away, he laughed as he headed down the court. He knew he was playing at the highest level in the sport he loved.

At his peak, Jack Nicklaus was like that. He was so much better than anyone else. His confidence level permitted him to perform near perfection. Though he wasn't the type like Michael Jordan to laugh or show other outward emotion, the same sort of inner feeling must have been present. When he dominated, Jack simply toyed with his opponents. As Tom Weiskopf said, "You knew he knew that you knew he was going to beat the shit out of you."

In addition to his records, Nicklaus will leave a collection of golf courses that will influence the way people play the game for generations to come. Like his predecessors, Jack's legacy of golf course design will show a caring man who developed highly playable courses carved out in harmony with the natural terrain of the land. Perhaps more than anyone else before him, his willingness to travel the globe and design courses in remote parts of the world will make the game accessible for many who otherwise would never have had the chance to enjoy it.

Added to Nicklaus's credentials with competitive golf and golf course design will be his business legacy. His golf centers, club design, management services, and other related golf ventures will impact the game for many years to come. He has been instrumental in starting the Golden Bear mini-tour that will provide young players the opportunity to hone their game in anticipation of the PGA Tour.

Above all, the real Jack Nicklaus story is one that will demonstrate to future generations that one man was able to be the best and still be an exemplary gentleman and a family man. Nicklaus has been a credit to the game of golf; a man who put family first and kept them first no matter what the temptations. He has shown love and respect for his wife, been there for his children, treated fellow competitors with respect and courtesy, and by all accounts, lived an exemplary life that would make anyone proud.

In the future, when the name of Jack Nicklaus is spoken, it will be with admiration of his competitive record and with awe of how he accomplished it. He is one of the greatest sportsman to have ever lived. A man who combined strong character and a fierce fighting spirit. A man who climbed to the top of the mountain and stayed there.

MARK SHAW

# Bibliography

*"And Then Arnie Told Chi Chi . . .",* Don Wade, Contemporary Books, Chicago, 1993

*"And Then Jack Said to Arnie . . .",* Don Wade, Contemporary Books, Chicago, 1991

*The Architects of Golf,* Geoffery S. Cornish and Ronald E. Whitten, HarperCollins, New York, 1993

*Arnie, Inside the Legend,* Larry Guest, Tribune, HarperCollins, 1993

*Arnold Palmer, A Personal Journey,* Thomas Hauser, Collins Publishers, San Francisco, 1994

*The Bear and I,* Angelo Argea with Jolee Edmondson, Atheneum/SMI, 1979

*The Birth of a Legend, Arnold Palmer's Golden Year 1960,* Furman Bisher, Prentice-Hall, Englewood Cliffs, N.J., 1972

*Buried Lies,* Peter Jacobsen with Jack Sheehan, Penguin Books, New York, 1993

*Bury Me in a Pot Bunker,* Pete Dye with Mark Shaw, Addison Wesley, New York, 1995

*Championship Media Guide,* United States Golf Association, 1995

*Following Through,* Herbert Warren Wind, HarperPerennial, New York, 1995

*Gary Player: World Golfer,* Gary Player with Floyd Thatcher, Word Books, Waco, TX, 1974

*Golf and All Its Glory, A Modern Look at an Ancient Game,* Bruce Critchley with Bob Ferrier, BBC Books, London, 1993

*Golf Anecdotes,* Robert T. Sommers, Oxford University Press, New York, 1995

*Golf Digest Magazine,* all issues, 1972

*Golf: The Great Ones,* Michael McDonnell, Drake Publishers, Inc., New York, 1973

*The Golf Immortals,* Tom Scott and Geoffrey Cousins, Hart Publishing Company, New York, 1968

*Golf Magazine's Encyclopedia of Golf,* HarperCollins, New York, 1993

*Golf My Way,* Jack Nicklaus with Ken Bowden, Simon and Schuster, New York, 1974

*Grand Slam Golf,* George Peper, Harry N. Abrams, Inc., New York, 1991

*Great Golf Stories,* Robert Trent Jones, editor, Galahad Books, New York, 1982

*Great Moments in Golf,* Nevin H. Gibson, A.S. Barnes and Company, New York, 1973

*Great Moments in Golf,* Dave Klein, Cowles Book Company, Inc., New York, 1971

*Great Opens: Historic British and American Championships 1913-1975,* Micahel Hobbs, A.S. Barnes and Company, New York, 1977

*The Greatest Game of All,* Jack Nicklaus with Herbert Warren Wind, Simon and Schuster, New York, 1969

*The Greatest Golf Shots Ever Made,* Kevin Nelson, Simon and Schuster, New York, 1992

*The Greatest Masters: The 1986 Masters and Golf's Elite,* Stephen Goodwin, Harper and Row, New York, 1988

*Hogan,* Curt Sampson, Rutledge Hill Press, Nashville, 1996

*The Illustrated History of Women's Golf,* Rhonda Glenn, Taylor Publishing Company, Dallas, Texas, 1991

*Jack Nicklaus, Facts and Figures of His Career,* Golden Bear International, 1996

*Jacklin, The Champion's Own Story,* Tony Jacklin, Simon and Schuster, New York, 1970

*Let Me Teach You Golf As I Taught Jack Nicklaus,* Jack Grout with Dick Aultman, Antheneum/SMI, New York, 1975

*The Masters: Golf's Most Prestigious Tradition,* Dawson Taylor, Contemporary Books, Inc., Chicago, 1986

*The Masters: Profile of a Tournament,* Dawson Taylor, A.S. Barnes and Company, New York, 1973

*The Memorial,* Executive Sports, May 27-June 2, 1996

*PGA Tour, Official Media Guide of the PGA Tour,* Triumph Books, Chicago, 1996

*The PGA World Golf Hall of Fame Book,* Gerald Astor with the PGA of America, Prentice Hall Press, New York, 1991

*Scioto Country Club, 75 Years of History,* Paul Hornung, Scioto Country Club, Ohio, 1993

*The Senior Tour and the Men Who Play It,* Steve Hershey, Doubleday, New York, 1992

*Sports Illustrated Golf,* Collector's Library, Oxmoor House, Birmingham, Alabama, 1994

*The Sports 100,* Brad Herzog, Macmillian, New York, 1995

*The Story of the Open Golf Championship,* Charles G. Mortimer and Fred Pignon, Jarrolds Publishers, London, 1952

*They Call Me Super Mex,* Lee Trevino and Sam Blair, Random House, New York, 1982

*Triumphant Journey, The Saga of Bobby Jones and the Grand Slam of Golf,* Dick Miller, Holt, Rinehart and Winston, New York, 1980

*The Ultimate Golfer,* Richard Bradbeer and Ian Morrison, Smithmark, New York, 1993

*The U.S. Open: Golf's Ultimate Challenge,* Robert Sommers, Antheneum/SMI, New York, 1987

*The Venturi Analysis,* Ken Venturi with Al Barkow, Antheneum/SMI, New York, 1981

*Who's Who in Golf,* Len Elliott and Barbara Kelly, Arlington House Publishers, New York, 1976

*The World Atlas of Golf,* Pat Ward-Thomas, editor, Gallery Books, New York, 1991

# Index